Books by Maria Elena De La Iglesia:

The Catalogue of Catalogues

The Catalogue of American Catalogues

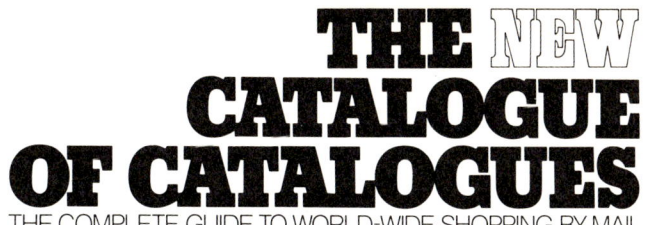

THE NEW CATALOGUE OF CATALOGUES

THE COMPLETE GUIDE TO WORLD-WIDE SHOPPING BY MAIL

MARIA ELENA DE LA IGLESIA

RANDOM HOUSE
NEW YORK

Copyright © 1972, 1975 by Maria Elena De La Iglesia

All rights reserved under International and Pan-American Copyright Conventions. Published in the United States by Random House, Inc., New York, and simultaneously in Canada by Random House of Canada Limited, Toronto.

Library of Congress Cataloging in Publication Data

De La Iglesia, Maria Elena.
   The new catalogue of catalogues.

   Published in 1972 under title: The catalogue of catalogues.
   Includes index.
   1. Mail-order business—Directories. I. Title.
[HF5466.D45 1975]   380.1'025   75–11985
ISBN 0–394–73079–8

Design: Charles Schmalz

Manufactured in the United States of America
9 8 7 6 5 4 3 2

Contents

Introduction		9
How to Buy		11
1	Antiques	13
2	Art	21
3	Books	32
4	Christmas and Other Celebrations	42
5	Cigars and Pipes	45
6	Clothes and Accessories	48
7	Collecting	64
8	Fabrics	69
9	Food, Spices, Candy, Wine, etc.	73
10	General-Department Stores and Mail-Order Houses	77
11	Handicrafts and Special Local Products	81
12	Hobbies	95
13	House	107
	Bathtubs	108
	Blankets	108
	Eiderdowns	108
	Flatware	109
	Furniture	110
	Modern Furniture	111
	Reproduction Furniture	115
	Garden Ornaments and Furniture	118
	Glass and China	120
	Hardware	127
	Household Objects and Gifts	127
	Kitchen	129
	Lace, Linen, Embroidery and Crochet	131
	Light Fixtures	133
	Pewter	134
	Rugs	136
	Do-It-Yourself Rugs	138
	Tiles	138
14	Jewelry and Silver	139
15	Music	145
16	Perfume and Cosmetics	149
17	Pets	151
18	Photographic Equipment	153
19	Services	
20	Special Needs	158
21	Sports Equipment and Clothes	162
22	Stereo Equipment	168
23	Toys	171
24	Watches	179
Appendices		
	Clothing Size Charts	181
	Additional Import Information	182
	Conversion Tables	183
	List of Customs Charges	184
Index		185

Introduction to New Edition

For this second edition of *The Catalogue of Catalogues* I have taken out the names of any shops that are no longer selling by mail, brought all addresses, information and prices up to date, and added the names of 300 new shops. Particularly interesting additions for the fearless are saunas and log cabins from Finland (suggested by a reader in Virginia), baths from England (requested by a Canadian reader who was very rude about the design of American bathroom fixtures) and boat sails made by an Irish firm (suggested by an English friend), but lots of smaller gaps are filled too—for instance, more countries are represented in the Handicrafts section.

Since the first edition of this book appeared I have written *The Catalogue of American Catalogues: How to Buy Practically Everything by Mail in America*, also published by Random House, and I have found that America is very good on sports equipment and clothes (specially for backpacking and camping), many hobby supplies (with the exception of yarn for knitting and weaving), food (there are some delicious regional specialties) and, of course, it is the place to buy reproductions from American museums, American Indian handicrafts and furniture in traditional American styles. Foreign sources are, perhaps, better for gifts and luxuries, among other things, and even though the dollar has been devalued, American importers raised their prices, so it is still worthwhile buying imports directly from abroad. But you do have to be careful and compare prices if you want to save money on imported versions of everyday things (English clothes for children, for instance, are no longer cheaper than American, but they are of much better quality for the same price, and children's clothes from Hong Kong are still real bargains). The advantages of finding better quality for the same price, and of finding many things that aren't for sale in America, also still hold when buying from abroad.

The first edition seemed to work out very well indeed. I got lots of letters from satisfied readers telling me about the bargains they had successfully bought through the book, other letters generously suggested more addresses (some of which have been included) and still others asking advice on where to buy silk stockings, hand-carved lazy Susans, metric wrenches and European automotive tools. Two people even got carried away and asked me for advice on what to do with their children.

And to calm the fears of anyone who, like the lady I met the other night, loved the book but would never dare use it, I got only eleven letters of complaints about things that had gone wrong, which is excellent considering the thousands of transactions that took place. Six of the letters complained about merchandise taking a long time to arrive, including one from a Canadian reader who ordered an automatic tea-making machine for Christmas that didn't arrive until January 21. Three other letters were about minor misunderstandings that were no one's fault, and two were more serious. One involved a personal check made out to "Cottage Industries" instead of Central Cottage Industries Emporium that never arrived. I haven't received any other complaints of this sort, but Indian shops have asked that letters containing payment be registered. The other involved Roger Elliot the fortuneteller (for an account of that complaint, see his listing).

The shops were mostly very pleased with their new customers and some smaller ones were delighted with the friendly letters and visitors they received (Kendal Playing Cards was even taken out to dinner and sent a can of maple syrup at Christmas by a traveling couple). Other shops complained that not enough of the people who sent for catalogues actually bought anything, so asked to be removed or decided to start charging for their catalogues. And practically all the shops wished that people would write their return address more clearly, and to repeat it in the letter as well as writing it on the envelope, and remember that surface mail takes several weeks each way . . .

HOW THIS BOOK ORIGINATED

I started buying by mail from abroad the way many people do—by writing to shops I had visited in other countries and asking for things I had seen and liked but not bought because of being in a hurry, overpacked or simply indecisive. After a trip to Sweden I wrote and ordered some blankets; after Denmark, some lamps; after France, perfume; after England, toys, glassware, pottery and yet more blankets; after Spain a leather couch and a carpet. Everything worked out so well that by this time I was hooked. I was also spending so much time giving out addresses to friends and friends of friends, and listening to people's stories about the odd things they buy from abroad (children's underwear from London and feather pillows from Geneva), that it occurred to me it would be very useful to have a list of all the shops abroad that sell by mail to other countries.

When I started writing to shops I wondered how many of them would be organized to sell efficiently by mail. I discovered, rather to my surprise, that there was a whole underground movement of mail-order shoppers busily at work. In fact, it seems that so many Americans returning from abroad have written back that they have caused the shops to produce catalogues and start an overseas mail-order business. Each country's enterprises have mushroomed in whatever the country does well—Italy, for instance, has masses of shops selling kid gloves by mail, but none for toys; Germany has toys galore but no furniture; Denmark has furniture but no perfume, and so on.

One of the great advantages of doing your own importing is that you get a tremendous choice of exotic, well-designed and useful objects that you just can't buy in America. Every section of this book, almost every catalogue listed, has goods that have never been imported (and many more that are available only in big cities). And even with things that are popular imports, you can get a much wider choice by writing to the source. When American shops import, they obviously have to restrict themselves to a few of the most popular models in each line—sweaters, for instance, available in four colors in New York are available in fifteen in Scotland.

The other great advantage to buying directly from abroad is all the money you save. Of the things I ordered, the Swedish blankets, the perfume, the leather couch and the carpet cost half of what they would have cost in New York *after* shipping costs and duty were paid. When American shops import, they pay duty, and also often pay exporters, importers and distributors as well. And on top of that they raise prices; there are many lines on which shops expect to make a 100-percent profit, and others where they expect to charge "what the market will bear."

But although by buying directly from abroad you nearly always save money, it's not automatically the case. In a few categories American prices are so low that it is not worth buying from abroad—for instance, certain less expensive wines. In other cases it would not be to your advantage to buy a single object (such as a coffee table or a doll house) which is too large to mail, though it might be worthwhile as part of a larger shipment. So when you are buying from abroad only to save money, always check local prices first and remember to allow for shipping costs and duty.

Another good thing about shopping from abroad is that it is very easy. The large shops with special export departments and catalogues in English are so efficient that it is almost less trouble to buy from them than to cross town and brave a crowded department store. Buying from small shops that sell one-of-a-kind handicrafts, pictures, antiques, etc., is obviously more of an adventure and more of an effort, as you have to write and ask about sizes, prices, shipping costs, etc. Nervous beginners should stick to shops which sell mass-produced articles and have catalogues in English with prices given in dollars.

The one real disadvantage to mail order from abroad is that there is no instant gratification—you have to wait for catalogues, and then you have to wait for the goods. And while small parcels can be air-mailed and received immediately, others take longer, occasionally leaving the worried shopper imagining that they will never arrive (this has never happened in my experience).

The addresses in this book were orginally taken from independent and reputable shopping guides to the specific areas, a few addresses were taken from government lists, and others were recommended by friends who had used them, (and I would be very pleased to hear about other shops that ought to be included in future editions). I wrote to over two thousand selected shops asking to see their catalogues. If the catalogues looked good, I sent a letter saying I was compiling a book, and asking various questions about how they sell to customers abroad and whether they can answer complicated letters in English (most can; there are warnings in the text about the exceptions). To many of the shops I then sent another irritating questionnaire asking for more details about prices of catalogues, when available, etc. From the shops answering these questions I chose those which seemed of most interest and included them in the book—there is no charge of any sort for being listed, of course. So all in all I hope that I have done everything possible to make sure that the listings are reliable. However, the book is intended as a guide to these shops, not an endorsement of them, and my descriptions are intended to give just an idea of the prices and the goods. Both of these are likely to change, so it is important to write for a catalogue or to check with the shop before ordering anything.

If, heaven forbid, the dollar should be devalued again, the goods in this book will go up in price; however, the same imported goods will go up in America too, so the price difference will usually stay the same.

Finally, the shops marked with crowns are royal warrant holders. Each crown means that the shop has supplied a member of the royal family with goods for at least two years and is allowed to boast about it—a handy indication that the shop is very reputable, but possibly expensive.

M.E.I.
May 1975

How to Buy

CATALOGUES

When there is a charge for a catalogue, the easiest, if riskiest, way to pay it is to *tape* coins onto a letter. If you prefer you can get international reply coupons at the post office, or you can pay with an ordinary check. When you make out the check (as with all amounts under $10 paid by personal check) you must add 75 cents for the bank charges that the shop will have to pay. However, shops seem to prefer cash for catalogues costing less than $2 because banks make it difficult to change checks for such small amounts. Most of the catalogues listed as free will come by surface mail and take four weeks or more to arrive. Do remember to send your requests by air mail if you are in a hurry; several shops have told me that they often get letters requesting catalogues to be sent immediately, and saying things like "as I want to buy a present for a birthday in June" and it is already July when the catalogue request arrives.

Some of the catalogue listings in this book include publication months; this is for shops which change a large part of their stock seasonally and allow their brochures to go out of print while the next one is being prepared. If you write just as a catalogue has run out, you may have to wait a couple of months before receiving an up-to-date one.

Most of the catalogues are in English; the exceptions are marked. Obviously foreign-language brochures are a nuisance if you don't know the language, as you have to write for more details, but for people who don't mind extra correspondence, they are very worthwhile, that is why I have included some.

ORDERING

When ordering from a shop whose description includes "prices in $" you will of course have no problem. For other shops the conversion tables at the back of this book should be a rough guide. At the time you want to send in an order and need to know the exact price in dollars, you can get the official exchange rate from a newspaper or bank, or buy up-to-date conversion tables from Perera, 636 Fifth Avenue, New York, N.Y. 10020. Or you can write to the shop and ask the price and shipping costs in dollars of what you are interested in. Don't forget to mention whether you want surface or air mail, and whether you want insurance.

Most of the shops will exchange things but this is troublesome, so when ordering, be obsessively specific about color, size, number, design, and so on. Be sure to keep the receipt for any duty you have paid, because if you do want to return a purchase, you will need it for the duty refund. I also find it very useful to keep copies of my orders to check dates, prices, reorders, etc., later on.

Make sure you order from an up-to-date catalogue, because prices and goods do change with the seasons.

PAYING

PERSONAL CHECK

This is the method that I always use because it is by far the easiest—you simply make out one of your personal checks, exactly as you would if you were paying an American firm, and mail it to the shop. The disadvantage of this method is that it is much slower than any of the others; most shops wait until their bank has cleared the check with your bank, which can take up to four weeks but is usually done in two weeks. If the amount you are paying is less than $10, don't forget to add the 75 cents which the shop has to pay in bank charges. If the check is for more than $10, shops usually pay the bank charges themselves. Payments to Indian shops should be sent by registered mail.

BANK DRAFT (INTERNATIONAL CHECK)

Although banks use the same methods of sending money abroad, they have their own names and charges for each method, so your bank may call "bank draft" something different. If you don't mind going to the bank and filling out a form, buy an international certified check there, made out to the shop you are dealing with, and air-mail it yourself so that the money reaches the shop within a few days. The charge at my bank for this is $1.20 for any amount under $300.

CABLE AND MAIL TRANSFERS

By these methods the bank air-mails or cables the money to the shop's bank, and the shop is immediately notified. If you don't know what bank the shop uses, your bank will choose a bank near the shop, and the shop will be told to collect the money. The advantage of a cable transfer is of course speed; it's the fastest method. My bank charges $1.90 for an air-mail transfer, and $1.70, plus the cost of a cable, for a cable transfer.

LETTER OF CREDIT

If a large sum of money is involved, you can pay with a letter of credit so that the money is guaranteed, but the letter is not given to the shop until the shop has shown certain documents to a bank. Decide first, with the shop, as to what documents are important—they could be the invoice stating exactly what you have bought and the bill of lading to show that it has been shipped, and a time limit can also be included in the agreement. Most shops want the credit to be "irrevocable," then the customer can't suddenly decide he doesn't want the goods while the order is being prepared. Any bank will arrange a letter of credit, but charges vary.

INTERNATIONAL MONEY ORDER

At the post office you buy an international money order made out to the shop you are dealing with, which the post office sends. At the moment the charges are: 45 cents for amounts under $10, 65 cents between $10 and $50, and 75 cents between $50 and $100.

SHIPPING

MAIL
Most parcels can be delivered exactly like domestic parcels, and if there is any duty it is paid to the mailman, along with an 80-cent handling charge, which the post office calls "postage due." However, there is a limit on the size and weight of a parcel that can be shipped by mail—it must not weigh more than 22 lbs., and the combined length and circumference of the parcel must not add up to more than 72". This means that the length of the parcel is measured in the usual way, but the width is measured with the tape right around the parcel.

AIR FREIGHT
This is used mainly for single objects which are too large to go by mail—framed pictures, large carpets, small pieces of furniture. Cargo of any size can be sent by air freight, and it is charged according to weight, volume and distance. Very roughly it works out at $1.70 to $2.05 a pound, and there is a minimum charge ($29 from Europe). The goods arrive at the airport nearest your address that has customs facilities, and you are notified of the arrival. You then go with identification and the bill from the shop (for customs) to the airport during office hours and see the parcel through customs (storage is charged if you don't go within five working days). If you want to employ a broker to get the parcel through customs, the airline can give you a list of firms.

SEA FREIGHT
This is only for large items such as furniture. Some of the shops in this book will arrange to have furniture delivered to your door by an agency, others just deliver to your nearest port. If furniture is delivered to a port, the steamship company will tell you when it arrives. You can then call a firm such as REA Express (formerly Railway Express) to see it through customs and deliver to your door, or you can save the flat fee of about $45 and get the furniture through customs yourself. If you do it yourself, you take the bill of lading and the bill for the furniture, both of which the shop will have sent you, and go to the steamship company to have the bill of lading stamped, then go to the customs house. Your crate will probably be opened, inspected and closed again, and you pay the duty. Then, with a certificate of clearance, you can take the goods away. If the package is too large, call someone experienced, like the REA people, who can tell you the exact cost of a job before they take it on; they charge by weight and distance. A few years ago I bought a couch from Spain and asked a small trucking firm to bring it over from the New Jersey docks to Manhattan. They charged by the hour, and as they were inexperienced, they kept arriving when the dock was closing, or at rush hour (and then consoling themselves with coffee breaks). I had to pay them $30 more than I would have paid REA. Big trucking firms such as REA are usually customs brokers too and take care of everything.

BRINGING THINGS BACK WITH YOU

If you are coming back from abroad by boat, you can save on shipping by bringing goods back with you as part of your family's baggage allowance (I have brought a sofa, an armchair, a bathtub and several smaller objects back with me this way without paying any sea-freight charges). Have whatever you buy abroad delivered straight to the steamship company's offices at the port. They will load it; you don't even see your purchases until you arrive at the port of entry to America, where you take them through customs and make arrangements with one of the shipping companies on the docks to deliver the things to your home. If you live in the same town, delivery should not be too expensive; mine has always been under $20. But if you live farther away, you should definitely find out about delivery costs, which can be high, before you even buy.

CUSTOMS DUTY

Duty isn't as high as you may think; for one thing, it is usually charged on the wholesale value of the goods (about 33 percent less than the retail value), for another, duty has been sharply reduced over the last few years and will probably remain at a new low level that was reached in January 1972. Gifts worth less than $10 are exempt from duty altogether, but only when bought by someone who is outside the country, so the very common practice of asking shops to mark parcels "Gift" is in fact illegal. However, I have found customs officers to be pretty lenient with small parcels—only one out of about ten toy or record parcels seems to be charged.

There is a guide to various rates of duty at the end of this book, but the rules for applying them are sometimes complicated, so you can't be sure what the exact charge will be until you receive the goods. If you ever think you have been overcharged, either refuse the parcel and write a protest to your postmaster, or accept the parcel, pay the duty, but send copies of the receipt for the duty and the shop's bill to the address given on the receipt. You may be able to get a refund, though not of the 80 cents post office handling charge called "postage due." If you ever want to return goods you have bought from abroad, write to the address on the receipt for duty to see whether and how you can get a refund.

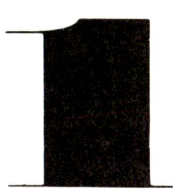# Antiques

Antiques

The shops in the Fine Arts section (below) are listed strictly for people looking for "significant examples of important styles in good condition"—"important pieces," as the shops call them. At these levels, prices in England are no lower than American prices; there are simply more pieces available.

If, however, you are simply looking for handsome pieces of antique furniture to furnish a house, then, in addition to having a wider choice, you should be able to find things at lower prices in the Furniture and General section than you can locally.

But except for one or two of the mail-order specialists, don't expect the same service from the small and personal antique shops that you get from the stores in the other sections. They can only answer requests for specific items, and if you don't get an answer you must assume that the store didn't have what you wanted.

No duty is charged for anything that is over a hundred years old.

ANTIQUITIES

G. Lambor, 345 Hangleton Road, Hove, Sussex, England
Subscription to six price lists, $1.

G. Lambor states that all the antiquities he sells are guaranteed to be what he says they are, and anyway, they are sent to his customers on approval (you get your money back on anything you return). He sends out ten short mimeographed lists a year. The one I looked at had forty-three items listed with short descriptions and twenty line drawings. The cheapest thing was Roman, a jeweler's crucible, of the Imperial Period, 3.2 cm. (1¼") high, and it was Ordinary (as opposed to Important/Superior/Interesting) and Defective (as opposed to Perfect/Signs of Wear/Badly Damaged). It cost $5. The most expensive thing was also Roman, a necklace of assorted beads rated Superior, with Signs of Wear. It cost $114, including postage.

ARMOR

The Armourer's Shop, 114 Buxton Road, Whaley Bridge, Near Stockport SK12 7JF, England
Catalogue, $1.

James Bernard Marsh, the owner of this shop of antique arms and armor, proudly proclaims that his customers frequently tell him he has the best catalogue in the United Kingdom. Arms come from all over the world, and in the catalogue I looked at, prices ranged from about $25 for a Victorian sword cane to about $550 for "a rare British military percussion musket of a type not previously encountered and probably experimental."

BEDS

Sheppard's Place Antiques, 23 Gloucester Street, Cirencester, Gloucestershire GL7 2DJ, England
Photographs and details, $1.

Brian Humphry specializes in antique fourposters in which, he says, he is the largest United Kingdom dealer and he has a large stock from the eighteenth and nineteenth centuries. He sometimes gets earlier, carved oak beds but they are becoming very rare. Some beds he has draped and upholstered and fitted with springs and new mattresses completely ready for use, but he says that beds with just the carved posts and frames are better for exporting because they are easier and cheaper to ship.

1
Strike One Very early Black Forest cuckoo clock. $400.

2
Strike One Eight-day American shelf clock in rosewood and gilt by Seth Thomas, Plymouth Hollow. Recently sold for $300.

CARPETS

Perez, 112 Brompton Road, London S.W.3, England
An excellent London shop specializing in fine, old, antique and expensive Oriental carpets and rugs, old tapestries, needlework and Aubussons. Their wares are too sought-after ever to reach the stage of being listed; but private collectors write from all over the world describing what they are looking for. When Perez finds something possible, they send photographs and a full description for the customer's approval.

CLOCKS

Strike One, 1a Camden Walk, London N.1, England
Descriptive list, free. Photographs on request.

"Clocks for decoration, interest and investment," Strike One says enticingly. Their specialty is an ongoing responsibility for their clocks even after the clocks are ticking away in the new owners' homes. Everything is thoroughly overhauled and sold in perfect working order with a one-year guarantee (you can mail them back to be fixed); a record is kept of key sizes, so that lost keys can be replaced by mail; a comprehensive repair service covers not only clockwork mechanisms, but also cases, dials, hands, weights—all the things that most repair shops refuse to handle. And mail-order customers are given a very good five-page booklet on how to set up and look after their clocks.

Some of the clocks are quite old; a seventeenth-century, one-handed lantern clock has a square brass dial decorated and signed "Thomas Parker" in beautiful copperplate writing. A Black Forest cuckoo clock in the earliest style has roses painted around the face, and the cuckoo pops out from a bouquet of flowers. All sorts of clocks are sold—wall, shelf and long-case—and prices are usually well over $200.

CURIOS

Boyne House (Kington) Ltd., 6 Bridge Street, Kington, Herefordshire HR5 3 DL, England
Price list, $3 (refundable with first order over $30). Prices in $.

The director of Boyne House tells me that he sells bric-a-brac and exports all over the world. Most popular with Americans, he says, are brass, copper, china and glassware, sewing items, dolls, interesting cans and advertising materials, though different states have different tastes. No dates are given for anything, and descriptions are minimal, so I guess this is a very superior, good old-fashioned junk shop patronized mainly by dealers.

The list I looked at had carnival glass, copper saucepans, candlesticks, toasting forks, sugar tongs, and things like "Pink china teapot, scroll edging, self color raised designs, gold bands and patterns, cherubs. Signed and impressed. Unusual shape 5½" high," and "11" diameter mahogany solitaire board complete with fairly early glass marbles"; and "Black leather box, gold edged, containing set of six mother of pearl handled knives, ornate patterned silver bands, blue velvet and satin lining." Many things cost less than $20; almost everything less than $50.

Edward Golemberski, 93 Whitemoor Road, Nottingham NG6 OHJ, England
Eight 28-page lists (published irregularly). Eight consecutive issues, $4.

An antique-and-curio catalogue (not illustrated) guaranteed to delight anyone looking for inexpensive, campy Victoriana to decorate their house or themselves. These are the things we were throwing out a few years ago, but with the rise of pop art have learned to love. For a mere $3.50 you can walk around wearing a large silver leaf-shaped pin saying "Mother," or hang on your wall an 1887 sampler with eight lines of religious quotation. For about $16, buy a rare nineteenth-century Staffordshire group in perfect condition of two girls asleep below a guardian angel; or a lidded tobacco jar inscribed with the owner's name and decorated with sprigged scenes of men smoking and drinking. There is blue, green, marigold and purple carnival glass, porcelain and pottery, watches and clocks, pipes, jewelry, beadwork and embroidery (a Victorian footstool embroidered with glass-bead flowers costs $15), and some miniature pictures and engravings of American interest—General Goffe repulsing the Indians at Hadley costs $1.80, Thomas Jefferson only $1.50.

A. Goto, 1–23–9 Higashi, Shibuya-Ku, Tokyo, Japan
Price lists, free. Prices in $.

An intriguing list of small Japanese things, most of which are just under one hundred years old. The list I looked at had netsukes (small hanging ornaments) made of all sorts of different materials, from incised yak horn (from Tibet) starting at $15 to Mongolian in jade and silver at $50 to $80. There were small antique figurines, jade hair pins and buckles, gunpowder holders and incense bottles, a limited quantity of carved wooden rice candy molds (would these do for cookie-mold collectors, I wonder?), brocade obis, and cast-iron or copper teapots from one hundred to one hundred and fifty years old for $6 to $12 each. Minimum order, $30. On a separate list, various raw materials such as exotic woods for carving were listed.

Thomas Humphrey Ltd., 24 Old Brompton Road, London S.W.7, England

Thomas Humphrey specializes in unusual antique objects and decorative oddities. A photograph of one of the rooms shows an appealing conglomeration of cherubs asleep on rose-garlanded cushions, naked women riding lions, galloping fairground horses, shining brass pots, and lots of smaller things that might be Elizabethan shoehorns, fairground scales, blacksmith's signs, ships' models, scientific instruments or almost anything else. If you are looking for anything special, Thomas Humphrey will try to find it.

FINE ARTS

Christie, Manson and Woods (U.S.A.), 867 Madison Avenue, New York, N.Y. 10021
Catalogue subscription list, free. Prices in $.

Sotheby and Co., P.O. Box 2AA, 34–35 New Bond Street, London W1A 2AA, England
Catalogue subscription list, free. Prices in $.

These grand English auction houses almost daily auction off "the things most worth living with," as one of them put it, frequently achieving world-record prices (I read recently in the *New York Times* that Christie's got a world-record price for an undrinkable old bottle of wine; the next week that Sotheby's got one for a Stradivarius). Comes the revolution, all this will be done away with, but meanwhile, in spite of the phenomenal record sales that get international publicity, there are plenty of things that people who are merely moderately well off can afford. You can subscribe to semi-illustrated catalogues throughout the season, more or less the academic year, for prices between $7 for something like musical instruments, and $72 for English and Continental antique furniture, ormolu, carpets, tapestries and textiles. Auctions are held of furniture, clocks, works of art, ceramics and glass, silver, jewelry, coins and medals, arms and armor, Art Nouveau, art deco posters.

You receive catalogues about two weeks before auctions, and if you want to bid you can write the house for an estimate of what the bids will be, and then send in your own. At the actual auction a member of the staff will bid for you. If you win, you are notified within two weeks and must inform the house where you want your prize shipped or stored. You can also subscribe to price lists that will arrive later telling you what each item finally went for, and who got them.

I asked a man who worked for Parke-Bernet, which is owned by Sotheby's, what the difference is between the two houses. He said that Christie's has a larger turnover, but no "better" than Sotheby's, and that Christie's has a "better record" on silver, while Sotheby's has a "better record" on French impressionists.

Antiques

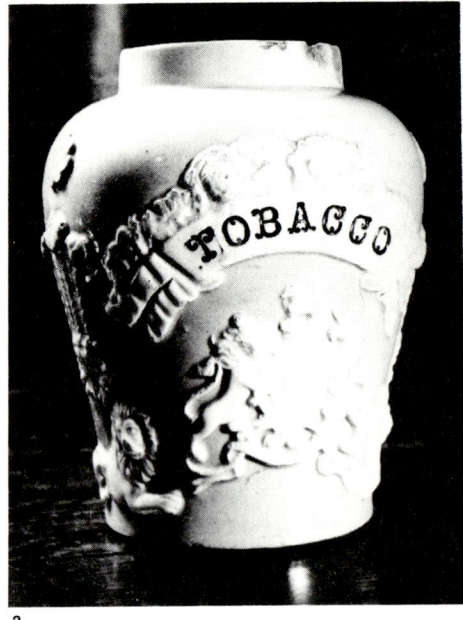
3

4

5

3
Edward Golemberski An early-nineteenth-century stoneware tobacco jar, decorated in white with lions and Prince of Wales feathers; chipped rim. $10.60.

4
Thomas Humphrey Ltd Rare Oriental processional figure in dry lacquer, late seventeenth century, possibly from Kansu province.

5
Thomas Humphrey Ltd 3'-high ivory-veneered cabinet from East India (circa 1750). Recently on exhibition at the Victoria and Albert Museum, London. $1,650.

6
Thomas Humphrey Ltd Eighteenth-century Italian carved wooden figure with original polychrome decoration 48" high. $900.

7
Spink and Son Ltd A rare George II mahogany commode chair (commode fitment removed), English (circa 1730). Recently sold.
photo Raymond Fortt Studio

8
Phillips Auctioneers Set on rare Bow "Seasons of the Year," each figure brilliantly decorated in polychrome enamels and gilded. The set of rare bow figures was recently sold for $2,168.

9
Crowther of Syon Lodge Ltd Stone groups of children with animals mounted on baroque pedestals; one of a pair of carved stone lions; one of a pair of terra-cotta jardiniers decorated with lion masks and swags of oak leaves.

10
Christopher Sykes A corner of the shop: Queen Anne padfoot oak side table (circa 1690), $250; stick barometer by P. Cossa $224; 1750 pewter chocolate urn, $100.

11
Christopher Sykes Rare 1790 Staffordshire figure, $75; small Staffordshire horse in yellow and brown, $23; red-coated Staffordshire huntsman holding fox. Firing crack on back, otherwise perfect, $36.

12
Eric Vejerslev Antique Russian candlesticks, over 100 years old. 21¾" high. The original glass shades have clear blue or red rims. About $185 a pair, plus postage.

Antiques

6

7

10

8

11

9

12

17

Antiques

Phillips Auctioneers, Blenstock House, 7 Blenheim Street, New Bond Street, London W1Y OAS, England
Subscription list to auction catalogues, free.

Puffing and blowing along behind the giants comes another auction house, 175-year-old Phillips Auctioneers. Indignant that the others get more publicity, they have made a movie about themselves showing behind the scenes at an auction house—they lend the movie free to interested groups (antique collectors and bankers mostly). All year there are daily auctions of furniture, paintings, porcelain, silver and art objects in their Bond Street auction rooms, with goods coming to them from all over the world and often going back to equally distant countries. But although you can attend these auctions when in London, the catalogues are seldom ready in time for mail order.

On the other hand, there are some auction catalogues that overseas collectors can subscribe to and receive in time to bid:

Two toy-soldier catalogues.

Six pot-lid catalogues (a few years ago Phillips Auctioneers got a world-record pot-lid price for "Washington Crossing the Delaware"). In the nineteenth century, English manufacturers often decorated the lids of pottery jars in which foods and cosmetics were sold, with full color transfers of famous people, events, humorous scenes or animals. These round lids, rarely larger than 5" across have become collector's items and are often framed for display.

Four stevengraph catalogues. In the middle of the nineteenth century Thomas Stevens, an English textile manufacturer, invented a way of weaving multicolored pictures in silk. These pictures of royalty, historical scenes, famous buildings, etc., are also collected.

Four Art Nouveau catalogues (glass, pottery and objects).

Not all of the catalogues are illustrated; subscription to most of the "special sale" auction catalogues is about $10.

Spink and Son Ltd.; 5–7 King Street, St. James's, London S.W.1, England

The omnipresent Spink's main enterprises are the fine arts sections, which contain only the most rare and important pieces. They send their old customers *Octagon*, a quarterly journal with articles and illustrations of new acquisitions (without prices). If you are serious and wealthy enough to want to become an old customer, write and inquire about your interests. Their Oriental Art is perhaps their best-known department, but they also have English silver and English paintings, and now a small gallery of early English furniture.

FURNITURE AND GENERAL

Antique Export Establishment, P.O. Box 21 498, LF 9493 Mauren, Liechtenstein
Catalogue, $5. September. Prices in $.

A fantastic collection of European antiques and antique reproductions are illustrated in the catalogue of this dealer, who exports to shops and to importers on orders worth over $200. You'll find old Austrian kitchen clocks in earthenware, porcelain, metal or brass; old American school clocks and cash registers ("It's the fashion for modern stores to use old American-made 'National' cash registers"); Charleston telephones ("used in the Roaring Twenties by Al Capone and his gang"); old Danish music boxes; painted peasant washstands; figureheads; horse-drawn carriages and working hurdy-gurdies (these start at $1,000); Dutch reproduction cookie molds and genuine street organs and orchestrations ("Please ask for special quotations"); English bisquit barrels, Victorian pressed glass, shaving mugs, brass miner's lamps, iron ship lamps and paintings "(all old and on canvas with old gold frames around). Special selected (can be sold for four times the amount in the United States)": German mirrors with gold-leaf frames, German hope chests with original paintings and date still on them, and dolls ("We specialize in dolls . . . From ordinary fifty-year-old ones especially from Germany to the expensive collector's dolls with French markings such as S. F. B. J. and Jumeau").

Somewhat horrifying for the average shopper are some of the descriptions of the reproductions which confirm one's worst fears about behind-the-scenes trickery in the "antique" world. For instance, from Pakistan, "Solid brass taxi horns reproduced to be sold by *Antique Dealers*, look handmade and old. We sell them as reproductions, but we know some of the dealers put them outside in the garden fourteen days and then even an expert can't see if they are old or new." At least in this catalogue reproductions are labeled as such, and it seems that the Antique Export Establishment sells reproductions of just about anything: early-American pine furniture, Victorian jewelry and silverware from Portugal, "Reproductions of Georgian silver, Sheffield silver or any item which you would like reproduced can be made at very moderate prices by Portuguese silversmiths. We are affiliated with a small factory which can handle any design." Seventeenth- and eighteenth-century styles of ceramics; and from Hong Kong, pewter plates (and tankards, and measuring sets), "dull color with old marks. Fantastic reproduction."

Prices are all extremely low, the owner says: "We are sure you will agree that Americans are now more interested in antiques than ever, especially when they can buy direct from the wholesalers in Europe and save up to 100%."

The Antique Lovers Coterie, Ingram Warwick Ltd., 6 South Molton Street, London W1Y 1DH, England
Price list, free.

Small antiques and collectible objects are described on the lists sent out every three or four months by this family business, established in 1912. The list that I looked at announced, besides about twenty-four other things, late-Victorian glass preserve jars at around $13 each; a Regency brass pestle and mortar for just over $100; a ship's chronometer (c. 1870) by John Fletcher for just over $1,000; and a restored 1830 liquor cabinet at the "come-at-able" price of $425. Pieces over one hundred years old are starred, and prices tend to start at around $30. Prints and maps are also listed.

Crowther of Syon Lodge Ltd., Busch Corner, Isleworth, Middlesex, England
Occasional catalogues (as I write, there is one available for $4). Photographs on request.

Crowther of Syon Lodge, a family firm with one of the largest antique businesses in England, specializes in statues and garden furniture, mantelpieces and grates, wrought iron and period-paneled rooms, mainly eighteenth- and early-nineteenth-century. As you can imagine, their clients are dealers, decorators or very wealthy people. If you happen to fit into one of these categories and are looking for something grand, you will probably find it at Syon Lodge. Most of the stock is not available in America, and Crowther's says that American dealers sell what they acquire from Crowther's for three times their purchase price.

In the catalogue that I looked at there was a room of Georgian paneling in perfect condition. If the customer's room size is slightly off, Syon experts can adjust the proportions of the paneling. (No price given!) Apparently there are usually about forty rooms waiting to be renovated, which is done by stripping off the layers of paint and stain, and finally wax-polishing the original pine.

The garden statuary is mainly eighteenth-century lead or

marble and very decorative: sundials, birdbaths and urns; lions, sphinxes, griffins and classical figures. A slim and graceful Apollo and Narcissus, a marble pair from the collection of Lord Leverhulme, cost $2,520.

Photographs of stock can be sent to you by return mail, and shipping costs can be given within two hours (presumably cabled or telephoned). Anything not in stock can be found.

Constance and Anthony Chiswell, 1 Market Place, Dunmow, Essex, England
Fountain House Antiques has dealt mainly with American dealers, but they will be very happy to answer inquiries from ordinary citizens as well. If you write and ask about their nineteenth-century decorative pieces—pottery, glass, silver and jewelry—they will tell you what they have, and if you place an order, mail it themselves. If you ask about rarer and more expensive things, such as eighteenth-century pottery and porcelain (English and Continental), English silver and rare glass, photographs can be sent with complete description and approximate date of manufacture. Expensive and fragile pieces are sent via London packers.

Margery Dean Antiques, The Galleries, Wivenhoe, Colchester, England
Information in reply to specific request, 5 International Reply Coupons.

Margery Dean, author of *English Antique Furniture,* has been selling reasonably priced English period furniture since 1947. Because of inflation she has stopped putting out a price list, but instead answers specific inquiries. Besides telling her what piece of furniture you need, don't forget to mention which period and which wood you want. If the information she sends you "proves acceptable," she will send a Polaroid photograph of the piece she has.

Furniture is stocked dating from 1600 on, including Victorian furniture and economical country furniture, so this is a very good place for people who want antiques that aren't too expensive. Prices at the moment are roughly $260 to $930, depending on size, for seventeenth-century gate-leg tables; $390 to $2,000 depending on whether they are made of oak, mahogany or walnut, for eighteenth-century bureaus; $60 to $230 for fruitwood side tables.

Abelardo Linares, Carrera San Jeronimo 48, Madrid 14, Spain
Probably now Spain's largest antique shop, Abelardo Linares is a four-generation family firm with a branch on Majorca. They have no catalogue of their antiques, but they do answer serious inquiries for paintings by old masters, sculptures, Spanish furniture, tapestries, paperweights, porcelains. However, be specific about whether you want an antique or a reproduction, as they have both.

Christopher Sykes Antiques, 11 Market Place, Woburn, Milton Keynes, Bedfordshire MK17 9PZ, England
P. Pottery and Porcelain Catalogue (English, Continental and Oriental): Staffordshire figures, Wedgwood, Worcester, Spode, Blue and White, etc.
T. Tavern Signs Catalogue (pub and shop signs, advertising signs, heraldic shields).
M. Metalware Catalogue (pewter, wrought iron, brass and copper), specializing in early Lighting, Cooking Utensils, Trade Tools, Apothecary Mortars, Locks and Keys.
S. Scientific Catalogue (microscopes, sundials, telescopes, sextants, levels, measuring instruments, clocks, medical instruments).
D. Doll Catalogue (toys, games, needlework, samplers, music boxes, mechanical, ship and horse models, musical instruments).
O. Oil Paintings and Watercolors Catalogue (seascapes, sporting, genre, landscapes, portraits, miniatures).
W. Wooden Articles Catalogue (Treen, tea caddies, military lap desks, miniature furniture, leather, carvings in wood, scrimshaw, ivory and horn).
G. Glass Catalogue (drinking glasses, decanters, bottles, colored glass, silver, Sheffield plate, snuffboxes and fine bronzes).
First catalogue, $3 (refundable), plus $1 (refundable) for each extra subject.

Christopher Sykes, who has often appeared on television and radio programs, has two large antique shops in Woburn village filled with antique pottery, porcelain, pewter, brass, copper, scientific instruments, tea caddies, etc., ranging in price from $30 to $1,000 each. He is wonderfully well organized to sell by mail, and since more than half his sales go to America, this is probably the best antique shop for you.

Erik Vejerslev, Hyskenstraede 7, Copenhagen K, Denmark
Photographs on request

Mr. Vejerslev sells old pewter, porcelain, lamps, mirrors, and pretty things for the house. However, *please* write only if you are seriously looking for something, because his letters are written out in longhand, in cautious English, and I can see that if he gets too many complicated inquiries, he'll have to shut the shop in order to answer them all. He does get a lot of American tourists, and says that Russian samovars and Russian brass candlesticks are a "big success" with them and usually available.

JEWELRY

N. Bloom and Son Ltd., 158 New Bond Street, London W.1, England
Monthly leaflets, free; a catalogue before Christmas, free. Prices in $.

A winged cherub on a Georgian heart-shaped brooch, a gold and turquoise bracelet "in the gothick taste," a Victorian "dearest" ring—N. Bloom sells unusual antique jewelry that ranges from the slightly odd, (an Egyptian-style, Victorian gold brooch with a scarab, $180), to the magnificent (a ruby-and-pearl watch with bow fob, obviously ex-royal property, $840). In between, there are some gorgeous pieces of antique and Victorian jewelry for a person looking for something more interesting than any modern jewelry. Prices start at $125 and go up to $8,000. Some of the Victorian pieces are the least expensive: a rich-blue enamel brooch with pearl flowers and gold decorations costs $350; an Etruscan-style bangle in gold and diamonds, $550; and an engraved gold-and-turquoise flexible bracelet, $310.

N. Bloom sends out a page each month illustrating about fifteen items from their stock, which, besides jewelry, includes English and some Continental silver, snuffboxes and nineteenth-century *animalier* bronzes and enamel.

JUDAICA

The Collector, 10 King David Street, Jerusalem, Israel
No catalogue or price list.

A rather nutty paean to collectors and collectors-to-be introduces the gallery owned by American-born and -educated Michael Kaniel: "You who adore the antique and value the unique, enveloped and enriched—with the fair and the fine . . . for the elegant you and your elegant home . . ."

Mr. Kaniel deals in jewelry, manuscripts and antiques of all sorts, but he is actually a specialist in Judaica and rare Jewish art. He has published articles on the subject in

Antiques

13
Keith Harding Antiques Completely overhauled music box by Nicoles Frères, with drum bells and castanets, sold for $550 in 1972. Now worth $1,200, according to Keith Harding.
photo Harvey Johns

14
Denise Poole 1793 cruet by Peter and Anne Bateman. The three larger bottles are original; the two smaller, Sheffield 1819. Mint condition, $230, sold in 1973. Now worth $360, according to Denise Poole.

15
Denise Poole Hester Bateman teapot, London 1787, crested on one side, $750. Hester Bateman sugar basket, London 1786. Mint condition, $245. Both sold in 1973. Teapot now worth $950 and the sugar basket $400, according to Denise Poole.

American and Israeli magazines, contributed to the *Encyclopedia Judaica*, formed the Judaism display at the New York World's Fair, and has had his private collection of antique Jewish art exhibited in American museums. He says that he has also assembled collections for clients over the world, so if you are seriously interested in Judaica or rare antique Jewish art, write to Mr. Kaniel with specific inquiries only.

MUSIC BOXES

Keith Harding Antiques, 93 Hornsey Road, London N7 6DJ, England
Lists of cylinder and disc music boxes, list of spare parts for antique boxes, list of books on music boxes, $5 (refundable). Prices in $.

The last lines on the Keith Harding music-box price list are: "You might think we go to a great deal of trouble to give you exactly what you want. We do." And this does look like a place where music boxes and music-box lovers will be equally cared for and cosseted. There are eight craftsmen working and four floors of showrooms, museum, workshop and storage, plus a main workshop in another building. Modern boxes are made there, and antique boxes are overhauled before they are sold, with a guarantee that they leave the shop in the best possible condition. Hymns, operatic selections, waltzes, popular airs, and even "the British Army Quadrille" in five turns. Inlaid rosewood or painted boxes by Nicole Frères and other makers from $500 to $5,000. Photographs and recorded tapes are available.

Customers' own music boxes are repaired and cylinders repinned at $9 per inch.

SCIENTIFIC INSTRUMENTS

Harriet Wynter, Arts & Sciences, 352 Kings Road, Chelsea, London S.W.3, England
Catalogues of ancient scientific instruments and books, free; $1.25 air mail.

The Wynter catalogues are a joy to behold, showing how lovely the working instruments of the past can be. The two current lists, of old microscopes and sundials, include some marvelous examples of early technology. Under such simple names as "English Universal Microscope" are pictures of beautifully simple brass instruments, as evocative an artifact of its time (1754) as much more pretentious works of art. The catalogues show a small part of the firm's holdings, but the store will also try to find items that either private or public collectors are looking for. Wynter believes it is the only such dealer in antique scientific instruments in the world, although, unless I am mistaken, there is at least one similar shop in Paris. Wynter is, however, the only one I know of that sells by mail-order catalogue. Prices for the instruments are available on request only, but the list of books on the history of science gives book prices.

SILVER

Denise Poole, South Thoresby, Alford, Lincolnshire, England
54-page catalogue, free. Prices in $.

Denise Poole sells choice eighteenth- and nineteenth-century English silver almost exclusively by mail and she is well set up for it. Mugs, jugs, spoons, salt dishes, wine labels, sugar baskets, teapots, trays and more are photographed and described in detail in the catalogue, and she has a mailing list to keep customers up to date on recent acquisitions.

2 Art

Art

Some galleries publish catalogues for people who aren't able to get to certain exhibitions, others specialize in selling by mail. One way or another, the shops, galleries and museums in this section broaden the choice available for everyone, because even people living in art centers like New York can't buy locally some of the works listed here.

Oil paintings are obviously the hardest to choose by mail, but collectors do it, and there are firms willing to supply anyone who wants to try. Reproductions are the easiest, and there are great bargains in those areas: see the famous Italian Alinari reproductions, for instance.

There is a section called Graphics, which lists shops that sell original prints made from a block, plate or stone on which the artist himself worked, and from which a high-quality small edition has been produced. Another section, Maps and Prints, lists original prints made the same way, but some of these prints have been produced in large editions for magazines and other mass media.

There is no duty on art.

DRAWINGS

Martyn Gregory, Gregory and Kruml, 9 Lancashire Court, New Bond Street, London W1 9AD, England
Exhibition catalogues, May and November, $7 for both.

Martyn Gregory's prices have gone up. He is now selling English drawings and watercolors at prices from $250 to $2,000. The catalogue shows lovely eighteenth- and nineteenth-century landscapes, looking as idyllic as watercolor landscapes can. I hadn't heard of any of the painters.

Alister Mathews, Fremington, 59 West Overcliff Drive, Bournemouth BH4 8AB, England
Catalogue, 8 International Reply Coupons.

I got a very emphatic letter (with important points typed or underlined in red) from Alister Mathews, who since 1937 has been selling original antiquarian drawings (not prints) from the nineteenth and twentieth centuries; drawings by book illustrators (not books, not prints); and English watercolors from the eighteenth to twentieth centuries. The catalogue I looked at described over one hundred works (and had about sixteen illustrations) with many prices from $25 to $200, including some works by Canaletto, Sir Edwin Landseer and Claude Monet, but most by lesser-known artists.

Mr. Mathews says that he has definitely NOT the time or inclination to send off catalogues unless he is sure they will be really appreciated, so he doesn't accept orders to "send all forthcoming catalogues."

Stanza del Borgo, Via Giacomo Puccini 5, Milan 20121, Italy
Catalogue "Five Centuries of Drawings of Architecture and Building Ornamentation," September 1972. $5 surface, $7 including air mail.
Catalogue "The Neo-Classical Echo," 1973. $7 surface, $9 including air mail.
Catalogue "Un po di Seicento," 1974. $7 surface, $9 including air mail.
Catalogue planned for 1975 which will include etchings, lithographs and drawings of the end of the nineteenth and beginning of the twentieth century from France, Great Britain, Germany and U.S.A.

The director, Liliana dal Pozzo, writes: "My gallery specialises in ancient art for collectors and I deal very much with international and national museums such as Louvre, museum of Stuttgart, museum of Berlin, museo Casa di Michel-Angelo, Memorial Museum in Los Angeles, Modern Art Museum in New York and many others."

GRAPHICS

Ganymed Original Editions Ltd., 11 Great Turnstile, London W.C.1, England
Mailing list for occasional illustrated prospectuses.

Ganymed publishes limited editions of graphic works by modern artists, usually between fifty and seventy-five copies. Publications have included suites of lithographs by Kokoschka, Sidney Nolan and L. S. Lowry, and etchings by Ben Nicholson and Arthur Boyd, all on handmade paper, carefully boxed and presented. Prices from $150 for a single print.

Kegan Paul, Trench, Trubner and Co., 43 Great Russell Street, London W.C.1, England
Occasional catalogues and lists, free.

One of the best dealers in the world in Japanese and Chinese prints, Kegan Paul issues lists and catalogues throughout the year on all aspects of Africa and the Orient, especially art. I have seen two illustrated catalogues, one of them from an exhibition of sixty Japanese drawings of artists known and unknown in the West from the first half of the nineteenth-century. The prices started at $36 for a fan painting of a pair of cranes by Toyo, and several other items at that price, including a few humorous drawings by Naohiki, a pupil of Shigehiko. A bird and tree trunk with a slight red wash and *sumi* by Nanrei cost $72; a Hokusai-school sketch of a girl by a lantern, $240; and the most expensive of all, a magnificent dragon by Hokusai, was $1,320. The other catalogue of Japanese prints had an exact description of the condition of each print, with prices starting at $180 for an eighteenth-century print—a picture by Torji Kiyomasu II of a nobleman inscribing a letter before a princess—though a more typical price was $300 for a print by Choskai of three girls under a flowering cherry.

Richard Kruml, 9 Lancashire Court, New Bond Street, London W1 9AD, England
$7 for a year's subscription to at least two catalogues.

Richard Kruml deals in "fine Japanese color prints" and once or twice a year sends a catalogue to the people on his mailing list. The catalogue I looked at was of Hiroshige landscapes and gave information on the quality of the impressions, the state of the prints, and the types of seal. About two thirds of the listed prints were illustrated, and prices were mainly around $300—though they went as low as $72 and as high as $700.

Lumley Cazalet Ltd., 24 Davies Street, London W.1, England
Exhibition catalogues, $2 each.
List for artists usually in stock, free.

Lumley Cazalet sells twentieth-century original prints by English and European masters. They hold exhibitions six or seven times a year and will put you on their mailing list to receive notice of all forthcoming exhibitions. You can then ask to have any exhibition catalogue air-mailed to you for $2.

Apart from the special exhibitions, Lumley Cazalet always has other graphics in stock, and have a standard list giving names of artists whose work is usually available, as well as approximate prices. To give you an idea (alphabetically): Bonnards start at $90; Braques at $200; Calders at $20; Chagalls at $12. These starting prices are for large, unsigned editions. The prints can be seen in standard catalogues on the artist, or if you can't get hold of one, Lumley Cazalet will send photographs. This gallery also receives many requests for rare prints which, if not in stock, are tracked down.

Art

1
Alister Mathews Elizabeth Walker (née Reynolds) 1800–1876. Miniature pencil and watercolor of "The Whitethorne Family." 16″ × 18¼″. About $250.

2
Alister Mathews Artist unknown. "Pocahontas." Mid-seventeenth-century oil on canvas 12½″ by 9¼″.

3
Richard Kruml Utamaro, a recently sold print.

4
Richard Kruml Hiroshige "Station 37 Miyanokoshi." A fine impression in very good condition. Sold for $660.

5
Lumley Cazalet Ltd Paul Helleu "Looking at the Watteau Drawings in the Louvre." 11¾″ × 15¾″. Signed drypoint (circa 1895). $910. Sold.

6
Lumley Cazalet Ltd Henri Matisse "Hindou, Jupe de Voile." 11″ × 14¾″. Signed lithograph (1929). $9,500.

Art

7
Louise King Typical of fashion plates for sale, about $10 each.

8
Louise King Johannes de Bischop (Dutch, 1646–1686) "Young Man Turning Around." Etching. $10.60. Typical of stock.

9
Louise King "Two Men Burning a Bishop." 1472 woodcut, heightened with color. Printed at Augsburg. $21.20. Typical of stock.

Orangerie Verlag, Helenestrasse 2, 5 Cologne 1, Germany
Catalogue with some color, $6; $8 air mail. In German.

This German publishing house and art gallery sells a vast number of prints both of its own making and printed by others. The catalogue is so extensive that collectors may be interested in it simply to see what the going prices are for their favorite artists. Such prices can be very high indeed, with a number of lithograph listings in the thousands rather than hundreds of dollars. The catalogue includes a great many graphic artists whose work I don't know, but on the other hand, just about all the leading modern names are there. The catalogue is well illustrated with some lovely color prints, but unfortunately, the text is entirely in German. While you will have no trouble figuring out what *"Original Lithographie"* means, it would be wise to check with Orangerie about the details of any print you may wish to buy.

The Red Lantern Shop, 236 Shimmonzen Street, Higashiya-Ku, Kyoto 605, Japan
20-page catalogue, free.

Red Lantern specializes in modern Japanese prints, all the works being carved and printed by the artists in signed and numbered editions. The styles range widely, and while a few are clearly modern versions of traditional wood blocks, others seem much more Western, with Redon or Dali or even, in one case, Keane as the influence. The artists vary so much that it is impossible to say what kind of taste the catalogue appeals to most. There are some traditional Christian subjects that would be quite suitable in a progressive church, while others are much more old-fashioned. Prices, in any case, are very reasonable, ranging from under $10 to one at $100, with the largest concentration in the $20–$40 range.

Signum Press Ltd., P. O. Box 1476, Station B, Montreal H3B 3L2, Canada
Leaflet, 1 International Reply Coupon.

Signum Press produces signed and numbered graphics "to offer the collector original graphics of high artistic and technical quality by internationally known artists at a lower price through increased editions, namely, three hundred, of which two hundred and seventy are offered for sale." The leaflet I have shows serigraphs by Alfred Hrdlička, Denis Juneau, Norman Laliberté, Almir Mavignier, Manfred Mohr, and John Roy—most of them abstracts—at prices between $60 and $100.

William Weston Gallery Ltd., 10 Albemarle Street, London W.1, England
A year's subscription to at least twelve brochures, $8. Prices in $.

Perfectly set up for mail order, the William Weston Gallery issues monthly black-and-white brochures of recent acquisitions. They stock original etchings, engravings, lithographs, etc., by nineteenth- and twentieth-century masters and hold occasional special exhibitions for which they also send out brochures. I was sent a current brochure and one from a recent exhibition. The monthly brochure illustrated seventeen works by artists such as Albers, Feininger, Manet, Munch, Palmer, Roualt, Vuillard, and a few others not so well known. Prices started at about $47 for an etching, "L'Intérieure au Canapé" by Vuillard, initialed on the plate, and went as high as $1,240 for an initialed color aquatint, "Clown Assis" by Roualt. The brochure for an exhibition of color lithographs and etchings by impressionists and post-impressionists had some illustrations in color, and the prints were more expensive, starting at $240 for "Aux Champs-Elysées" by Henri Edmond Cross, apparently one of the few pointillist lithographs, and going up to $2,450 for a signed linocut, "Picador et Taureau," from an edition of fifty by Picasso.

The Yoseido Gallery, 5–15 Ginza 5 Chome, Chuo-Ku, Tokyo, Japan
100-page catalogue with some color, $3; $5.50 air mail. Prices in $.

A first-rate catalogue of limited-edition, signed wood-block prints by modern Japanese artists. As the wood block is still highly valued and much used in Japan, and as the Yoseido Gallery handles the works of all the best-known Japanese artists using this medium, the catalogue shows a huge and varied collection that should please all but the choosiest of customers. Most modern styles are represented, and many pictures show overwhelmingly Western influences — some look like Klees, others like Calders, there is even a blue-purple "Chicago — Night View" by Fumio Kitaoka. Prices are generally between $10 and $50, and there are also about fifteen unlimited, signed prints at $13 each.

MAPS AND PRINTS

Collectors Treasures Ltd., 91 High Street, Amersham, Buckinghamshire, England
List of maps, $1.

This is a list with only brief descriptions of some of the types of maps available, so you have to know what you want. Decorative maps by Tallis (c. 1850) of most of the world cost between $16 and $36 and are adorned with views of notable buildings, local costumes, etc. Another decorative series, by Thomas Moule (c. 1836–43), shows the counties of England with vignettes, heraldry, sometimes first railways.

Ernst Geissendorfer, Postfach 33, 8803 Rothenburg ob der Tauber, Germany
Christmas-card brochure, catalogue of etchings by Hans Figura, catalogue of etchings by Ernst Geissendorfer — all three $1 surface mail, $2 air mail.

This print shop in the market square of the old town of Rothenburg in Bavaria sells at very modest prices, under $10 each, etchings in black-and-white or hand-colored by the owner of the shop, Ernst Geissendorfer. Most of the etchings, which are in a very precise, traditional style, are of old views of Rothenburg, but at slightly higher prices there are views of other German and of Italian towns by Paul Geissler, and of Yale and Princeton universities. Another artist, Hans Figura, has a freer style, and his views of European cities and snow-covered landscapes are more romantic. Etchings by all three artists are available reproduced on Christmas cards. This firm was recommended to me by a reader, Roberta J. Frus, who says the service is very prompt.

Louise King, 36 Gloucester Circus, Greenwich, London S.E.10, England
Catalogue, $1; $2 air mail.

Mrs. Louise King sells original, inexpensive prints and engravings by mail, and publishes two riveting catalogues a year listing about a hundred items from her very varied stock. She gives fairly detailed background information and an illustration or two for each type of print; otherwise, prints are just listed and described. There is an approval service for old customers, and new customers may return anything they don't like.

The catalogue that I looked at had, for under $20, modern color mezzotints and etchings by the once unpopular Stefano della Bella, 1610–1664 (a thousand proofs and fine engravings of his, belonging to the Duke of Cambridge, were sold at Sotheby's for $10 in 1904, but Louise King claims he's now being "belatedly recognized"). At various prices below $200 there were etchings by Edouard Manet, James McNeill Whistler, Alfred Sisley, Giambattista Piranesi; and at prices below $500, woodcuts by Dürer and a lithograph by Gaugin.

The Parker Gallery, 2 Albemarle Street, London W1X 3HR, England
Catalogue, free; $1.50 air mail. October.

The oldest established firm of picture and print dealers in London has an enormous collection of prints and publishes a semi-illustrated catalogue each October. The catalogue I looked at listed the kinds of prints in stock at the shop: marine, military, topography, sporting, transport, trades, caricatures, weapons, family portraits and decorative; but the catalogue also listed specific "views of the world," for sale with most prices between $12 and $60. The Parker Gallery is willing to send prints "on approval," and will look for anything special you want that is not in stock.

Paul Prouté, S.A., 74 Rue de Seine, Paris VI, France
Catalogue, $6. Available March – May only.

Paul Prouté is well known for its immense stock of half a million prints, which are sold to private individuals and American dealers. Stock ranges from the fifteenth-century to contemporary artists, and includes old-master prints, views of cities, portraits, old maps.

P. J. Radford, Sheffield Park, Uckfield, Sussex, England
50-page map catalogue: Americana, free.
50-page map catalogue: British Isles, free.
50-page prints catalogue, free.
General catalogue, free. Any catalogue, $5 air mail.

P. J. Radford, author of *Antique Maps*, published in England, has a magnificent stock of prints and rare maps, especially Americana, described and displayed in his temptingly well designed catalogues. Even nonmap collectors might be seduced by some of these; indigenous inhabitants, ships in full sail, sea monsters, mythological figures, the seasons and the elements crowd the maps with decorative activity. Prices for rare maps start at about $70 and seem to depend partly on how much demand there is for the country. A map of Bohemia, for instance, in spite of marvelous pictures of cities and costumes of all the social classes, tends to be less expensive than, say, of America. Near the top of the price scale, at $425, comes something like "Novissima Totius Terrarum Orbis Tabula," by Nicolao Visscher (c. 1685), with full original coloring. The world is shown in two hemispheres (with California as an island), and the whole is surrounded by a profusion of allegorical figures representing the elements and the signs of the zodiac.

If you want to pay much less, ask for the prints catalogue and look at the nineteenth-century prints of Europe and America, about $20 each. Taken from engravings, they were often used as tourists' mementos, and show a blissfully unspoiled, pastoral world.

Sifton, Praed and Co. Ltd., 54 Beauchamp Place, Knightsbridge, London SW3 1NY, England
No catalogue.

Sifton, Praed and Co. writes: "We have one of the best collections of antique maps in Britain and, although we do not do a catalogue as our stock turns over too fast, we are always willing to send our lists on any particular area or cartographer."

Uchida Art Co. Ltd., Kyoto Handicraft Center, Kumanojinja-Higashi, Sakyo-Ku, Kyoto, Japan
Color leaflet, free. Prices in $.

This firm sells the kind of modern Japanese wood-block prints you often see on Christmas cards and calendars. Here the prints are larger, for framing, and subjects are mostly birds, flowers, horses, Japanese landscapes, and figures in Japanese costumes. Each one costs about $6.

Art

10
P.J. Radford A map of Virginia by Henry Hondius (1636). $300.

11
P. J. Radford Typical of early-nineteenth-century horse prints for sale. Hand-colored. Smaller sizes from $20, larger sizes from $30.

12
P. J. Radford Typical of flower prints for sale with original hand coloring, issued in the 1850s and 1860s. From $30.

10

11

12

13

14

13
Old Hall Gallery Ltd Henry Howard R.A. exhibiting 1794–1804 "Caroline Carey" oil painting in the original frame. This picture comes with a letter describing its history. $1,400, including delivery to the customer's nearest airport. Sold.

14
Old Hall Gallery Ltd George Morland (1763–1804) "Bargaining for Fish" 27" × 35". This oil painting has been exhibited at the Victoria and Albert Museum, London, and comes with two books on George Morland in which the picture is mentioned. $1,750, including delivery to the customer's nearest airport. Sold.

15
Educational Graphics "The Sky at Night." Poster. About $2.

15

Art

16
Lecuyer Original American Depression poster. $15, including postage.

17
Lecuyer Original American Depression poster. $15, including postage.

18
The Lords Gallery Ltd Poster by Greifenhagen in red, white and black. $38. Typical of stock.

PAINTINGS

Christie, Manson and Woods (U.S.A.) Ltd., 867 Madison Avenue, New York, N.Y. 10021
Catalogue subscription list, free. Prices in $.

Sotheby and Co., P.O. Box 2AA, 34—35 New Bond Street, London W1A 2AA, England
Catalogue subscription list, free. Prices in $.

The subscription lists give information on the price of subscriptions to catalogues for sales in each field. Christie's and Sotheby's, England's two leading auction houses, have art auctions throughout the season (September to June) in which Monets are sold to the Metropolitan, Géricaults back to the French, and Rembrandts to collectors from Los Angeles, all for thousands of dollars and so much publicity that closed-circuit television has been installed to accommodate all the would-be buyers. Anyone who can't be there, may bid by mail. Subscribe to a season's worth of catalogues for any favorite category, and the partly illustrated catalogues will arrive about two weeks before the sales. Then, if anything catches your fancy, you can ask the house for an estimate of the bids and send in your own. At the appropriate time a staff member will bid for you. You can also subscribe to price lists that arrive later and tell you who bought each item and what they paid.

Both houses sell old-master and modern paintings, drawings and prints in various combinations. At Christie's this year there were twelve art categories: a subscription to catalogues for old-master and modern prints cost $7; impressionist, modern paintings, drawings and sculptures, altogether $20; old-master paintings up to 1900, $40. At Sotheby's there were nine categories: catalogues for eighteenth- and nineteenth-century drawings and watercolors cost $7; old-master drawings, $16; and impressionist and modern paintings, drawings and sculptures, $41.

G. Cramer, Javastraat 38, The Hague, Holland
Current catalogue in two parts, $10, including air mail postage.

"Oude Kunst" says the stately Cramer letterhead, but "paintings by old masters" is a closer description than "old art." The Cramer catalogues, with one illustration per page, are clearly aimed at museums and very wealthy collectors. The current offerings include several paintings by Jan Steen, two Rembrandts, a Rubens, a Cranach, etc. Cramer writes that the listing is "for a very specialized public [and therefore] there is no printed price list but every serious inquiry will be replied separately." A fascinating look at the caliber of work still available for sale, but not for the casual browser.

Euston Gallery, 126—130 Drummond Street, London N.W.1, England
Catalogue, free.

The Euston Gallery boasts of a stock of over one thousand paintings, costing from $3 up, and the catalogue gives but a small sampling of its collection. A number of items are of the kind that you would expect to find at the Washington Square annual exhibit, but others are of earlier versions of the genre, some from the Victorian period or even older. The cover of their current catalogue shows a 1930's (?) portrait of the Queen Mother which, if you acquired it, may not be the ideal way to make your money grow but may be just what your living room needs.

Art

Fortune Hand Work Family Co. Ltd., P.O. Box 6066, Kowloon, Hong Kong
Catalogue with some color, free. Prices in $.

If you fancy a "touch of the Orient" (to quote the text) in your home, send for this catalogue, which illustrates small touches such as hand-painted pictures of misty mountains and birds on blossoming branches; ceramic reproductions of Tang Dynasty animals and Buddha figures; stone rubbings and Chinese scrolls. If you'd like a really dramatic touch of the Orient, look at the hand-painted wallpapers, which are Chinese scenes painted on four panels which, when put together, make a picture of about 10′ high by 18′ long. If the size isn't right, then wallpaper can be made to your own size, and even your own design (European designs accepted). Prices go from about $20 for framed stone rubbings to about $500 for the wallpaper. Hand-painted and Coromandel screens are sold, but will be more expensive to ship.

Old Hall Gallery Ltd., Iden, Rye, Sussex, England
48-page catalogue, $1. Prices in $.

The Old Hall Gallery is a small family firm that sells seventeenth-, eighteenth-, and nineteenth-century paintings, but specializes in the "rising field" (though all the art fields seem to be "rising fields") of Victoriana. They supply museums and galleries; in England they have supplied institutions such as the Victoria and Albert, London, and the Ashmolean, Oxford, and in America, the Capitol Museum, Washington State, the Princeton Museum, and others. Everything is efficiently organized: catalogues with black-and-white photographs of framed paintings are published several times a year, prices include air freight to America, and there is an explanation of terms of attribution generally used in the London Art World (their capitals). "Signed," for instance, means a signature of the artist, whereas "signature" means a signature which *may* be by the artist. After seeing the catalogue, ask for color slides of any picture you are interested in.

Subjects are much the same as the Giles Gallery's, but almost all the painters were successful enough in their lifetimes to exhibit in London, and prices are correspondingly higher—mostly between $800 and $2,000, though there are several above and below those prices.

Margaret E. Wolverson, Wychelm, Atwick Road, Hornsea, North Humberside, England
Price list, free.

Margaret Wolverson paints miniature oil paintings on a variety of set subjects, many of them horsy ones. "The Meet at a Country House," "Riding in the Snow," "Welsh Mountain Pony" are typical titles. But she will also paint a picture following an idea of your own, or a miniature portrait if you send her a photograph. She says that paintings of horses and dogs, and hunting and snow scenes are her most popular subjects.

The paintings are oval-shaped and really tiny; with the mount and frame they measure 4″ by 4″. Miss Wolverson's standard scenes cost $13 in a square frame, and $25 in an oval frame. Her portraits to order cost from $20 to $45. Paintings are sent on approval; if you don't like the one you get, you can send it back and have either your money returned or another painting submitted.

Mark Rimmell, Willow Cottages, 34b Willow Road, Hampstead, London NW3, England
Send a photograph of a horse or ship for an estimate.

Mark Rimmell has two artists specializing in ships and two specializing in horses who will paint in oil on canvas a portrait of your horse or ship from a photograph. The style of the pictures, judging by the photographs he sent me, is a rather pleasant, dignified, eighteenth-century style with a touch of the primitive. Prices are between $75 and $125 according to the size of the picture. Excellent presents for a doting horse or ship owner.

POSTERS

Arts Council Shop, 28 Sackville Street, London W1X 1DA, England
34-page publications price list, 20-page visual-arts price list, 50 cents each.

The British Arts Council's new shop is an exciting new listing for those interested in the arts. This handsome showplace, on a small street between Piccadilly and Regent Street, is still unknown to most Londoners, but for both visitors and mail-order shoppers alike, it is an ideal source for a wide range of materials which were practically unobtainable before. The store sells posters, prints, books, records, slides, photos, catalogues, just about everything that might normally be found in a well-stocked museum shop in America, but here the inventory represents material from every museum in England. In addition, there are the Council's own special projects—books, catalogues, poetry broadsides, posters, specially commissioned prints. Here are posters for the Royal Shakespeare Company's various productions, or those of the Royal Opera or Sadler's Wells, ranging in price from $2 to $3. The same prices apply to extremely well reproduced art posters announcing exhibits of Russian Revolutionary posters, French symbolists or Chinese paintings. In addition, some of the provincial museums have come up with beautiful posters which until now would have been available only if you had visited Manchester or Birmingham or Coventry.

The Council has also printed a series of handsome poetry posters, featuring a poem by Ted Hughes or Sylvia Plath or even Coleridge, costing for the most part $1.50 each. The shop has a smaller selection of art reproductions, on the whole inexpensive by American standards, as well as a series of Inigo Jones architectural drawings that I hadn't seen elsewhere. Slides, some five hundred lovely postcards from various museums, folios of photographs and a number of museum reproductions are all available, as well as a good collection of books and catalogues described in the Books section. It would be nice if our own excellent museum stores went one step further and followed the Council's example. As it is, the store is a delight, and the easiest way I've found of buying gifts that I know none of my friends can possibly have found for themselves.

Caldron Promotions, 98 Mill Lane, West Hampstead, London NW6 1PA, England
Color leaflets, 3 International Reply Coupons; $1 air mail.

A colorful collection of posters and patches for children and teenagers. Many of them are imported from America, but others are English or Continental, and particularly with the patches, there is a much wider variety than most local shops carry.

Dodo, 185 Westbourne Grove, London W. 11, England
Brochure planned, $1.

Dodo, which has all sorts of fashionable things like pub mirrors available in its shop, sells old, if not antique, paper decorations by mail. They have masses of huge 1930's English pantomime posters (the English Christmas show in which the leading man is played by a girl, and the comic turn is a female played by a man, and a good time is had by all), leggy Robinson Crusoes and bow-mouthed Red Ridinghoods, for between $10 and $50. Dodo also has old chemist posters,

28

Art

19
Adachi Institute of Woodcut Prints Cover of catalogue showing five hundred reproductions of Japanese woodcut prints. Price of catalogue $8 including surface postage.

20
Mary Potter Designs Knight and lady from medieval church brasses reproduced as two wall hangings 7" × 20". Black design on white cotton, about $3 each. Black design on orange or mustard, about $3.50 each. Air mail 50 cents for one, 75 cents for two.

21
Mary Potter Designs A scene from the Bayeux tapestry reproduced on a wall hanging. $12 and up.

which are described as "very amazing and *original*," for about $5 each; French jam labels; English wine labels; American orange- and lemon-crate labels; and cigar-box labels.

Educational Graphics Ltd., 43 Camden Passage, London N1 8EB, England, or P.O. Box 798, Oak Park, Illinois 60302
Leaflet, 25 cents; air mail 50 cents.

This English firm (formerly Posters by Post) had so many orders after its listing in the first edition of *The Catalogue of Catalogues* that it has now organized an American warehouse. The stock consists of a very good collection of posters and educational charts for children's rooms and schools. For decoration there are some beautiful animal photographs, and posters by Arthur Rackham, the famous illustrator of children's classics, and by Alfonse Mucha, an Art Nouveau painter. More educational, or at least practical, are posters to teach kids primary skills such as counting and time telling, kitchen nutrition and calorie charts, historical charts, and a collection of hobby charts illustrating subjects like postage stamps of the world, the history of steam engines, the history of sailing ships, and racing cars—these last make excellent presents for older children. All posters and charts are in color and cost around $2 each.

Lecuyer, 107 Avenue Louise, Brussels 5, Belgium
Lecuyer has a fantastic collection of original American depression posters, '30's artwork and ironically Pollyanna-ish sentiments make them fascinating comments on the time: "WHO SAID CAN'T?" "SOMEONE IS ALWAYS DOING SOMETHING SOMEONE ELSE SAID WAS IMPOSSIBLE. TRY TRYING." "STRUT YOUR STUFF. YOU'VE GOT THE GOOD'S— STEP OUT AND SHOW'EM." "ARGUING WASTES TIME— SPOILS TEMPERS—KILLS TEAMWORK—STALLS PROGRESS. LET'S AGREE TO AGREE." "PLUCK MAKES LUCK." "ONLY HITS WIN." "MEAN IT AND YOU'LL MAKE IT." There are fifty different posters at about $15 each, including post and packing. Lecuyer also has original Art Nouveau and art deco posters, including old ads and old theater posters, of varying prices.

London Transport Poster Shop, 280 Old Marylebone Road, London NW1 5RJ, England
Leaflets describing posters, London Transport publications and souvenirs, free.

For years London Transport has been responsible for the best public-information service that I have ever seen. Its posters, guidebooks, leaflets do more than show you the way; they embody a determination to add unlikely beauty to the humdrum aspects of daily life and to share with the public a contagious enthusiasm for the minutiae of its inner workings. London Transport assumes—correctly, I suspect—that people are interested in how the mass-transit system works, how it was built and how it has changed; accordingly, London Transport has published a series of books ranging from *The Horse Bus as a Vehicle* to *A History of London Transport*. In addition, it has issued a series of extremely popular guides to London and its neighboring countryside. All these, plus slides and a series of souvenirs aimed at the Transport enthusiast, are available from its shop. Though the number of outsiders wanting to buy a London Transport tie or cuff links may be limited, I imagine there would be many a customer for the two LP records of bygone buses and trams, and even more who would want to buy the souvenir dishes, each decorated with a different vehicle and costing some $4 for six.

Of all these efforts, however, none match the popularity of the underground (subway) posters. Starting in the 1920's, some of England's leading graphic artists were commissioned to do a series of posters about London that remain a remarkable achievement to this day. From E.

McKnight Kauffer's "Old London engulfed in a blaze of Fire" to Epstein, the posters are so handsome that you'll very likely want to put some up — something that can be said of very few examples of outdoor art. A great many of them are ideal for children, including those by such well-known illustrators of children's books as John Birmingham. At under $2 each, the posters are an exceptional bargain even if you care nothing for London or its Transport system. Even though London's subways are no longer what they used to be — the employees being understaffed and underpaid — the original vision remains, and the ideal of a city made exciting and beautiful by its public services is worth remembering.

The Lords Gallery Ltd., 26 Wellington Road, St. John's Wood, London N.W.8, England
Catalogues available at the time of writing, $2 each. Prices in $.

"Patriotic Posters: World War I" (149 illustrations)
"Chéret Posters" (94 illustrations)
"U.S. World War I Posters" (65 illustrations)
also "Schwitters" (13 illustrations), which costs $24.

The Lords Gallery specializes in rare, old, original posters, many designed by famous artists and unobtainable elsewhere. Lautrec, Bonnard and Beardsley are here, and styles range from marvelously intricate *fin de siècle* theater posters and book jackets to bathetic advertisements for Eno's Fruit Salts.

There are heavily tressed women, windswept Edwardian couples, period exhortations, and an extraordinarily gloomy poster of St. Paul's and London silhouetted against the night sky with the legend, IT IS FAR BETTER TO FACE THE BULLETS THAN TO BE KILLED AT HOME BY A BOMB. GOD SAVE THE KING.

Prices start at $25, but most of the really attractive posters cost over $50, and the Lautrecs are in the $1,000's.

Plaistow Pictorial, 3 New Plaistow Road, London E15 3JA, England
Leaflet, free.

An odd collection of posters — military and transportation (racing cars, English trains, and World War I airplanes). Also a collection of famous newspaper front pages, from a special edition of *Völkischer Beobachter* on Hitler's annexing of Austria to the Dallas *Morning News* announcing Kennedy's assassination. This firm also publishes a quarterly magazine called *After the Battle*, which has "then" and "now" photographs of World War II battlefields.

REPRODUCTIONS

Adachi Institute of Woodcut Prints, CPO Box 362, Tokyo, Japan
Catalogue, including surface postage, $8. Prices in $.

A few of these very fine reproductions of Japanese woodblock prints are on sale in American museums, but this is the only place where you can get the whole range. Reproductions of the works of Moronobu, Hiroshige, Sharaku, and other masters of ukiyo-e, are carefully done. The originals are perfect specimens in the Tokyo National Museum, the materials used are specially prepared and similar to those of the originals, and only the most skillful engravers and printers work on them. Prices range from $13 to $50 per print, including surface postage and insurance.

Fratelli Alinari, Lungarno Corsini 24 R, Florence 50123, Italy
44-page catalogue with some color, free. Prices in $. August.

The magnificent Alinari reproductions are widely exported and can be found wherever good reproductions are sold, but they can be bought for a fraction of the price directly from the makers. Color reproductions of paintings cost only just over $2 each, while beautiful and unusual reproductions of drawings cost half that. Both can be mounted on wood with gold-leaf borders so that they don't need frames and still only cost $4.50 and $5.50. Most of the painters are Italian — Giotto, Fra Angelico, Botticelli, Piero della Francesca, Da Vinci, Michelangelo, Raphael, et al. — and there are some interesting Etruscan frescoes and Pompeian mosaics, and some painters from other countries, including the French impressionists. Religious paintings and drawings mounted on triptychs and diptychs finished in gold leaf cost $14 and $17.

Pictures also decorate a stunning collection of objects for the house: trays, boxes in various shapes and sizes. book ends, and lamps with reproductions on the shades and hand-carved bases finished in gold or silver leaf, at $33.

Bookshop, Greater London Council, The County Hall, London S.E.1, England
Price list, free.

The Greater London Council sells fine-line black-and-white lithographic reproductions from the collection in the Council's library at very low prices. There are sixteenth-, seventeenth-, and eighteenth-century maps of London in black-and-white for $1.30 each, and various old views of London: the Tower, Westminster and Whitehall, the Dockyard at Deptford (a view of the Royal Dockyard with its ships), and various London scenes by Hogarth — all of these for about $1 each. Also of interest is "Buck's Long View," a set of five panoramic views of the Thames published in 1749 by the brothers Buck. These can be bought as a set or singly for $1.30 each. Postage will be quoted by the Council when you tell them what you want.

Medieval English Brasses, 2 Thurlow Road, Hampstead, London NW3 5PJ, England
Brochure, 2 International Reply Coupons.

Brass plates gracefully engraved with the figure of a person to be remembered were first produced in England in the thirteenth century, and it is the only country where they are to be found. Rubbings of these striking church brasses have become popular decorations over the years. John Henderson makes his own rubbings; they are taken directly from the plates in black on white paper or in gold or silver on black paper, and are sold at prices between $8 and $25.

Misrachi, Avenida Juárez 4, Mexico 1, DF, Mexico
Color brochure, free. Prices in $.

Color reproductions of paintings by modern Mexican artists — mostly Rivera and Siqueiros, but also some big-eyed, soulful children by Gustavo Montoya, all $4.80 each. For $6 each there are two books of plates for framing of Mexican birds and flowers with the text in English; and for $10 each, delightful old views (1628) of Mexico City, Acapulco and Veracruz.

The National Gallery, Publications Department, Trafalgar Square, London WC2N 5DN, England
32-page color brochure, 60 cents.

A good brochure of small reproductions with a separate price list. The National Gallery is intelligently pessimistic about rising prices and advises customers to ask for a new price list if the brochure has been around for more than six months.

The actual reproductions are of 138 famous and favorite European masterpieces from Fra Angelico's "The Rape of Helen by Paris" to Monet's "Pond with Water Lilies," both about 10 square inches and both 65 cents. Prices go by sizes, and range from 25 cents for pictures around 6 square inches to $6.50 for pictures 2' by 3'. But there is very little choice in the largest sizes. Postcards also available.

National Palace Museum, Mail Order Division, Taipei, Taiwan
Price list of Publications and Reproductions of the National Palace Museum Collections, free.
Price list of Color slides, free.

Probably mainly of interest to specialists, these two price lists have no illustrations whatsoever. The publications available are, with very few exceptions, *in Chinese* and consist largely of catalogues of the art in the museum and a certain amount of calligraphy. The price lists give no indication of the size or number of colors in the plates reproducing paintings (they may be postcard-sized and black-and-white, for all I know), but the titles are so intriguing that they might be worth trying: "Eighteen Scholars in Fairyland," by Ch'iu Ying, Ming Dynasty; "Sitting up at Night," by Shen Chou, Ming Dynasty; "Literary Gathering in the Mountains," by Wang Fu, Ming Dynasty; and "Children Playing Games on a Winter Day," anonymous, Five Dynasties, cost just over $1 each. Other pictures are reproduced as postcards and cost from about 50 cents to $2 per set: "Ten Prized Dogs," by Lang Shih-ning (Guiseppe Castiglione); "Prized Steeds," by the same artist; "Portraits of Emperors and Sages"; and "Ancient Flower and Bird Paintings." The reproductions of the "antiquities" are even more tempting, and include all sorts of little carved lacquer boxes, carved lacquer plates, food and wine vessels (for example, "Chih, wine vessel decorated with coiled hornless dragons, Spring and Autumn Period"). Personally I like the sound of "Ting, cooking utensil decorated with stylized reptiles, Western Chou Dynasty (1122–722 B.C.)," but I'm afraid prices for the reproductions of the antiquities start at around $100 and go up into the thousands.

Mary Potter Designs, Hunters Wood, Laughton, Lewes, Sussex, England
Leaflet, 25 cents.

Facsimiles of knights and ladies on medieval church brasses have been made into wall hangings by Mary Potter. Silk-screened in black on white, red, orange or gold cotton. Prices from $3 to $15, including air-mail postage. There are also hangings based on the *Bayeux tapestry* — stylized little pictures of William's ship and Harold riding to Bosham — which cost about $1 each, while a 6-foot-long frieze of the Battle of Hastings on orange or red cloth costs $15, including postage.

Stedelijk Museum, Reproduktie Afdeling, Paulus Potterstraat 13, Amsterdam, Holland
Price list, free.

Amsterdam contains some of the world's most impressive museums, which publish marvelous reproductions, postcards and catalogues. The Stedelijk is of special interest to those buying by mail, for it offers a good choice of reproductions of paintings with a tempting selection of the Van Goghs for which the city is so well known. For slightly over $1, for instance, you can get a set of eleven Van Gogh drawings or many of his better-known paintings, and for up to $10 you can get works by earlier painters as well as contemporary Americans. Unfortunately, the mimeographed list does not have any descriptions, so you have to be able to remember pictures just by their titles. The museum catalogues are mainly on modern artists; about twenty-five appear each year.

The Tate Gallery, Publications Department, Millbank, London S.W.1, England
Publications catalogue, $2.50.
Color-slides catalogue, $2.50.

Another of England's national museums sells reproductions, here mainly of English and modern French paintings. The publications catalogue rather annoyingly has pictures of the books listed (37 books, mainly about the Tate Gallery and English artists), but not of their 82 reproductions, which are only named. Prices for reproductions of Blake, Gainsborough, Turner, Dali, Klee, Dufy, et al., range from $1.25 for drawings to about $6 for largish paintings. Available and illustrated in the catalogue is an unusual three-dimensional reproduction of Ben Nicholson's "White Relief, 1935" in a chrome frame.

The Tryon Gallery, 41/42 Dover Street, London S1X 1HB, England
Catalogue, free.

The Tryon Gallery publishes natural-history and sporting pictures mechanically reproduced by photolitho in editions of two to three hundred and with prices for signed "artists proofs" at between $40 and $75. In the catalogue I looked at there were animals of Kenya by Joy Adamson, the author of *Born Free*; fishing pictures by the well-known humorist Norman Thelwell; reproductions of racing paintings from the Jockey Club, Newmarket; and other, sometimes romantic, pictures of birds and other animals in their natural habitats.

3 Books

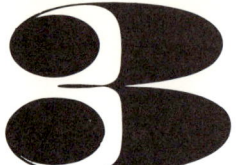

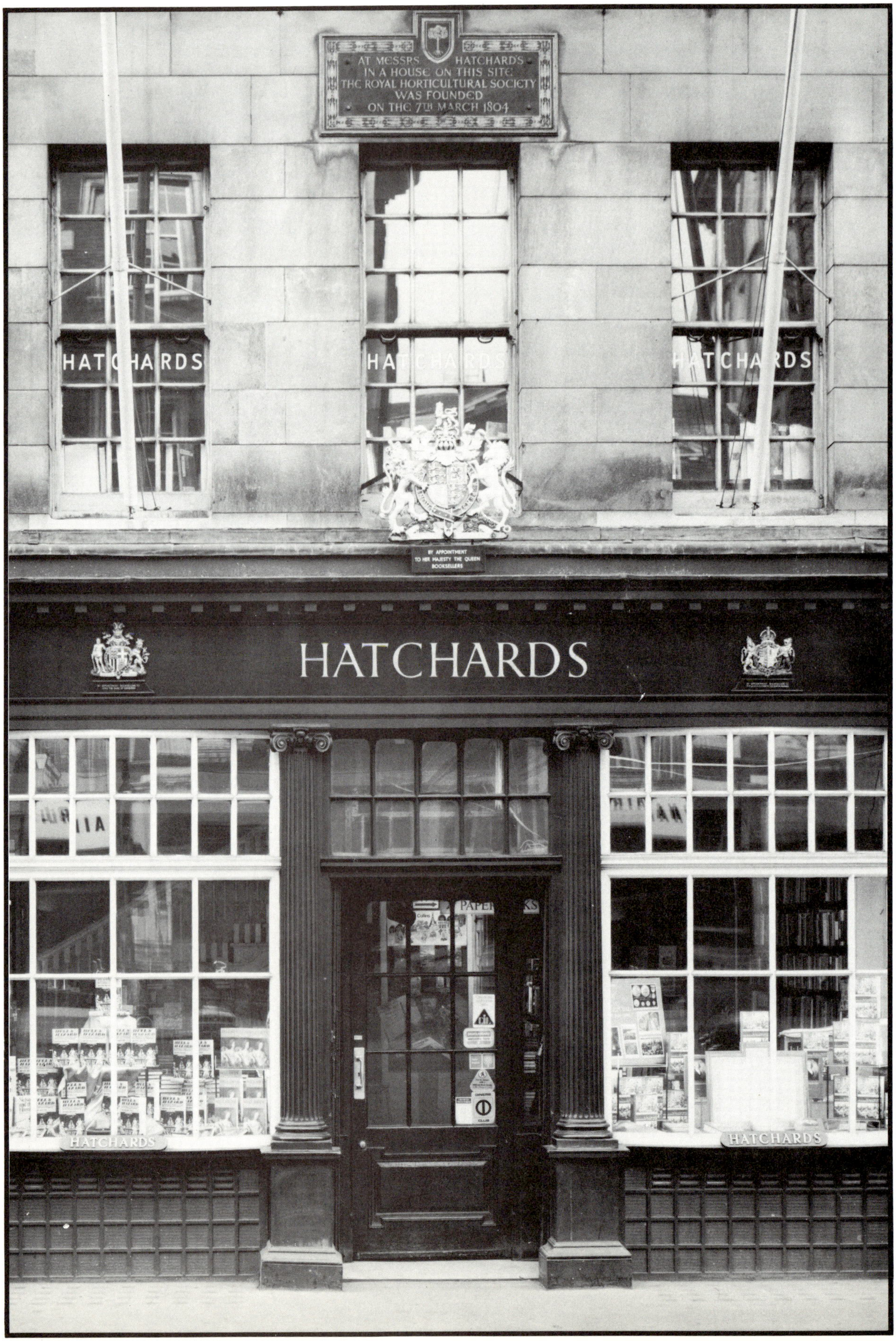
AT MESSRS HATCHARDS
IN A HOUSE ON THIS SITE
THE ROYAL HORTICULTURAL SOCIETY
WAS FOUNDED
ON THE 7TH MARCH 1804
HATCHARDS
HATCHARDS
HATCHARDS
BY APPOINTMENT
TO HER MAJESTY THE QUEEN
BOOKSELLERS
HATCHARDS
HATCHARDS
HATCHARDS

Books have traditionally been sold by mail, and a system of catalogues and mailing lists has been developed to a very impressive extent. There are dealers for practically every kind of book and it is possible to do all one's buying by mail. This is, in fact, the way most university libraries now build up their collections, and their budgets explain in part why mail-order bookselling has continued to prosper as it has. As you leaf through an exceptionally elaborate catalogue—in itself an impressive example of the bibliographers' craft—you may reflect that this is due to the lavishness of some of our own state university systems. The Texas taxpayer may well be the unwitting patron of your ability to buy just about any book by mail.

For Americans, the most efficient bookselling comes from England. While each country has its own network of antiquarian book dealers, the English are the most proficient when it comes to selling current books by mail. It would be hopeless to try to list the hundreds of Continental specialists in old books, so I have limited this section to a few such dealers, besides listing some of the major British ones. Before describing these, a few words on *what* it makes sense to buy from abroad and *why*.

CURRENT BOOKS

Several of the English booksellers listed below can supply you with any new British book, and for many an American book lover it is worth buying from abroad just to get the marvelously complete catalogues issued by these firms. The English dealer will still service customers in ways that few American stores bother with, and in many cases, this alone makes it worth buying by mail. Out-of-the-way books, out-of-stock titles, and of course, out-of-print titles, can be bought in this way with no trouble at all. However, you should note that the time when British books were automatically cheaper than American ones are now past. Specialized titles in nonfiction now tend to be about the same price; the English edition may even be more expensive, and the physical product—paper, binding, etc.—may well be better in the American edition. Certainly American bindings are better suited to the overdry and overheated atmosphere of most American homes. On the other hand, novels and some children's books are still considerably cheaper in England. There is also the fact that a considerable number of books, particularly those for children, are available in inexpensive or paperback editions from England. It's practically impossible to buy paperbacks by mail from an American bookseller, and in this respect British stores offer exceptional service. The children's-book dealers listed below have no American equivalents.

BOOKS IN SPECIAL FIELDS

Because so many British booksellers deal with universities, in addition to the far-flung alumni of the British universities they are able to supply you with lists of titles that simply cannot be found in the United States. Certain catalogues, such as those of Hammersmith Books, are works of exemplary scholarship in themselves and offer readers a service that goes far beyond the mere provision of books. The major university booksellers all offer specialized catalogues, and if you are interested in keeping up not just with new titles, but with bibliographic research in certain fields, then you should get on these mailing lists.

ANTIQUARIAN BOOKS

This is, like prints or works of art of all kinds, a field all its own. Prices vary enormously and collectors will want to compare them on an international scale. Bargains are possible, of course, but chances are that the dealers involved will know more than you do, and your chances of finding an unnoticed first edition are probably better if you browse through the stalls on lower Fourth Avenue in New York City. On the other hand, the catalogues that are available will keep you up to date with both prices and what is available on the market. Since so many old books include illustrative material, this is also a useful way of looking for prints and related material.

ESOTERICA AND EXOTICA

The days when, as in Ogden Nash's poem, lovers of such books needed the service of Railway Express to avoid the frowns of the post office, are now past. Pornography is widely available domestically and the need to look through old French masters to find a bit of erotica is now past. Today, such material is sold openly at Parke-Bernet; but the lure of books to enter forbidden fields is still there. For some reason, the unknown is still thought to be contained in these mysterious old tomes, and a large number of stores still specialize in the mystical, the magical and the supernatural. One such store is listed below, again largely English, though as in other categories foreign works are usually available through British dealers devoted to the supernatural.

At the end of this section you will find shops specializing in *Children's Books* and listings of *Booksellers on the Continent, Bookplates, Magazines, Maps* and *Useful Paperback Guides*.

CURRENT BOOKS

THE BIG FOUR

Most Americans who have gone to England to study, along with a vast number of other colonials, usually leave their name with one of the major university booksellers they have patronized; keeping an account at, say, Blackwell's is a way of keeping in touch with old memories. These stores are quite used to dealing with Americans; their letters to me all charmingly assured me that they are more than accustomed to mail-order selling—a bit like the family butler assuring the uncertain guest that he is indeed in professional hands.

W. Heffer and Sons Ltd., 20 Trinity Street, Cambridge CB2 3NG, England,
is the major bookseller in that town but also a leading international supplier. It has just moved from its rambling thirties quarters to a very handsome new building facing Trinity College, and like the galling zip code at the end of its address, symbolizes the modernization of English bookselling. Like the other stores in this section, Heffer's can supply you with any new British book (along with a number of American ones).

Heffer's issues a large list of specialized catalogues, covering just about any field, such as archaeology, management, chemistry, linguistics, etc. Chances are that your particular interests will be served.

Blackwell's, Broad Street, Oxford Ox1 3BQ, England,
is the Oxford equivalent of Heffer's, and has also recently moved to ultramodern and rather soulless quarters, where on endless underground floors you are likely to find any book in print and a great many that aren't. Their stock allows them to fill almost any orders on receipt; if not, the book is ordered from the publisher or the order is kept until the title shows up. Blackwell's specifies that they will bill you upon receipt of order, and the charge for postage, insurance, etc., tends to run about 7 percent of the cost of a book. Again, specialized catalogues are available in many fields.

33

Books

Dillon's University Bookshop Ltd., Malet Street, London WC1E 7JB, England,
is the London equivalent of these university stores. Because of its location in the heart of London, near Russell Square, it is the one bookstore that most visitors may have happened to come across. There is a sense of excitement for any book lover in discovering Dillon's and finding that what looked like one store goes on and on, to cover several buildings, each housing departments that are complete stores in themselves. Here, as in the others mentioned above, one finds not just a complete stock of books but pamphlets, little magazines, teaching aids, etc. Dillon's stocks 75,000 new titles, besides maintaining a substantial second-hand department, and they too cover most academic fields with special strength in areas such as psychology, languages, education, history and the sciences.

Hatchard's, 187 Piccadilly, London W1V 9DA, England ♛♛♛
For those with less academic interests, Hatchard's is probably as good a store as any to keep in touch with British general publishing. Located on Piccadilly next to Fortnum and Mason, they cater to the carriage trade and are very much the literary equivalents of these splendid purveyors of gastronomic self-indulgence. They call themselves The World's Finest Bookshop and I suppose "fine" must be read in the context "of social quality." Certainly their stock cannot compare with the above-named stores, but if you want the latest British novel, mystery or gift book, they are most likely to have the book you want in stock. Their letter to me refers to hundreds of parcels that go to America each week, and their catalogue (illustrated) gives you a fair sample of the new and popular, which, as I said, is also most likely to be less expensive. The latest, albeit short, Mary Stewart is listed at under $2, and a number of gift items are less expensive than they would be in America. Hatchard's also has an out-of-print department and a special stock of leather bindings. A unique aspect of their service is that you can order any book to be bound in full or half leather.

1
Hatchards Hatchards Bookshop, 187 Piccadilly, London. Established in 1797.

BOOKS IN SPECIAL FIELDS

AFRICA

Chas. J. Sawyer, 1 Grafton Street, London W1X 3LB, England
Price list, free.

Sawyer's is one of London's most distinguished dealers in rare books, autographs and manuscripts, but as a specialist in Africana, it may be of most interest overseas. The firm specializes in books on Africa throughout the years and issues a special catalogue on that area.

ANARCHY

Freedom Bookshop, 84B Whitechapel High Street (in Angel Alley), London E.1, England
Price lists, free.

My letter to this famous anarchist bookshop brought back not only their price lists but a copy of *Freedom,* the anarchist weekly, and a selection of pamphlets and posters. These give some of the flavor of the original, but a visit to the store itself is far better if you are ever in London and are interested in the history of left-wing movements or simply feel intrigued by visiting the world of Conrad's *Secret Agent.*

The Angel Alley shop is crammed with old books, many of

Books

them published earlier in the century, and happily, its fantastically inexpensive items have not yet been discovered by book collectors and university libraries. So, here is most of what Kropotkin wrote or *Mother Jones' Autobiography* or Shelley's *Mask of Anarchy*. Ironically, many of the books are available in American paperback reissues, but there is still much here that would be difficult to obtain elsewhere. In addition to the classics, it is fascinating to see the number of authors, from Martin Buber to Wilhelm Reich, Noam Chomsky to Sir Herbery Read, who have been linked to the development of anarchist theory and practice.

ARCHITECTURE

Paul Breman Ltd., 1 Rosslyn Hill, London NW3 5UL, England
Various catalogues (see below).

PB (a friend who has given some impressively knowledgeable advice for this book section) was one of the founder-members of the first antiquarian bookshop to specialize entirely in architectural books and drawings. He now works by catalogue, mail and personal offers only, and his interests are wider than before—but he still writes a monthly column on architectural books for the Journal of the German Architects Society, and the main strength of the firm remains the same: architecture, with special emphasis on the early twentieth century, on bridge building and on fortification. Catalogues on these three specialties are issued once a year, and recently the first list of original posters appeared. Requests for catalogues are welcome and so are wants lists.

ART

Arts Council Shop, 28 Sackville Street, London W1X 1DA, England
34-page publications price list, 50 cents.

This new shop, described in detail in the Arts section, is a particularly helpful source for those seeking books in the arts. The shop is well stocked in all the arts, selling books by all publishers, but its main contribution is to disseminate catalogues of exhibits held in museums throughout England, and in some cases, in the United States and on the Continent. Though I suspect you could ask for any book in the arts, the catalogue stresses these last-mentioned holdings. Here are catalogues of a great many exhibits which never made their way to America, including some stunning ones that were part of England's entry into the Common Market, such as a very imaginative book on the Impressionists in London. Given the price of art books these days, many of the catalogues are remarkably inexpensive: the book on the Impressionists is only $3; a 232-page, heavily illustrated *Pioneers of Modern Sculpture* is about $6.

But the prices of these obviously subsidized works are a secondary attraction. The main interest is the subjects which range from the relatively classical subjects such as Munch or Cézanne to specifically English areas such as Burne-Jones or *British Sporting Painting* and to a number of younger painters and sculptors whose works are barely known here. There are also numerous catalogues of exchange exhibits from countries such as Russia or Hungary, and many books of particular interest to collectors, such as catalogues of Chinese ceramics or Indian miniatures.

The list includes the less prestigious arts, from landscape gardening to bookbinding. A useful complement to the Council's art and poster list, but very useful in itself.

A. Zwemmer Ltd., 76-80 Charing Cross Road, London WC2H 0BH, England
Price list, free.

Zwemmer's is probably London's best-known art-book store. Located as it is right in Charing Cross Road, its windows are seen by hundreds of thousands of tourists, but it was only recently, thanks to a reader of my first edition, Ruth M. Goldstein, that I learned that the store also publishes a mail-order list. The store sells primarily new books and has an excellent stock of art books from all nations; it also does some publishing of its own. Its current price list offers a reasonable selection of books, but I am sure that the store could supply any art book in print. Like its American counterparts, it also lists a small selection of remaindered art books, particularly useful during this period of increased book prices.

AVIATION

The Aviation Bookshop, 656 Holloway Road, London N19 3PD, England
36-page price list, free; $1 air mail.

This store thinks it is the only one in the world devoted exclusively to aviation and is obviously a prime source for those interested in airplanes, whether real or model. The shop's list is international, and in addition to books, includes magazines, plans, charts, photos, prints, and modeling books and periodicals. Besides such basic categories as civil, military and private aviation and the various wars, the store stocks such unique items as facsimile reprints of official pilot's notes.

BUILDING

The Building Bookshop, 26 Store Street, London WC1E 7BT, England
32-page annual price list, free.
Catalogue, free. September.

The Building Bookshop, located in the Building Centre, is an exceptionally useful source of books for all those interested in the practical aspects of construction. Emphasis is on the technological, with a wide choice of engineering and other texts. There are selections of books on architecture and its history, but here again, the focus is relatively specific. While some of the books deal with legal aspects of construction peculiar to England, there is still a great deal of interest to American home owners.

FILM

Cine Books, 692A Yonge Street, Toronto, Canada
Catalogue published each fall, $2.50.

This firm specializes in books and related materials on the film in all its aspects and has already developed a large American clientele. (It was recommended by a reader, Ruth M. Goldstein.) In addition to books, they stock sound tracks, posters, magazines and 8-mm. films.

Filmdocumentatie, 57 Stadionplein, Amsterdam 1009, Holland
Price list, free.

Film bookstores seem to be as international as film itself, and this Dutch firm issues a ten-times-a-year book list in English

Books

2
Bertram Rota Ltd A typical selection of first editions:
Saul Kain (pseudonym for Siegfried Sassoon), $66;
Edith Sitwell, $132; Beatrix Potter, $198; Marianne
Moore, $66. Sold.

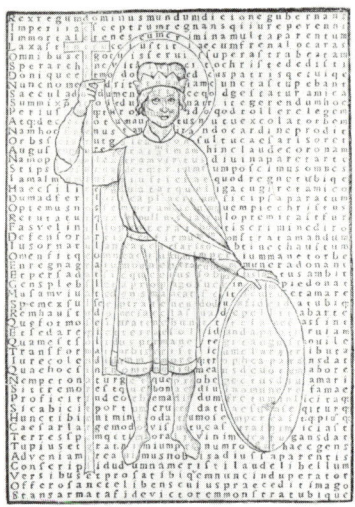

3
Branners Bibliofile Antikvariat First edition of "Rabanus
Maurus" (1503) in red and black with Roman letters,
two large woodcuts and "figure poems." One of the first
printings from Pforzheim.
photo John U. Duurloo

that should be of real interest to American film buffs (it was also recommended by Ruth Goldstein). Established in 1948, the firm has books on all aspects of film and film making in addition to selling stills, periodicals and even records. In this last category is featured a list of original Vitaphone records of *The Desert Song, On with the Show,* and other favorites.

GARDENING

Daniel Lloyd, Heather Lea, 4 Hillcrest Avenue, Chertsey, Surrey, England
92-page annual price list, 25 cents; $1 air mail. Prices in $.

Lloyd's list of gardening and botanical books, they assure me, is the most comprehensive in the world, and the firm has hundreds of American customers. It deals in out-of-print and old as well as new books, and lists both technical works and those primarily of interest because of their color plates and illustrations. The firm will also search for out-of-print books without charge. On the whole, prices seem very reasonable. There are many entries under $5, and with the rising cost of British books, this is clearly an area where older and sometimes rare books may be less expensive than new ones.

GENEAOLOGY

Heraldry Today, 10 Beauchamp Place, London S.W.3, England
Catalogues of new and old books sent free, but $2.50 is charged for subscription to regular mailings.

This store is both a publisher of new books on heraldry and geneaology and dealer in a wide range of older books on the subject. "A great many American clients" are particularly interested in tracing their own ancestors, but the store adds that "we are not a reference library and our books are purely for sale." New titles range from the intriguing *New Extinct Peerage, 1884–1971*, with the promising subtitle "Extinct, Dormant, Abeyant and Suspended Peerages with Geneaologies and Arms," to *A Dictionary of Scottish Emigrants to the U.S.A.* Close to a thousand older titles are also listed, covering much of Europe. In addition to the more traditional books on coats of arms and pedigrees, there are more plebeian lists of parish registers or transcripts of lists of *Passengers who Arrived in the U. S.*, which may interest humbler folk seeking to trace their family history.

MILITARY

P. G. de Lotz, Bookseller, 1 Baptist Gardens, Chalk Farm, London NW5 4ET, England
Various annual catalogues, free.

"Books on the history of warfare, all aspects and periods" is De Lotz's description of his huge collection of books on military history. Each annual catalogue lists some two thousand books, from classical times to the Vietnam war, many of them out of print.

NATURAL HISTORY

Wheldon & Wesley Ltd., Lytton Lodge, Codicote, Hitchin, Hertfordshire SG4 8TE, England
Catalogue, free.

This firm specializes in books on natural history, and the

catalogue is the most thorough in that field that I have seen. Primarily specialists in old books, they do a bit of reprinting themselves (their current catalogue advertises their reissue of *A Guide to the Snakes of Uganda*), but theirs is a much more general list with the greatest strength in zoology and botany. They are also agents for the Natural History section of the British Museum and stock a number of the museum's publications now out of print.

Of more general interest is their offering of fine illustrated books, which includes items from *A Monograph of the Pheasant* at just under £1,000 to a much more modest £50 edition of *La Zoologie Agricole*, published in Paris 1854–56. There are over 1,700 books in the current catalogue, and as is always true of any good bookstore, a surprising number of titles (a collection of *Redoute Roses, Captain Cook's Voyages*) that could lure any browser.

POLITICS

Hammersmith Books, Barnes High Street, London S.W.13, England
Judging purely from catalogues, Hammersmith Books must be an extraordinary place to visit. Their catalogue tells you how to get to the outlying part of London in which their vast stock is located, and it must be worth the trip to meet the kind of people who compile their catalogues. Their letterhead simply says, "Scarce literature on social economic movements, Afro-Asian-Soviet Affairs, War, Revolution and Peace," and their catalogues live up to that comprehensive heading. Their latest, on the Middle East, includes a wider range of material than one would have thought possible to collect, all meticulously annotated, and it is reasonably priced. These are obviously the people to get in touch with if you are interested in contemporary politics and international affairs, or in the history of the modern left.

Collett's, 39 Museum Street, London W.C.1, England,
has a number of books in English published in Russia and the other East European countries, as well as a large stock of Russian-language material and English-language books on Russia. Catalogues are available.

TRANSPORT

Chater & Scott Ltd., Mail Order Department, Syon Park, Brentford, Middlesex TW8 8JF, England
28-page catalogue, 25 cents and self-addressed envelope; $1 air mail.

"All new and second-hand books on transport," it says on the letterhead, but the firm's real strength is in books on motor vehicles. Their catalogue, *The World of Motoring*, lists new as well as old books and has helpful sections on remainders and new titles. The firm has a strong line of books on American cars, but many of these are of American origin. American car buffs may be more interested in the British and European selections, as well as some more out-of-the-way listings on Australian and South African cars.

See also the listing for London Transport under Posters in the Art section.

Motor Books and Accessories, 33 St. Martin's Court, St. Martin's Lane, London W.C.2, England
Price lists, 30 cents; $2 air mail.

The "Accessories" in this store's name is as important as the "Motor Books," since in addition to books about cars they also have extensive lists of books on aviation and aircraft as well as arms and armor. Motor Books is one of the tiny, dark shops that line this very popular tourist walk in London, and there would be no way of guessing from glancing at the store that its holdings would be as extensive as they are. They stock a huge and relatively international selection ranging from French books on the uniforms of Louis XV's army to Soviet accounts of their tanks. The price lists are unfortunately classified by publisher, which is very inconvenient unless you intend to plow through anyway. On the other hand, it may be helpful to know that there is a substantial Australian literature on fighter planes or that an English publisher called Foulis has a massive list of books on cars, including one of the Volkswagen by a Mr. Hopfinger (a variant that James Bond apparently never considered in his lust for larger vehicles).

ANTIQUARIAN BOOKS, MANUSCRIPTS, ETC.

Since this is a category that could include literally hundreds of names, the following is but a sampling. Starting your own bookstore is the ambition of a vast number of people, and England is obviously the ideal place to deal in antiquarian books. Lists of such bookstores are available and journals such as the *Times Literary Supplement* will carry ads for a great many of these. Here are a few:

N. V. Boekhandel & Antiquariaat B. M. Israel, N. Z. Voorburgwal 264, Amsterdam, Holland
Various price lists, averaging 100 pages each, on different subjects.

B. M. Israel's catalogues are among the most impressive I have seen in the field of rare books. His specialties, to quote him, are "Medicine, Old Sciences, Old Technology, Geography" as well as manuscripts, autographs, illustrated books, etc. The price lists are in English, though the books listed are, of course, in various languages. Prices are not low, but these are rare books, and on the whole I was surprised at the number of items under $10, though of course the most interesting volumes were much more. The History of Medicine and Psychology catalogue ranged from bloodletting and craniology to Freud's early articles, available in early (1882–88) copies of the *Neurologisches Zentralblatt* of Leipzig. Current catalogues include one of the history of the exact sciences, technology and transport, and another of books on the fine arts. An impressive series of lists, of clear interest to serious collectors in these fields.

Dawson's of Pall Mall, 16 & 17 Pall Mall, London SW1Y 5NB, England
Price list of Atlases and Travel Books; other lists available.

This antiquarian bookshop specializes in books on the history of science but stocks books on other subjects as well. Its collection of ancient atlases and travel books is of particular interest. The current list is extensive but also expensive and is recommended only to those ready to spend a good deal of money. A rare first edition of a 1765 atlas, for instance, is priced at close to $2,000, while the 1856 first edition of Perry's voyage to Japan is nearly $500. There are less expensive items, such as Cobbett's *Rural Rides* for about $100, but this is a 1930 edition.

Francis Edwards Ltd., 83 Marylebone High Street, London W1M 4AL, England,
offers a number of very satisfactory specialized catalogues in a number of classic fields of interest in which England has always excelled, such as military books, economics, industry,

Books

technology and transport, family history and heraldry, etc. The economics catalogue, for instance, includes sections on agriculture, brewing and wool. Mostly older books, and including such items as autograph letters, etc.

Henry Sotheran Ltd., 2 Sackville Street, Piccadilly W1X 2DP, England
Catalogue 75 cents; $1.50 air mail.
One of London's oldest booksellers (est. 1815), this shop specializes in early printed works and color-plate works, especially in natural history. They also stock old bindings of standard authors, letters, maps and old views of British scenery.

Charles W. Traylen, Castle House, 49–50 Quarry Street, Guilford, England
This store specializes in its own reprints of old prints, maps and scholarly works (such as Ackerman prints) reissued at very reasonable prices, as well as having an extensive stock of out-of-print titles, particularly of the classic English interests in sport, travel, natural history, naval and military history, and theology.

Covent Garden Bookshop, 80 Long Acre, London W.C.2, England
This very attractive, airy store in the midst of the theater and operatic district specializes in modern first editions, of which they claim to have the largest stock in England. They also have a number of British first editions of American authors such as Pound and Hemingway, and their attractive 150-page catalogue is filled with the fascinating footnotes of modern literary history, from a first edition of Virginia Woolf's *A Room of One's Own*, signed, one of 492 copies, for $100, to the carbon copy, also signed, of Henry Miller's "apparently unpublished" preface to an early Parker Tyler book ($88).

Bernard Quaritch, 5–8 Lower John Street, Golden Square, London W1V 6AB, England
This shop specializes in the publications of various learned societies and is an excellent source for the reports of everyone from the British Museum to the Royal Horticultural Society. Some of these items are reprints, others cover the original output of such diverse groups as the Egypt Exploration Society or the Librairie du Liban. It is, obviously, for specialists.

They also have a very extensive collection of materials on English literature, including private letters and manuscripts, which, as always, offers intriguing insights into the lives of people whose letters are worth keeping and selling, and sometimes give you the feeling should have remained unread by outsiders, e.g., T. S. Eliot, letters and telegrams "describing the mental and physical collapse of his wife and his own unhappiness and illness" ($960.00), or somewhat less moving, Norman Mailer's three letters to Alexander Trocchi, complaining about what Hollywood does to your novels: "It came out as if they'd run a garbage truck over the pages of the book . . ." ($432).

Bertram Rota Ltd., 4–6 Savile Row, London W.1, England
A leading dealer in modern first editions, letters and manuscripts, who has dealt with special needs of customers in all sorts of areas, ranging from first folios and whole libraries of scholarly books. As with many dealers, if you are looking for a specific rare book, you can write and see what is available at what price.

4
Book-Care Bookplate no. 21, gray-green on white, type style B.

5
Book-Care Bookplate no. 22, mauve on white.

6
Book-Care Bookplate no. 23, dark brown on white, type style B.

7
Book-Care Bookplate no. 24, gray on white, type style A.

8
Book-Care Bookplate no. 25, light brown on white, type style A.

9
Book-Care Bookplate no. 26, green on white.

10
Misrachi (see Art section) A portfolio of twelve pictures of Mexican flowers suitable for framing with text in Spanish and English. About $6.

L. A. Wallrich, Books, 25 Whitehall Park, London N.19, England
Quarterly price lists, $1 per annum, surface mail; $4 air mail.

Larry Wallrich, who used to run one of Greenwich Village's most attractive old bookstores, now works from London, specializing in modern first editions and English and American literature. His price list includes many of the "classic" moderns—Auden, Eliot, Lawrence, Joyce—but also has a section devoted to contemporary work, including concrete and visual poetry. His is also the first book catalogue that I've seen listing audio recordings and tapes. An excellent list for those interested in the avant garde, past and present.

ESOTERICA

Watkins Bookshop, 19–21 Cecil Court, Charing Cross Road, London WC2N 4HB, England
Entering Watkins Bookshop is like stumbling into a tea party given by Alistair Crowley, the self-styled English magician and eccentric. Located just off the major theatrical and second-hand-book area in London, Watkins represents a vast enclave of esoteric and fascinating expertise. Here is that unique English blend of magic and religion, of psychology and alchemy, of the erudite and the exotic. The shop has expanded into two buildings, accommodating youth's vast new interest in magic, alchemy and related subjects. The selection is a serious and professional one; the mysterious can be sold efficiently, and the store and its catalogue command both respect and attention. The latest catalogue includes a variety of titles in various religions, serious works in psychology, as well as a selection of their vast stock of books on alchemy, cabala, tarot, occultism, diet and health, and "astrology, palmistry, graphology, numerology and allied subjects."

CHILDREN'S BOOKS

Children's Book Centre Ltd., 140 Kensington Church Street, London W.8., England
Quarterly newsletter, $5 (refundable).

There is unfortunately no American equivalent of the Children's Book Centre, and anyone who has ever taken a child into this marvelous place will know what a loss that is both to parents and children. Every city should have its own version of this splendid institution, even though they might not be expected to stock the five thousand titles that are on display in the Centre. The Centre will sell you all its books by mail and will supply you with its four reading lists at 75 cents each: one for two-to-five year-olds, one for six-to-eights, one for nine-to-elevens, one for twelves and up. Each one is an excellent 40-page annotated brochure containing 28 pages of descriptive material, so that it is possible to buy by mail with ease. A great many English children's books are not available in the United States, and also, a great many titles are available as inexpensive paperbacks. The first-rate Puffin list published by Penguin Books offers an enormous selection for young readers. English children's records also on sale here.

Heffer's Children's Bookshop, 27 Trinity Street, Cambridge, CB2 1tb, England
While much smaller, the Heffer's store is an excellent model of what a college bookstore of any size should be able to offer to its community. Heffer's will supply you with some of the publishers' brochures and has a good stock of most popular titles.

The Folio Society Ltd., 202 Great Suffolk Street, London SE1 1PR, England
This is in a separate category, but should be listed here as another way of buying books from England. Like the American Heritage Club, the Folio Society publishes its own illustrated and deluxe editions of books, but it puts out a large number of titles itself. The society says it has a growing number of American subscribers and offers an American catalogue of its books, which cover a wide variety of areas and are very reasonably priced. For example, *Homage to Catalonia*, by George Orwell, illustrated with contemporary photos, sells at $4.75, less than an ordinary American edition of the book would sell for. Most of the titles are of more classic genres but are certainly good bargains for those seeking the kind of book that used to be available, for instance, in the illustrated Modern Library.

BOOKSELLERS ON THE CONTINENT

Each country has its own leading bookstore and each country its own network of second-hand bookdealers. A list of stores as long as the one for England could be compiled for the rest of the world, but that would lead to a separate book. I am therefore confining myself to just a handful of stores; if you're looking for a more complete list, you can write to the New York commercial attaché of the country in which you're interested, or simply look at the ads in the literary journals published in each language. Books are always easy to order and there is little room for confusion, even if you're ordering in English. Anyway, here are a few additional names.

DENMARK

Branners Bibliofile Antikvariat, Bredgade 1o, 1260, Copenhagen K.
Copenhagen is one of the world's great book cities; it has more good English bookstores than many an American town, as well as a host of second-hand stores. Looking for a rare old book can be as international a process as looking for an old print, and it is worth keeping stores like Branners in mind when one is searching. Branners deals with many American individuals and libraries, and is typical of the kind of store, outside of England, where books in English can be found.

FRANCE

Brentano's, 37 Avenue de l'Opéra, Paris II,
is probably the most famous bookstore as far as Americans are concerned and their English-speaking staff should be able to supply you with any current French title, whether book or periodical. They have an excellent stock of gift books, and carry the specialized French fashion and decorating magazines.

La Joie de Lire
is known in France and among visitors to Paris as the best serious bookstore in that book-filled capital. Just about any book in the social sciences, literature or the arts can be found there, including rare university-press books in French. This is not the store for fancy non-books, but you should be able to get any current French-language title in the above fields, as well as books on the film, paperbacks, a very wide selection of political journals and all books on Marxism and left-wing political thought. The store has now established a special mail-order address, 44 rue Vieille du Temple, Paris IV, and an idea of its range can be had from the following list of catalogues, available at this writing: Marx and Engels, Lenin,

Flaubert, The Commune, Contemporary Greece, Czechoslovakia, Children's Books and Periodicals.

GERMANY

Marga Schoeller Bücherstube, Knesebeckstr. 33 (Ecke Mommsenstr.), 1000 Berlin 12,
is a bookstore which over the years has come to supply customers all over the world. While not specializing in mail order, as does Van Stockum, they do periodically mail their customers lists of new titles in such fields as literary criticism, history, education, sociology, psychology, etc.

HOLLAND

W. P. Van Stockum, N.V. 36 Buitenhof, The Hague,
is a specialized bookseller similar to Dillon's or Blackwell's in England, as well as serving by appointment to the Queen of the Netherlands. They are one of the leading general and scientific bookshops in Holland, a country noted for the quality of its bookstores, and are equally strong in the sciences and in the humanities. They can be paid through their account with Chase Manhattan Bank in New York.

HUNGARY

Kultura, P.O.B. 149, Budapest 62,
is the agency in Hungary specializing in the export of all books and periodicals published in that country. Other East European countries have similar organizations, but Kultura is of particular interest because it has made a point of publishing specialized material in English, particularly in the sciences. Of course, it is to them that you should address orders for anything published in Hungarian, but you may wish to see their English-language catalogue of foreign-language materials, which includes an impressive list of medical literature, e.g., *Critical and Theoretical Pictures of Some Renal Diseases*, 313 pages with many illustrations, $10. Kultura also distributes the English-language Corvina publications, books for the most part on art and literature, which may include many Hungarian literary works, as well as an extensive list of picture books on Hungarian paintings, crafts, music, cooking, etc. Probably the most extensive literature in English of any of the East European countries.

BOOKPLATES

Book-Care, 8 Porchester Place, London W.2., England
Book-Care sells six decorative plates which cost, including surface postage: $16 for a hundred, $20 for two hundred, $30 for five hundred. All the plates come plain (without inscription), or printed with either of two type styles at no extra cost. When ordering, remember to give the quantity that you want, the number of the plate, the letter of the type style, and in clear capital letters the inscription you want, e.g., "JOHN BLOGGS," "EX LIBRIS JOHN BLOGGS," or "EX LIBRIS."

MAGAZINES

Wm. Dawson & Sons Ltd., Cannon House, Folkestone, Kent CT19 5EE, England
The Little Red Book, a guide to the press of the world, free.

Dawson's *Little Red Book* provides an extremely useful guide to the world's magazines, and the firm specializes in supplying journals on a subscription basis throughout the world. The list contains a selection of "5,000 more popular journals," but Dawson's computer contains over 26,000 titles, "thus enabling us to supply any journal from any country in the world . . . provided the journal is normally available to the public." For anyone with a hobby or specialist interest or for any library, the Dawson list is therefore of great use. The House of Lords *Parliamentary Debates* is listed right next to the Australian *Pastoral Review and Graziers Record*, both harder to find here than the *Peking Review*, which follows. Dawson's will try to compile a list of magazines in your field if you don't find what you want in their catalogue.

MAPS

Edward Standford Ltd., 12–14 Long Acre, London W.C.2, England
List of recommended maps for any one area in the world, free.
International Maps and Atlases in Print [Bowkers], $37.50.

The largest and best-known map retailers in the world can solve any map problem put to them. Modern maps of every kind: road maps for tourists, town plans, geological and thematic maps, maps for sales and educational purposes, and maps printed to order. Also magnetic maps, maps mounted on board or cloth to order, maps dissected for the pocket, atlases, globes, and guide books.

USEFUL PAPERBACK GUIDES

INTERIOR DESIGN
The Council of Industrial Design, 28 Haymarket, London S.W.1, England
Publication list, free.

The government-sponsored Council of Industrial Design sells various magazines and books of interest to designers, or anyone interested in design, and have a collection of books published by the Design Centre that should be useful to anyone building, remodeling or furnishing a house. Although the books recommend specific English products, some of which are available by mail, they are mainly helpful because they give the kind of unbiased, factual information that amateur interior decorators need on subjects such as children's rooms, kitchens, storage space, lighting. The book on kitchens, for instance, compares the advantages and disadvantages of different kinds of flooring materials, wall coverings, work surfaces; tells you the most convenient heights for different appliances and where they should be in relation to each other and storage; how much of a splashback you need in each area, etc. The books cost about $1.60 each, plus postage.

VACATION
Barton Children's Holidays, West Woodyates Manor, Salisbury, Wiltshire, England
Brochures, free.

Parents who would like to combine a family trip to Europe with a fling without the kids might think about leaving their children in an English "holiday home." People have occasionally asked me about riding holidays in England, and indeed, last year when I was on vacation in deepest Devonshire I discovered a couple of New York girls who had been deposited on a remote moorland farm for two weeks' riding while their parents went to France. (The girls were very happy.) But American children in English "holiday homes" must be quite rare, as Peter Hopper of Barton Children's Holidays writes: "Three young American children came to stay with us for six weeks of last summer while their parents 'did' Europe; they are coming to us again for six weeks [next year]! As costs are relatively less in England and it is a tradition for American children to go to (expensive) summer camps, I believe an American parent could send a child to us and the cost including the air fare would still be surprisingly low." Basic fee in 1974 was about $75 per week, with extra charges for a few optional activities such as tennis and riding lessons. English study courses are arranged for foreign-language children in one of the centers. Barton's Holiday Homes are for boys and girls of five to sixteen.

Boat Enquiries Ltd., 7 Walton Well Road, Oxford OX2 6ED, England
A Lazy Man's Guide to Holidays Afloat, $2. October.

A Lazy Man's Guide to Holidays Afloat lists boats for rent on the English canals and coast, and a few in France, Holland, Germany and Scandinavia. It also lists hotel boats which take you through the canals and stop for land excursions as you go (prices start at about $150 for seven days, all included). A certain amount of information is given in the booklet, such as where to go to combine fishing with your sailing, and prices. Extra free brochures are available about the individual firms listed, and you can also book through Boat Enquiries if you like.

Farm Holiday Guides Ltd., 18 High Street, Paisley, Scotland
Farm Holiday Guide
Britain's Best Holidays
Furnished Holidays in Britain
Scotland's Best Holidays
Holidays in Wales
Each guide costs $1.50 including postage, and is available from January to May.

Bearing in mind that British food and summers are both likely to be watery, people with young children might think about a fairly inexpensive vacation in the English countryside. The 600-page *Farm Holiday Guide* lists farms and country houses all over Britain which take guests. These places pay for inclusion in the guide, but have filled out questionnaires both about their own facilities and about local sports available, such as fishing or pony trekking. Prices start at $27 a week per person for bed, breakfast and supper (lower for children).

There is a special section on riding holidays with thirty-three residential riding schools in England, Scotland and Wales listed.

Furnished Holidays in Britain gives details of places for rent, but most, though not all, of these are on caravan sites (trailer courts) or seaside resorts, so you'd be surrounded by other holidaymakers. Trailers start at $27 per week, and houses at $55.

The Inland Waterways Association, 114 Regents Park Road, London NW1 8UQ, England
Leaflets and price lists, $1.

There are three thousand miles of navigable rivers and canals in Britain, and the I.W.A. is a voluntary organization devoted to their care and development. It is not just a boating organization, since it is equally concerned with fishing, walking and other activities that can take place on riverbanks. Its shop sells a wide variety of maps, guidebooks, navigation guides and history books as well as general books for adults and children. These include both the basic, practical guides needed to plan a vacation trip and more esoteric background reading. If you join the I.W.A., you are entitled to buy their tie, brooch and burgees (whatever those are). Dishtowels, postcards and other souvenirs are also available.

* * *

Incidentally, no one should take a holiday in England without first arming themselves with the *Good Food Guide*, which contains reports on the best value-for-the-money places to eat all over the country recommended by local food lovers. It is on sale in most bookshops in England, and in a few of the larger ones in New York.

Another book of interest to anyone planning to tour the British countryside is *Visitor's Guide to Country Workshops*, which lists craftsmen and craft shops all over England, Wales, Scotland and Northern Ireland. It is available, free, from the Council of Small Industries in Rural Areas, 35 Camp Road, Wimbledon Common, London S.W.19, England.

Rélais du Silence, Hôtel les Oiseaux, 38640 Claix, France
Guide to quiet French hotels, 75 cents; $2 air mail. In French.

The Network of Calm and Tranquillity is probably the best translation for this appealing chain of hotels. The guide lists inns and hotels throughout France, located both in the countryside and in the city, where "you will find the peace and quiet you will not wish to do without any more." Each hotel is photographed in color, and many are ravishingly old. All details of size, price, etc., are included. French hotels are still among the less expensive in the world; three-star hotels are listed where a room can cost well under $10 a day per person. Rates at the Norman beach resort of Royan, for instance, start as low as $7 off season, with full pension available for another $10. Though prices will undoubtedly rise, government regulations still make these among the rare travel bargains left.

Research Publications Services Ltd., Victoria Hall, East Greenwich, London S.E.10, England.
Residential short courses, $2. March and September.

If you are already planning to go to England and would like to add a touch of intellectual stimulation, try a weekend of antiques, archaeology, architecture, dancing, drama, flower arranging, music, needlework, photography, pottery, writing or discussion. Each year the National Institute of Adult Education compiles a list of two- to seven-day courses held from April through August. Many of the courses are held in universities or big country houses, and besides, hopefully, being interesting in themselves, are a good way to meet the English. Prices start as low as $13 for certain weekend courses.

Starfish Books Ltd., Starfish House, Brook Farm Road, Cobham, Surrey, England
Farm and Country Holidays.
Devon and Cornwall.
Self Catering Holidays.
Bed, Breakfast and Evening Meal.
January; $2 each, including surface postage.

Starfish Books also sells a guide to farm and country holidays. Theirs is much smaller than *Farm Holiday Guide* (above), but it is very good on background information. Each paid entry tells you whether the farm is a working farm (most are), what animals there are, how many people the farm has room for, and a bit about the nearest town or village, population, atmosphere, buildings worth looking at, etc.

4 Christmas and Other Celebrations

Christmas and Other Celebrations

Even though people grumble about Christmas having become commercialized, it is still possible to find some lovely handmade traditional decorations in small shops abroad. And shopping by mail is particularly agreeable for Christmas, when instead of tramping endlessly around crowded stores full of jostling, pushing people in search of inspired gifts, you can sit comfortably at home and with a flick of the wrist look through catalogues with tempting offerings of stores all over the world. You must do this no later than October, though, since unless you want to pay for air-mail postage, orders should be in by the very beginning of November.

DECORATIONS

Akios Industries, P.O. Box 219, Quitó, Ecuador
75-page catalogue, $1. Prices in $.

Akios sells Ecuadorian handicrafts made locally or in its own workshops, and has some beautiful Christmas decorations: a bread-dough Nativity set, very decorative and very inedible, as the figures have been painted, varnished, "sanitized" and preserved against mold. This technique must be quite widespread, for I have seen bread-dough figures from Czechoslovakia too, but the South American versions are the most colorful. Twenty-two pieces cost $16. Also small straw Nativity scenes for $4, and pretty straw Christmas-tree decorations: birds, fish, pigs, bells, dolls, flowers, angels for only $1.50 a dozen, plain or colored.

Akios also sells Christmas cards for $22 the hundred, hand-painted or embroidered with Indian figures and local scenes, but *everything* takes a minimum of eight weeks to arrive, so you should order way in advance.

Fortnum and Mason, Piccadilly, London W1A 1ER, England
40-page Christmas catalogue in color, free. September.

In their abundant Christmas food and gifts catalogue, Fortnum's has a page of very fancy snappers (an essential part of English Christmas). Dazzling gold or silver froths of net and flowers contain hats, headdresses and novelties for adults, $18 for a box of six. Dark-green snappers hidden by an overgrowth of holly and berries contain headdresses and novelties for the whole family, $16 for twelve. Then there are snappers just for ladies, snappers just for gentlemen, snappers containing only jewelry; and snappers just for children, decorated with toy animals on the outside, are $8 for twelve. The least expensive snappers for the whole family are also $8 a dozen. And for any time of the year, a children's-party centerpiece; in 1970 it was a white elephant filled with twelve hats, twelve balloons and twelve toys, about $9.

Hamleys of Regent Street, 200–202 Regent Street, London W.1, England ♕ ♕
39-page color catalogue, free.

The catalogue of London's largest toy shop has a couple of pages of party and Christmas things for children. Surprise snowballs and snappers, each containing a hat, a novelty and an indoor fireworks, cost $5.50 for twelve; a fairy for the top of the Christmas tree, $5; also shatterproof tree decorations; Christmas stockings (empty or full); party favors, party novelties, party jokes and party games (a pack with ten games for children aged three to ten, $5); masks and dress-up clothes.

Klods Hans, 34 Hans Jensensstraede, DK-5000 Odense, Denmark
14-page brochure, $1. Prices in $.

A neat and appealing little brochure showing handmade decorations at about one half of their New York prices. For Christmas: star, elf and angel tree decorations; choirboy candlesticks, musical angels, pottery elves and snowy cottages; mobiles, wall hangings, and calendars (one cotton calendar has twenty-four little girls with pockets in their aprons for small gifts, $5.60). An artless Nativity scene in hand-painted wood, $19.

For Easter there are hand-painted wooden eggs, chicks, rabbits and candlesticks, and wooden mobiles; and for any other time lots of little things that are bound to please children: face egg cups with hat cozies, people pencil holders, tiny ceramic animals, pinafores with appliquéd dolls in cradles—and a wall hanging with a dollhouse or farmyard on it and a removable doll, $7. For adults: brass candlesticks and oil lamps, and Royal Copenhagen figurines.

Hobby Horse Ltd., 15–17 Langton Street, London S.W.10, England
Catalogue, 65 cents, $1.40 air mail.

This general crafts catalogue has a section with materials for Christmas decorations. There are fine chip-wood strips from Finland for curly designs to hang on the tree, kits to make wooden stars, kits to make small wooden Father Christmases, straw for making stars and angels, wooden figures to paint, and metal foil in assorted colors. Leaflets and very good booklets with pictures and instructions are also on sale.

G. G. Lang sel. Erben, P.O. Box 28, 8103 Oberammergau, Germany
Christmas catalogue, $2. In German.
Main catalogue, $5. In German.

Wood carving has been a traditional craft in the mountain village of Oberammergau ever since the middle of the seventeenth century, and before the days of catalogues, traders would carry a "Kraxen," wooden frame, on their backs to foreign trading centers, displaying the carvings for sale as they walked. "The Woodcarving Workshops of G. G. Lang's Heirs" was started in the late eighteenth century and is still producing hand-carved sacred and "profane" (as they put it) works from native German woods. Probably their best-known works are their crèches, where single figures or groups can be bought in plain wood, painted or even dressed in fabric clothes. These are "heirloom" crèches, perhaps to be gradually assembled if you like them but the prices daunt you—a complete set with seventeen 6" figures and crèche in natural wood costs just under $100; painted, $193.

For Christmas-cookie molds, see Handicrafts: Holland; for Christmas embroideries, Hobbies: Eva Rosenstand; for commemorative Christmas plates, Glass and China: Focke and Meltzer.

CARDS

Fratelli Alinari, Lungarno Corsini 24 R, Florence 50123, Italy
44-page catalogue with some color, free. Prices in $.

This firm, famous for its reproductions, issues twelve cards a year, each one a color reproduction of an Italian painting on handmade paper. Some of the cards have religious subjects—Raphael's "Madonna of the Chair," Fra Angelico's "Group of Angels," etc.—but not all of them are religious, and as cards are available with or without Christmas greetings, they can be used for other occasions as well.

Christmas and Other Celebrations

Konn's Fine Arts, Mail Order Department, The Hong Kong Hilton Hotel, Hong Kong
Samples, free. Prices in $.

Hong Kong's leading mail-order card firm produces Americanized Chinese-style cards with your name and address and any message you choose printed inside. $16 per hundred (including postage) for birds, flowers or landscapes hand-painted on silk, or $18.50 per hundred for portraits of children, junks and harbor scenes reproduced from oil paintings. For $1 more, all the envelopes can be printed with your name and address too. These prices include postage.

Treasures of Italy, P.O. Box 1513, Florence, Italy
Christmas card leaflet, free. Prices in $.

Christmas cards, notes and stationery. The cards ($1.75 per box of twelve, including postage) are illustrated with scenes of the Nativity, the Adoration, the Annunciation by Botticelli, Raphael, Da Vinci and other famous Italian painters. The pictures are bordered by a classic Florentine scroll in gold, red and cobalt copied from Renaissance manuscripts. The scroll motif is repeated on the inside of the envelopes and on stationery. There are also cards for other occasions.

1
Klods Hans Red, white and blue hand-painted wooden elves with handknitted caps. About $1.13 each.

2
Klods Hans White paper angel mobile on brass wires. About $1.56.

3
Klods Hans Straw Christmas-tree star. About 22 cents.
photos Gunnar Larsen

4
Klods Hans Christmas hanging, with bell.
photo Gunnar Larsen

5
Folklore (see Handicrafts section) Decorative bread-dough figures (nonedible), under $2 each; fifteen-piece Nativity set, about $11.

6
Treasures of Italy Christmas Card "Choir Angles" by Guarnacci, from a box of twelve assorted cards. About $1.75 per box, including air-mail postage.

5 Cigars and Pipes

Cigars and Pipes

Astley's Ltd., 109 Jermyn Street, London S.W.1, England
18-page catalogue, free. Prices in $.

"You shall avoid all evil company, and all occasions which may tend to draw you to the same; and make speedy return when you shall be sent on your master's or mistress's errand," apprentice pipe makers were instructed in the seventeenth century. Astley's pipe shop displays the original document along with famous and not-famous antique pipes, some of which are for sale. However, their catalogue shows just their well-known new briar pipes and explains the distinctive characteristics of each one. Prices, including postage, vary between $14 for their Crusty and Atlantic briars and $44 for Super Straight grained briars. Lots of shapes are shown, and there is a pageful of unusual designs with a pipe made out of briar *root*. Also available are meerschaum pipes, special tobacco blends, pipe cases, tobacco pouches, smokers' knives and a repair service by mail for pipes of any make.

Davidoff et Cie, 2 Rue de Rive, 1200 Geneva, Switzerland
List of Cuban cigars, in French, free.

Davidoff et Cie is best known for its Cuban cigars. In fact, one line of Cuban cigars is named after the owner: Davidoff's Nos. 1 and 2, about $50 for twenty-five 6" cigars. Owing to U.S. government restrictions, Cuban cigars aren't allowed into the country, so if they are found being imported, they are confiscated. However, Canadians can buy them without fear, and Americans can either send them to friends in other countries or console themselves with cigars, cigarillos, cigarettes and pipes from any other country in the world, as Davidoff stocks them all (the cigars in special controlled-temperature cellars). He also counts as a free port when the cigars are sent out of Switzerland and they are exempt from the original Swiss import taxes.

Hayim Pinhas, P.O.B. 5000, Istanbul, Turkey
36-page brochure. Prices in $.

Meerschaum is a mineral found only in Turkey. It makes excellent lightweight, porous pipes which smoke turns dark-brown in time. Here you can get hand-carved pipes direct from Turkey and much cheaper than anywhere else. You can buy a sober "English style" or plain with straight or curved stem for $5.50. But if you would like to be more flamboyant, there are carved creatures—a busty "sea-girl" with hair flowing back over the pipe bowl, $10; Cleopatra; Abraham Lincoln; Shakespeare; Bacchus; a priest; a fisherman; an Indian; a Viking; and for $22, a hunting dog with prey in its mouth. Carved cigarette holders cost $1.50. Air-mail postage for each pipe is $1.50, but the minimum order is two pipes.

Inderwick and Co. Ltd., 45 Carnaby Street, London W1V 1PE, England
Leaflet, free.

Inderwick's was established in 1797 and has belonged to the same family ever since. They are very proud of their old age and illustrious past and say that although they don't have a catalogue, people write to them telling them what kind of tobacco they want and "we go from there." Tobacco is what they mainly sell by mail, though they also have pipes (shapes illustrated on a leaflet, but without prices or details) and a popular world-wide pipe repair service.

W. Larsen, Amagertorv 9, DK 1160 Copenhagen K, Denmark
Brochure, $1.

Besides being purveyers to the Royal Danish Court, this fifth-generation family firm says it is *the* pipe shop of Europe. The handmade pipes are made from only well-seasoned, aged briar in sand-blasted or smooth-grained finish, hand-polished,

1
Davidoff et Cie Mr. Davidoff in his Geneva cigar shop.

2
Hayim Pinhas Hand-carved meerschaum pipe "D'Artagnan." $10.

3
Pipe Dan "The Tulip." Both machine-made and hand-carved pipes are on sale here.

and there are over forty designs to choose from in prices starting at about $25.

Mohilla, A 8693 Mürzsteg 47, Austria
Leaflet, free.

The leaflet claims that after a decade, Austria is again able to offer the world a Bruyère (briar) pipe of the highest quality. Designs are based on the classical tradition with that "special Austrian touch," and each model "with a surface no machine can ever give you" is available in smooth and shell. A couple of pipes come with sterling-silver stems. Prices about $30–$50.

Pipe Dan, Vestergade 13, DK-1456 Copenhagen, Denmark
20-page leaflet, free.

Sixty-four pipes are photographed in this clear leaflet. Many of them are of unusual shapes, and they are divided into types: big bowls, verticles, chimneys, light-weight shapes, etc. Prices start at about $6 for a standard mini, and for the handmade pipes vary between $16 and $55. You can buy Danish pipe tobacco here, and pipes made by other Danish manufacturers if you give the number or sketch the shape of the one you want. And there are several unusual services: you can have a name or initials stamped on the pipe for free; you can have a pipe of your own design made up from your own sketch; or Dan will send you the raw materials and you can make your own pipe.

G. Smith and Sons, 74 Charing Cross Road, London WC2H OBG, England
Price list, free.

I was once offered some snuff on the New York subway (of all unlikely places) by a man who had given up smoking and was taking snuff instead. Smith the Snuff Blenders produce a price list which not only describes their many blends and various packagings but also includes answers to your queries. To your question "Why is snuff taken?" they answer: "Most snuff takers take snuff because it is refreshing and invigorating and because it counteracts the mental fatigue caused by the stress and strain of modern life. Others take snuff because it keeps them free from colds and gives relief from catarrh and similar complaints. It has also been said that snuff stimulates the mind." To your question "What other advantages are there?" they answer: "Over the years, snuff has been the start of many great friendships. The passing of a snuff-box will 'break the ice' in many a social gathering, serve as an introduction, and create a talking point to the mutual advantage of all snuff takers."

Shannon Airport (see General section) stocks Peterson pipes.

6 Clothes and Accessories

Clothes and Accessories

Although it seems so tricky to buy clothes by mail, they are in fact popular mail-order buys, both with people who know they can slip easily into standard sizes and, at the other extreme, with people who like clothes made to measure. If you like classic clothes you can do really well by mail. There is a wide and impressive choice of good tweed skirts, silk shirts (from Thailand), and lamb's wool and cashmere sweaters—often at marvelously low prices.

Great Britain, which has long had a worldwide reputation for good workmanship and excellent tailoring, has really latched on to the idea. Selling Scottish knitwear by mail is a booming business; posh Savile Row tailors and Jermyn Street shirtmakers send representatives over to measure their customers each year; and the rest of the country seems to be busily sending out brochures, self-measuring charts and swatches.

Hong Kong is another main source for clothes by mail. The tailors there are well known for their capacity to copy old suits—there are jokes about new suits coming back with carefully reproduced cigarette burns. However, although their workmanship is generally praised, the fabric swatches for men's suiting I was sent looked rather flimsy to me. But if anyone feels like trying these tailors (all listed in reputable American shopping guides), write and tell them what weight suit you want, and they will send you fabric swatches and self-measurement forms. Or if you prefer, send them an old suit to copy. The shoe shops, too, will copy any shoes you have grown fond of, and they will also copy purses, either your own or from photographs cut out of magazines.

The women's and children's clothes from Hong Kong look like great bargains—for one thing, they are made of fabrics such as silk which China has specialized in. The styles are all-American, the colors mainly pastel for children and strong for women—turquoise, hot pink, kelly-green, yellow.

Clothing sizes differ from country to country (see charts at the back of the book), so I think it best, while you ask for a certain size, always to enclose a drawing with your measurements. But never take your own measurements, and if you are having something made to measure, either send something that fits well to be copied, or have a tailor measure you.

FOR MEN AND WOMEN

W. Bill Ltd., Mail Order Dept., 93 New Bond Street, London W1Y 9LA, England
General color brochure, free. Prices in $.
Pringle and Barrie knitwear brochures, free. Prices in $.

This firm, which is well known to American visitors in London, runs a big mail-order business in clothes and fabrics, and puts out a brochure showing a little of everything. For women there are knit dresses and sweaters with skirts to match; for men, sweaters and tweed jackets from W. Bill's own exclusive tweeds. A Shetland sports jacket, illustrated in the current brochure, comes ready-made or made-to-measure for $100, postage and insurance $3 extra.

Cambrian Factory Ltd., Llanwrtyd Wells, Breconshire, Wales
Color leaflet and self-measuring chart, free. Prices in $.

At this factory, tweeds are made from Welsh wool by disabled people, and the entire process of wool sorting, dyeing, spinning, etc., can be watched by visitors. The tweeds are of high quality, and colors are fairly earthy: beige, mustards, gray, greens, in herringbone or checks. The tweeds are sold by the yard: the 8/10 oz. tweeds in 29" widths cost $6 a yard, including postage. There is also a made-to-measure service: women's skirts cost $20 to $24; men's sports jackets, $65; two-piece suits, $98—all these prices include postage.

J. C. Cording and Co. Ltd., 19 Piccadilly, London W1V OPE, England
Catalogue, free.

Top English clothes for the sporty country life; hunting, shooting and fishing, or just walking; both ready-made and made-to-measure (self-measurement charts enclosed). The catalogue explains in admirable detail the various features of each of its classic models: the Yeo coat, "the original waterproof riding coat, often copied but never equalled"; 'Grenfell' golfwear, cut from the cloth originally made for Sir Wilfred Grenfell, "heroic doctor/explorer," to wear in the arctic wastes of Labrador; the "Barlows" Norfolk jacket, based on the original Norfolk jacket; etc.

Creation Boutique, Duke Street, Dublin 2, Ireland
24-page brochure, $1. Prices in $.

The director of this shop, who was formerly with Marshall Field, Chicago, has put together a neat little brochure with just a few choice items: two Irish handloomed dresses in off-white for about $66; two sheepskin coats, $120 for women and $135 for men; and four Donald Davies shirtwaist dresses for $46 each. Donald Davies dresses are made in featherweight tweed in the most magnificent colors: various shades of everything bright—blues, mauves, reds and yellows, either solid or checks or stripes. These dresses are sold in New York for $60 and up.

P. Cutler Ltd., 95 Upper Street, Islington-Green, London N1 ONP, England
Catalogue, $3.

This firm, which sells boots, shoes, wigs and some clothes for female impersonators, says that they have a world-wide mail-order service.

David and Joe Trading Co., P.O. Box 8189, Kowloon, Hong Kong
Catalogue of beaded sweaters and handbags, free.
Catalogue planned of men's and children's knitted sport shirts, free.
Both catalogues together, 50 cents surface mail; $1 air mail.

I have just seen the catalogue of the inexpensive beaded cashmere sweaters (under $15 each) and beaded handbags (under $5 each), but the mail-order manager, Mr. Frederick, says that since sports/T shirts are very successful with their mail-order customers, they are planning to put out a catalogue of these which will be ready by the time this book is published.

Irish Cottage Industries Ltd., 18 Dawson Street, Dublin 2, Ireland
30-page brochure, free. Prices in $.

This shop puts out a nice amateurish brochure, with all the people from next door modeling clothes and looking as though they are trying not to laugh. Clothes include several shapes and designs of the colorful, woven crios belt; the traditional, heavy, off-white Aran sweaters; gossamer-weight tweed dressing gowns ($43.50); lumber jackets; hand-knitted socks for men; string gloves; and stoles, scarves and ties made out of gossamer-weight tweed in so many shades that they can't be listed.

Tweed is sold by the yard, and samples are sent on request for specific colors and weights.

Clothes and Accessories

1
W. Bill Ltd Shetland-wool roll-collar dress, made to measure, in dark aqua, green mist, barn red, camel, blue haze, green lovat, olive green and misty blue, or almost any other color. About $26.
photo Dudley Harris

2
Creation Boutique "Paddy Sprung," a Donald Davies handwoven featherweight tweed dress, available in checks, stripes, plaids or solid colors, in sizes 8 to 16. About $46.
photo Photographic Services

3
Moffat Weavers All-wool Welsh tapestry coats. About $65 each, including surface postage.

S. and M. Jacobs Ltd. Exports, 20 Dawson Street, Dublin 2, Ireland
12-page brochure, free; fabric swatches, $1. Prices in $.

A huge mail-order business in made-to-measure suits and coats for men and women. Styles are good, classic, but not dowdy. The fabrics are 100 percent wool, Irish handwoven tweed in rich colors: reds, blues, purples, and the prices are quite low: about $23 for a fully lined skirt; about $68 for a lady's suit, coat or cape; and $95 for a gent's coat. Jacobs says that no size or figure problem is too difficult for them. They also sell tweeds by the yard.

Jahn-Markl, Residenzplatz 3, A-5020 Salzburg, Austria
Catalogue, free.

An extremely old family firm saying "we do business with American customers since decades" puts out a rather staid catalogue illustrating their Austrian-style suede and leather clothes. I heartily recommend it to people who are serious about buying because there are measurement charts, suede samples and background information on types of leather and their care. However, there are no prices at all and each article has to be inquired about individually, so please don't ask for this catalogue unless you mean business.

Victor Laurence, 62/64 Hampstead Road, London NW1 2NU, England
32-page catalogue, 75 cents; $2.50 air mail.

Laurence is England's largest dealer in government surplus clothing and equipment, and also stocks a wide range of outdoor and camping gear. The catalogue is filled with the familiar British military fashions at extremely reasonable prices and should, I suspect, appeal enormously to many people, especially teenagers, who have never considered the possibility of strenuous outdoor activity. Government Wellington boots cost $7.50, for instance; military greatcoats are under $20; and new, nonsurplus clothing is in the same price range. Obviously, ideal for anyone who wants to look like the hero of a wartime movie, but also perfect for people simply seeking inexpensive, serviceable clothing (such as NATO long johns for $2).

In addition to clothing there is a great variety of other equipment, including school and lab supplies, government surplus medical instruments, tools, camping gear, etc. While any one family could probably find bargains in a dozen different categories, this catalogue could also launch an excellent group undertaking. One family might try the pith helmets, another the ornamental cannon doorstops, another the earthenware chamber pots. A marvelous mixture, ideal for large families.

Loden-Frey, Maffeistrasse 7–9, 8 Munich 1, Germany
24-page color catalogue in German, free.

This German lodenwear is more international, more fashionable and more expensive than the Austrian. A man's classic coat costs about $90. A woman's straight-cut scarlet coat trimmed with braid, $51; a maxi-coat, $90; and a stunning embroidered dark-brown (antelope) suede suit, $280.

There are all sorts of variations on the dirndl theme, including some unorthodoxly low-cut ones, and one mauve-and-pink maxi-dirndl that looks fashionably peasanty and costs about $40.

Children's coats shown here are $19 and up; and dirndls for girls, $14.50 and up.

Clothes and Accessories

Moffat Weavers, Ladyknowe Mill, Moffat, Dumfriesshire, Scotland
Color catalogue, free.

Besides making clothes, this small manufacturing and retail firm sells clothes in tartans and rather undistinguished tweeds. For men there are sweaters or two sports jackets and durable-press pants in standard sizes, while women have much more to choose from. Sweaters, skirts, dresses, suits, coats and raincoats in classic styles; coats in richly colored Welsh tapestry; or capes and long skirts in mohair. A sports jacket costs about $30; a partly lined skirt made to measure, about $13.

The Scotch House, Knightsbridge, London, S.W.1, England
24-page color catalogue, free. Prices in $.

The largest and most glamorous of the shops dealing in Scottish goods. The Scotch House sells all sorts of sophisticated variations on the Scottish theme that will appeal to people without a trace of Scottish blood in their veins. Full-length evening kilts, $53; tartan blazers, about $44, a tartan dinner jacket with a black satin shawl collar, $80; wool tartan capes for little girls, $34. And a Viyella dressing gown for $33 that looks identical to one I have seen in New York for $57.

This is also a very good place for well-made and fairly expensive clothes in Scottish wools and tweeds. For men: jackets, trousers, suede vests and deerstalker hats. For women: classic coats, skirts and sweaters. For children: smart little coats, $36–$47.

Swan and Edgar Ltd., Piccadilly Circus, London W1A 2AY, England

Swan and Edgar's front doors on Piccadilly are a favorite meeting place for Londoners, partly because they are opposite an enormous clock, and tourists seem to magically discover the doors, too. The shop is a large fashion store which sells most good, medium-priced English clothes, many of them known to Americans as they are sold in the United States: Rodex, Aquascutum, Dannimac and Quelrayn Coats; Ricci Michael dresses; Braemar, Pringle and Morely knitwear. And there are three departments dealing exclusively with Jaeger, Berketex and Windsmoor clothes. Jaeger's are perhaps the most popular of all in England: excellent medium-priced classic tweeds and knitwear for men and women; coats, suits, sports jackets, trousers, skirts — everything. All these clothes are much less expensive in England, and although Swan and Edgar has no catalogue, they answer individual questions and try to send manufacturers' brochures when they are available.

Charles Veillon SA, P.O. Box 1032, 1001 Lausanne, Switzerland
Color catalogue, $1; $3 air mail. Spring, fall. In French.

This mail-order firm publishes two very large (over 200 pages) catalogues a year of clothes for men, women and children. It's a useful basic source book with mainly rather standard classic clothes but also a few quite smart ones. In the catalogue I looked at there was a nice cream-colored suit with a belted jacket and pleated skirt; brightly colored raincoats that would do as lightweight coats; and some very attractive psychedelic nylon jersey two-piece swimsuits for women. For children, besides the usual dresses and pants and tops, there were some smart overalls in red or blue with white stitching and flared trousers with snazzy stripes below the knee. For men, very lightweight zippered jackets with pants to match; and for everyone, bright red, blue and yellow cotton underwear. A good collection of classic shoes, too.

4
The Scotch House Kilt skirt in any tartan, about $103, velvet vest, about $33; blouse, about $35.

5
The Scotch House Reversible Buchanan cape, available in many tartans, about $100. Solid-color cashmere pants, about $75. Tartan trousers, about $30; cashmere sweater, about $40.

6
Leather School Leather purse in bone, natural tan, medium or dark brown, red, navy blue, black or white. $47 plain, $48 with Florentine gilding.
photo Style

Clothes and Accessories

BALLET

Ballet School Supplies Ltd., 25 Queen Street, Newcastle upon Tyne NE1 3UG, England
Color leaflet, free.

The stocker for leading ballet-clothing manufacturers, this firm supplies ballet schools in England and abroad as well as "keep-fit enthusiasts" with clothing. Besides the usual leotards in several colors, they have frilled leotards, leotards with separate skirts, and Grecian tunics as required by some ballet schools. They also sell ballet shoes in infant-to-adult sizes, tap shoes, gymnastic pumps, ballroom dance shoes and shoes to dance the Irish jig in.

GLOVES, BAGS AND LEATHER

Anticoli Gloves, Via del Tritone 143, Rome 00187, Italy
30-page brochure with some color, free. Prices in $.

A good, illustrated selection of gloves, wallets and belts at very low prices.

Catello D'Auria, Via Due Macelli 55, 00187 Rome, Italy
12-page leaflet, free. Prices in $.

A smaller and slightly more expensive selection than Anticoli's but in a wider variety of leathers. Here there are gloves in pigskin, sheepskin and doeskin as well as kid. Wrist-length kid gloves cost just over $4 for women and so do doeskin.

Denise Francelle, 244 Rue de Rivoli, Paris I, France
Price list, free. Prices in $.

Finest Roger Fare and Kislav gloves that are hard to find in America start at $13. Also doeskin, suede, velvet and calf gloves, each kind in four lengths, and bags, scarves and umbrellas. For children, gloves and purses that match, but are unillustrated.

Jannabags, 1 Prince of Wales Crescent, London N.W.1, England
Leaflet, 50 cents.

These tough canvas bags have had an admiring press in England and have become increasingly popular since the firm was started by Janna Drake in 1970. In fact, with all their pockets, their strong, clear colors, and their flexibility and low price, they are a tempting replacement for stiff, old handbags and suitcases. Seven bags are illustrated with line drawings on the leaflet, and prices go from about $7 for a small shoulder bag to about $17 for the biggest bag, intended to replace a small suitcase. It has plenty of outside pockets for tickets, passports, etc. Weekend bags, shopping bags and everyday bags come in oatmeal, denim, black, yellow, red, green or brown.

Kristine Leather Goods Workshop, 18–20 Fulham High Street, London S.W.6, England
6-page catalogue with crocodile-skin samples, free. Prices in $.

Classic crocodile handbags ranging in price from $176 to $200; also crocodile wallets, $41; billfolds, $23; key cases and glass cases. Postage and insurance included in prices.

Leather School, Piazza Santa Croce 16, Florence, Italy
32-page color catalogue, free, Prices in $.

The Leather School in the cloister of the Santa Croce Church was founded by monks to produce a complete line of Florentine leather goods and to technically prepare young boys who wish to specialize in this type of work in a morally sound atmosphere. (The atmosphere isn't so morally sound, however, as to prevent whoever wrapped my parcel from writing "*Niella valore*" on the customs form.)

There is a very wide range of wallets in calf, crocodile, lizard and tortoise skin (starting at about $5.75), and cigarette cases, glass cases, photograph albums, photograph frames, etc., in the gold-tooling-on-colored-leather that is typical of Florence. In cut velvet there are jewelry boxes, wastepaper baskets, picture frames, handbags. And in calfskin there are belts for men and attaché cases at about $80, and a wide range of handbags both tooled in gold (for about $35) and plain, including some chunky, casual, sport, and shoulder bags ranging in price from $22 to $65. A seven-piece desk set, gilded or plain, costs $73 and comes in all colors.

Loewe, Barquillo 13, Madrid 4, Spain
Color brochure, free. For Christmas only.

Spain's poshest leather shop sells only exclusive designs made in its own workshops. There is a branch in London but none in America yet, so they can sell by mail. Prices seem high unless you compare them with similar top shops in other countries. A wallet with a coin purse costs about $20, and an attaché case about $90. Some styles are decorated with embroidered ribbons or contrasting leathers, others achieve noble simplicity. Besides the usual colors, there are lovely, unusual ranges of browns—grayish browns, toasted beiges, tobaccos, and burgundys.

HATS

Herbert Johnson Ltd., 38 New Bond Street, London W.1, England
18-page catalogue for men, leaflet for women, free.

Herbert Johnson opened his hat shop in the '90's at the suggestion of Edward the Prince of Wales, and now the shop justifiably prides itself in combining the best of old and new. There are hats to convince the most adamant hat haters. Besides every sort of classic hat for men they carry all-purpose felt, town and formal wear, tweed and leather hats and caps, sporting headwear, seasonal hats "for warmer times or cold comfort." They have a smashing collection of "character hats," including "the poet," "the artist," and the "38," originally sold by Herbert Johnson in the '20's. ("The fact that this style is immediately associated with the gangster just means the wearer can never be disregarded.") Felt hats cost between $13 and $33, and tweed caps are about $12.

The English *Vogue* uses lots of Herbert Johnson's hats for women in basic shapes and fashionably, completely undecorated styles. Prices are from $15 to $30.

Carlo Lambardi, Via 4 Novembre 157 B, Rome, Italy
10-page brochure, free. Prices in $.

Instead of answering any of my letters, Carlo Lambardi has simply sent neat little brochures giving instructions on how to buy his Borsalino hats by mail. So I assume that he does have a mail-order business but that whoever answers the mail doesn't understand English. The impeccable brochure shows sixteen classic Borsalino models for men and women, lists colors and American sizes available, and contains a handy order form. Men's hats are around $30 and women's around $20, both including postage and insurance.

Clothes and Accessories

7
Hayashi Kimono Cotton apron in any color $6 including surface postage.

8
Hayashi Kimono Silk kimono in any color. $28.50, including surface postage.

9
V. Juul Christensen and Son Sweaters for men and women cost between $25 and $55.

10
Wilson of Hawick Lyle and Scott's most classic sweaters available in merino wool, lamb's wool or cashmere, and thirty different colors. Prices from about $17.

11
The Scottish Merchant Authentic Fair Isle sweater knitted to order (takes six to eight weeks). Suggested color combination: mostly blue and red with some yellow on natural background. $75 and up.

12
Burberrys Ltd Terylene and cotton gabardine in oyster, sand, black or navy. Styles change each season, but similar raincoats are usually on sale for around $100.

Clothes and Accessories

KIMONOS

Hayashi Kimono, Tokyo Hilton Hotel Arcade, 2–10–3 Nagata-Cho Chiyoda-Ku, Tokyo, Japan
Brochure with some color, free. Prices in $.

A top Tokyo shop for antique kimonos which has a mail-order service for Westernized Japanese clothes, marvelous for exotic wear around the house. Full-length, flower-embroidered silk kimonos in almost any color cost between $28 and $40. Happi coats, which are less spectacular but more practical, since they are knee-length and have narrower sleeves, cost $21 to $30 in silk, $16 in rayon, and $12 in cotton. The cotton ones cost about $10 for children. Happi coats also come with trousers as lounging pajamas for men and women. Prices for men's clothes are mysteriously lower than for women, and are embroidered in gold with dragons or Japanese characters. Westerners have been impressed with the beauty of the black cotton coats Japanese firemen wear, and these are on sale for $21 with wide gold bands around the waist, and the name of the firehouse on the back, in a Japanese character. All the above prices include surface postage; air postage is given and is around $2 extra.

KNITWEAR

V. Juul Christensen and Son, Livjaegergade 17, 2100 Copenhagen, Denmark
Color brochure, free.

Juul Christensen, which appeared in the first edition as Copenhagen Handknit, says they had trouble with Danish retailers and are now selling only by mail. They continue to make lightweight and heavyweight traditional Norwegian hand-knitted sweaters in beautiful and subtle color combinations. They also make woven Norwegian "vams" (sort of tunics) with trimmings and pewter clips; Danish machine-knitted sweaters in jacquard patterns; Icelandic hand-knitted sweaters in natural wool and natural colors; and hand-knitted Aran sweaters—so they've gone International. Prices are from $25 to $55.

Heather Valley Ltd., Brunstane Road, Edinburgh EH15 2QL, Scotland
12-page color brochure and swatches, free.

Heather Valley's own made-to-measure lamb's-wool and Shetland sweaters with tweed skirts to match. The designs are all classic, the colors unusual. There are pinks, mauves and dusty blues that the internationally famous manufacturers don't make—you might prefer these. Sweaters cost around $17 each, skirts cost from $20 to $35.

Ancrum Craig Knitwear Co. Ltd., Jedburgh TD8 6UN, Scotland
*Lyle and Scott brochure.
Price list for children's sweaters, and tweed and yarn packs, $1; $2 air mail. Prices in $.*

Hunt and Winterbotham Ltd., 4 Old Bond Street, London W.1, England
Barrie and Pringle brochures and "color toned" fabrics, free.

W. S. Robertson Ltd., 13/15 High Street, Hawick, Scotland
Braemar, Pringle brochures and wool samples, $2 a year. Prices in $.

Romanes and Patterson, 62 Princes Street, Edinburgh, Scotland
Barrie, Braemar, Pringle brochures and wool samples, free.

Wilson of Hawick, 30 Drumlanrig Square, Hawick, Scotland
Lyle and Scott brochure and wool samples, $1. Prices in $.

All the above shops sell knitwear by famous English and Scottish manufacturers by mail. Tell one of them which manufacturer you are interested in, and they will send the current brochure. Each manufacturer has two brochures going at once, one with sweaters for men and another with sweaters for women. The men's brochures show sweaters in merino, camel's hair, lamb's wool and cashmere, with prices from about $17 and up. The women's brochures have not only sweaters from about $17, but also skirts—either in exactly the same color, or else in tweeds to match, from $16.50. If you sew, you can buy skirt packs in matching fabric for about $22. You can save *roughly* one third of the price by buying from Great Britain and another advantage is the enormous range of styles and colors to choose from: each manufacturer has about twenty-four styles in around fifteen colors each.

Eileen's Handknits, Ardara, Co. Donegal, Ireland
Brochure, free. Prices in $.

Twelve Aran sweaters and jackets for men and women are photographed in this brochure; prices are a few dollars lower than at the other shops. As I write, they go from $19 to $25.

Kennedy's of Ardara, Ardara, Co. Donegal, Ireland
Brochure, free. Prices in $.

Kennedy of Ardara sells traditional Aran sweaters knitted by the farmers' and fishermen's wives in their homes. Prices are slightly lower here than in many stores; at this writing, sweaters for men and women cost $25 each, handwoven satin-lined tweed skirts and slacks $15 each. Tweeds are sold by the yard; write for cuttings.

Kløverhuset, Strandgaten 13, 5001 Bergen, Norway
12-page color catalogue, free. Prices in $.

This shop started as a small dry-goods store in 1852, but has gradually expanded to become Bergen's main fashion store, with a gift store that opens during the tourist season. The handy catalogue shows mainly traditional hand-knitted Norwegian sweaters and jackets in full glorious color. Children's sweaters and jackets cost $23–$33 according to size; sweaters for adults, $50; jackets, $51; caps and gloves, $8.

Glen Lockhart Knitwear, Aberdour, Fife, Scotland
38-page brochure with some color, free.

Made-to-measure knitwear—sweaters, skirts and dresses, tartans and tweeds at low prices. In the brochure the fabrics are photographed in color, but swatches can also be sent if you ask for specific fabrics after seeing brochure. A pure-wool ribbed dress costs about $22 and a lamb's wool sweater and knitted skirt (lined) together are $55. A kilted mini-skirt is about $19, and a kilted evening skirt is about $30.

Millhaven Knitting Services, Knowstone, South Molton, Devon, England
Details, 3 International Reply Coupons.

Millhaven will knit or crochet anything to your own measurements. Send them a picture and details of whatever

Clothes and Accessories

you want, together with the measurements, and they will tell you how much it will cost. They buy English yarn and don't mind using the finer ones.

Una O'Neill Designs, 30 Oakley Park, Blackrock, Co. Dublin, Ireland
Leaflet, 25 cents; 50 cents air mail. Prices in $.

Una O'Neill sells hand-knitted, traditional, off-white Aran fisherman sweaters and jackets. The complicated symbolic stitches evolved centuries ago and are so distinctive that in case of accident a particular design of a sweater could identify the wearer's home village.

The Scottish Merchant, 16 New Row, London WC2N 4LA, England
Leaflet, $1.

Scottish Merchant specializes in very carefully authentic Scottish knitwear, often copied from antique Fair Isle knits now in museums. Apparently the Fair Isle patterns evolved when Scotland was under Norse rule, which is why the designs look somewhat Scandinavian. Patterns were modified as time went by, and when in the sixteenth century one of the Spanish Armada ships was driven ashore on Fair Isle, the local knitters copied the Spanish heraldic designs. Since then, true Fair Isle patterns have incorporated those symbols, including the Armada cross.

Le Tricoteur, 3 St. James' Street, St. Peter Port, Guernsey, Channel Islands, England
Leaflet and samples, free. Prices in $.

Loose, long casual sweaters in styles used originally by smugglers and sailors, and knitted on the island of Guernsey, traditionally a great knitting island. Guernsey men have been exporting their hand-knitted stockings since Queen Elizabeth's day. Mary Queen of Scots wore them. The sweaters are made from partly oiled worsted wool and are still good for sailing, fishing and smuggling. They come in plain colors: red, blue, navy, beige, white, and are priced according to size from $11 for a 22" chest to $27 for a 48" chest.

Westport House, Westport, Co. Mayo, Ireland
Brochure, $1. Prices in $.

Westport House is the stately home of the Marquess of Sligo, who like many stately home owners has flung his doors open to the public in order to pay for upkeep. The mail-order enterprise has developed from the boutiques, shops and centers connected to the house, all of which are carefully watched over by the Marquess' son, the Earl of Altament. The most fetching things in the catalogue are some hand-knitted clothes—a cloak, a fringed hostess skirt, a shawl and two dresses—in large, loose patterns and in either black or white. Prices go from about $30 to just over $100. Sizes: small, medium and large.

RAINCOATS

Burberry's Ltd., Haymarket, London S.W.1, England
12-page brochure, free.

Twenty-four of Burberry's famous coats and raincoats for men and women are shown in the brochure. Prices range from $77 for "ladies' walking Burberry" to about $250 for "Frome," a pure-cashmere coat for men. For about $39 there is a detachable fleece lining that fits into all the weatherproofs. Styles change each season.

South Bucks Rainwear Co., Iver, Buckinghamshire SLO 9BA, England
Brochure, free; $1 air mail. Prices in $.

"Make tomorrow your black and shiny day" says the brochure of this firm, which sells ravishing rain gear for men and women. Dashing capes and trench coats are made from rubber or rubberized cloth, and apart from the popular black, can also be bought in white, navy and red. Prices under $40. Also on sale are ponchos, exercise suits, skirts, pants, etc.

SHEEPSKIN

The Sheepskin Rug Shop, Mail Order Dept., P.O. Box 12175, Penrose, Auckland, New Zealand
Brochure and coat catalogue, free.

The brochure illustrates toys, slippers and rugs, and the loose-leaf catalogue shows coats made of New Zealand sheepskin. Coat styles are unusually varied, from rough-looking, long-wearing "ranchers" through jerkins and leather-trimmed Astra lambskin jackets to rather glamorous, fluffy evening capes. Prices for coats start at $120.

For more clothes, see Fabrics: Thailand, and the shops listed in the General (Lace, Linen & Embroidery) and Handicrafts and Special Local Products sections.

SHOES

A. T. Hogg (Fife) Ltd., Strathmiglo, Fife, Scotland
Catalogue, 50 cents; $1 air mail. Spring, September.

Sturdy-looking walking shoes and boots for men, women and children. The director of A. T. Hogg says that heavier walking shoes and lighter boots are very popular with American customers. I also see rubber boots for women and children which cost under $5 and look very much like imported boots that sell for $17 in New York.

Kow Hoo Shoe Co. Ltd., 19–21 Hennessy Road, Hong Kong
Style leaflet, self-measuring chart, free. Prices in $.

Men's shoes starting at $25 for calf skin, but also in Du Pont Corfam, lizard skin, lizardgator skin, sea-turtle skin, ostrich skin, and French baby-alligator skin. Women's shoes starting at $22; purses, $30.

Lee Kee Ltd., 65 Peking Road, Kowloon, Hong Kong
Style leaflet, leather samples, free. Prices in $.

Men's shoes in the same leathers as at Kow Hoo (above), starting at $21 for West German calfskin. Women's shoes starting at $18, purses at $25.

A. W. G. Otten, Albert Cuypstraat 102–104–106, Amsterdam-Zm, Holland
Leaflet, free. Prices in $.

The wooden shoe is thought to have originated in the South of France, and was once worn all along the European coast of the Atlantic Ocean and North Sea from Spain to Scandinavia, especially where there was marshy ground. The shoes used to be worn not at home, but by people who were working and needed protection against dampness or injury. Recently it has been only in Holland that wooden clogs (or *klompen*, as they are called in Dutch) have been worn. A. W. G. Otten sells clogs, both the all-wood kind and the kind that has recently become popular again, wooden soles with leather uppers. The leaflet lists them in red, white, black and yellow, and prices are about $4 to $7.

Clothes and Accessories

UMBRELLAS

Swaine Adeney Brigg and Sons Limited, 185 Piccadilly, London W1V OHA, England ♕♕
*20-page general catalogue, free. $1.50 air mail.
Saddlery and riding equipment catalogue, free.*

This very prestigious old firm has been making whips for English monarchs since George III, and provides everything necessary for the civilized country life—whips, canes and drinking flasks.

After six pages of mean-looking whips come things of more general interest: elegant canes, including swagger canes, and a Swagger-Dagger cane with a hidden dagger. Discreetly sober umbrellas in best silk with Malacca handles and gold or silver bands, or in nylon with lizard-skin handles; many different seat sticks, seat umbrellas and golf umbrellas; hunting and shooting accessories including silver-plated sandwich boxes; picnic baskets and race hampers for two, four or six people; "sporting gifts"—spoons and cuff links with animals on them.

At the end of the catalogue there is an impressive leather section, showing fitted beauty cases, jewel cases, briefcases, gentlemen's fitted dressing cases, writing cases, passport cases and purses.

No prices available as they are in the process of being revised, but you can guess they are high.

SHIRTS

FOR MEN
Ascot Chang Ltd., 34 Kimberley Road, Kowloon, Hong Kong
Style sheet, self-measurement chart, free; fabric swatches, $3. Prices in $.

Shirts, shorts, pajamas and robes.

Atkinson-Ward Shirts, 21 Rainhall Road, Barnoldswick, Colne, Lancashire, England
Leaflet and fabric samples, 20 cents.

This firm specializes in custom-made shirts using the finest quality cotton, though pajamas are made to order as well. The simple leaflet includes a number of very handsome striped and plain cloths; the current price is only about $15, considerably less than ready-made cotton shirts cost in London. In fact, this is now about the price for the usual cotton-and-synthetic-mix shirts. Satisfaction is guaranteed, and the firm stresses its use of the finest material, etc.

A. Garstang and Co. Ltd., 213 Preston New Road, Blackburn BB2 6BP, England
Measuring charts and swatches, $1 refundable on first order.

Shirt and pajama specialists. Various styles of shirts can be made in twelve types of material with spare collars and cuffs, either from charts sent to you or copied from an old shirt you send them. Delivery time is five weeks, and prices range from about $20 for all-cotton to $31.25 for silk. The plentiful swatches are in conventional checks, stripes and plain colors.

Harvie and Hudson Ltd., 77 Jermyn Street, St. James's, London S.W.1, England
Fabric swatches, free.

Nowhere else in the world is there a street like Jermyn Street, crammed with astronomically expensive, ineffably elegant men's haberdashery stores. The mind boggles—who on earth buys himself $26 shirts? If you'd like it to be you, try Harvie and Hudson, a firm with many American customers which will

13
Cleo Munster cloak in navy blue, maroon, green, purple or black wool. $112.50.
photo Bill Doyle

Clothes and Accessories

send you swatches of current fabrics—stripes, checks and plain colors in cotton voiles, zephyrs, poplins, broadcloths and oxfords. Prices for ready-made shirts, about $20; for made-to-measure, $30–$33, with a minimum order of three shirts.

Liberty and Co. Ltd., Mail Order, Regent Street, London W1R 6AH, England
List of available fabrics and swatches, free.
Swatches of shirt fabrics, swatches of tie fabrics, free.

Liberty sends out swatches of all their famous fabrics, including Tana lawn for shirts, and flowery cottons for their fashionable ties. But order promptly and give second choices, as the goods move quickly. Prices are about $13 for shirts and $3.50 and up for ties.

Turnbull and Asser Ltd., 71–72 Jermyn Street, St. James's, London S.W.1, England
Fabric swatches, free.

Like the Savile Row tailors, Turnbull and Asser, another Jermyn Street shirtmaker, sends a representative to Philadelphia and New York each fall to measure customers and show them the latest "shirting materials." Once customers' measurements are taken, more shirts can be ordered by mail with the help of fabric swatches if necessary. Prices are, roughly: poplin, $20; voile, sea island cotton, $25; silk, $39 and up. Ready-made shirts are about $16.50–$20.

SHOES

John Lobb, 9 St. James's Street, London S.W.1, England
♕♕♕♕♕
Tour schedule, free. Prices in $.

John Lobb is far and away the most prestigious shoe makers in the world. They have made shoes for at least three English kings and one American president (President Johnson). Each spring and fall a representative tours America taking measurements of new customers, and showing their latest models to old customers. Once measurements have been taken and permanent lasts have been made, customers can order new shoes by mail, with the help of photographs if necessary. Handmade shoes in calf leather start at $216, rarer skins are more expensive.

Alan McAfee, 38 Dover Street, Piccadilly, London W.1, England
Color brochure, 25 cents. Prices in $.

Very good English shoes of every sort for men. Prices mostly between $50 and $60, and insured postage is $4 for one pair, $5 for two.

TAILORS

H. Huntsman and Sons, 11 Savile Row, London W1X 2PJ, England ♕♕♕♕♕♕♕
Tour schedule, free.

A Huntsman representative tours America and Canada each spring with samples of cloth and models of "all types of riding coats, waistcoats, breeches, suits and evening dress wear." He visits thirteen American cities and two Canadian, measuring customers for suits which they will later pick up in London or which will be mailed to them. The Huntsman people feel that considering the workmanship, their prices are very reasonable, and even after duty is paid, compare more than favorably with American prices. Prices for a two-piece suit start at $485, and for a three-piece suit at $515.

14
Highland Home Industries Hand-knitted in the outer Hebrides from home-grown wool and hand-spun yarn, a Shetland sweater with a Fair Isle yoke. Available with background in black, white, dark brown, navy, traditional beige or other colors. $18.75 to $22, according to size.

15
Highland Home Industries Mohair coat stole in coral, ruby, orchid, pink, flax blue, jade, turquoise, ice blue, oyster, French navy, black or white. $52.50.

Clothes and Accessories

16

17

18  19

Clothes and Accessories

16
Cornelius Furs Australian fox coat. Maxi-length up to 54", $1,175 (length up to 40", $395).
photo Ian Morgan Pty Ltd

17
Pels Backer Natural Norwegian bluefox cape "Albatross." $435.

18
Maternity Kits Kit to make camel-colored pants suit in gabardine Trevira, on the left, about $30. Kits to make dark-brown gabardine Trevira pants, on the right, and off-white polyester-and-cotton gabardine, top; each about $16.

19
Clothkits Kits to make cotton canvas shorts, from about $5. Ready-made T shirts, from about $2.50. Both in children's and adult sizes.

20
Clothkits Beach outfit in stretch toweling. The shorts double as swimming trunks, the elasticated sleeves stay above elbows for playing in the sand, and there is a hood for protection against the sun or wind. Styles change each season, but kits to make similar outfits are usually available for around $8 for ages up to eleven.
photo Alistair Creer

21
Clothkits A typical outfit. Kits to make similar clothes are usually available in gold on pink, turquoise on blue, purple on blue, or tan on natural needlecord.

22
Mothercare Ltd Machine-washable maternity dress, pink pattern on white background. Similar dresses are usually available for around $18.

23
Mothercare Ltd Bright red three-piece waterproof suit—dungarees, double-breasted raincoat and sou'wester, for children up to 40" tall. About $9.

Clothes and Accessories

Henry Poole and Co., 10–12 Cork Street, London W1X 1PD, England
Tour schedule, free.

Henry Poole were originally the first tailors established in Savile Row. Each spring and fall a director of the firm tours America with a large selection of new fabric swatches and takes customers' measurements. The measurements are sent back to Cork Street to be made up, and usually the customer comes over to London for a fitting. But suits can be completed without a fitting, in which case any necessary small adjustments can be made by certain American tailors at the expense of Henry Poole. Prices start at $325 for a three-piece suit.

Walter Wright, Flat G, 42 Croxteth Road, Liverpool 8, England
Brochure, 3 International Reply Coupons.

"Specialist in leather and rubber gear for enthusiasts." Enthusiasts can have shirts, jeans, shorts, belts or even a cap made to measure in leather or rubber. About twenty possibilities are illustrated with line drawings on the mimeographed lists.

William Yu, Room 112, Peninsula Hotel, Kowloon, Hong Kong
Style sheet, self-measurement chart, fabric swatches, free. Prices in $.

Two-piece suits in English worsted, $110–$250.

DRESSES, SWEATERS, ETC.

FOR WOMEN

Cleo, 3 Molesworth Street, Dublin, Ireland
Color leaflet, $1. Prices in $.

Cleo sells flamboyant clothes based on traditional Irish styles to boutiques in America and also by mail. Aran knitting appears in all sorts of colors and shapes—as ponchos, full-length hostess skirts, knickerbockers, trouser suits and even as bedspreads. Bright crochet patterns and handwoven fabrics are used for skirts, vests, capes, hats and bags. And for evening wear there are colorful new versions of tinker's shawls, and the full length sixteenth-century hooded Munster cloak which used to be worn in southern Ireland. Most of the prices are under $40.

Estelle, 82 High Street, Walthamstow, London E17 7LD, England
Catalogue, 1 International Reply Coupon; $2 air mail.

Their letter to me calls it Provocative Glamorous Ladies Underwear, the catalogue calls it Scandalous Lingerie. Anyway, everything is frilly and lacy and either transparent or cut out, and the text describing these "torrid temptations" (Be a pussy cat and catch your little mouse!!!) is a good laugh. Enough fancy dresses from "slave girl" to "naughty nineties" to add verve to the most boring sex life. They say they have thousands of delighted customers all over the world. . .

Highland Home Industries, 94 George Street, Edinburgh, Scotland
10-page brochure, free. Prices in $.

A beautifully organized nonprofit organization that encourages Scottish crafts. Their well-designed little brochure shows just a few attractive pieces for women. Shetland and Fair Isle sweaters, about $17 each; heavy Hebridean hand-knitted sweaters, $35; fully lined made-to-measure tweed skirts, $22. A mohair coat-stole, poncho, mittens and hat.

May Fashion House, P.O. Box 6162, Kowloon, Hong Kong
Brochure planned, $1; $3 air mail.

I haven't seen the latest May Fashion House catalogue (which is still in the works as I write), but the general manager says that besides the usual silk dresses in American styles, there will be beaded belts, beaded trim by the yard and also Oriental brassware.

Merion Mill, Dinas Mawddwy, Machynlleth SY20 9LS, Wales
Brochure with some color, 30 cents; 75 cents air mail.

This small Welsh weaving mill was brought back to life by an Englishman with a great interest in Wales and a Welsh wife. They bought the mill in 1966 and since then have developed a woolen cloth in traditional Welsh design and several attractive color combinations. The cloth is sold by the yard or in made-to-measure clothes (a full-length evening skirt, about $30, looks terrific in this fabric), and bedspreads are made in all sizes. Samples are on view in the Design Centre, London.

Pettits, 191–195 Kensington High Street, London W8 6ST, England
4 brochures a year, $1.

Pettits sells women's clothes in larger sizes and this is how the stock is described: "We are not an up-to-date fashion house but more the 'mums' type of business. Many of the items are useful rather than decorative. Just the sort of article that older people love to buy, but in this age when everything is for the 'young,' they do not know where to get the type of wear they have had in the past."

So if you are looking for baggy cotton underwear, warm nightgowns, lisle stockings, flannelette sheets, or anything else of that sort which you've had trouble finding lately, try Pettits.

Elsie Tu Ltd., 121 Chatham Road, Kowloon, Hong Kong
50-page brochure with some color, free. Prices in $.

Beaded and hand-embroidered sweaters.

Wallis Woollen Mill, Ambleston, Haverfordwest, Pembrokeshire, Wales
Brochure, 75 cents; $1 air mail.

This small mill publishes a slender brochure showing just a few of the things they make in their own version of the traditional Welsh tapestry design. The brochure has line drawings only, and the color descriptions are maddeningly unsuitable for buying by mail—"Seascape," "Firefly," "moorland" and "mountain rainbow," etc., etc.; however, I hope they'll be more explicit if you write and ask.

This firm makes Welsh tapestry in a special light weight which is shown at the London Design Centre and from it they make floor-length skirts with matching shawls and some very nice chunky handbags with straps and edging in matching suede. Crib and baby-carriage blankets are made from heavyweight tapestry.

FURS

A. C. Bang, 27 Østergade, DK-1100 Copenhagen K, Denmark
Brochure, free.

This internationally known firm publishes a catalogue yearly of their *haute couture* furs. Prices are given only when you tell them exactly what you want, and although they say, "concerning our prices there is a reasonable good saving considering the high quality and workmanship of our furs,"

Clothes and Accessories

24
Mothercare Ltd Blue and white suit to fit children up to 40" tall. Similar outfits usually available for around $4.

25
The Scotch House Viyella dress from about $30. Shorts and vest about $12 each.

you must understand that A. C. Bang is a top firm with top prices, so you can only tell yourself you're saving money if you'd otherwise be buying from an equally prestigious American firm.

Cornelius Furs, 72 Castlereagh Street, Sydney, Australia 2001
Color leaflet and fur samples, free. Prices in $.

Kangaroo, Australian lamb, Australian fox, sueded sheepskin in coats and jackets—you choose your own fur, color, length and style. A sleek tailored midi-length kangaroo fur coat with leather trimming and buttons costs about $400. A horizontally worked Australian fox costs about the same. Also fur hats and bags at about $50. These are not shown in the catalogue, but photographs are sent on request.

Pels Backer, Kongens Gate 31, Oslo, Norway
No catalogue.

I suppose it is easier to buy a fur cape by mail than a fur coat. Pels Backer has a natural Norwegian selected blue-fox cape (which they say is their best seller) at about $435. Besides saga mink coats, they have broadtail, beaver, ocelot, otter and mole, and also fur-lined coats. They say that if customers tell them exactly what they want by letter, Pels Backer will make an offer. They write: "We have the largest and most beautiful stock in ready-made furs here in Norway and possess our own five-story building in the shopping center of Oslo . . . the firm was established in 1856 and is now owned by Mr. Lars Backer, the grandson of the founder . . . American customers tell us they have to pay at least 30 percent more for the same goods after having paid the duty of 18½ percent."

J. A. Sistovaris and Sons, 14 Voulis Street, Athens, Greece ♛
18-page brochure, free.

Greece has a thriving fur industry and specializes in making coats out of fur scraps at reasonable prices. J. A. Sistovaris, the leading manufacturer, has a very good reputation. The brochure I have seen shows various fancy styles in Persian lamb, mink, stone marten, fox and other furs.

MATERNITY CLOTHES

Maternity Kits, 136 Kensington Church Street, London W8 4BH, England
Brochure, 25 cents; 50 cents air mail. March, September.

Maternity Kits, a newish firm, has been started by two young women who recently "between us have had three children" (if you see what they mean) and who "during our pregnancies couldn't find the sort of clothes that really appealed to us— either the price was right and the style was wrong, or vice versa." They have worked out two small collections of kits to make maternity clothes. The kits include thread and everything you need, and are said to be very easy and quick to make, even for people who don't usually like sewing.

I have seen the two brochures they have produced so far. The first was illustrated with color photographs and showed a pants suit, three dresses, two smocks and two pairs of pants — all in solid colors, very pleasant styles, machine-washable and costing between $14 and $25. In the spring collection there were pants in several colors, a denim pants suit, a dress in white polyester cotton with navy dots, and two smocks. Prices between $15 and $25. All kits are for sizes 10 to 16, and some for sizes 18 and 20 too.

For more maternity clothes, see Mothercare Ltd., under Children's Clothes in this section.

Clothes and Accessories

CHILDREN'S CLOTHES

Clothkits, 2 Mount Place, Lewes, Sussex, England
12-page brochure with some color, 25 cents. March, September.

Clothkits was started by a housewife in her own home, and is a great idea for people who want to keep their children dressed in colorful and fashionable clothes without going bankrupt. Clothes for children aged one to sixteen are screen-printed directly onto the fabric and come ready to cut out and sew up with all the necessary haberdashery and easy-to-follow instructions.

No party clothes or Sunday best—everything is very casual—denim for summer and needlecord for winter, but the styles are the latest English eye-catchers and the colors are brilliant mixtures of anything dazzling. All prices are within the $4–$15 range.

Jillian Junior Fashions, Drake Circus, Plymouth, Devon PL1 1QE, England
Brochure, 25 cents. Spring, fall.

A small shop in the west of England stocks regular and discontinued lines of clothes for children aged two to thirteen. The small brochures are illustrated with black-and-white line drawings, and show mostly well-made and cheerful-looking clothes by Ladybird. The regular clothes almost all cost under $15, and the clothes in discontinued lines are under $10—usually well under.

Gertrude Liechti, Storchengasse 13, 8001 Zurich, Switzerland

Gertrude Liechti stocks a whole range of children's clothes, but says that the one with most appeal to American customers is her Swiss dirndl. These dresses, in sizes for ages one to ten, have white blouses and red skirts with embroidered black velvet straps. Being 100 percent cotton, they are machine-washable.

Mrs. Liechti has no catalogue, but here are the prices, which include surface postage and insurance: ages one to three, $20; four to six, $23; seven to ten, $26.

Julie Loughnan, 18 Beauchamp Place, Knightsbridge, London S.W.3, England

Julie Loughnan makes the kind of classic English party dresses that are almost unobtainable in America. Very pretty, individually designed, hand-smocked dresses in Liberty lawn, voile, etc., for children aged two to twelve cost from about $35 to $45. Enthusiastically recommended by a friend of mine.

Mothercare Ltd., Cherry Tree Road, Watford WD2 5SH, England
180-page color catalogue, free. Spring, fall.

A terrific chain of over a hundred stores selling everything for mothers, babies and children up to the age of five—at lowest possible prices. I can't think of any other shop as efficiently and thoroughly geared to mothers and babies. Anyone who is about to have a baby or who has just had one should look at this catalogue.

Starting with pregnancy, you can get attractive maternity dresses for $15; then colorful stretch suits, play tops and pants and dresses for children up to 44" tall, all for under $5. There are coats, shoes, boots, and various other things such as wool blankets, toys, baby plates, cups and jugs, and a special medicine cabinet (for poisonous drugs) that cannot be opened by a child.

Pollyanna by Post, 660 Fulham Road, London S.W.6, England
6-page color brochure, $1. August and February.

A smallish English organization that designs, manufactures and sells "better designed, more amusing" children's clothes and likes to think they have done for this age group what Mary Quant and Carnaby Street did for adult clothes. In fact the clothes, though very "now," are not revolutionary. They *are* well designed and co-ordinated—colors match and tops look good with bottoms. A small collection of medium-priced dresses, skirts, trousers and shirts (no coats) is put out each spring and fall. Size is determined by the height of the child. Prices for these clothes, which are really very sophisticated and well made, start at about $15 for dresses and $13 for pants.

Rowes of Bond Street, 120 New Bond Street, London W1Y 0BN, England
Self-measurement chart, free.

I went to look at Rowes clothes at the Hotel Pierre in January and saw what must have been a typical Rowes customer—reed-thin and stunningly dressed, choosing some clothes for her children that their grandmother had forgotten in London (understandably, as the grandmother annually buys complete wardrobes for ten children). Rowes sells its classic English clothes and shoes to the international set, who pass them around between siblings and cousins. Dresses tend to be flowered or hand-smocked ($60 and up). Coats and boys' clothes are very traditional ($96 and up), perhaps the best known being the Rowes coat, or the coat now known as the John-John coat worn by John Kennedy, Jr., and widely copied by other manufacturers. Clothes can be bought in London or Paris, otherwise write to Rowes with your requirements, and they will reply with self-measurement forms drawing of models you might be interested in, fabric swatches and prices. If you prefer to look at the actual clothes, Mr. Kenneth Barnett comes to New York, Washington, Middleburg, Philadelphia, Boston and Chicago in January and June, takes measurements and orders. Summer clothes are ordered in January and winter clothes in June, and if you want to choose for a year or two ahead (styles barely change), orders can be taken and measurement charts sent at the appropriate time.

The School Shop, Yorkshire House, Shambles Street, Barnsley, Yorkshire, England
Catalogue, 40 cents or 4 International Reply Coupons; air mail 70 cents or 7 International Reply Coupons. May.

A useful collection of hard-wearing and inexpensive school clothes are stocked by this large shop, which is the official supplier to several English schools. The clothes are usually only available in school-uniform-type colors: navy, bottle-green, gray and maroon, and in very plain classic styles. But the neat raincoats, skirts, pants, shirts, blazers and sweaters, underwear and sports clothes are made by well-known English manufacturers. Leather school bags, scout and guide uniforms, and science aprons are also on sale, and the catalogue is published each year at the end of May in good time to organize school clothes well ahead of time for the following September.

George Sim Mfg. Co., 9 Carnarvon Road, Kowloon, Hong Kong
12-page leaflet, free. Prices in $.

Little girls' embroidered polyester-and-cotton dresses about $4; women's embroidered polyester-and-cotton blouses, $5.

Clothes and Accessories

Strength and Co. Ltd., No 130B, Deck 1, Cheung Chau Gallery, Ocean Terminal, Kowloon, Hong Kong
30-page brochure, fabric samples, free. Prices in $.

Very inexpensive nylon rainwear for adults and children. Baby's snowsuit, $9; children's lined and cotton-filled jackets, $9. Colorful sleeping bags, around $18.

The Young Idea, 9 Kingsbury, Aylesbury, Buckinghamshire, England
Brochure, 25 cents; 50 cents air mail.

Although the famous English Ladybird clothes aren't quite as modern and good-tasty as you might wish, they are certainly above average. I've bought lots in my time and found them far better-wearing and longer-lasting than most of the American children's clothes I've picked up, so I was terribly pleased to find this firm, which sells perfect Ladybird clothes in discontinued lines at bargain prices.

Young Idea produces three brochures, illustrated with line drawings, each year. They all show dresses, shirts and pants for boys and girls up to the age of thirteen, a few baby clothes (sometimes by the famous British make Bairnswear), sometimes frilly nightdresses and fleeced pajamas, and sometimes coats. There is also usually an "Odd Box" page with a few jackets, socks, pants, etc., at especially low prices but available in only one color each. Typical prices in the last brochure I looked at had dresses and pants for children up to the age of six at $4.50, pants for thirteen-year-old boys at $7, and pants suits for ten-year-old girls at $7—not bad, considering that the clothes are very well made. The only trouble with this firm is that as the clothes are from discontinued lines, there is usually a limited choice of colors, and you can't dawdle about ordering after getting a catalogue because certain styles sell out.

7 Collecting

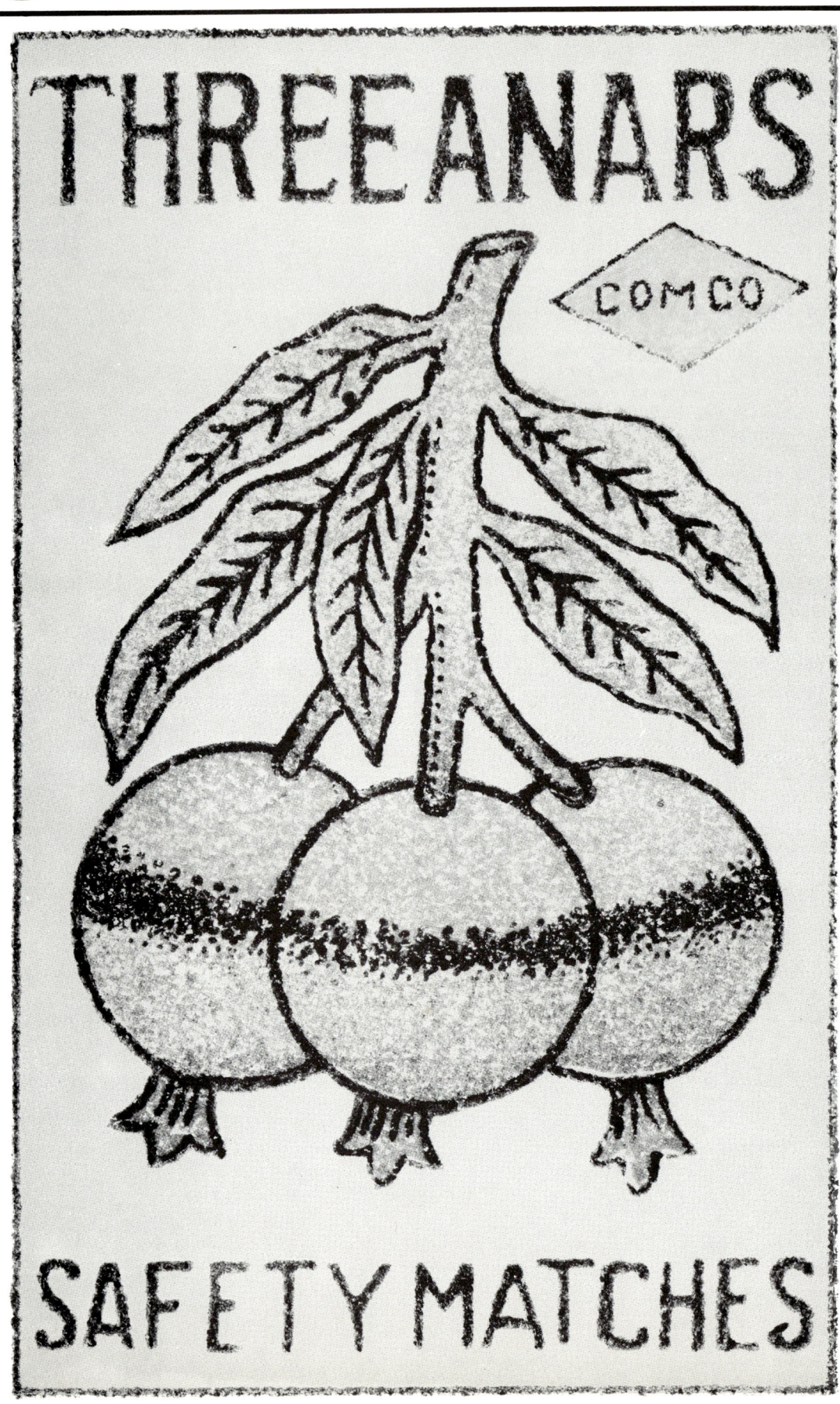

THREE ANARS

COMCO

SAFETY MATCHES

AUTOGRAPHS

R. Saggiori, 51 Avenue de la Chartreuse, F-38240 Meylan, France
Quarterly price list, free. In French.

This firm specializes in autographs, historical documents, illustrated books and old prints, and does business with American collectors. Their holdings are basically international, their current list ranging from Mussolini to Tchaikovsky, and including a thank-you note from Franklin Roosevelt for $12, which seems reasonable by American prices, as does the signed photograph of Hermann Hesse for the same price. As in many fields, collectors of Americana may be better off buying from abroad.

CIGARETTE CARDS

London Cigarette Card Company Ltd., Cambridge House, 34 Wellesley Road, Chiswick, London W.4, England
Catalogue and handbook Part II dealing with all known cigarette cards issued in the United Kingdom between 1918 and 1940, numbered and autographed edition, $5.85.
Mini abridged catalogue, 25 cents.

Apparently cigarette cards originated in America (the earliest known card is in the Metropolitan Museum, New York). However, they were dropped here early in the century, while they grew more popular in England. Anyway, the London Cigarette Card Company says that it is the largest and most reputable dealer in cartophilic items in the world. Besides catalogues they put out a friendly magazine, *Cigarette Card News*, for $9 a year. The issue I looked at had, among other more serious articles, a piece describing kinds of cigarette-card collectors, including the swopper, the fanatic, the specialist (mortal enemy of No. 5, who is only interested in pretty pictures), the perfectionist, and Mr. Average Collector, whose "cards are not particularly immaculate—neither are they grubby," and who sorts his cards only when he feels like it. In the post-1940 list, prices range from about 25 cents to $1.20, and it covers a fascinating variety of subjects from Batman to Budgrigars.

COINS

Spink and Son Ltd., 5–7 King Street, St. James's, London S.W.1, England
Numismatic Circular, twelve volumes, one year's subscription, $13.
Modern Coins and Banknotes, five journals a year, $6.50.

Spink's, a three-hundred-year-old family firm, is not only mentioned in *The Lost World*, by Sir Arthur Conan Doyle, but they were delighted and amused to find their name dropped by "M" in a James Bond novel: "As Spink and the British Museum agree . . ."

They send their two illustrated journals by air. *Numismatic Circular* has a catalogue of Greek, Roman, Byzantine, English and foreign coins, war medals and books offered for sale, and it also has articles, reviews, news and correspondence of interest to collectors.

Modern Coins and Banknotes is more of a catalogue of Spink's modern coins and bank notes of all periods—the issue that I saw also had three short articles.

GLASS FIGURES

Svenskt Glas, Birger Jarlsgatan 8, S-114 34 Stockholm, Sweden
Leaflet, free.

Orrefors and Kosta agents have been leaning on Svenskt Glas and won't let it appear in the Glass and China section (I suppose the agents would like U.S. customers to buy at higher prices in America). However, Svenskt Glas says it can appear in the Collecting section for its crystal figures of endangered species. Together with the World Wildlife Fund it is bringing out a model of an animal from an endangered species each year and hopes to contribute about $16,000 to the World Wildlife Fund. The first animal in the series is the musk ox by Göran Warff of Kosta, who has signed each one. As only four thousand are produced ($42.50, including postage), Svenskt Glas thinks that the musk ox will be sold out by the time this book appears, but you should be in time for the next animal.

MINERALS

W. D. Christianson, 200 Napier Street, Barrie, Ontario, Canada
Price list, 10 cents.

Mineral specimens ("avidly sought after" by collectors) from all over the world, especially Canada and the United States.

MINIATURES

Bruce Coombes, Lamyatt, Shepton Mallet, Somerset, England
Leaflet and information, 2 International Reply Coupons.

Bruce Coombes writes: "I make models to special order of any type of building, large or small, anywhere. Prices vary according to size and quantity of details required." He makes models for business houses, commercial promotions, and model villages for amusement parks. His brochure has line drawings of a seventeenth-century coaching inn, a seventeenth-century clapboard house, an eighteenth-century Georgian town house, a nineteenth-century villa, a post mill and a farm wagon, but it doesn't give details or prices, so the best idea if you want something special is to write and ask Mr. Coombes about it, enclosing 2 International Reply Coupons for an answer.

Joan Faulkner Miniatures, 47 Harvest Road, Englefield Green, Surrey, England
Price list, 25 cents.

A short list of 1" to 1' miniatures for collectors—copper kettles and coffeepots with wooden handles cost $7 each, and a warming pan with a wooden handle costs $10. Joan Faulkner also makes shops in Victorian and Edwardian styles; a butcher's shop complete with sides of meat, tools, counter, etc., and one room upstairs furnished in period style costs $300. A similar baker's shop costs $250.

Minutiques, 82b Trafalgar Street, Brighton, Sussex BN1 4EB, England
Catalogue, $1.50.

It is clear that this shop, which has a $25 minimum for overseas orders, is strictly for serious collectors, indeed it calls itself a collector's shop and dolls hospital. For doll collectors there are human-hair wigs that can be fitted over the old wig and removed for a shampoo. The catalogue suggests you take your doll along to a local hairdresser and have him set the wig. There are straw bonnets, and antique-style doll clothes made by a "retired British nanny."

For miniature collectors there are quite a few things that I haven't seen in American catalogues: sterling-silver miniatures, silver-plated miniatures, caneware for the kitchen, Staffordshire ornaments, and some marvelous leather books and family photographs. Minutiques also has single rooms made to your own specifications in case, after looking at the

Collecting

1
Spink and Son Ltd Edward III gold noble (circa 1363–1369).

2
Minutiques Wax household, seven dolls, about $38.

3
Les Bâteaux Leclerc Inc. Bluenose available complete $225, or in kit form $65.

4
Kendal Playing Card Sales "America" court cards show pre-Columbian art; "Comedia," a modern Swedish pack; pack designed for Simpson's of Piccadilly.
photo Kevin Kirby

prices, you don't feel up to a whole dollhouse but would like to make a period room to hang on the wall. The shop also has some exceptionally attractive miniature families in all sorts of different materials. The one I like best is a complete Victorian household of seven wax dolls which costs $37.

Den Young, 63 Earith Road, Willingham, Cambridgeshire CB4 5LS, England
Price list, 2 International Reply Coupons.

Den Young says he makes dollhouses and miniatures to order, and he says that his work is in some of the world's finest collections. He is known on radio and television and in the press as one of the foremost craftsmen in the field. He will make any period houses at prices from $250 up and will even reproduce your own house in a scale of 1″ to 1′. He will also make any piece of furniture from a drawing or photograph or picture cut out of a magazine. His brief price list includes rocking horses, chess sets, fourposters, harps, violins and grand pianos, and he has several chairs for around $12 each. He can also provide sets of stairs, window frames, and set-scene wall boxes (these cost about $125 each).

MODEL AIRPLANES

Aero Nautical Models, 39 Parkway, Camden Town, London N.W.1, England
Send 2 International Reply coupons for an answer to your letter, $5 for manufacturers' brochures for boats or aircrafts.

A very wide range of the best aircraft- and boat-modeling goods from England and all over the world. Sweden, Italy, Japan, and especially Germany, Austria and France are main sources of supply for aircraft, boats and engines, every sort of kit and all the materials needed. They are official agents for most well-known brands with a knowledgeable staff, who, when asked, likes to give advice and solve problems. Their letterhead encouragingly says: "Phone, write, or call, the SERVICE is the same for ALL."

Argyle Models, 247 Argyle Street, Glasgow G2 8 DN, Scotland
Price lists, 20 cents each.

Argyle Models offers a large line of aircraft and armored kits for plastic modelers. They carry very specialized fittings for aircraft conversions—one uses a conversion in conjunction with a basic kit to make the desired type of equipment. And for the final touch, one may consult their enormous selection of military decals. Argyle's products are generally not available in this country.

Henry J. Nicholls and Son Ltd., 308 Holloway Road, London N.7, England
Price list, 50 cents; $1 air mail.

Model aircraft—mainly ones that are radio controlled. They import from every European country and have had a mail-order department for over twenty years.

Spielzeug-Rasch, Gerhart-Hauptmann-Platz 1, Hamburg 1, Germany
Toy catalogues in German, $1.
200-page model catalogue, $4.

Spielzeug-Rasch's illustrated special models catalogue is extremely imposing, and a must, I would think, for anyone interested in model planes or ships. Modern planes and famous old ships (the *Santa Maria*) are shown, as well as all sorts of engines and spare parts, in two-hundred professional-looking pages.

Collecting

MODEL RAILROADS

Cherry's Ltd., 62 Sheen Road, Richmond, Surrey, England
Price list, $2. Prices in $.

Cherry's, which has become known and thoroughly visited by American model railway buffs, specializes in very high-class, second-hand working steam engines of all types, most of them not obtainable in America. Their list gives a detailed description of each model, including marine models, traction engines, locomotives, steam plants, boilers, vertical engines, horizontal engines, miscellaneous combustion engines, Stuart Turner (used, completed models and also new products), useful accessories and pressure gauges, and "special items" which, in the catalogue I looked at, were a generating plant, $156; a nineteenth-century, six-pounder field gun, $84; and a working steam-driven replica of a 2-2-0 Birmingham Dribbler, $60.

Hamblings Ltd., 29 Cecil Court, Charing Cross Road, London W.C.2, England
Price list $1 (no checks).

The largest and oldest established "oo" specialists, and probably the only firm in Great Britain that manufactures, wholesales and retails exclusively model railroad products, parts and accessories. They stock British prototypes which are almost impossible to buy in America; although, strangely enough, there is a demand. Anyway, any model railway lover should be deliriously happy here, for there are the most detailed and perfect kits and parts of every kind on which an infinite amount of care can be taken (how about a scale lattice girder section, "Just the thing for those who enjoy soldering"), though lazier enthusiasts can buy a completely painted train and track. There are scenic models and accessories for building, about 30 cents each card. Signal boxes, loco coaling stages and entire villages can be built, complete with half-timbered or Georgian houses, modern bungalows, blocks of flats, fire stations, schools, libraries and churches. In fact, these villages and their landscape backgrounds might inspire people who don't have model railways. Tools and books and magazines about model railroads are also listed.

Millholme Models, Woodborough, Nottingham NG14 7DX, England
Set of three black-and-white booklets, $1.30 air mail.

This firm specializes in scale model-railway equipment. They offer a large selection of British prototypes, from "Z" scale to gauge "O." The catalogues provide an assortment of loco, coach and wagon kits for the serious modeler. There is a list of detail castings as well as a control-equipment section which features their own brand of transistorized power packs. If you are ready for the big splurge, inquire about their limited editions of brass locos.

MODEL SHIPS

Les Bâteaux Leclerc Inc., St. Jean Port-Joli, Cte L'Islet, P. Quebec, Canada
Catalogue, $1. Prices in $.

Very beautiful historic ship models are produced by this firm, which was founded by Honoré Leclerc, whose father had been building model ships since 1927. About ten delicate wooden models with or without sails are photographed in the catalogue, with short histories of the original ships. Several models are available in kit form at various prices between $10 and $50. The made-up boats in lengths between 16" and 38" are more expensive. Models include copies of the *Cutty Sark* and *H.M.S. Bounty* as well as lesser-known ships.

5
Joseph Kober Model of Franz Josef I. Just over $2.

Collecting

PLATES

Gilbert Hansen, Vestergade 10, Tune, 4000 Roskilde, Denmark
Price list, free. Prices in $.

A list of old, commemorative plates by Bing and Grøndahl, Sv. Jensen and Royal Copenhagen that starts with an 1895 Bing and Grøndahl Christmas plate for about $100.

PLAYING CARDS

Kendal Playing Card Sales, 3 Oakbank House, Skelsmergh, Kendal, Cumbria, England
Regular list and Once Only list, free. Prices in $.

Two playing-card collectors sell by mail new playing cards from various countries. Some of the packs sound fascinating even for noncollectors. From Spain there is a double pack for about $3, *Discoverers and Explorers of the Americas*, with a named portrait on every card, Columbus' ships on the backs and an explanatory booklet. From France, *Versailles* ($2.65 for a single pack) shows the courts of kings, queens and statesmen associated with Versailles, and the aces show buildings in the Versailles gardens. Also from France, *Napoleon* ($8 for a double pack produced for the bicentenary of his birth) with members of the Bonaparte family on the court cards and the insignia of various orders on the aces. Or you can be put on waiting lists for cards from Iceland—some have figures from Icelandic mythology on every card, with mythological sea creatures on the back ($2.65); others have characters from the Icelandic sagas on the court cards. There are also magician's packs (seven extra cards), solitaire packs, and eleven different kinds of tarot cards including the *Ancien Tarot de Marseille*, the most famous of all. Books about cards, too.

STAMPS

Stanley Gibbons Ltd., 391 Strand, London W.C.2, England
Price list, free.

World-famous for their stamps and authoritative catalogues, they will send lists of albums, stamp catalogues, accessories, and books that are available.

TOY SOLDIERS

Joseph Kober, Graben 14–15, A 1010 Vienna, Austria
Price list in German, $1 (refundable).

Using turn-of-the-century molds, this toy shop in the middle of Vienna hand-makes the military units of the Austro-Hungarian Empire and civilians of the time. The figures are made out of tin and lead and are hand-painted. Although the list is in German, most of it consists of names, so it isn't too hard to figure out that a "*Trompeter*" in the "*Gardetruppe*" costs about $2.25 as do "*Husaren*," "*Dragoner*" and "*Ulanen*" cavalry officers, and Kaiser Franz Josef I in "*Galauniform*." A set of "*Infanterie im Marsch—Offizier, Fahne, Trompeter, Trommler und 10 Mann*" costs about $22.

Phillips Auctioneers, Blenstock House, 7 Blenheim Street, New Bond Street, London W1Y OAS, England
Subscription list to auction catalogues, free.

This well-known London auction house holds two auctions a year of lead toy soldiers and say they have many American customers who bid by mail.

WEAPONS

Arima, Francisco Guzmán 3, Apartado 14008, Madrid 25, Spain
Color brochure, 2 International Reply Coupons.

Arima makes reproductions of old pistols and crossbows which can be bought in pairs in ornamental boxes or with plaques to display them on the wall.

IA Produkter AB, Utställning, Renstiernasgatan 22, 116 31 Stockholm 4, Sweden
No catalogue.

Sweden's largest weapons shop sells antique and reproduction weapons by mail. The reproductions are imported from Germany, England, Italy and Spain, as the Swedes only go in for collecting, not manufacturing.

WINE LABELS

Wyatt Druitt, Donstan House, 14a St. Cross Street, London E.C.1, England
Brochure, $1.

Apparently decanter labels were all the rage from 1730 until 1860, when they were replaced by paper labels on wine bottles. During that time the great silversmiths made beautiful labels, very hard to find and mostly already being tucked away in collections. Wyatt Druitt has started reproducing some of these labels by famous Georgian silversmiths such as Hester Bateman, Paul Storr, Benjamin Smith and Edward Farrell. At the moment there are sixteen hallmarked sets, and prices for each individual label start at about $60 for sterling silver and $68 for silver gilt.

8 Fabrics

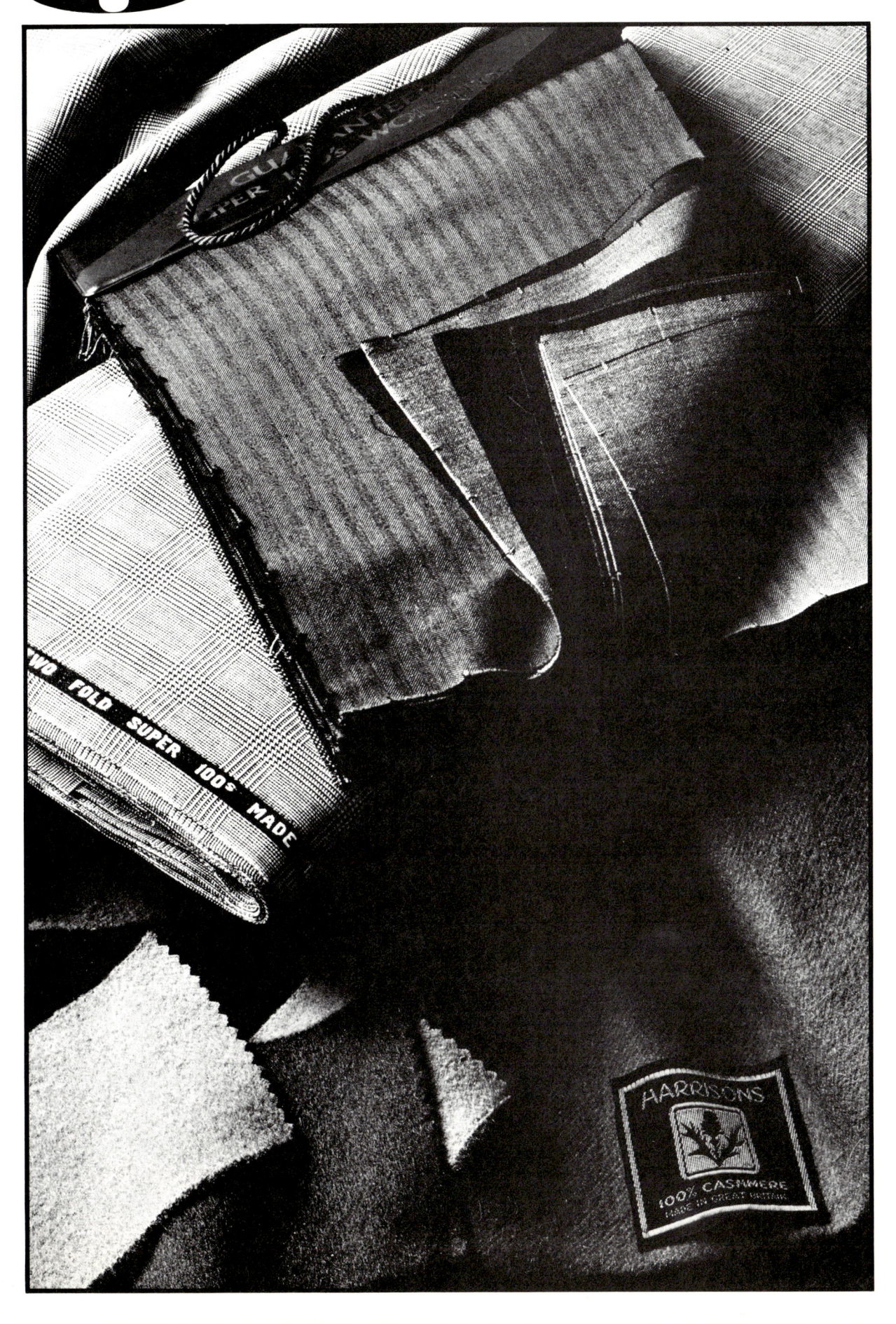

Fabrics

CANADA

Cottage Crafts Ltd., St. Andrews, New Brunswick, Canada
Price list with fabric and yarn samples, free. Prices in $.

Beautiful tweed fabrics are woven in New Brunswick country homes and sold at the Cottage Crafts shop, with knitting yarns in one and two ply to match. No patterns, just pale and pretty solid colors which come in suit- and coat-weight tweeds. Compare prices and colors with those of Pinecraft Fabrics (listed in *The Catalogue of American Catalogues*), as colors are similar and the American firm may have lower prices.

ENGLAND

W. Bill Ltd., Mail Order Dept., 93 New Bond Street, London W1Y 9LA, England
General catalogue, free; swatches, free. Prices in $.

W. Bill has a large mail-order service to America. They sell clothes, knitwear and also good fabrics for clothes. Harris tweed from $6.70 per yard; Shetland and Irish tweeds from $9; worsteds from $23; cashmeres from $48; and many others.

Hunt and Winterbotham Ltd., 4 Old Bond Street, London W.1, England
Swatches free. Prices in $.

Hunt and Winterbotham, not very modestly, claims to make the "world's finest cloth." Still, the company is very old (over five hundred years) and very well thought of, and stocks over six thousand wool patterns, including men's light and heavy suiting, Harris tweeds, Shetlands, gabardines, flannels, cashmere and vicuna. Also tweeds and woolens for ladies, and Pringle and Braemar sweaters.

Liberty and Co. Ltd., 210–220 Regent Street, London W1E 5LE, England
Swatches free, price lists (no illustrations). Spring and fall.

Liberty is one of London's most imaginatively stocked department stores, but it is best known for magnificent fabrics, especially their own dress-weight printed cotton lawns and silks. They have what they call an "extremely large and efficient" mail-order service in dress and upholstery fabrics and send out tiny swatch books on request. If customers want larger samples they are charged $1.30, which is refunded when the sample is returned. Fabrics $1.30–$8 per yard.

Pater Textiles Ltd., Rampart Street, London E.1 2LD, England
Price list, 25 cents; 50 cents air mail. March, September.

An old firm that advertises itself as the largest direct-to-customer textile service in England is recommended by several English women's magazines as a good place for inexpensive fabrics. The newspaperlike price list describes most kinds of fabrics, usually synthetic, including lace, velvet, jersey with lurex, raincoat material, anorak material, tailor's canvas, fur fabrics, etc., etc. Also some woolens. The prices are almost all $2–$5 a yard.

Redpath Campbell and Partners Ltd., Harescombe, Gloucestershire, England
8-page leaflet and swatches, 25 cents surface mail, 65 cents air mail.

One of the very few firms that sells suede and leather in small-enough quantities for the home dressmaker, Redpath Campbell has a helpful leaflet/price list for people who have

1
Central Cottage Industries Emporium Crewel-embroidered fabric from Kashmir, hook woolen embroidery on a cotton base, $7.50 a yard. Also available as drapes.

Fabrics

never sewn leather before (which must be most of their customers), describing the different leathers, what they are best used for, and clear hints on how to sew each type. They tell you how to adapt ordinary patterns for use with leather, and they also sell their own patterns for a skirt and a short or long waistcoat. Eighteen colors in leather and suede, sheepskin and chamois, a fashion material which hangs like wool and looks like suede. Enough leather for a mini-skirt costs about $8; a larger skirt up to midi-length, $16. You can also buy cut suede and leather patches to make the patchwork skirts and coats (or bags and cushions) that are so incredibly expensive ready-made.

Theatreland Ltd., 14 Soho Street, Oxford Street, London WIV 6HB, England
Price list, 2 International Reply Coupons.

London's largest stocker of ballroom and theatrical materials sells silks, nets, lace, velvets, sequins, feather trimmings, leotards and tights. So anyone in need of fluorescent satin or gold and silver skin suits, opera hose or tights, or handmade cup-sequin motifs for a theatrical do, need search no longer.

FRANCE

Rodin, 36 Champs-Elysées, Paris VIII, France
Swatches, free.

This very large fabric shop on the Champs-Elysées, well known to Americans, can sell *haute couture* silks and wools as well as upholstery fabrics by mail to America. However, their choice is so wide that you have to be very specific in describing what you want, and prices are quite high.

GREECE

Argalius, 7 Filellinon Street, Athens, Greece
Leaflet, free.

Argalius sells raw silk by the meter. "PURE NATURAL GREEK SILK spun and woven by HAND . . . it is of the best, the most ELEGANT material for LADIES' and GENTLEMEN'S suits and clothes . . . They do not wrinkle, the more they are WASHED, the more their quality improves; therefore, for years on end you will not get tired of them." The leaflet says: "Your orders may be carried out by MAIL"; however, I predict that this shop will be very hard to buy from, since when I wrote to ask about prices and colors, I received the same leaflet I had already been sent, with a note saying: "Thank you for your letter." I suggest that people who are seriously interested in raw silk (which is not smooth and shiny like regular silk, but has a rougher weave) do *not* send for the above leaflet, which gives no useful information, but write (preferably in Greek) sending a sample of the color that they want matched and ask the current price per yard. The fabric is 30"–32" wide.

INDIA

Central Cottage Industries Emporium, Janpath, New Delhi 1, India
22-page color catalogue, $1.50; swatches, free.

The catalogue has some color photographs of the really unusual fabrics gathered from all over India at this government-sponsored handicrafts shop. For furniture: cottons, raw silks and crewel embroideries from $4 to $8 per meter. For dresses; hand-blocked cottons and silks costing up to $8 a meter, and Banaras silk with silver or gold motifs, $8.

IRELAND

Brown Thomas and Co. Ltd., Grafton Street, Dublin 2, Ireland
38-page general catalogue, 50 cents, prices in $.

Brown Thomas sells church, table, bed and dress linen by the yard in various widths and weights. The dress linen comes in shell green, primrose, eggshell, peach, pink, beige, gray, blue, tan, coral, lilac, apple green, red, brown, navy, charcoal, black, and white. A 36"-wide fabric is $3.50 per yard. Also Irish tweeds.

Kevin and Howlin Ltd., Nassau Street, Dublin 2, Ireland
Swatches, free.

Handwoven Donegal tweeds in 29" width cost only $7 a yard here. Designs are very sober and classic: misty blues and earthy browns in checks and herringbones and traditional Donegals. Fabrics for men's clothes only.

SCOTLAND

MacGillivray and Company, Muir of Aird, Benbecula, Outer Hebrides, Scotland PA88 5NA
Price list and swatches, free. Prices in $.

A popular source for low-priced fabrics, MacGillivray has been selling handwoven Harris tweed by mail for many years and has gradually begun to do other things too (they say that they will give you advice on vacations in the Scottish Highlands or islands). Hand-knitted Harris and Shetland wool socks, hand-knitted Harris wool sweaters, blankets, bedspreads, Fair Isle sweaters and gloves, Aran and Norwegian sweaters and made-to-measure clothes are all described but not illustrated on their price list. Fabrics cost about $4–$5 per yard. Recommended by Joan D. Fettes.

St. Andrews Woolen Mill, The Golf Links, St. Andrews, Scotland
Leaflet, free.

This leaflet invites you to join the St. Andrews Mill band of happy mail-order shoppers. Tweeds woven at the Mill are sold by the yard at prices between $3 and $15. Send a snippet of any color you want matched and give an idea of what price range you are interested in. Tartans by the yard, kilts and knitwear are also for sale.

THAILAND

The Thai Silk Company, GPO Box 906, Bangkok, Thailand
Price list and swatches, free. Prices in $.

Gorgeous Thai silks are some of the most astounding bargains I have seen. Iridescent, stylized flower designs, checks and solid colors are all magnificent; if you can find them in America, they cost several times as much. Upholstery-weight cotton, $2.10 a yard; silk, $5–$9 a yard, depending on weight. Prices of the fabrics made up: men's ties in classic shape, $3.20; in last year's narrow shape with square ends, $2; in *this* year's superwide 5" shape, $3.25; cummerbund, $6.35, and matching bow tie, $5.50, sports shirt, $11; neck scarf, $1.50; 16" by 16" cushion cover, $5; eight cocktail napkins, $4, and a luncheon set of eight place mats and eight napkins, $24.

I should add that air mail from Thailand is expensive and parcels by sea take two months, so to save as much money as possible, order way ahead of time—in September for Christmas presents.

For more fabrics, see the stores in the General section.

Fabrics

WALES

Felin Newydd, Gellywen, Carmarthen, Dyfed SA33 6DY, Wales
Price list with samples, $1.

Anne de Boisgelin lives in an old mill by a trout-and-salmon stream, keeps goats, geese, ducks and chickens, and grows all her own vegetables. She makes and sells silk with her own batik patterns, which are inspired by natural phenomena such as gallic manifestations, water formations, and the general ebb and flow of the universe. Her dress lengths in pure shantung silk cost about $13 a yard, and the swatches I saw had cloudy designs in subtle, dusty colors.

9

Food, Spices, Candy, Wine, etc.

Food, Spices, Candy, Wine, etc.

H. L. Barnett, Brunswick House, Torridge Hill, Bideford, North Devon, England
66-page catalogue, free; $1 air mail.

A general gift catalogue that has a food section worth mentioning here. From October to December they export Lochinvar Scottish smoked salmon in various weights up to 4 lbs. (at the time of writing, 2 lbs. cost $17, including air-mail postage to the United States). All year round they export excellent Floris and Bendicks chocolates; fruit cakes, shortbread and plum puddings from the well-known Ormeau bakery in Belfast; English specialties such as Eccles, Bakewell, mince pies and various gift hampers. Within Great Britain they also send out hams, turkeys, geese and game, cases of wines and spirits, and boxes of fruit, including Cox's Orange Pippin apples.

Buderim Ginger Factory, Buderim 4556, Queensland, Australia
Hamper price list, free.

Australia's only ginger factory is visited by thousands of ginger-loving tourists a week, who shop at the ginger shop and eat at the ginger bar—ice cream with ginger topping, and hot scones with cream and ginger marmalade. Ginger connoisseurs in other countries can send for ginger in every shape and form, from one-pound presentation gifts of crystallized ginger for about $6.25, including postage, to large hampers that sound a bit excessive. One costs about $17, including postage, and contains crystallized ginger, young stem ginger, ginger marmalade, ginger topping, ginger date-nut spread, ginger in syrup, and rosella and strawberry preserves. It comes, like the other hampers, with a recipe booklet that tells you what to do with it all—"new ideas for *every* meal," the brochure hopefully announces.

Charbonnel et Walker, 31 Old Bond Street, London W.1, England ☙
18-page color brochure, free; 25 cents air mail. September.

A posh little shop in Old Bond Street selling chocolates in lacy, velvety, flowery boxes—most suitable for a romantic gesture. The brochure says these chocolates are a compliment to the discriminating taste of both sender and recipient. Besides the elaborate boxes (some of which are designed to be used afterward for tissues or cigarettes) there are two gratifying services: one is foil-covered chocolates with letters on top that can be used to spell out a message— the message can be as banal as "Thanks for a Lovely Weekend" or as interesting a quotation or private allusion as you can make—provided you can be brief. The other service is that centers are numbered so you can choose your own favorites (and avoid whatever you don't like). In my case, I think soft centers are too perfumed at Charbonnel et Walker and advise nuts, etc. Prices start at about $5 a pound. As well as chocolates, you can buy Marzipan Amandé in the Lubeck tradition, Marzipan Gingembre, marzipan with assorted nuts, crystallized peppermint creams, crystallized ginger, glacéed pineapple, marron glacé, burnt or sugared almonds, etc.

Chocolaterie Dauphine, Peter Reynhoudt, 25 Prof. Oranjerstraat, Amsterdam, Holland
Catalogue, $1. Prices in $.

Even though liquor chocolates are not legally for sale in the United States, they are apparently sure-fire presents for all those notorious people who have everything. Anyway, this group of shops, which specializes in sending gift parcels abroad, says that the Ringers liquor-filled chocolates are their most popular item with American customers. Other Dutch goodies that look almost as appetizing include cherries in

1
Confiserie-Schatz Pistachio-marzipan, hazel-nougat chocolate-covered "Mozartkugeln." Packed in a box decorated with an old engraving of Salzburg.

2
Chocolaterie Dauphine Ringers 2-lb. box of assorted chocolate "Flower Market." About $16.50, including postage.

3
H. L. Barnett Bendicks handmade chocolate in presentation boxes. Prices from $8 for a 1-lb. box to $12 for 2-lb. box. Other kinds of Bendicks chocolate in regular boxes from $3.
photo A. C. Littlejohns

Food, Spices, Candy, Wine, etc.

liqueur covered in chocolate, big chocolate letters (should appeal to children) and bonbon assortments by Driessen, Droste, Rademakers and Ringers in Dutch-inspired gift boxes.

Chocolaterie International, Damrak 65, Amsterdam, Holland
Price list, free. Prices in $.

This firm sends boxes of delicious Ringers full-strength liqueur chocolates in wooden export boxes (at the moment 200 grams, $5, including surface postage). It is illegal to import these into America (though a friend of mine did it for years until I told her she was breaking the law). They can, however, be sent to friends in other, luckier countries.

Confiserie-Schatz, Getreidegasse 3, A-5020 Salzburg, Austria
Price list, free. Prices in $.

Salzburger Mozartkugeln are filled with pistachio marzipan and hazelnut nougat and coated with chocolate in the form of a ball. I can happily report, having received a free sample, that they are *very* rich and *very* delicious. Each one is wrapped in silver foil with a rather blurred picture of Mozart on it and packed in a box which shows an old engraving of Salzburg and is tied with a ribbon with the colors of the Austrian flag. They cost, including surface postage (it takes about five weeks), $7.90 for a mini package (15 pieces); $14 for maxi (32 pieces). A suitable present for a musical gourmet or a greedy music lover.

Christie, Manson and Woods (U.S.A.), 867 Madison Avenue, New York, N.Y. 10021
Catalogue subscription list, free. Prices in $.

Sotheby and Co., P.O. Box 2AA, 34–35 New Bond Street, London W1A 2AA, England
Catalogue subscription list, free. Prices in $.

Both these illustrious auction houses have sales of all kinds of fine wines usually unavailable in America, which you can bid for by mail. Subscribe to a season's worth of catalogues, roughly October to July, which will tell you what is being offered. When you receive each catalogue, you can ask the house what their estimate of the bids is, then send in your own bid. You can also subscribe to lists that arrive after the auctions which tell you what the wines actually fetched. Friends of mine who have bought wines from Christie's (they sell more than Sotheby's) tell me they used to make fairly low bids and were quite often lucky, but prices are going up and low bids aren't as rewarding any more.

But check whether you are allowed to import your own wine into your state, as this is illegal in some states. There are no formalities in the others, just customs duty and state taxes to pay.

Danfood Ltd., 37 Raynham Road, Industrial Estate, Bishop's Stortford, Hertfordshire, England
Price list, free.

This is obviously an unlikely address from which to buy Danish food, but this British firm stocks an excellent variety of packaged and canned Danish goods at very reasonable prices. As would be expected, various fish—herring, mackerel, brisling, mussels, etc.—head the list. But there is a good choice of meats, cheese, vegetables and even Danish jams which I've never tried but which look tempting and reasonable (a pound of black-currant jam for $1). There are a number of other things that are not specifically Danish, like coarse salt, but not easy to find elsewhere.

Fauchon, 26 Place de la Madeleine, Paris VIII, France
Export leaflet, free. Prices in $.

Fauchon is France's Fortnum's (see below) with the difference that when in 1970 Maoist students looted Fauchon and distributed their goodies to the poor, Fauchon refused to prosecute. When Emily Pankhurst and the suffragettes smashed Fortnum's windows, Fortnum's merely sent a hamper of delicacies to sustain them in prison.

The general catalogue austerely and simply lists the many foods that they import and export, some of which will be no great treat to Americans—"Rice Krispi" and "Coco Pops," for instance. However, everything is neatly divided into categories and countries (Congo, Malaisie, Mexique, Indonésie), so it easy to find things that one could hardly find anywhere else: Coffret Safari: (Tigre-Eléphant-Serpent) and Nopalitos Finos (Feuilles de Cactus en escabèche).

The little export leaflet is more useful, as it simply lists the goods most popular with American mail-order customers. Ten kinds of goose liver from $24 for 7 oz.; truffles from $4.50 for ½ oz.; glazed chestnuts, $10 for 14 oz.; currant preserves; French tuna fish; French sardines; biscuits; herbs (these eighteen times cheaper than in my local supermarket—though, presumably, that isn't the reason people buy them from France); white peaches; French asparagus; mustards; snails; dried mushrooms; cheeses (Munster, Camembert, Brie, each $1.75 for 8 oz.); and, of course, pâtés (hare, thrush, baby wild boar, deer, pheasant, partridge, blackbird, and lark), each $2 for 4½ oz.

R. W. Forsyth, Food Hall, 3 St. Andrew Square, Edinburgh EH2 2BG, Scotland
Christmas list, free.

Forsyth's, the Edinburgh department store, has lower-priced delectable local foods useful for small presents. Cheeses in earthenware jars, honeys and preserves in china pots, stem ginger (costing $5.50, half as much as at Fortnum's), rum-and brandy-flavored mincemeat, Scottish shortbread, Bendick's mint crisps and bittermints, Christmas puddings, and completely iced and decorated Christmas cakes.

Fortnum and Mason, Piccadilly, London W1A 1ER, England ☙
Color Christmas catalogue, free. September.

Started in 1707 by Hugh Mason and William Fortnum (royal footman with excellent connections at the palace), Fortnum's have purveyed food to royalty and top people ever since. They are thoroughly experienced in mail order to Englishmen abroad, officers in the Napoleonic wars would rely on their hams, tongues, butter and cheese, and write desperately: "Candles are articles dreadfully in request and you have sent none"; "No news yet of your hams, which I must regret, for my housekeeping is now ruinous." In the Crimea, officers wrote and begged Fortnum's to stop stenciling their name on crates as it led to an "undue leakage of luxuries during the voyage." Queen Victoria sent Florence Nightingale crates of concentrated beef tea through Fortnum's; and Charles Dickens, describing a Derby day, wrote about their famous hampers: "If I were on the turf and had a horse to enter for the Derby, I would call that horse Fortnum and Mason, convinced that with that name he would beat the field. Public Opinion would bring him in somehow. Look where I will—in some connection with the carriages—made fast upon the top, or occupying the box, or peeping out of a window, I see Fortnum and Mason. And now, Heavens! all the hampers fly wide open and the green Downs burst into a blossom of lobster salad."

Now Fortnum's has expanded into a small department store, and the lavish, sybaritic Christmas catalogue has a little of

Food, Spices, Candy, Wine, etc.

the best of everything. The food pages are magnificent, with full-color photographs of caviar and paté, English and Scottish cheeses, salmon, nuts, desert fruits, and crystallized fruits prepared exclusively in France, ginger and honey, handmade chocolates, and of course, the hampers—famous as Christmas gifts complete with champagne and cigars.

And if you are looking for presents and have money to fling carelessly away, this is a place to buy even more things for those people who have everything, provided they have a taste for luxury. This is the place for silver—leaf-shaped ashtrays, fish-shaped peppermills, for old-fashioned rocking horses, black-velvet suits, and eighteenth-century cushions. But the Fortnum's label is costly and identical articles cost less in any other English shop. Probably the only bargain in this store is the super scale electric Blower Bentley car, which can be driven by child or parent. It costs around $700 here and $1,500 in a New York toy store.

Health 4 All Products Ltd., P.O. Box 307, Willowdale, Ontario, Canada
Price lists, 15 cents; 25 cents air mail.

This Canadian firm has been in the herb business since 1888 and assures me that it is under the direction of herbalists and pharmacists to assure quality. They have a very thorough herb list but also stock vitamins, tinctures, fluid extracts and essential oils, and import Korean ginseng products.

Matthes Ltd., Englands Lane, Gorleston-on-Sea, Great Yarmouth, Norfolk, England
Leaflet, free. October.

Matthes sells two traditional Christmas foods, a Norfolk fruit cake and a Christmas pudding (made with brandy). The cake weighs 2 lbs., the pudding slightly more. Each costs about $7 postpaid, the two together about $10.

M. M. Poonjiaji and Co., 42 First Marine Street, Bombay 400002 India

For $20, M. M. Poonjiaji will mail twelve bottles or cans of their Sweet Sliced Mango Chutney, Hot Mango Chutney, Major Grey's Mango Chutney, Sliced Mango Pickle, Lime Pickle, Combination Pickle, or Curry, in powder or paste—whichever you choose—by registered parcel post.

Ritchie Bros., 37 Watergate, Rothesay, Bute, Scotland

A family firm on the Isle of Bute that has been air-mailing their own bland, cured, smoked salmon to fastidious American gastronomes since a mention in the *New York Times*. Mr. Ritchie sent me a letter from a grateful lady in New York saying that the salmon is always of excellent quality and she keeps it refrigerated for three to four weeks with no problem at all. She also says that the speediest delivery took eight days after she wrote and the slowest took three and a half weeks (for a friend in Florida), but it was ordered in mid-December.

A two-pound side of salmon will probably cost $24, including postage, by the time this book appears, but if it costs less, Ritchie will send a little more salmon.

Schiphol Airport, Tax-free Shopping Center, Amsterdam, Holland
Cheese leaflet, free.

Schiphol Airport will sell you Dutch cheeses, Edam and Gouda, in various sizes. They'll send an order form with up-to-date prices that include mailing costs.

Seaweed Ltd., Kylbroghlan, Moycullen, Co. Galway, Ireland
Price list, free.

There are not that many good sources for seaweed these days, so seaweed lovers or health-food addicts may wish to get in touch with this Irish firm which has been dealing in seaweed for twenty-five years. Seaweed has been used in Ireland for hundreds of years as a food supplement and can also be used to relieve rheumatic pains. Packets are available for use in footbaths and regular baths. Packets of Carrageen and Dislisk are seaweed prepared as a jelly or as a food supplement.

Mail Order Department, Shannon Free Airport, Ireland
Catalogue with some color, free; $1 air mail. Prices in $.

The Shannon Airport Shop will send you a side (about 2½ lbs.) of Irish smoked salmon cured by the oldest curing house in Dublin, Thomas Murphy. As I write, the price, including air-mail postage, is $21. Cookies, Irish whiskey cake, and Indian tea packed in scenic caddies are also for sale.

10 General–Department Stores and Mail-Order Houses

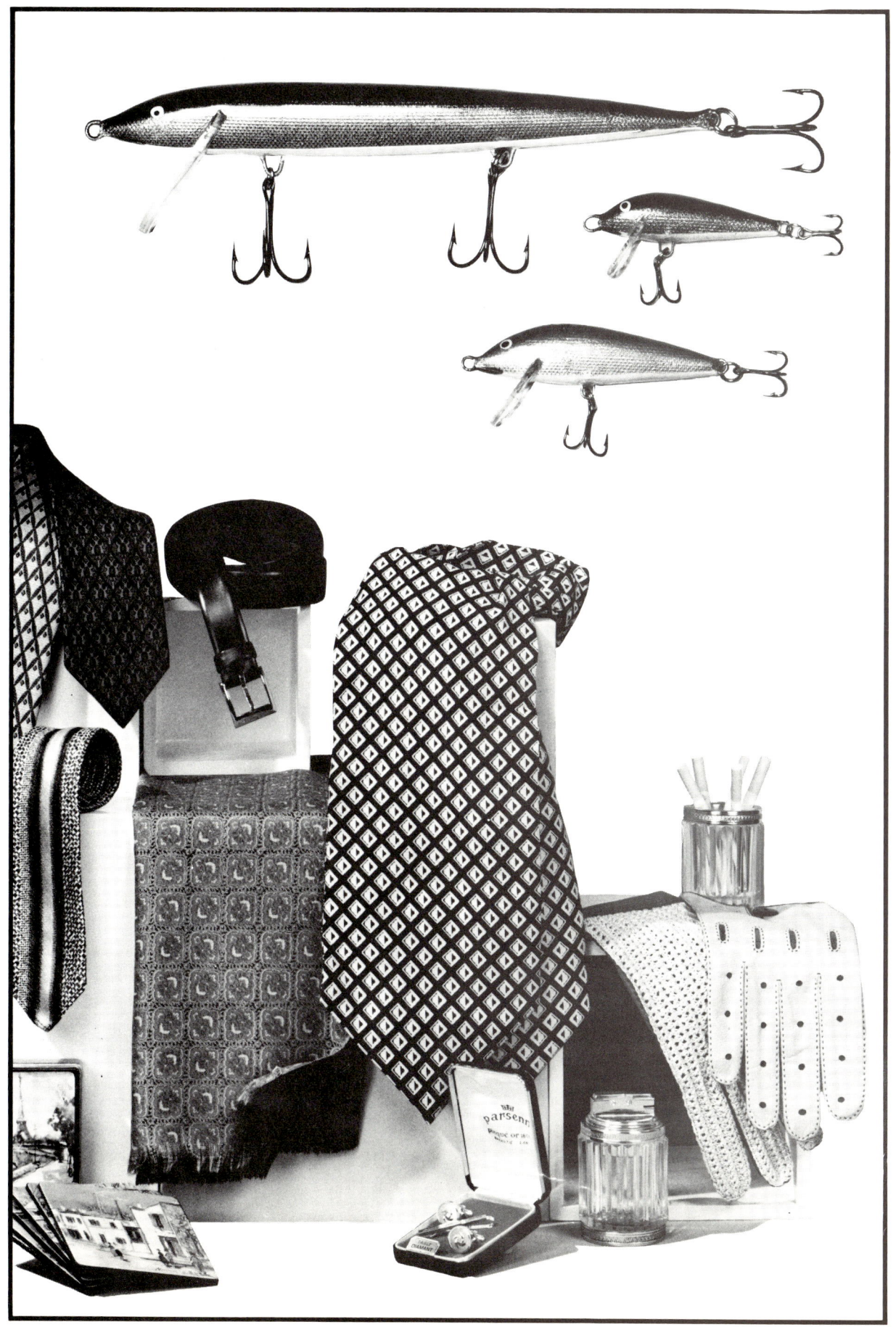

General—Department Stores and Mail-Order Houses

This is the section for real mail-order maniacs, the people who read the Sears, Roebuck catalogue in their bath, and send away for anything as long as it is new and out of the ordinary. People who aren't looking for anything special will have lots to mull over in the large catalogues from the big stores and mail-order firms in this section where almost everything looks just slightly different from the things you see in America.

But this is also a useful section for inexpensive basics, more clothes are illustrated in full color in these catalogues than anywhere else, more shoes, raincoats, fabrics, pots and pans, lamps. And if you are looking for something special from a certain country that isn't in any of the other sections, it might be here.

ENGLAND

Freemans of London, 139 Clapham Road, London S.W.9, England
800-page color catalogue, $4. Spring and fall.

One of England's biggest mail-order firms, Freemans puts out two whopping catalogues a year of their own products and of other manufacturers'. The catalogues should give mail-order addicts many happy browsing hours. Glancing through them, I see a lot of things (such as furniture and appliances) not worth buying, but amusingly different from things you see in America.

The clothes are mostly rather ordinary, but there are certainly some perfectly pleasant clothes: solid-colored pants, skirts that look well cut (some for under $10), tweed suits and wrap-around coats for women, three-piece suits and corduroy jackets for men, a good selection of clothes for children, all at low prices, and a large section of shoes by well-known English manufacturers.

Harrods Ltd., Knightsbridge, London S.W.1, England ♛♛♛
Color brochure, free. Prices in $. November.

London's most established, most establishment department store has a special export brochure for Americans showing famous British goods. The brochure concentrates on quality rather than economy and the one I looked at had Harrods own silver reproductions, London charms, fine bone china, rural-British-scene place mats, traditional-style embroidery kits, reproduction pewter tankards, suit and coat fabrics, sweaters, ties, shirts, dressing gowns, blankets and gloves.

They are an outstandingly well stocked store (in the higher price ranges) and they will open an account for you, but they are not very good at answering letters (they haven't answered any of mine lately, but I do happen to know they're still there).

FINLAND

Stockmann, Export Service, 52, Aleksanterinkatu SF00100 Helsinki 10, Finland
Manufacturers' brochures for Arabia china, glass and enamel cookware, Iittala glass. $3. In Finnish.

Finnish design in some ways seems to be more with-it than Scandinavian design—brighter, bolder colors and shapes. Their children's furniture is particularly nice and is not too expensive if bought from Finland in quantity; ask to see the Muurame brochure. However, Helsinki's biggest department store, Stockmann, advertises a thriving export department but does not, alas, put out a catalogue. They seem to stock most of the famous Finnish furniture, rugs and fabrics that are exported, so if you already know what you want, write and ask.

FRANCE

Au Printemps, Relations Clientèle et Commandes, 64 Boulevard Haussmann, Paris IX, France

One of Paris' largest medium-priced department stores, Au Printemps is at your disposal to answer questions about any articles you are interested in. Unfortunately, like Finland's Stockmann, they don't produce a general catalogue. A great loss, because most of their departments stock goods with a typically French high level of design and color. But try them for any special French products you are looking for. French prices are generally high for Europe, but many exports get a 20 percent discount.

GERMANY

Mail Order House, Quelle Inc., 6050 Kennedy Boulevard East, West New York, N.J. 07093
750-page color catalogue, $3 ($2.40 refundable). Spring, fall.

I strongly recommend Quelle, Germany's largest mail-order house, which is streets ahead of its competitors in standards of design. Whatever the section, their goods are easier on the eye than the goods in similar catalogues from other countries.

Quelle has an office in New Jersey, advertises here, and although the catalogue is in German, it comes with a complete translation for the clothes and linen sections (the most popular in America). Very clear instructions, including a full table of exchange, so there is virtually no calculating to do.

One of the reasons that their clothes are much more attractive than clothes of American and English mail-order houses is that the styles are new-looking yet pared down, casual, and the colors, too, are subtler. Everyday winter dresses cost from $25 to $35, with good selections for pregnant women and larger figures. Men's winter suits cost from $75, and there are plenty of children's clothes, from dresses and pants for young children to separates for older ones up to the age of fourteen for under $10, and ski clothes for everybody. In other sections there are bicycles with motors, kitchen gadgets and bright-enameled saucepans, toys, Christmas decorations, and a marvelous food section with all sorts of German candies and cookies packed for Christmas and wrapped for hanging on the tree. There is also furniture, and in fact almost anything that an American mail-order house would have, Quelle has too. You're almost bound to find several things you want here. Minimum order, $22.

IRELAND

Mail Order Department, Shannon Free Airport, Ireland
60-page catalogue with some color, free; $1 air mail. Prices in $.

Shannon Airport has a famous tax-free shop at which, the *New York Times* says, our Secretary of State buys sweaters and ambassadors do their Christmas shopping. The shop has a vast and superbly organized mail-order business, with a very efficient catalogue showing popular brand-name items at greater savings than any other shop, and including an estimate of the American duty you'll have to pay on each item.

The goods on sale are always things that have proved popular and include English china, Irish porcelain, Irish lace and linen, Irish jewelry, Peterson pipes, knitwear (although the selection is smaller than at the English knitwear shops, their

General—Department Stores and Mail-Order Houses

prices for Pringle are several dollars lower), Viyella blouses and robes (at half their New York prices), Irish rugs and rug coats, mohair and mohair coats, and even golf balls. Shannon will also undercut on imports—French perfume, Swiss army knives, Italian wood figures by Anri, Dutch blue Delft, Norwegian pewter and Icelandic knitwear in the catalogue I looked at.

NORWAY

A. S. Sundt and Co., Export Department, P.O. Box 1063, 5001 Bergen, Norway
Brochures for crystal figurines, hand-carved wooden figurines, enamelware, hand-knit sweaters, pewter, quilts, all free. Prices in $.

Sundt exports about two thousand packages of Norwegian-made goods a year and says that the quilts are getting more and more popular, while the handmade traditional Norwegian knitwear is becoming less and less popular (they think maybe the prices are getting too high—between $40 and $50 for adult-size sweaters). Sundt is a good place to get the brilliantly colored enamel gifts by Emalox; I haven't seen them in any other catalogue. Bowls, napkin rings, candlesticks, salt and pepper shakers, table lighters, and even an electric wall clock are shown in the brochure. They come in eleven colors and make good presents. Many pieces cost under $10, and almost everything is less than $20.

I haven't seen the small carved and painted wooden figures anywhere else, either. Postcards have color photographs of trolls, peasants in local and working costumes, and a few slightly Christmassy figures—a choir girl candlestick and some skiing children. Depending on size, these cost from about $6 to about $20. Sundt also sends out the Hadeland lead-crystal figurines. They are small and chubby animals—hedgehogs, mice, seals, fish, snails and ladybugs—all under $10 each.

SWEDEN

PUB (Paul U. Bergströms AB), Export Department, Box 40 140, Stockholm 40, Sweden
Leaflets for glass, flatware and souvenirs, $1.50 for all. Prices for all of these in $.

PUB is a large co-operative department store in Stockholm with a very efficient export service. They have no general catalogue, so you have to write and ask about any Swedish thing you are trying to track down. They mainly sell to America stainless-steel tableware and Swedish glass: Orrefors, Kosta and Skruf, and a few Swedish souvenirs such as dolls and painted Dalecarlian horses.

TRINIDAD

Stechers Ltd., 62 Independence Square, Port of Spain, Trinidad
Leaflet, free.

Stechers, which claims to be almost a landmark for Caribbean tourists, has been widely written up in the American press as a great spot for bargains. They handle internationally known glass, china, watches, perfumes, stainless steel, pewter, binoculars, etc. They will send you a leaflet listing the manufacturers they handle and then will give you their price for any specific thing you ask about. If they do not have what you want in stock, they can order it.

1
Stockmann Lapp dolls: 14" high, $11; 6" high, $10.30.

2
Stockmann Woman's wool cardigan "Revontuli," about $44. Child's sweater, $22–$27 according to size.

3
Stockmann Palaset cubes: small, $4.30; large $12.20. Plate, cup and saucer "Paratiisi" breakfast set, $7. Candles, $1–$6. Stand under the heart candle, $4.

4
Stockmann Make-it-yourself lampshade kit in natural-colored chip wood. $4.50.
photos Kalevi Hujanen

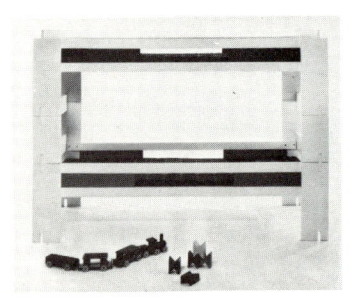

General—Department Stores and Mail-Order Houses

5
Stockmann Muurame painted beech bunkbed "Jetti," designed by Pirkko Stenros. Several color combinations available. $153.

6
Stockmann Iittala glasses. A set of six costs about $16.

11 Handicrafts and Special Local Products

Handicrafts and Special Local Products

This section is a hodge-podge of shops that sell very traditional, handmade local crafts, and also shops that sell a whole range of products that their country happens to make especially well or inexpensively. So even if you detest anything ethnic, look through this section, as you might like the highly metropolitan perfumes and gloves in the French shops. For people who do like crafts, there are lots of marvelous and inexpensive things here.

CANADA

Iroqrafts Ltd., Box 3, Ohsweken, Six Nations Reserve, Ontario, Canada
Catalogue, 50 cents (no checks please). Prices in $.

A serious firm that sells traditional and ceremonial Iroquois crafts to museums as well as shops and individuals. Many of the crafts are the highly decorative beaded and fringed things that have suddenly become popular: headbands, bracelets and necklaces, tasseled belts, flower-embroidered gloves, fringed and patterned bags, $3–$20; sheepskin slippers with white rabbit-fur cuffs and beaded toes, $6.25 children, $8.25 adults, and moose-hide jackets.

For the hundreds and thousands of children studying Indian at school there are instructive little models, totem poles, canoes, teepees, dolls in traditional costume; and a full-color wall map showing fifty Canadian tribal groups in typical surroundings, $2.50 including postage. For more serious collectors: hand-sculptured ceremonial false face masks "sold only on the understanding they will not be used pseudo Indian ceremonies or other sacrilegeous ways" and, on the collectors lists (irritatingly illegibly mimeographed), a whole lot of scarcer items: one-of-a-kind clothes, pillows, quilts, paintings, pottery, full-size canoes, etc.

Shuttles and Seawinds Limited, New Germany, Nova Scotia, Canada
Color brochure, $1; $2 air mail.

A collection of color cards illustrate the locally made apple dolls (decorative dolls made with heads of dried apples), patchwork quilts and tablecloths, comforters, pillows, shower curtains, bags and a few clothes sold by this crafts shop. Judging by the photographs, the quality of the work is extremely high; the carefully thought out color combinations and elaborate quilting give a sophisticated look that is quite different from the cheerful country look of most patchwork that is popular now—some of the white quilts appliquéd with flowers in red and green would look more at home in a mansion than a cottage. Prices are correspondingly high, starting at under $200 for single-size machine-made quilts, and at over $400 for the handmade quilts. The smaller things on sale, such as apple dolls, place mats, crib-size comforters, bun cozies and oven mitts are less expensive, of course, and more popular. Four place mats with napkins to match start at about $16, but you can buy the napkins alone for $2 each.

DOMINICAN REPUBLIC

Santa Rosa de Lima, Inc., Cesar Nicolas Penson No. 111, Santo Domingo, Dominican Republic
Catalogue, 50 cents. Prices in $.

This private social-welfare institution has several departments. One trains social-welfare volunteers, another runs a school and training workshop for deaf-mutes, another sells clothes at low prices to the local poor. One department has started teaching local women macramé to do in their homes, has formed a cooperative staffed by volunteers, and is marketing the macramé. The catalogue shows handbags, shoulder bags, belts, cushion covers and wall hangings in natural cord or white nylon. Most things cost less than $10, and the president of the organization says that the macramé "is very high quality, very finely and skillfully done."

ECUADOR

Akios Industries, P.O. Box 219, Quito, Ecuador
59-page catalogue, $1. Prices in $.

A good catalogue for anyone who likes colorful South American handicrafts, Akios Industries is chock full of vividly decorated handicrafts. Magnificent woolen evening skirts with wide bands of hand embroidery, $22; jackets embroidered all over, $33; slacks with embroidery up the edges, made to order, $22. Handwoven, brightly patterned ponchos, $7; fringed vests, $5 for adults, $3 for children; belts, ties; and slippers. Over thirty bags of all sorts—calfskin or fabric—decorated with colorful handwoven ribbons, one for little girls is in the shape of a doll, $3. There are also embroidered cushions, $2.75; a receiving blanket with birds and flowers, $15; tablecloths and place mats. Sixty Inca-inspired carpets, similar to Folklore's, are light-fast, color-fast, and cost $50 a square yard—one, 6" by 8" costs under $220. Colored drawings can be sent.

And for decorating the house: carved and painted wooden dolls; shiny bread-dough figures; Inca wall masks, $1.20 and up; straw hats; mats; dolls; Indian musical instruments; onyx free-form ashtrays, $3.25 and up; chess sets with Inca figures, $13; oil paintings of local scenes and figures, $13.

Folklore—Olga Fisch, P.O. Box 64, Quitó, Ecuador
Rug color brochure, $3. Prices in $. Handicrafts brochure, $1. Prices in $.

Folklore has now produced a very appetizing brochure of carefully chosen handicrafts, and it's illustrated with photographs. I thoroughly recommend it. Straw figures, bread-dough figures, silver jewelry, embroidered pillowcases and bedspreads, painted gourds, woven hangings and dramatic clothes designed by the owner's niece are all illustrated.

EGYPT

Yahya el Miligi and Co., 12 Moh. Mahmoud and Salah El Din Street, Dounzo Building, Port Said, Egypt
Photographs and prices in $, free.

I don't know how many mail-order dealers there are in Egypt, but this firm claims to be one of the leading ones (they've been at it since 1960, they say). Photographs and carefully typed descriptions of goods for sale are always available. I was sent pictures of sterling-silver jewelry set with genuine turquoise, coral and amethyst stones at very low prices; wooden jewelry and cigarette boxes inlaid with mother-of-pearl and ivory, at $5 to $40, including postage; calfskin hassocks decorated in gold with Arabic and Islamic designs, at $10 to $30, including postage; and also camel stools. I quote the description of one of the camel stools: *"Camel Stool with Two Carved Heads*, made of very solid beech wood, hand carved, it is ornamented with four big silk tassels and long silk fringes on both sides, the leather cushion is made of fast color calf skin with very beautiful Arabic gold printed designs, the legs are decorated with very unusual designs, body color as you desire, the stool folds for easy storage." The letterhead says that other things such as Arabic coffee sets, silver and copper trays, and Oriental ladies' dresses are

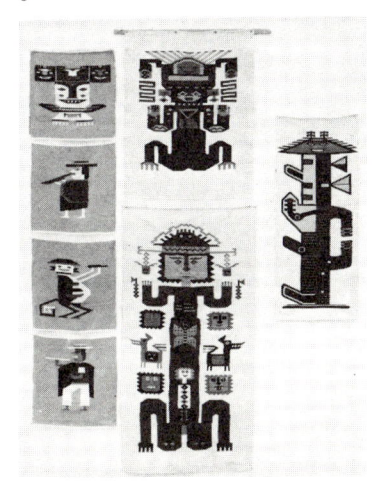

Handicrafts and Special Local Products

1
Folklore Cuenca cross, wrought iron, used on roofs of newly built houses for good luck. $12.50.

2
Folklore "Uma Devil," Indian fiesta mask, gray or blue cloth, hand-embroidered in bright colors, 26" by 12". About $25.

3
Folklore "Guano" bedcover. Handwoven merino sheep's wool, background in orange, off-white, black or purple with multicolor embroidery. Single-bed size, $49.

4
Folklore–Olga Fisch Wall hangings woven by Salasacan Indians. The small are $1.20 each, the medium $2, the large $10 and up.

5
Yahya el Miligi and Co. Sterling-silver set, with genuine turquoise, coral and amethyst stones. 2557-A earrings, $16; 2557-B necklace, $35; 2557-C bracelet, $40. Add 15 percent if gilt with 18-carat gold. Prices include air-mail postage.

also stocked, but you would have to ask specifically about them.

ENGLAND

Artwork, Woodlands, Ivybridge, Devonshire PL21 9HF, England
Leaflet, 25 cents.

The Victorian craft of making flower pictures has been revived by this firm, which says that the pictures shouldn't be confused with dried-flower pictures, as colors and textures are preserved by setting the flowers in a deep frame, not by pressing them. Bouquets on a background of velvet come in a variety of traditional frames and sizes at prices from $12 to $20. The leaflet that was sent me was unfortunately blurry, and though you can get an idea of the style of the pictures, it is in black-and-white, so you get no sense of the colors.

Country Cousins, Gorse Croft, Ranmoor Lane, Hathersage, via Sheffield S30 1BW, England
Price list, 50 cents (coins only).

Mrs. Muriel Brown designs most of Country Cousin's toys, cushions, aprons and oven gloves, which are made up in gaily colored cottons by local people working at home. She says the cushions are by far the most popular with Americans and Canadians. First, the 17" square "Officers and Gentlemen" cushion with gold, scarlet, blue and black eighteenth-century soldiers printed on one side, and a solid color on the other, $10; then, patchwork cushions based on old English designs copied from museums: "Flower Garden" (top left) is a design used by Elizabeth Fry, who taught prisoners patchwork in Newgate Gaol before they were transported to Australia. The cushions, except for "Mosaic," which has a mixture of jolly colors, are made in predominantly brown, pink or turquoise-blue tones, but any other colors can be made, and customers' own fabrics used. Patchwork quilts are made to order after a discussion of types and colors (single, $116), and old quilts can be restored.

Luis Grosse Ltd., 36 Manchester Street, London W1M 5PE, England
Church vestments leaflet, free.
Church fabrics price list, free.

This firm has been making church furnishings since 1783, and at the moment is making a set of copies for St. Paul's Cathedral in London designed by John Piper. The firm believes that furnishings should blend with their surroundings, so the leaflets, illustrating copes and chalices and vestments, and listing other things such as small linens and "Bishops' Requisites," are just for inspiration, as each inquiry is dealt with individually. The church fabrics, embroidery supplies, emblems and metal fringes, etc., that are used in the Luis Grosse workrooms and which they can thoroughly recommend, are also sold separately.

Douglas Hart, Aiblins, Cott Cross, Dartington, Totnes, Devonshire, England
Brochure, $2; $2.25 air mail. Prices in $.

Douglas Hart, an old friend of mine, is a professional woodturner and makes very simple, beautiful things out of ash, beech (light woods) and orangy brown teak. Waxed salad bowls from $25, polished bowls from $20, cheese board and knife from $10, a hanging salt box for $5.25, a bird house, $5.25. There are fifty-five items altogether, including lamp bases from $5.25 up, but these would need altering to fit American bulbs.

Handicrafts and Special Local Products

6
Country Cousins Patchwork cushions based on old English designs. *Reading left to right and starting at the top:* "Flower Garden," $13; "Autumn," $13; "Little Boxes," $13; "Morning Glory," $13 (these four made in mainly brown, pink or turquoise-blue tones). *Bottom:* Two "Mosaic" (in a mixture of colors), $13 each.

7
Country Cousins 17" square "Officers and Gentlemen" cushion, $10; 13" square "Train" (or "Ship" or "Rocking Horse") cushion in red and pink, $8; 6½" mouse with removable red cloak and blue apron, $2.

8
Taylor of London Pomander in pale blue or green Jasper by Wedgwood, with a fragrance made from a sixteenth-century recipe claimed to last for fifty years. About $15.

The International Model Mail Order House, 327-3, Camphill Products, Central Sales Department, Bolton Village, Danby, Whitby, Yorkshire YO21 2NJ, England
Catalogue planned, 75 cents; $2.50 air mail.

I haven't seen the catalogue produced by this sheltered workshop for handicapped people because it wasn't quite ready when I wrote, but the catalogue is published annually in the late summer. Engraved glass, beeswax candles, enameled copperware, rugs and baskets, dolls and toys, woven goods and dyed silk are made in the workshops, and I hope that most of them will be illustrated in the catalogue.

Patches, Daylesford, Wellington Square, Cheltenham, Gloucestershire, England
Brochure, free; air mail 2 International Reply Coupons.

Clothes and furnishings in a modern version of patchwork are made and sold here. The patchwork is sewn by machine, and each article is made in one color but with squares of different fabrics with different designs on them. You can find floor-length skirts, floor-length aprons, children's dresses, men's shirts, curtains, tablecloths, fabric by the yard, and of course, bedspreads. Prices are a bit high, considering that the patchwork is machine-sewn, the hostess skirt, for instance, costs $45, and the single-size bedspread $70, but if you'd like something slightly less countrified than traditional patchwork, then Patches will probably have just what you want. You can buy things in all blue, all red, all green, all pink, or in combinations of pink/purple, brown/orange, or black/white.

Chris Reekie, Old Coach House, Stock Road, Grasmere, Westmorland, England
Leaflet planned, 50 cents. Prices in $.

These handweavers make stoles, rugs, capes and coats from soft and warm mohair. Their leaflet isn't ready at this writing, but I have seen photographs of their goods in pale tartans and light colors. Prices are very reasonable. A scarf costs about $3, and a travel rug about $25.

Somerset House Wedmore Ltd., Station Road, Cheddar, Somerset, England
Leaflet, 50 cents.

The craft of making idols out of grain, corn dollies, is thousands of years old and was inspired by the belief that a spirit lived in the wheatfield which died when the grain was cut. In order to preserve the spirit and make sure of a good harvest the following year, an idol was made from the last sheaf of grain. The corn dollies, handmade in Somerset and sold by this firm, are not to be confused with American cornhusk dolls. These are traditional English abstract patterns which can be hung on the wall as decorations, or if you believe in magic, as symbols of peace and prosperity.

Audrey Taunton, 63 Bellingham Road, Cumbria LA9 5JY, England
Leaflet, 25 cents; 50 cents air mail. Photographs, $1 each.

Audrey Taunton has exhibited her work in England and France and as yet hasn't found anyone else doing the same thing. She makes pictures of birds with the actual feathers of the bird shown. Feathers of dead birds are provided by aviaries, zoos, breeders and airlines, and Mrs. Taunton places and sticks the feathers individually, using no artificial coloring or any other faking. She has a list of birds on sale including mallards, short-eared owls, swans, and she says that American birds will be made to order if she can get hold of the right feathers. The birds are mounted on a silk background and framed. Most of them are very small — around

Handicrafts and Special Local Products

5" wide—and most of the pictures cost between $75 and $150. There is only one illustration on the leaflet, but photographs can be sent on specific request.

Taylor of London, Perfumery Shop, 166 Sloane Street, London S.W.1, England
Leaflet, free.

Taylor of London says they have been making *status* scents for royalty and the cream of English and Continental society for the past eighty years. Gardenia, lily of the valley, carnation and lilac are hand-distilled and made into soaps, bath essences, dusting powder, cologne and perfume, and during the summer, delivered in a horse-drawn brougham to customers in London's West End. Taylor also makes sachets to perfume drawers and potpourris of flowers to be emptied into bowls to perfume rooms for several months. But most popular of all are their Crown Staffordshire and Wedgwood pomanders filled with an Elizabethan essence, guaranteed to last for fifty years.

Wilkinson and Gaviller Ltd., Pembroke House, Wellesey Road, Croydon CRO 2AR, England
Leaflet, free.

In 1851 Thomas Smith showed some of his "trugs," now known in America as willow-wood garden baskets, at the Hyde Park exhibition, where they won gold medals and were admired by Queen Victoria who ordered some for the palace. Smith's Famous Sussex Trugs are still being produced, and as the leaflet says: "There is no Garden, Farm, or Home where they can not be used to advantage." Traditionally, the oblong baskets made of wide willow-wood slats are used in the garden, but they are now also made in bowl shapes for storage and in larger sizes for log baskets. Trugs for flower gathering cost about $6 each, and for log baskets they cost about $8 each.

ETHIOPIA

The Olive Wood and African Curio Shop, P.O. Box 878, Asmara, Ethiopia
Color leaflet, 50 cents. Prices in $.
Catalogue, $5.

A highly designed and colorful leaflet announces an "accurate and prompt" mail-order service to any part of the world. The leaflet shows some decorated knives, barbed spears (the spears about 80 cents each), dolls, horn cups and birds, crocodile handbags and a leopard-skin hat and handbag. There is also the shop's specialty, olive wood, from naturally seasoned trees that have been standing dead for two to four hundred years. The olive wood has been carved into spoons, or turned (on a lathe, presumably) into smooth bowls, plates, candlesticks, pipe racks, sometimes decorated with inset bands of black and white porcupine quills. Almost all the olive wood items cost under $5, and most of them are about $2.

If you are at all interested in handicrafts, then its well worth sending for the $5 catalogue, which is in fact a booklet put out by the Ethiopian Tourist organization illustrating goods being produced. And very tempting the goods are too, much more interesting than the African crafts that usually reach the shops. There are used or unused *kook mawoocha* (ear cleaners), heavy earrings, hand-engraved bracelets in metal, handwoven wool rugs with strong designs or angular Ethiopian lions on them; brightly colored primitive Christian paintings, or on wood triptychs; musical instruments; weapons; colored woven baskets; odd bulgy painted wooden vessels; glossy beeswaxed handbuilt pottery (the wheel has only recently been introduced); and very lovely metal Coptic crosses. The rugs cost under $10 a square meter, and most of the things illustrated cost under $10, although in some categories, such as the paintings, it is possible to pay much more.

FINLAND

Alajarven Huvilaveistamo, 62900 Alajarvi, Finland
Catalogue, $4.

Originally it was the carpenters who traveled around to build log cottages; now it's the cottages that travel. This firm sends cottages as far away as Japan along the Siberian Railway. They are made either in the oldest way, with round logs, or with squared-off logs, which is now more popular because you can get better insulation. In either case, the logs cross through each other at the ends, giving an attractive, primitive look to the buildings. The cottages are built largely by hand, then they are taken apart for transportation in containers. You get the cottage ready for assembly with bores and dowels. Logs are numbered for reassembly, and instructions are supplied. Sizes go up to three-bedroom cottages, one or two with separate dining rooms, and one with an upstairs room that will take three single beds or bunks. Fittings such as cupboards and benches can also be supplied. Sauna prices start at just under $1,000, "guest" cabins with bedrooms only start at $1,500 for a two-bedroom version, and regular cottages start at just under $3,000 for a model with two bedrooms, a living room and a porch, and go up to around $10,000 for the very largest sizes.

Kause Oy, 28120 Pori 12, Finland
Color brochure, free. Prices in $.

"A prefabricated log cabin and sauna is a quick and economical solution for you who are planning to build a summer and weekend cabin of your own," says the Kause Oy brochure. This forty-year-old firm employs three hundred men making planed pine-log saunas and cabins and cottages. There are six saunas and ten cabins to choose from, all in the same agreeable, straightforward style with large windows and slightly sloping roofs. Sauna prices start at $920. The smallest log cabin, with a sauna, porch, living room and two alcoves with room for a single bed or a bunk each, costs under $3,000; the largest and most expensive cottage of all, with a sauna, changing room, eat-in kitchen, living room, two bedrooms (one double-bed-sized) and a porch, costs just over $7,000. The brochure illustrates a version of their cabins they send to Switzerland whose small panes and shutters give the Alpine-cottage look. Kause Oy will make any other changes you want in the cabin. They will make cabins according to your own drawings at the same "fair" prices as in their serial production and will give you all drawings needed for planning permission.

FRANCE

Freddy, 10 Rue Auber, Paris IX, France
New brochure planned, free. Prices in $.
Price list, free.

There are several shops in Paris that specialize in tax-free gifts for tourists. They are expert at packing and shipping, and have well-established mail-order services for popular French goods at *around* half the price they are abroad.

The Freddy brochure has a perfume price list and also eight pages of gifts illustrated in colorful glory: mauve umbrellas lined with pink roses; purses embroidered with bouquets; gold-and-blue Limoges cigarette cases; famous-

Handicrafts and Special Local Products

9
Holland Handicrafts "St. Nicholaas" traditional hand-carved Christmas cookie mold, 13" × 9". $13, including surface postage.

10
Central Cottage Industries Emporium Inexpensive decorative toys: two string puppets from Rajasthan; on the right, string puppets from Andhra; rocking horse in red with Saurashtra mirror embroidery; Rajasthan doll carrying pitchers; satin elephant from Poona; snake charmer.

11
Central Cottage Industries Emporium Traditional Indian jewelry: silver Mina necklace with real stones on the left, $65; in the center, gold-plated necklace with synthetic red stones, $65; on the right, white metal folk necklace, $16; Thapa mirror, $6; top, brass and copper Thapa pendant, $7 and up; Kundan ring, $2.10.

12
Nepal Craft Emporium Dragon mask, $6.50.

13
Andrzey Szczepka 10"-high Polish dolls, about $5 each.

Handicrafts and Special Local Products

name silk scarves; Dior and Fath ties; and souvenir dolls in regional costumes.

Grillot, 10 Rue Cambon, Paris I, France
Price list, free. Prices in $.

Grillot has a price list with no illustrations, but besides perfumes, well-known French cosmetics are listed, and this is a good place to buy Lacoste (he clothes with the crocodile emblem): shirts sweaters and dresses The different sty es are listed and measurement across the shoulders are given in inches. Prices for Lacoste seem to vary between half and a third off American prices. Also "Rigaud" candles are on sale at much lower prices than abroad (if you can find them abroad).

Obéron, 73 Champs-Elysées, Paris VIII, France
20-page catalogue with some color, $1.50 (refundable). Perfume price list, free.
Prices in $.

A good catalogue with excellent illustrations and an exhortation to ask for anything you don't see, as there are thousands of articles not shown. (Obéron says that they redo the catalogue each year "considering the requests of their customers.") A few pages of gifts "for him" and "for her," fancy gloves, petit-point handbags, designer scarves, and the rest of the space is given over to china and glass objects. Lalique and Baccarat figurines, table items, smokers' sets and ashtrays. In china there is palatial Limoges, countryish Porcelaine de Chantilly, and Fourmaintraux, very kitcheny hand-decorated earthenware.

GERMANY

Kunstschmiede Manfred Bergmeister, August-Birkmaier-Weg 2, 8019 Ebersberg bei München, Germany
Catalogue, $1; $3 air mail.

Bergmeister specializes in handsome modern church objects, the liturgical arts covering a wide field which in some instances must be called sculpture in others artisanry His catalogue depicts a number of extremely attractive rugged candlesticks that could easily be used outside a church context, while other items are suitable only to Christian places of worship. This is obviously a list of primary concern for progressive religious groups, but the artisanry involved is so exceptional that people particularly interested in working with metal may wish to see the catalogue as well.

GREECE

Avis Avouris and Co., 23 Apollonos Street, Athens 118, Greece
Brochure planned, 30 cents; 60 cents air mail. Prices in $.

Avis Avouris has exported Greek handicrafts since 1957. Now the firm is planning to sell by mail order, too. They sent me a few pages of their brochure-to-be with black-and-white pictures of tagari drawstring bags with Greek motifs; Cretan bags, some in natural colors, others embroidered in red and orange; woven pillows; embroidered woolen striped bedspreads; a sailor's cap; Spartan sandals with leather thongs; slippers; off-white Aran-style knitwear; and several different kinds of small rugs from different areas in Greece.

National Welfare Organization, Handicrafts Dept., 6 Ipatias Street, Athens 117, Greece
22-page crafts catalogue with some color, free.

This fetching catalogue, showing the best Greek handicrafts, is put out by the official craft-encouraging National Welfare

Handicrafts and Special Local Products

Organization under the title "Hellas." The big hitch is that prices are not given, and when you write to ask it turns out that half the things aren't available any more. However, I did buy a nice silver bracelet that only cost $12, including airmail postage. (I wasn't charged customs duty.) Besides that bracelet (the rest of the silver jewelry and ashtrays are "off" at the moment), there are handsome, simple brass candlesticks along with copper jugs and coffeepots; some richly colored velvet slippers trimmed with gold; and a smart duffle coat, plain on the outside, but lined inside with a handwoven design. Most of the other things will probably only appeal to people who like distinctively local crafts: linen tablecloths with bird-and-flower regional embroidery; fish, mermaid and boat design needlepoint cushions, about $8 (these cost $25 and up in New York); embroidered purses; and multicolored square wool tagari bags.

GUATEMALA

Manuel Antonio Pilón, P.O. Box 268, Guatemala City, Guatemala, Central America
Catalogue, free. Prices in $.

Native handmade Guatemalan products, announces this small catalogue, offering such goodies as "typical men's cotton shirts, typical ladies' overcoats, and curios seed necklaces." It is a shame that the catalogue is in black-and-white because these as well as the multicolor woven shopping bags and "beautiful women" dress lengths (fabric by the yard) are described as having "nice colors" and probably have to be seen in color to be appreciated (actually you can get samples on request of the dress lengths). Easier to appreciate in black-and-white are the long silver-colored and gilt necklaces. Most prices are under $10, but there is a $20 minimum.

Sombol, P.O. Box 119, Guatemala City, Guatemala, Central America
Leaflet, $1 postal order, refundable if you order within a month. Prices in $.

Sombol has been exporting Guatemalan handicrafts since 1942, and in 1962 opened a retail shop in Guatemala City. At the moment they sell ponchos, capes, wall hangings and place mats in local designs woven in cotton and acrylic yarn by native Indian weavers, and also beautiful metal belts and metal wedding chains which are worn by the girls of the mountain city of Cobán when they get engaged to be married. As Sombol has so far been dealing with importers and retailers, they have good descriptive pages illustrated with line drawings, and by the time this book is published, will have printed information on prices and postage costs for individual mail-order customers.

HAITI

Holy Trinity School Gift Shop, Box 857, Port-au-Prince, Haiti
Catalogue, free; $1 air mail. Prices in $.

The Holy Trinity School is run by the Episcopal Church and has a nonsectarian enrollment of over 1,300 students from varied backgrounds. The idea of the school's gift shop is to give parents and students a chance to earn part of the cost of tuition to the school. Nice and chunky bowls, plates and cheese boards are made by fathers from Tarverneau and caracoli woods. Place mats, guest towels, baby clothes are embroidered with voodoo symbols by mothers, while students make banana-bark stationery and seed-bead jewelry. Haitian dolls, wooden animals, metal patio lights, hand-spun natural-colored cotton upholstery fabric, and hand-spun yarn for weavers are all sold here too, and prices are very low (practically everything except the embroidered linen costs less than $4).

HOLLAND

Holland Handicrafts, Dept. R, Pruimendijk 24, Rijsoord, Holland
8-page brochure, $1. Prices in $.

Adrienne Trouw, an American living in Holland, sells, at Holland Handicrafts, a collection of Dutch products: a shiny old-fashioned brass iron you can put plants in, $14; sterling-silver Dutch charm bracelets from $5; pewter ashtrays in the shape of old brandy tasters, $6; small reproductions of old Dutch paintings in antiqued frames, $7 each. And, much the prettiest—hand-carved traditional Christmas-cookie molds. The molds are usually hung up as decorations, but they can also be used to cut patterned cookies—the recipe comes with them. Prices for molds start at $4, and all the above prices include postage.

Pottenbakkery 't Spinnewiel, O.Z. Achterburgwal 195, Amsterdam -C, Holland
Leaflet planned, free.

Apparently giving a newborn baby a decorated tile is an old Dutch custom. The Pottenbakkery makes birth tiles with the name, weight and place of birth of a baby worked into a picture of an infant in a crib surrounded by flowers.

HONG KONG

Candlelight Associates, P.O. Box 1243, Hong Kong
Catalogue with some color, free; $2 air mail. Prices in $.

It calls itself The Shoppers Paradise, and it does have a particularly well organized, colorful catalogue that has a more tempting look than the other Hong Kong catalogues, even if the selection isn't quite as big (but get them all to compare prices). This one starts off with slinky Chinese-inspired/American-influenced embroidered-silk evening dresses and pants suits for prices up to $50; hand-smocked children's clothes for around $5 each; men's silk pajamas for around $13; rayon brocade dressing gowns for around $10; and men's silk shirts for around $5 and $10. The catalogue also shows beaded and petit point evening bags, jewelry, Omega, Rolex and Seiko watches, photographic equipment, transistor radios, lace, linen, hand-painted porcelain, ivory chess sets, furniture, original oil paintings, silk embroidery pictures, and hand-painted picture-wallpaper.

Swatow Weng Lee Co., P.O. Box 5972, Kowloon, Hong Kong
50-page brochure, free; air mail $1. Prices in $.

This fifty-year-old firm has just put out a new mail-order catalogue in which they say they will "strife further to elevate our strict standards of service and bring prolonged satisfaction like its been before to our clients always." The catalogue, which represents but a portion of their ability to delight, shows a fairly typical Hong Kong selection at typically Hong Kong low prices: rayon pajamas for men and women, $8; brocade robes and housecoats, around $20; Canton embroidered coats for $40. Also European-style needlepoint handbags at well below European prices (around $20); gold jewelry; ivory carvings; Chinese dolls; and other local gift-type things.

Handicrafts and Special Local Products

Union Handiwork Co., S.P.O. Box 8329, Kowloon, Hong Kong
Catalogue with some color, free; $2 air mail. Prices in $.

A good place to look for popular Hong Kong goods, as the handy catalogue has most popular exports illustrated. Lace and embroidered tablecloths, cotton sheets and pillowcases that can be monogramed, beaded handbags, woven-silk and embroidered hangings, dolls, snuff bottles, mah-jong and chess sets, jade flowers, brass trays and lamps, gold and enameled jewelry, porcelain plates and tableware sets in Oriental designs are all shown. And there is not only the usual selection of Chinese-inspired silk robes and nightwear for men and women and children, but also classic Western-styled clothes—dresses and pants suits for women in Swiss linen, or double-knit car coats and suits for men. The clothes can all be made to any measurements.

Welfare Handicrafts, Deck 1, 176 Samum Gallery, Ocean Terminal, Salisbury Road, Kowloon, Hong Kong
Leaflet, free.

All the handicrafts on sale through this nonprofit organization are made by handicapped or needy people, and besides seeing that all the money from sales goes back to the craftsmen, the organization also makes sure that a high standard of manufacture is kept up. On the leaflet, goods are listed and some are illustrated with line drawings, but prices are only given in response to specific requests. Things on sale include ivory chess sets; pewter jugs, dishes and cigarette boxes; brass dinner gongs and candlesticks; mother-of-pearl butter knives and pickle forks; desk sets; lingerie cases and toilet bags in Thai brocade or cotton; hand-embroidered cotton clothes for adults and children; hand-knitted ski sweaters; Chinese dolls; and a great deal more.

ICELAND

Icemart Mail Order Dept., P.O. Box 23, Keflavik International Airport, Iceland
48-page color brochure, free; 50 cents air mail. Prices in $. Food price list, free. Prices in $.

This airy, modern shop in the free-port area of Iceland's international airport is owned and run by several of the country's leading manufacturers, and sells their products as well as local foods such as canned caviar, smoked salmon and cheeses.

The brochure for mail order is one of the most delectable I have looked at, with a stunning collection of expensive-looking clothes that use traditional Icelandic designs and materials together with modern shapes. This year there are gorgeous maxi- and midi-skirts, sweaters, vests, long tunics, ponchos and slacks, knitted or woven in white lamb's wool, edged with bands or designs in subtle mauves, browns or black. The ponchos and maxi-skirts cost about $64, the sweaters about $40. There are long, fluffy black or white knitted coats made of long-haired Icelandic lamb's wool and then teased, at about $110; smart sheepskin coats (a brown coat for men, $319), and lots of other sheepskin—hats, bags, boots and muffs, and some cushions that at around $20 are almost half the price of the ones I have seen in New York. In addition to the clothes, the brochure shows Icelandic wool blankets in natural colors, three medieval-style chairs, handmade lava ceramics, a few souvenirs, and some silver jewelry: charms, witchcraft symbols on pendants, reproductions of ancient ornaments, filigree and modern pieces.

INDIA

Central Cottage Industries Emporium, Janpath, New Delhi 1, India
22-page color catalogue, $1.50.

A gorgeous, tempting catalogue of handicrafts from all over the country (oddly entitled "Paradise Shopping in Instant India") is put out by this main government emporium. The large, air-conditioned building houses twenty-six departments, including a shipping department, and a vast assortment of beautifully chosen goods—an ideal shop for anyone looking for something new and interesting. (Unfortunately, the catalogue is a general review with only approximate prices, so every item will have to be inquired about individually. In fact, you can skip the catalogue if you know what you want.)

For the house there are all sorts of rare and wonderful decorations: ashtrays, cigarette boxes; and although some of the metalwork has been seen around a lot, there are still plenty of things that haven't: hand-painted papier-mâché, ivory, alabaster, filigree silver. A fretted copper bowl cost $9, and a silver filigree bowl, $25, a small silver box studded with moonstones, $40; and a square marble plate inlaid with a regular pattern of flowers in semiprecious stones, $35. There is a department for lamps, hand-painted, ceramic or metal, with silk or cotton shades made to order.

I have described the fabrics in the Fabrics section, but there are also table linens and bedspreads, a white cotton bedspread from Jaipur, hand-blocked with a delicate design of little olive-green and pink flowering shrubs, $7 single size; a silk bedspread with orange stripes on hot pink costs $30, single size.

For actual wear, there is what the catalogue calls a "flamboyant color riot" (in American sizes) for evenings or lounging around the house. A pink tunic with bell sleeves, handsomely printed in mauve and black, costs up to $8; a raw-silk cocktail dress embroidered around the bodice and hem, about $40. For children, tunics and trousers in cotton or silk (among other things), and for men, some dazzlingly colorful (some more sober) raw- or printed-silk ties; foulards; cotton bush shirts for $6, and silk shirts, $12. Cotton dressing gowns cost from $7, and silk dressing gowns start at $20, going up to $60 for a rare brocade.

Tibetan Self Help Refugee Center, 65 Ghandi Road, Darjeeling, India
Catalogue, $1. Prices in $.

I do hope this catalogue is still around when you write for it. My copy looked a bit yellow and faded, as though it had been pulled out from underneath a pile of dusty and forgotten papers. This center was organized in 1959 to give work to the Tibetan refugees who came to India. The main specialty is carpets, and they can make carpets of any design, size and color from the wool of the same sheep that are used in Tibet and from natural dyes imported from Tibet. The rugs shown in the catalogue have angular-flower, bird-abstract and even dragon designs not often seen in the West. Unfortunately, the catalogue isn't in color, but the designs are striking. The rugs shown are all 3' by 6' and vary in price from $36 to $100. Apart from the carpets there is a heavy sweater, two rough wool jackets, fur hats (one a Tibetan soldier's hat), embroidered leather boots, all for extraordinarily low prices under $20. At the end of the catalogue is some metal at prices around $20—a nice brass soup stove, a copper coffeepot (it's called a kettle, but it's coffepot-shaped), and a copper kettle, all decorated. Tibetan dolls are also for sale, but they are not illustrated, and the Center says that it breeds rare and pure Tibetan Apso dogs. Orders can be booked in advance.

Handicrafts and Special Local Products

IRELAND

D. J. Cremin and Son, Kenmare, Co. Kerry, Ireland
Color leaflet, free. Prices in $.

A small collection of popular Irish products are illustrated in color in this leaflet: handwoven stoles, woolen capes, mohair rugs, tweed hats, hand-embroidered tablecloths, blackthorn walking sticks, blackthorn shillelaghs and Irish dolls. There is also Belleek china and Waterford crystal, but supplies of these are low, so there might be a long wait if you order Waterford or Belleek from here.

Emerald Crafts, Slaney Place, Enniscorthy, Co. Wexford, Ireland
6-page brochure, only partly illustrated, free. Prices in $.

A cottage shop, with a small brochure of Irish crafts, which in spite of being visited by tourists has steered clear of souvenirs in favor of genuine local products: rushwork baskets, wooden bowls, crystal, marble and pottery. Shangarry jugs, black with brown rims and white inside, cost $1 to $5, and a pottery coffee set, freely hand-painted with flowers and fruit, costs $24.

Donegal tweeds, still woven by hill farmers, although centrally designed, cost about $4.50 a yard. In addition to crocheted blouses, mohair stoles and cashmere sweaters ($28 to $33), there are heavy, creamy Aran sweaters for only $33 (in New York they cost $50) and unusual dark-brown sweaters in oiled, undyed wool from black sheep.

James Hanna Workshop, 11 Greenwell Place, Newtownards, Co. Down, Northern Ireland
Brochure, 35 cents; $1 air mail.

A small company that makes really lovely small things in copper by hand. My favorites are some Georgian "measures" (jugs of different sizes) and some very plain, workmanlike tinker jars, a kettle, and a tea "drawer" (not quite sure what that is, it looks like a covered jug), all made by a tinker in the traditional way. All of these things are useful and fit very well with the back-to-the-earth clay and wood kitchenware that is popular now. The firm also makes reproduction arms and armor in copper and copper figurines.

H. Johnson Ltd., 11 Wicklow Street, Dublin, Ireland
Price list, free. Prices in $.

Walkers and lovers of Ireland might want an Irish Blackthorn walking stick or shillelagh (the "traditional weapon"). H. Johnson Ltd. has been making them since 1872 from the hard wood of the slow-growing blackthorn trees and bushes that cover the Irish hills. The wood can only be cut during a few weeks in mid-winter, and it is then seasoned for two years before being straightened, sanded and polished. The prices of the walking sticks vary from $7 to $15, according to "the regularity and number of thorns, shapeliness of the knob handle, taper, balance, and general character." Only one or two in every thousand sticks are nearly perfect. If you want one of the nearly perfect ones, they cost $25 to $50 each.

Fergus O'Farrell Ltd., 60-63 Dawson Street, Dublin 2, Ireland
32-page catalogue.

Gifts, often with an Irish connection, are designed and made in the Fergus O'Farrell workshops. There are 12" copper figures from Irish mythology, reproductions of Celtic crosses, wooden chess sets (Irish v. Danes), and silver and copper jewelry with Celtic designs. Also wooden things for the house, such as eggcups and ashtrays, which have no connection with Ireland beyond being made there.

Mairtin Standun, Spiddal, Co. Galway, Ireland
Leaflets, free. Prices in $.

Maire Standun writes chatty letters saying that the Irish Tourist and Export Board will vouchsafe the excellence of her Aran sweaters. Apparently the knitters who purl and knit away by the fire through the long winter nights are not allowed to finish the sweaters—that is done by eight sewing experts, who put the pieces together and add the buttons. Besides sweaters, the shop stocks seven kinds of knitted Aran hats for adults and children from a funny leprechaun cap to a workman-like thatcher's hat, $5.

Other clothes not illustrated include featherweight wool blouses and dresses, kilts ($11), cashmere sweaters, ties, crocheted shawls and gloves. Various other handmade objects, such as tweed table mats and knitted tea cozies, are on sale, and there are Irish souvenirs as well as an illustrated leaflet of Foxford tartan travel rugs.

Sales Director, Switzers Department Store, 92 Grafton Street, Dublin 2, Ireland
Brochure planned, 50 cents.

Switzers let their previous catalogue go out of print, and the new one is not yet ready. But they tell me that it will cover the "most important items of Irish merchandise," namely china, Waterford crystal and other glassware, Irish linens, Irish tweed, Royal Irish silver, Celtic jewelry, clothes for children and adults, and Irish arts and crafts.

ITALY

Al Pellegrino Cattolico, Via di Porta Angelica 83, Rome, Italy

No catalogue, but this shop has lots of mail-order customers for religious articles, any of which can be blessed by the Pope. Rosaries of wood, crystal or mother-of-pearl set in metal cost from 25 cents to $4; set in silver they cost $5 -$25. Rosaries with semiprecious stones: lapis lazuli, coral, amethyst, topaz etc., set in silver, $30 – $135; stones set in 18-carat gold, $150 – $350. Also medals and chains in metal, silver, gold; crosses, pictures, statues and Papal Blessings.

KENYA

Cottage Industries, P.O. Box 45009, Nairobi, Kenya
Catalogue planned, $1.

Because of reorganization, Cottage Industries is now selling the clothes described in the first edition under the Home Industries Center. These are gorgeous cotton dresses based on traditional African styles and are, or at least were, very inexpensive. Cottage Industries is planning a catalogue that will list five to six hundred handicrafts made in Kenya.

E. Fioravanti and Co. (Kenya) Ltd., P.O. Box 84867, Mombasa, Kenya
22-page brochure, $2.50. Prices in $.

This export brochure shows reproductions of antique African sculptures and modern Westernized African-style sculptures rather indiscriminately mixed together. The brochure says that Fioravanti borrows works from museums and private collectors to copy them, and does research into the background of these pieces; a little of the research is given in the price list. Most of the pieces cost between $4 and $25, but there are some large wall panels of what they call modern (and I call Westernized) warrior scenes that can be made into doors, and

Handicrafts and Special Local Products

cost $215 each, as does an unusual set of Congolese carved coffee table and chairs. Hand-embroidered leather also sold.

Kuja Crafts, Ltd., Hotel Intercontinental, Sgt. Ellis Avenue/Uhuru Highway, P.O. Box 49176, Nairobi, Kenya.
Price list, free. Prices in $.

A good selection of things from Kenya, but no pictures. Besides the usual game trophies, skins and ivories, there are things I haven't seen listed anywhere else: batik and tie-dyed fabrics, $5 (each piece is different); two yards of Kitenge material, $10; beaded belts and necklaces, $5 each; beaded hats for ladies, $11; for men, $13; dressed dolls, $5; African decorated walking sticks, $15; musical instruments from different tribes, $32; zebra-skin drums up to $25. Also zebra belts.

LEBANON

Antranig S. Chiluirian, P.O. Box 11–1129, Beirut, Lebanon
Catalogue, $1. Prices in $.

Illustrated in this catalogue are some handsome, rough cowhide handbags made in this firm's own leather workshop. At under $10 they are tempting, although, as the catalogue is not in color, buying one will be a bit of a gamble. Other handmade things illustrated include dolls in local costumes, hassocks, camel stools, embroidered slippers, boxes and tables inlaid with mother-of-pearl, ornamental, *very* ornamental, brass lamps and candlesticks, and silver jewelry which, besides standard designs, can be made to customers' own designs. Prices are all very low wholesale prices, and "sample" or "trial" orders, as small orders are called, are subject to an additional handling charge.

MEXICO

Vicky, Popular Arts and Embroideries, Apartado 1, Avenida de las Americas S/N, Pátzcuaro, Michoacán, Mexico
Price lists for clothes, furniture and rugs, 25 cents. Prices in $.

An American living in Mexico has a shop which sells three kinds of goods that are popular with visitors to Mexico. Unfortunately the lists Mr. Gray sends out for mail order don't illustrate or describe the goods, although he hopes to have an illustrated list soon. However, he can supply photographs, for which he charges.

One list is for colorful Mexican embroidery on handwoven fabric: shirts, blouses, robes and dresses of all sorts, most of them for under $15; bags, aprons, potholders and place mats for under $5. Another list is for Spanish colonial-style furniture made out of Brazilian walnut (this takes about three months to make, as it is made to order). There are screens, tables, writing desks, chairs, bedroom furniture (including headboards), frames for paintings or mirrors, and also cane furniture in modern colonial style. Prices are very low and range from $40 for a gossip chair ("low, comfy") to $308 for a 9'10"-long dining table that seats twelve (dining chairs with leather seats and ornamental nails cost $40 each). The final list is for hand-braided and handsewn Henequen rugs in various designs, colors and sizes of your choice. These cost $18 per square meter (1 sq. m. = 1.2 sq. yds.).

NEPAL

Nepal Craft Emporium, G.P.O. Box 1206, Kathmandu, Nepal
Catalogue, $2. Prices in $.

A homemade-looking catalogue carries snapshots of the exotic little gold-gilt things studded with fake stones that the Nepal Craft Emporium exports. Elaborate jewelry. Tibetan tea kettles, holy-water jars, ceremonial pipes and miniature dragons for people who want something very unusual. For others there are more practical cigarette boxes, matchboxes and ashtrays. Prices are low; almost everything is under $10.

PHILIPPINES

Tesoro's International Inc., 1353 A. Mabini Ermita, Manila, Philippines D-406
Catalogue with some color, $2. Prices in $.

The catalogue put out by this chain of Manila stores shows all the Philippine products beloved of tourists. Carved monkeypod woodwork including such fantasies as a lazy Susan in the shape of a huge rose, laminated bowls of oyster shells and wood, embroidered dresses, shirts and tablecloths, colorful thonged slippers and handbags, Tiffany-style lampshades, all sorts of straw and cotton place mats, silver filigree jewelry and bone-inlaid furniture. All at very low prices. The hitch is that there is a whopping great $50 surcharge on orders worth less than $1,000, so this is another case where a group of friends should buy together to split the surcharge.

POLAND

Andrzey Szczepka, Pulawska 132/12, 02–715 Warsaw 13, Poland
Price list, 3 International Reply Coupons. Prices in $.

Andrzey Szczepka sells collector's dolls and carved wood spoons, mugs, and salt and pepper boxes. "All items are handmade by Polish Folk Artists and they are very genuine," he says. The dolls sound nice. They are in Bulgarian, Polish or Russian national costume, or Polish historical costume at various prices, all under $10, including air-mail postage. Russian nesting dolls and rugs for dollhouses are also for sale.

SCOTLAND

Kinloch Anderson and Sons Ltd., 14/16 George Street, Edinburgh 2, Scotland ☺☺
20-page Scottish gift book, free. Prices in $.

This catalogue shows basically the same sorts of things as the Tartan Gift Shops, but not everything is repeated. Anderson's has horn spoons and necklaces around $7 each, deerskin bags, reproductions of seventeenth-century maps, $5, and place mats with reproductions of old prints of Scottish views, $5 each. And instead of illustrating tartan clothes, Anderson's has a special brochure for its made-to-measure skirt service showing nine different styles that can be made up, tweed and tartan samples on request.

Handicrafts and Special Local Products

R. G. Lawrie Ltd., 38 Renfield Street, Glasgow C 2, Scotland ♛

16-page "Highland Dress" color catalogue, free. Prices in $.
Handwrought-silver brochure, free.

There seem to be almost as many shops catering to exiled Scotsmen as to nostalgic Irishmen. R. G. Lawrie (By Appointment to Her Majesty the Queen, bagpipe maker) says they have a worldwide reputation as authorities on Highland dress, and put out an extremely informative catalogue with descriptions of correct Highland dress for both evening and outdoor wear, as well as pipe-band uniforms. The catalogue finishes with a list of their most frequently requested books dealing with "things Scottish": clans, tartans, songs, dances and food.

A catalogue for handwrought silver has traditional Celtic jewelry and some exclusive new adaptations of old silver: necklaces, spoons and forks.

Paisley Limited, 72–96 Jamaica Street, Glasgow C 1, Scotland

16-page brochure, free. Prices in $.

This catalogue starts with authentic Highland dress and ends, apologizing, with incorrect Highland dress. The incorrect Highland dress consists of four different styles of tartan skirts that can be made to measure (around $22 each), sweaters to match with the chosen tartan, tartan slacks, dressing gown, car coat and Viyella shirts (from $10.50). Prices generally lower than Tartan Gift Shops (below) and Kinloch Anderson.

Tartan Gift Shops, 96 & 96a Princes Street, Edinburgh 2, Scotland

28-page catalogue, free; 75 cents air mail.
Color brochure, free. 75 cents air mail.

Not only kilts, but all sorts of women's clothes are made in tartan and illustrated in this brochure—hostess skirts, of course (about $30 each), capes, vests, pants suits with sweaters to match. Over three hundred tartan cloths are sold by the yard.

14
Kinloch Anderson and Sons Ltd Child's party or wedding kilt. Price according to size.
photo Tony Cleal

15
Tartan Gift Shops Saxony cape available in most tartans. $50. Surface postage $3.60.

16
Trade Exchange (Ceylon) Ltd. Batik wall hanging of a lion and of entwined male and female cobras, symbolizing ferocity and vengeance. Black, yellow, ocher and green. About $12, including air-mail postage.

17
Bangkok Dolls Completely handmade decorative dolls representing characters in Thai classic dance-drama. The White Monkey General and the Black Monkey General (10" high), $15.50 each.

Handicrafts and Special Local Products

SPAIN

Pascual Iniguez Montoya, Hnos-Quintero 3, Albacete, Spain
Color leaflet, free.

This manufacturer of *botas* (wine bags) says that although they welcome sample orders so long as they are accompanied by a check, they normally export in quantities of at least fifty. The *botas* are the traditional Spanish containers for carrying wine into the countryside (you hold one in the air and squirt the wine into your mouth so several people can drink without glasses). The *botas* come either in nice, plain, rough skin at about $2 each, or shiny skin with Spanish or sporting scenes painted in color. (At no extra cost the Montoya painters can reproduce any pictures you submit "referring to your own business, location, etc."). As the firm says: "Latex lined wine bags are suitable to hold not only wine but all kinds of drinks, juices, and even milk, never lending a strange taste to the contents. They are soft, light, air tight for which they give an unvaluable [*sic*] service to carry drinks in out-of-doors life and sports, games, picnics, camping, etc."

SRI LANKA

Trade Exchange (Ceylon) Ltd., 72 Chatham Street, Colombo, Sri Lanka
Catalogue and fabric samples, $10 (bank draft only).

In exchange for a $10 bank draft made out to Trade Exchange (Ceylon) Ltd., you will get an assortment of line drawings, mimeographed lists and fabric samples trying to convey an impression of the batik cotton fabrics, clothes and hangings produced by Lak Looms. The batik fabric is sold by the yard for about $4 and is decorated with beautiful and subtle color combinations. Fabric is also sold made up in cushion covers, scarfs, bags, saris, all for under $4, and clothes such as bell-bottom or hipster trousers, party dresses, fully lined capes, skirts and shirts are around $12 or under. The batik wall hangings are pretty inexpensive, too. I was sent a photograph of a hanging in black, red, green, purple, brown, orange and yellow, annotated thus: "Every year when the Esala moon is up in August the Kandy Perahera takes place with the Sacred Tooth Relic of Lord Buddha being taken on the back of the temple elephant in procession with dancers and torch bearers and Kandyan Chiefs in attendance." This hanging costs $2, others cost even less.

SWITZERLAND

Berner and Co., P.O. Box 8023, Zurich, Switzerland
Leaflet, free. Prices in $.

Very old clocks are reproduced by this firm but are not "intended for those of us who desire above all to have the exact time of a chronometer. We leave them to the modern industrial mass products. But for those people who would like to make their homes more decorative and friendly, who know how to appreciate the work and skill of the artisans, and who, at the same time, find pleasure in the inventiveness of our forefathers." The Wheel Clock is a wooden and iron reproduction of one of the first mechanical clocks, and there are also Gothic, Renaissance and Baroque clocks made of iron with bronze or painted faces. These clocks, handmade in a Swiss Alpine village, cost between $40 and just over $100. Clocks treated to look "amazingly old" cost between $150 and $250.

Schweizer-Heimatwerk, Rudolf-Brun-Brücke, 8023 Zurich, Switzerland

An official shop for carefully chosen Swiss handicrafts, Schweizer-Heimatwerk has no catalogue. They do have beautifully made goods, however, so write to them if you have something in mind, otherwise here is a list of a few of the many things they stock: cowbells on leather straps, decorated with brass ornaments and colorful wool trimming; gold, red, blue or silver metal Christmas-tree balls that play "Silent Night"; a collection of eighteen different rocks or minerals from Switzerland. Also hand-painted music boxes playing folk music; regional dolls and wooden hand-carved cheese or cake boards.

THAILAND

Bangkok Dolls, 85 Rajatapan Lane, Makkasan, Bangkok, Thailand
Color brochure, $1. Prices in $.

In the distant past, Thai ladies amused themselves making decorative dolls dressed in classic Thai costumes. In 1957 Mrs. Chandavimol, the wife of a Thai government official, revived the world-famous but degenerating craft and started a small business making really beautiful handmade dolls in classic costumes copied from museum displays. Her most sumptuous dolls represent characters from Thai dance-dramas and are dressed in splendid, glittering costumes, but there are also dolls dressed in working clothes of different Thai regions, with handwoven fabrics and baskets made by the people who made the originals. And there is a group of "cuddly" dolls, also in Thai costumes—the only dolls actually meant for children. Dolls are 8" to 13" high and cost between $7 and $18 each.

T. Seng and Son, 511/9-10 Phetchaburi Road, Bangkok, 4, Thailand
Color leaflet, free. Prices in $.

A small assortment of popular Thai goods is listed: princess rings at prices between $30 and $50; rings set with birthstones; gold and silver charms; bronze goblets and flatware sets; Thai dolls for under $10; and Thai silks—twelve solid colors are illustrated, $6 per yard. Recommended by a reader, Ane Denmark, who says she has had very satisfactory dealings with T. Seng.

TUNISIA

Office National de l'Artisanat, Ministère des Affaires Economiques, Den Den, Tunisia.
68-page color catalogue, Vol. I, "Tapis" (Rugs), $4.50.
100-page catalogue, Vol. II, "Divers" (Miscellaneous), $1.50.

The government handicrafts office trains craftsmen, controls quality and sees to it that Tunisian crafts while remaining true to the "purity of their original inspiration" don't stagnate but are allowed to develop freely. Consequently, the crafts shown in the beautifully produced catalogue are a mixture of old and new. Marvelous hammered copper pots and plates, painted wooden chests, pottery, vases, silver jewelry, regional embroidery and lace, and a palatial bird cage all look very traditional, while gold-tooled leather boxes, wrought-iron barbeque sets, hand-painted silk cushions, ceramic lamps, and dolls dressed in Tunisian wedding dresses look definitely modern. However, in spite of the glossiness of the catalogue, no prices or details are given, so determined shoppers must write, preferably in French, and be prepared to receive an answer in French.

Handicrafts and Special Local Products

WALES

Cadwyn y Cwch Gwenyn, Llangadog, Dyfed, Wales
Leaflet, 25 cents.

Occasionally this firm, dedicated to stimulating the Welsh craft industry, will put out a bilingual sheet illustrating some of the things they can sell by mail; for instance, embossed leather bags, decorative candles, handmade soft toys, baby shawls, fishermen's smocks in wool (about $25), or a traditional three-legged milking stool (about $10). The leaflets I looked at were amateurish and not very easy to buy from, but Ffred Ffransis says: "We will guarantee to answer individually all enquiries, and send relevant leaflets and price lists. The enquiree should, therefore, indicate which range of products he is interested in, and a money order for 25 cents will cover all our costs."

Brian and Cherie Smazlen, Llanlleban Farm, Hermon, Glogue, Pembrokeshire, Wales
Brochure, 30 cents; 75 cents air mail. Color photograph of the spoons, 60 cents.

A husband and wife make carved Welsh spoons (the Smazlens are really farmers, but say: "As the farm is less than forty acres, we make ends meet with woodwork squeezed in between the farming chores"). Some spoons are round and rough cawl spoons ("cawl" is a Welsh stew) that cost about $2.50 each, others are very pretty love spoons based on the spoons that traditionally young Welsh men gave their sweethearts. Modern versions have designs of hearts and crosses (the original spoons might also have symbols that showed where the maker lived or his trade), and are made from light woods: elm, lime or sycamore. They are rubbed with oil for use in the kitchen but are really well worth hanging on the wall as decorations—several together would look lovely. Spoons are up to 24" long, and cost as much as $25.

Workshop, Lower Town, Fishguard, Pembrokeshire SA63 9LY, Wales
Leaflet, 25 cents; 50 cents air mail. October to March only.

A crafts shop which tries to sell the best quality crafts made by men and women working in Wales. The leaflet shows wooden bowls and bottles, leather bags and belts, silver rings and cuff links, one or two cloth toys and the Glyn-y-Mel natural moisturizing cream packed in hand-thrown, creamy-colored pottery bottles (and, incidentally, sold at Neiman-Marcus in America).

Llyswen Welsh Craft Center, Llyswen, Brecon, Wales
Catalogue, $2 (refundable). Prices in $.

An inexpensive collection of clothes and bedspreads made from handwoven Welsh tapestry and flannel, also those fabrics by the yard. Tapestry is heavier than flannel and is suitable for coats; 56" wide tapestry costs $8 per yard, flannel is lighter and 54" wide flannel costs $4.50 per yard. The basic traditional design of the fabrics is a small honeycomb square woven into wool of another color, but there are all sorts of variations on that pattern, and different color combinations, too: rich new purples and pinks, or blues and greens, or natural-looking browns and seaweedy colors. Tapestry bedspreads cost $34 for single size; $39 for double; $44 for larger than double (measurements not given). Some of the clothes are bargains: tapestry coats for women, $47; flannel skirts, $20; hooded anoraks in tapestry lined throughout in rainproof nylon, $37; capes for children, $21 and up. The center also sells tapestry purses, Welsh socks, tea cozies, sheepskin goods, Welsh dolls and souvenirs.

Ron Scarpello, Ystumllyn, Criccieth, Sir Gaernarfor, Wales
Leaflet, 50 cents. Photographs, 25 cents each. Prices in $.

Ron Scarpello makes, by hand, simple and handsome cigarette boxes, ashtrays, backgammon sets and chess sets from local slate and marble. The leaflet illustrates only one chess set but gives prices for everything (from about $12 for a cigarette box to $156 for a backgammon-cum-chess set). You can ask for photographs of anything you are interested in.

Welsh Cottage Craft Shops, Orders by Post Dept., 516 Mumbles Road, Oystermouth, Swansea, Wales
Color catalogue, $1.

Skirts, dresses, capes and coats are illustrated in this catalogue, most of them in pure-wool Welsh tapestry with variations of the traditional Welsh honeycomb design. Some of the styles can be made in tweed or flannel, and some can be made in any size to measure. Tapestry capes cost about $50 each, and long-sleeved blouses in colored flannel, about $20 each, made to measure.

12 Hobbies

Hobbies

BATIK, CANDLEMAKING AND TIE-DYEING

Candle Makers Supplies, 4 Beaconsfield Terrace Road, London W. 14, England
List of supplies for batik, candlemaking, and tie-dyeing, 50 cents.

Here you can get a beginner's candlemaking kit, which contains acid, dyes, wicks, 5 lbs. of paraffin wax and an instruction booklet, for about $7, including postage. Or if you want to buy things separately, paraffin wax is about 22 cents a pound; beeswax about $1.65 a pound; wicks in all sizes; and perfumes for the candles in pine, lilac, lavender, etc. There is a helpful booklet for 25 cents, *Introduction to the Art of Candle Making*, which, among other things, tells you what to do about all the things that might go wrong.

Another beginner's kit is "Introductory Batik," $12, including postage. A little booklet, *Introduction to Batik*, describes batik as "an old Javanese method of fabric printing." You paint designs on your fabric with melted wax and then dye the fabric. The parts covered by the wax (which is later removed) don't take the dye but keep the original fabric color. You can do it on almost any kind of material and use the results for roller blinds, lampshades, dresses, scarves, wall hangings, etc.

There is no beginner's kit for tie-dyeing, but books and plenty of supplies are available, including the hard-to-get and highly-thought-of French Sennelier silk dyes.

BRASS RUBBING

Phillips and Page, 50 Kensington Church Street, London W.8, England
Price list, 10 cents.

Rather like shading or drawing over a penny under paper, taking "rubbings" from medieval monumental brasses and gravestones has become a popular pastime in England. (Schoolchildren even do it with manhole covers, the result is often a surprisingly decorative design.) Anyone thinking of rubbing brasses in European churches, gravestones in New England churchyards, or even manhole covers on city sidewalks, should write to Phillips and Page first, probably the only shop in the world to specialize in equipment and books for these activities. They have specially made sticks and cakes of "heelball" in colors as well as gold, bronze and silver. Lots of different kinds of paper in all the right sizes and colors, special crayons, erasers, and other useful equipment. Also books about every aspect of the subject, where and how to do it for beginners; history and documentation for addicts.

BUTTERFLIES

Worldwide Butterflies, Over Compton, Sherborne, Dorset, England
Color leaflet, 65 cents. Spring, winter, plus occasional lists.

Worldwide Butterflies sends live and dead specimens to collectors and schools all over the world, and it is clear that the firm is run by enthusiasts. The wonderfully detailed catalogue not only lists the stock and equipment but is full of extra advice and information on how everything should be cared for and used. The livestock includes stick insects, praying mantises, and eighty-eight kinds of butterflies for breeding. You can get the necessary import permit for live specimens from the Animal Health Division, U.S. Agricultural Research Service, Hyattsville, Md. 20782.

Worldwide Butterflies has a wide variety of entomological

1
Phillips and Page Rubbings taken from English manhole covers.

2
Worldwide Butterflies Danaus Plexippus (Monarch Butterfly), one of the many species bred each summer.

3
Priscilla Lobley Flower Kits Giant poppies made up. Two versions of this kit are available, one in red, orange and pink, the other in blue and green. Just over $6 each.

equipment: breeding cages, boxes, cabinets and nets, books, and various kinds of display cages with or without exotic butterflies. In the summer the Lepidopterists Rearing Outfit, "a complete outfit for the keen beginner," is on sale for about $12. And for those who like to go all the way with their hobbies, there are butterfly dishcloths, place mats, table napkins, wall charts, jewelry and carrier bags.

BUTTONS, BELTS AND BUCKLES

Deane and Adams, 10 Summers Row, London N.12, England
Catalogue, free. Prices in $.

"Stamp out the buckle" is the motto of this firm, which manufactures brass Tiffany-style buckles and sells them individually and in wholesale quantities. Write to Deane and

Adams if you want several buckles (as I write, buckles cost $5 including surface postage if you order twelve or more). But if you want fewer than twelve, prices are higher, so you might as well buy from an American source (see "Leather," Hobbies section in *The Catalogue of American Catalogues*). The buckles can also be made in sterling silver, or a buckle die can be made from your own design for about $1,000.

Paris House, 41 South Molton Street, London W1Y 2HB, England
Jewelry, belt and button catalogue, $2.50; $5 air mail. January and July.

Twists and twirls of beads and filigree, leather roses, and braided daisies—all on buttons. This shop is a prize for an ambitious home dressmaker or anyone who likes to change buttons and belts on store-bought clothes for more dressy ones. The buttons are handmade on shank fittings, many available with holes and almost all with screw-on detachable fittings. Each season the catalogue has a page or two of classic shapes and then there are pages and pages of the most exotic and ornate buttons—pleated and gathered, hand-stitched in fabric, leather braid or cord, or made of beads or metal. They can be made in any color, and many can be made in the customer's own fabric.

Classic belts can be made in any width, but there are also very unusual pleated, twisted, fringed belts made out of soft suede or kid, and tied instead of buckled; beaded rouleau tie belts made in gold or silver lamé; grosgrain or ottoman twisted belts tasseled with beads.

The jewelry is heavy and frankly fake, in keeping with the new English extravagance in dress. For about $33 there are "chatelaines"—cascades of chains and beads that hook on the belt of an evening dress; gold or silver neckties with bead tassels that can be used as hair ornaments; chokers of pleated silver and gold lamé with interwoven pearls, $22.

CHESS

Henke Schachspiele, P.O. Box 408, D-353 Warburg, Germany
Color catalogue, free.

A magnificent collection of about sixty different sets of chessmen, in various kinds of woods, metals or buffalo horn, bone or porcelain. Styles range from primitive hand-painted sets in bright colors through hand-carved wooden sets in classic or modern shapes to "Ming Dynasty" Chinese-style sets. There are also travel sets, magnetic sets, chess tables, chess boards and a few other games such as mah-jong, backgammon and roulette. There are sets in all price ranges, and mostly lower than they would be for similar sets if available in America, but there is a minimum order of $150.

CLOCKMAKING

Selva Technik, P.O. Box 1260, D-7220 Schwenningen, Germany
Color catalogue, $1; $2 air mail.

This now large and thriving firm was started almost by chance by Karl Christian Schlenker, the great-grandson of a traveling clockmaker. Herr Schlenker, who lives in "the clock town" on the eastern edge of the Black Forest, used to be asked so often by friends in other towns to send clock parts for replacements that he realized there was a need for a shop that would stock all the different parts from different manufacturers. From a small brochure a big catalogue has developed, and also a keen following of amateur clockmakers who sometimes want to build the kind of unusual and individual clocks that clock factories no longer find it economical to produce. For beginners, however, there are simple kits, such as colorful plastic clock kits for children, and "Bim-Bam gongs" to be installed instead of doorbells because they make a more agreeable noise. So altogether, this is an excellent catalogue, with a huge supply of tools and supplies for both repairing old clocks and for making new ones, from the latest digital clocks to the most fanciful antique-styled clocks.

CRAFTS

Hobby Horse Ltd., 15–17 Langton Street, London S.W.10, England
Catalogue, 65 cents; $1.40 air mail.

The Hobby Horse was started by a husband and wife who found it impossible to find good-enough-quality craft materials, so they started importing their own. Anyone working on hobbies at home will find the clear little catalogue very useful, because although only the basics for each activity are listed, they are always the best. Beads are a specialty—many of them are made for Hobby Horse—and there are supplies for macramé, jewelry making, leatherwork, modeling, artificial flower making, painting on wood (plain eggcups, candlesticks, boxes, etc., provided), mobile making, cold enameling, plasticraft (making things out of clear plastic) and Christmas decorations. The excellent French Sennelier dyes for batik are stocked, and vibrant Danish EM/ES dyes for batik and fabric painting. They also carry English Rowney and Reeves paints. Plenty of good and very inexpensive instruction booklets are stocked.

FLOWER ARRANGING

Ikebana International, CPO Box 1262, Tokyo, Japan
Explanatory leaflet, free.

A nonprofit international organization for people interested in *ikebana* (Japanese flower arranging) with chapters all over the world. If you are interested in joining, write to the head office and find out whether there is a chapter near you. If there is, you can join, whether you are a beginner or more experienced.

Ikebana International offers three different publications to members. The magazine published in English provides features on flower arranging in color, along with articles on other cultural aspects of Japan. The News Sheet constitutes a link between the head office and the world-wide membership. The Hana Kagami is an illustrated, step-by-step flower lesson provided by headmasters of the leading flower schools. A year's Regular Chapter Membership costs around $10. Each chapter varies in its activities, but most have flower-arranging classes, demonstrations and study groups. People who do not live near a chapter can become Members At Large for around $10 and pay their yearly dues directly to the head office in Tokyo, Japan.

The Ohara School, 7–14 Minamiaoyama and 5-Chome, Minato-Ku, Tokyo, Japan
Price list, free. Prices in $.

The Ohara School, whose flower-arranging style is more traditional than Sango's (below), sells a helpful-sounding book, *Creation with Flowers*, by Houn Ohara (about $13 including sea postage). It covers fundamental styles, color-scheme arrangements, nonrealistic arrangements, tone arrangements and small flower arrangements. For about $2.95 per set, including postage, there are twenty cards, in color, of arrangements in the Moribana style or the Heikas style by the same author. And in slides, "Ikebana for Beginners" and "Elementary Ikebana," both with step-by-step explanations. Also, an Ohara Study Program is available as a quarterly magazine, about $1.75 per copy. Contents include elementary course and middle course, essays, articles about Japanese traditional art, and a section described as "Things Japanese."

Sango Inc., c/o Sogetsukai, 2—21, 7-Chome Akasaka, Minato-Ku, Tokyo, Japan
8-page color brochure, free.

Sogetsu is the most modern of the leading *Ikebana* schools and through them you can buy everything you need for Japanese flower arranging (or plain flower arranging). A wonderful selection of beautifully simple and unusually shaped containers in restrained colors: black, white, mustard, brick, black and gold. Some expensive lacquerware—a set of five containers that can be piled on top of one another costs $55; also "scissors," which are actually special little shears. Over thirty shapes and sizes in "needlepoint" metal flower holders, and plenty of illustrated, instructional books and magazines in both Japanese and English. Also notebooks, calendars and postcards decorated with photographs or arrangements.

FLOWERS—PAPER

Yvonne Docktree, 28 Mile House Lane, St. Albans, Hertfordshire, England
Illustrated brochure, free.

Yvonne Docktree sells a kit ($2.25 surface, $4 air mail) which she designed herself for making five bright and decorative tissue-paper flowers. You can choose between gold, flame, pink, scarlet, turquoise, violet or autumn tints. When you finish the tissue paper and stems provided, you can buy more from her or anyone else, and go on using the instructions and patterns. I made two flowers quite easily with my six- and eight-year-old daughters (they did the cutting and I did the trickier bits).

Priscilla Lobley Flower Kits, 72 South Ealing Road, London W.5, England
Leaflet, 50 cents.

Very refined kits for making lifelike paper flowers to decorate the house: Oriental poppies, mixed roses, and giant sunflowers. The kits have been tested on all ages from "teenagers to grannies," and although some are for beginners, none are for children. Complete with instructions and everything needed except scissors, each kit costs just over $6, including postage. *Flower Making*, a book by Priscilla Lobley, is also on sale.

GARDENING

An importation permit is not needed for bulbs or seeds, but it is needed for plants, and should be obtained before plants are ordered. There is no charge. The Permit Section, Plant Importations Branch, U.S. Department of Agriculture, 209 River Street, Hoboken, N.J. 07030, gives out permits and has a circular with information on the details you should give when applying. Ask for "Suggestions to Applicants for Permits to Import Plant Propagating Material under Quarantine No 37."

GARDENING—BULBS

C. A. Cruickshank Ltd., The Garden Guild, 1015 Mount Pleasant Road, Toronto, Ontario M4P 2 M1, Canada
Catalogue, free.

This fifty-year-old firm specializes in bulbs, having a large stock of its own as well as being the Canadian representative of the Dutch firm of Van Tubergen, which is listed separately below They also have a very large selection of their own plants, seeds and gardening accessories. Theirs is a large and comprehensive catalogue with a particularly large range of seeds. Cruickshank also sells a number of items not easily

4
Tulipshow Frans Roozen A view of the nursery and show garden, where a thousand varieties of spring flowers can be seen from April 10 to May 15.

5
Thompson and Morgan Ltd Seed and bulb catalogue cover.

available in the United States, including English gardening tools and a portable polyethylene greenhouse, which seemed an excellent, reasonably priced aid for gardeners who can't think of building a real, old-fashioned version.

Dutch Gardens, Inc., P.O. Box 30, Lisse, Holland
Catalogue, free. Prices in $.

This firm clearly does a lot of business with the United States and their catalogue concentrates on the bulbs that are the most popular in America—tulips, daffodils, crocuses, etc. Their prices are somewhat lower than many of their competitors', but their choice is more limited. As with other Dutch firms, they seem very well organized, and their bulbs are inspected both in Holland and here.

J. Heemskerk, c/o P. Van Deursen, P.O. Box 60, Sassenheim, Holland
Color catalogue, free.

Neat little catalogues with lots of illustrations and descriptions of daffodils, narcissi, tulips (eighty-eight varieties, including wild tulips and parrot tulips, etc.), hyacinths, crocuses, lilies, anemones, Dutch irises, and miscellaneous Dutch bulbs. And for $53, including delivery, you can buy a "complete garden collection"—500 bulbs in 25 named varieties with a group to flower in each month from February to June. Half the quantity can also be bought.

Schiphol Airport, Tax-Free Shopping Center, Amsterdam, Holland
Leaflet, free. Prices in $.

Not as interesting for serious gardeners as the other bulb catalogues but good for people who like simple decisions, the Schiphol Airport leaflet includes just a few basic bulbs that come in lots of 50 or 100: daffodils, hyacinths, narcissi and tulips. Prices are $17–$23, including postage.

Tulipshow Frans Roozen, Vogelenzang, Holland
24-page color catalogue, free. Prices in $.

This catalogue is not as convenient as Heemskerk's because the illustrations are larger but fewer, and the plants are only listed and not described. It includes varieties, however, that I haven't seen listed anywhere else, and there are gift selections for sale at $8 and up. Each variety is separately packed, with full gardening directions in each parcel. Bulbs are shipped for planting time in September and early October only.

Van Tubergen, Koninginneweg 86, Haarlem, Holland
Catalogue, 30 cents.

Van Tubergen offers one of the most detailed and extensive Dutch catalogues and clearly does a great deal of trade with England, since there is a special list with English prices. It may be a little difficult to compare these with the Dutch prices elsewhere, but the difference between firms is never great and this catalogue ought to be of particular interest to those wanting a really broad choice of tulips and all other related flowers. There is even a section charmingly titled "Bulbs for the Wild Garden" listing all sorts of flowers, some from southern Europe, that I've not seen elsewhere.

J. B. Wijs & Zoon, Singel 508–510, Amsterdam, Holland
Brochure, free.

Another source of popular bulbs from Holland. Like Dutch Garden, it concentrates on basics but offers mostly large selections, such as a hundred tulips in ten different varieties. A good choice for beginners or as presents.

GARDENING—PLANTS

Alpengrow Gardens, Micaud & Co., 13328 King George Highway, Surrey, B.C. V3T 2T6, Canada
32-page price list, 25 cents.

Alpengrow has specialized in Alpines, flowering shrubs and dwarf conifers for many years, and the catalogue lists a number of rare plants unavailable elsewhere. Their slow-growing conifers are, they feel, their most interesting offering. Nearly everything in their catalogue can be imported to the United States, though special permits are required for a few varieties. Most of the plants listed cost about $1 each.

Anderson's Rose Nurseries, Cults, Aberdeen AB1 9QT, Scotland
62-page color catalogue, free. Prices in $.

Anderson's does a thriving business with American and Canadian customers and says that their roses do very well in North America. Before export permission is granted by the U.S. Department of Agriculture and its Canadian equivalent, the roses undergo three different inspections, so there is no possibility of diseased plants being shipped. Anderson's nurseries grow over a million rose bushes annually, and their catalogue illustrates a very wide variety. Bush roses cost from under $1 each to $2, with smaller-sized floribundas and others costing as little as $5 a dozen. Larger standard roses are under $5 each.

Bodnant Garden Nursery, Tal y Cafn, Colwyn Bay LL28 5RE, Wales
Price list, 10 cents, or 1 International Reply Coupon.

This is one of the very beautiful gardens run by the National Trust, the private group that preserves a number of the United Kingdom's stately homes and gardens. A number of ornamental trees and shrubs are available by mail at very reasonable prices.

Broadleigh Gardens, Barr House, Bishops Hull, Taunton, Somerset, England
Two catalogues a year, 50 cents each; air mail, $1, or 2 or 4 International Reply Coupons. January and June.

Broadleigh Gardens are specialists in small bulbs with a broad selection suitable both for country and city gardeners. Their spring list, mailed in January, features cyclamens, snowdrops, triliums, etc., while their main, June catalogue has crocuses, tulips, daffodils, irises and many other dwarf bulbs. There is a minimum of $12 for overseas orders, which will, for example, buy you one hundred of the more expensive tulip bulbs. For half that amount, you can buy an assortment of twenty-two miniature hybrid narcissi or a similar collection particularly suited to window boxes. Each catalogue includes a charming preface by the firm's owner, Lord Skelmersdale, who describes the progress of his small and personal enterprise.

Leo Cady's Cacti Gardens, P.O. Box 88, Kiama 2533, New South Wales, Australia
Price list, free; $1 air mail.

Cady's plants some two million cacti seeds a year in addition to five thousand rock-garden plants and a selection of orchids and other botanical rarities. They already export to the United States and find that American customers are particularly interested in their African succulent plants, of which they have a large variety.

Hillier and Sons, Winchester SO22 5 DN, England
A. *Manual of Trees and Shrubs, hardback, illustrated, $11.*
B. *Manual of Trees and Shrubs, paperback, $6.*
C. *Abridged Version of the Manual of Trees and Shrubs (adequate for most gardeners), $1.*
D. *Tree and Shrub price list for all plants in above publications also hedging, plants, free.*
E. *Roses and Fruit catalogue, 25 cents.*
F. *Roses and Fruit price list, free.*
G. *Hardy Perennial and Alpine Plants price list, free.*
J. *Aquatic and Bog Plants, free.*
K. *Uncommon Bulbs and Corm, free.*

Founded in 1864, and nurserymen and seedsmen to the Queen Mother, Hillier's is one of the most impressive botanic establishments in the world. The firm cultivates some fourteen thousand different plants and publishes, as one botanist put it, "an absolutely essential reference work . . . available at an absurdly low cost." This is how the Hillier catalogue describes it: ". . . contains representative descriptions of approximately eight thousand woody plants, which we believe to be the most comprehensive publication of its kind ever published.

"The individual descriptions include details of eventual height, habit, leaves, flowers and fruits, country of origin, date of introduction of first known cultivation, and also R.H.S. awards if any.

Hobbies

"The numerous anecdotes, little known facts, cultural hints, and educational information make the manual more of a reference book than a nurseryman's catalogue. In addition to the descriptions are several sections covering such subjects as selections of trees and shrubs suitable for various sites and soils, and those noted for their habit and other special features such as ornamental bark and autumn color; Nomenclature and Classification; Pruning; Planting Instructions; Plant sexes and Plant Collectors."

Hillier recommends that export orders be shipped in their most dormant season, November to February. They are perfectly willing to handle small export orders of only one or two plants (as well as larger ones, of course), but for small orders they charge at least $10 for the extra work involved in special packing and documentation.

Holly Gate Nurseries Ltd., Billingshurst Lane, Ashington, Sussex RH20 3BA, England
Catalogue, 35 cents; air mail, 5 International Reply Coupons.

Holly Gate specializes in cacti, succulents and bromeliads, and has a very large overseas following, much of it American. They attribute this in part to the number of plants they sell available nowhere else and also to the competitiveness of their prices. Thousands of plants are grown by Holly Gate, others are imported. The list is an impressive one, and any gardener interested in the field should have no trouble meeting the minimum of $2.50. The firm also publishes a bimonthly magazine, *Ashingtonia*, an annual subscription to which costs $7.50.

Quinta Fdo Schmoll, Cadereyta de Montes, Qro., Mexico
Price list, free. Prices in $.

This cactus farm has a mimeographed list of the many cactus plants and seedlings for sale. There are no descriptions, just names and prices, but if the names don't mean anything to you, ask for offers number one or two—both of which are ready-chosen assortments. Prices start at $13 for fifty seedlings, including postage (you can also get smaller quantities). Anyone interested in show plants can write for additional information.

Otto Richter & Sons Ltd., Locust Hill, Ontario, Canada
Catalogue, 50 cents.

Richter's feels that they are the most famous herb plant and seed distributors in North America, and their list is far more complete than many available south of the border. Both seeds and plants are offered, most of the seed packets being 35 cents and the plants $1 each. The names are by themselves reminiscent of other times: weld, woad, woodruff, wormwood. One thinks of Shakespeare rather than the modern world and realizes how limited the choice is in our own herb garden. There is much more to plant than basil or thyme. Verbena or vervain for herbal tea, or perhaps some sorrel for soup or coriander for Mexican or Indian recipes. Richter's also sells various gardening aids—an herb starter set and, for people who can't wait, a selection of herbal teas.

GARDENING—SEEDS

Allwood Bros. Ltd., Clayton Nurseries, Hassocks, Sussex, England
32-page catalogue, free.

A marvelous shop for carnation and pink lovers, Allwood specializes in selling by mail. Worthwhile for American buyers, according to Allwood, are carnation, pink and dianthus seeds, many of which are not generally available in America.

Blackmore and Langdon Ltd., Bath BA2 1 NA, England
Catalogue, free; 50 cents air mail.

These are famous specialists in begonias, delphiniums, cyclamens, polyanthus, etc., but their list of permitted exports is limited to begonia tubers and their full range of seeds, which cost $2 per packet, including air mail. The choice of begonias is wide, with many of the rarer varieties costing $5 and up each. However, there are less expensive selections, and a mixture of a dozen medium-grade unnamed one-year tubers can also be bought for $5. Seeds for all the above-named flowers are available, by color or in mixed lots.

Robert Bolton & Sons, Birdbrook, near Halstead, Essex CO9-4BQ, England
General catalogue, free. December.
Sweet-pea list, free. August.

"Bolton's, The Sweet Pea Specialists, Awarded 336 Gold Medals," states the letterhead, and each August a special sweet-pea list is published. A general seed catalogue is available each December with a full range of flower and vegetable seeds. The sweet peas include the standards plus a constant stream of new varieties. Though British seeds are obviously of greatest interest because of the choices unavailable here, they are also considerably less expensive than American seeds. A special booklet on growing sweet peas is also available for 15 cents.

Bushland Flora, 2 Cecily Street, Bluff Point, Geraldton 6530, Western Australia
Price list, 3 International Reply Coupons

Margaret Hargett sells by mail Australian native plant seeds which, she says, are becoming very popular overseas. The seeds are gathered from all over Australia by qualified collectors and are known for their viability (this firm supplies many Australian nurseries). Unfortunately, the list is just a list of seeds available with no descriptions whatever, so you have to either know something about Australian plants or be willing to take a chance.

L.S.A. Goodwin and Sons, Goodwin's Road, Bagdad, Sth 7407 Tasmania, Australia
Price list, 50 cents in U.S. postage stamps or 4 International Reply Coupons; air mail, $1.50 in U.S. postage stamps or 8 International Reply Coupons. List with one packet of Royal Polyanthus Primrose seeds, $2 in U.S. bills.

Mr. Goodwin says that his lists are used by universities, national parks, trust gardens, and nurseries all over the world. He sells tree, shrub, vegetable and flower seeds (many of them rare) which include sought-after Australian varieties. One specialty is the Royal Polyanthus Primrose, which has 2¼" flowers, and colors and variations not found in many other strains. If you send $2 in bills, Mr. Goodwin will send you his price list plus a packet of Royal Polyanthus Primrose seeds.

Kandelka Native Seeds, Post Office, Valley Heights, New South Wales 2777, Australia
Price list, 50 cents air mail.

This is a source for seeds for native Australian plants, primarily sizable bushes and trees.

Sutton and Sons Ltd., The Royal Seed Establishment, Reading, England
98-page color seed catalogue, free.

England's most famous seed company sells a wide variety of flowers, vegetables and herbs in special vaporproof laminated packets. The catalogue contains two pages of sundries.

Hobbies

Thompson and Morgan Ltd., London Road Ipswich, 1P2 OBA, Suffolk, England
160-page color catalogue, free. November.

This firm claims to have the reputation of listing more seeds in their catalogue than anyone else in the world, which may be true. Anyway, it is impressively extensive, with some interesting vegetables and unusual flowers.

Flowers are divided into categories such as "The Flower Arranger's Garden," "Everlasting Flowers," and others with seeds I haven't seen at all in America—"Ornamental Grasses" and "Bonsai Trees."

There aren't as many vegetables, but they are worth looking at, too, as strains are different, and there is a "Vegetables with a Difference" selection which includes asparagus-peas, globe artichoke, red brussels sprouts, celtruce (combines the use of celery and lettuce with four times the vitamin C content of the latter!) and scorzonera.

W. J. Unwin Ltd., Histon, Cambridge, England
68-page color catalogue, free. Spring.

There is a homey tone to Unwin's catalogue. In the introduction this, the third largest seedsman in England points out that it is the only seed firm of any size in England that is a family enterprise, and that all the photographs in the catalogue have been taken from plants grown on land plowed by ordinary methods, so there is no reason why customers shouldn't do at least as well in their own gardens.

I asked Unwin's what was especially appealing to American gardeners about English seeds, and they replied that Americans like to buy varieties that are not available in the States. Besides "the very best and most popular garden and greenhouse flower" seeds there are lots of sweet peas, a nice selection of easy-to-grow house plants, alpine plants, vegetables that are especially good for freezing, a "cottage" collection of vegetables for the small garden, and some plants, including Harry Wheatcroft's famous roses.

Vilmorin-Andrieux, Export Department, 49750 La Menitre, France
Catalogue, free.

A friend of mine who has lived in France was entranced by this catalogue, which has seeds for flowers and, better still, the French versions of everyday vegetables. Ambitious gardeners and gourmets might get together to order seeds from this place, which has a very high ($50) minimum order for export.

Watkins Seeds Ltd., P.O. Box 468, New Plymouth, New Zealand
Catalogue, 50 cents; air mail $1.

Adventurous gardeners may wish to try some of these attractive-looking New Zealand plants. A great many of the flowers are surprisingly familiar. New Zealand gardens apparently blossom with geraniums or marigolds, just as ours do. But there are also more exotic blooms, and only a few vegetable seeds are forbidden for export. Prices overall are very reasonable, and the firm has the unique and very helpful touch of telling you how many seeds each packet contains. Some contain as many as a thousand seeds at the same price charged for other, less common plants; so, comparatively speaking, there are some real bargains here. A note of warning: Prices are quoted in dollars, but New Zealand dollars.

6
Seldon Tapestries Ltd 5' × 4'1" rug kit, available in six pieces or in one. Background Chinese blue. $280 with the design painted on the canvas, and wools.

7
Clara Weaver 23½" × 17½" Children's Christmas Calendar 8-3027 with rings for small gifts, one for each day from December 1 to 24. Linen, chart, yarn, rings and ribbon, around $9, ready-made, around $43.

8
Clara Weaver 19½" × 15½" Sampler 8-3591. Linen, chart and yarn, about $7, brass rods, about $2.60; ready-made, about $56.

GEMS

Australian Gem Trading Co., 294 Little Collins Street, Melbourne, Australia
16-page price list, free. Prices in $.

A good catalogue for beginners, with information on the composition of stones sold, detailed descriptions of the different qualities, and instructions for cutting. Not only that, but the catalogue says: "We gladly invite correspondence on gem stones, gemmology, and minerals generally, and if we can at any time advise on technical or other problems, we are only too ready to do so." The catalogue lists many different sizes and types of rough and cut opals, the cheapest being lowest-quality opal chips at $1 per ounce. Australian sapphires are also sold in great variety.

Deepak's Rokjemperl Products, 61, 10th Khetwadi, Bombay 4, India
Price list, free. Prices in $.

Under the above name this firm sells cut and polished gemstones, beads, bead necklaces, silvery filigree jewelry and small ivory carvings. From the same address and from the same price list, but under the name *Shah's Rock Shop*, the same firm sells rough gemstones.

Kernowcraft Rocks and Gems Ltd., 44 Lemon Street, Truro, Cornwall, England
Color catalogue, $1; $2.15 air mail.

Although this catalogue does not have nearly as much as the big American jewelry-making catalogues (and indeed many of the tumbled polished gemstones are imported from the United States), there are a few English and Continental rough gemstones for tumbling and cutting, very simple, modern, stainless-steel, or silver mounts, and a good book list that might be of interest to American jewelry makers.

New Central Jewelry Stores, 61 Main Street, Colombo, Sri Lanka
Price list, free.

Dealers in Sri Lanka gems, this firm sells blue sapphires, yellow sapphires, star sapphires, star rubies, cat's-eyes, also semiprecious stones such as aquamarines, amethysts, garnets, moonstones and topaz.

Yogini Gems, 81 Marine Drive, Bombay 2, India
Price list, free. Prices in $.

Yogini Gems sells different kinds of agate beads, cabochons, eggs (18" of beads on a string, about fifty to sixty, costs $6); then garnet, smoky quartz, amethyst, citrine topaz, green onyx all as beads. Different moonstones, garnets and amethysts as cabochons, and smoky quartz, citrine topaz, amethyst, garnet faceted. They do not sell rough stones. Those are handled by Keshavlal Mohanlal E. and Sons at the same address on a wholesale basis only.

JEWELRY MAKING

Bede Brown (Metal Craft), 17 Birch Street, Jarrow, Tyne and Wear, England
Catalogue and sample ring shank, $1.

Jewelry makers who want modern stainless-steel findings for their jewelry will be very pleased with this manufacturer, who makes perfectly plain cuff links, rings, bracelets and chokers in shiny 8/10 stainless steel. Prices vary from 25 cents for a specially designed "non-nipping" adjustable ring to $1 for a 1"-wide choker with a setting for a stone in the center.

KITES

Yachtmail Co. Ltd., 7 Cornwall Crescent, London W11 1PH, England
Illustrated price list, free. Prices in $.

Yachtmail sends out an illustrated list of ten impressive cloth and wood kites well described and with flying hints. Start with a 32" by 30" war kite for about $11.15, highly recommended for beginners because it is the easiest to fly. Then advance to a black bat kite, about $8.13, which hovers and dives, or a hawk kite which flaps its wing pieces and looks like a hovering hawk. You can also get reels and string, and a parachute attachment for 47 cents which rides up the string and lets go automatically when it gets to the top. All these prices include surface postage.

KNITTING

R. S. Duncan and Co., Cliffe Mills, Bartle Lane, Bradford, West Yorkshire BD7 4QJ, England
16-page color catalogue with samples, $1.

Each year R. S. Duncan and Co. puts out a splendid catalogue illustrating in color some attractive knitting patterns for children, adults and fatties, with actual samples of two of England's best-known yarns: Falcon, and Jaeger at prices that they say are below normal retail prices in the United Kingdom. There are nineteen types of Falcon illustrated, and about three hundred colors and two types (fourteen colors) of Falcon listed. Tweeds to make into skirts, trousers, waistcoats, or whatever, to match with the knitting, and yarn in large batches for knitting machines are also sold.

John Lees (Nottingham) Ltd., Drury Walk, Broad Marsh Centre, Nottingham, England
Wool samples and leaflet, $3 surface mail.

John Lees says that English yarns are both better and cheaper than other yarns. He now stocks Sirdar, Wendy, Patons and Penguin knitting yarns.

Hall Green Wools, Hall Green, Wakefield, Yorkshire WF4 3JT, England
Catalogue with yarn samples, free. Prices in $.

A mail-order firm that sells about eighteen different kinds of inexpensive knitting yarn in nylon and wool.

Millhaven Knitting Services, Knowstone, South Molton, Devon, England
Price list, 3 International Reply Coupons.

Millhaven sells everything except the yarn for machine knitting: stitch patterns, original punch card motifs, foreign magazines, pattern books, tools and "sundries" (whatever they may be). No order too small, they say.

Snowflake Kit, N-1315 Nesøy, Norway
Color brochure, free. Prices in $.

Complete kits to make lovely Norwegian sweaters in pure wool. Each kit contains absolutely everything you need, including knitting needles and pewter buttons or clasps, and the instructions are very easy to follow (apparently this firm has five thousand American customers, some of whom have ordered as many as twelve kits). There are sweater kits for men and women as well as children at prices from $10 to $20, and hats and mitten kits for much less. Norwegian knitting yarn is also sold.

LEATHER

J. T. Batchelor and Co., 39 Netherhall Gardens, Hampstead, London NW3 5RL, England
Price list, 55 cents or 4 International Reply Coupons; air mail, 80 cents or 6 International Reply Coupons.

This firm supplies Her Majesty's government and various schools and colleges with quality leather, tools and fittings, and will be delighted to supply you too. They stock buckles, skins (including python) and leathercraft kits for beginners, but they think that their "high quality English saddlery tools" are of most interest.

Hobbies

MAGIC

L. Davenport and Co., 51 Great Russell Street, London W.C.1, England
Brochure "Demon Telegraph," free.
98-page catalogue "Children's Magic and Close-Up Magic," $1. Prices in $.

For children, parents and professionals—"tricks of infinite jest that will bewilder the brain." This third-generation family firm (there is a photo of Betty Davenport lifting a white rabbit from a top hat) supplies snappy routines to professional conjurers all over the world, but also manufactures humbler pranks: stinky scent, goofy teeth, dirty nose drops, and squirting chocolate suitable for party favors or "the man who likes pocket tricks (and who doesn't?)" at lower prices than comparable articles in America, they say. There is a small brochure to start you off, with books and popular jokes such as multiplying matchboxes and diabolical dominoes, but anyone who really wants to make an impression should send for the 98-page "Children's Magic and Close-Up Magic" (first in a series of specialized catalogues), which lists tricks with coins and money, dice, matchboxes, and miscellaneous delights such as "Improved Omelet in a Hat," and Chinese Finger Choppers. And for children's parties: spinning balloons, springing sausages, bewildering blocks, whimsical wands, chameleon clowns and, thank goodness, the old favorites, disappearing rabbits and appearing doves.

MOVIES

Mailmaster Film Productions, 69 Long Lane, London EC1A 9EJ, England
64-page catalogue, $2.

"Beware those weak hearts! We can only warn you of the unbelievable horror contained in this film, we cannot stop you watching it." Portland Films says that they have the largest 8-mm. home-movie, mail-order house in the United Kingdom, yet manage to reply to letters by return mail. They stock around 2,000 silent and some sound black-and-white and color titles but no pin-up or glamour movies, though there are a few silent little X movies with titles like *Summer Heat* and *Captive Woman* ("Big Jack Devlin was a bully and his job suited him down to the ground. Boss of a women's prison, he used his power to buy himself Love and Lust"). And if you feel like watching with fright as the horrible monster turns on his master and stabs him to death, then holding your breath as the deformed monster carries a girl along the edge of the castle's highest tower, buy *Castle of Death*. However, it must be said that most of the rest of the movies look thoroughly suitable for family viewing and children's parties. Fifty feet Cagneys, Bogarts, Harold Lloyds, Laurel and Hardys, and Chaplins for about $2.20 each. Also lovable Shirley Temple, who in *Polly Tix in Washington* "will bring a grin to every face." Cartoons, travelogues and animal movies. Two-reelers cost about $16.

NATURAL SCIENCES

Brunings (Holborn) Ltd., 133 High Holborn, London WC1V 6PX, England
Price lists, free.

This British firm specializes in new and secondhand microscopes and microscope accessories, and a full range of slides, stains, etc. The company also sells accessories for astronomical telescopes and a number of books in related areas. The slides are suitable either for students or professionals, though the firm has special school kits. A list of particular use to schools and to dedicated amateurs.

9
Clara Weaver 15″ × 17″ Owl Cushion 1-3864. Linen, chart and yarn, about $10; ready-made without inside cushion, about $53.50.
photos Koefoed Fotografi

10
Eva Rosenstand Felt and fabric to make four pixie children decorations. About $5.

11
Eva Rosenstand Kit to make Christmas letter box in cross-stitch. About $12.
photos Strüwing Reklamefoto

Watkins and Doncaster, Four Throws, Hawkhurst, Kent, England
52-page catalogue, 50 cents.

The letterhead says that this ninety-eight-year-old firm sells "the finest equipment for all the Natural Sciences." R. J. Ford adds that it is cheaper for Americans to buy their products direct rather than through American firms. Of fairly general educational interest are bird, mammal, and "Life in the Oglicene Period" charts for about $1 each, and demonstration cases illustrating different methods of seed dispersal, common objects at the sea shore, etc. Apart from that, there is the necessary equipment for the study and practice of botany, dissection, geology, oology and taxidermy, and being specialists in entomology, Watkins and Doncaster can provide exclusive entomological items such as moth traps, which, they say, they alone manufacture.

NEEDLEWORK

In embroidery a design, often in a variety of stitches, is sewn on a fabric, but the fabric always remains visible as background. In needlepoint (known as tapestry in England) the final surface is entirely covered by small, regular stitches sewn on a canvas. There are four kinds of needlepoint kits available: *charted*—a plain canvas comes with a "chart," or diagram, which you transfer onto the canvas by counting stitches as you sew; *painted*—the design has been painted

Hobbies

on the canvas; *trammed* or *trammé*—the design has been understitched on the canvas, and you fill in stitches with the appropriate colors; *part-worked*—the complicated parts of the design have been completed, with only the background left to be filled in.

Art Needlework Industries Ltd., 7 St. Michael's Mansions, Ship Street, Oxford, OX1 3DG, England
Six Aran knitting brochures, $2.50.
Ten English needlepoint brochures, $2.50.
Prices in $.

This is by far the most scholarly and serious of these needlework shops, and the owner, Heinz Edgar Kiewe, has spent over forty years writing books and researching historical designs. He makes a few nasty cracks about "prefabricated bargain basement kits" and says his kits are not for neurotics who want to finish something overnight but require discipline, respect and love from the embroiderer. Anyone who feels up to Mr. Kiewe's standards should write for his very informative brochures, which come with samples of specially dyed wools and describe and illustrate hand-painted and/or charted kits.

Mr. Kiewe says that he has gathered many of his unpublished designs from customers, including one allegedly embroidered by Mary Queen of Scots, and another said to have been worked on by Marie Antoinette in prison. These two complete kits for chair seats cost $33 each, including postage. Other interesting old designs include medieval French miniatures, Georgian birds, William Morris designs, and a hand-painted seat or panel set for $72 of "The Unicorn Caught," one of the Cluny tapestries at the Cloisters branch of the Metropolitan Museum in New York. And there are several charted needlepoint rugs about 3' by 4' costing about $83, including postage: a Persian "serail" rug, a late Regency rose rug, and a Smyrna hunting rug.

The knitting brochures include wool samples, illustrations and descriptions of Aran sweaters, jackets and hats. Prices, $19–$25 per kit. Also Icelandic, Shetland, camel's-hair and cashmere sweater kits.

Aux Gobelins, 352 Rue Saint-Honoré, Paris I, France
Price list for rug squares, free.

No catalogues are produced by this shop, so it will be a difficult one to order from (and remember that French prices are much higher than English ones), but I am including it because French petit point and wools have such a high reputation. Aux Gobelins sells painted and trammed canvas for armchairs, panels and rugs. They say Americans write and tell them what period work they want, and sometimes specify the color and design (if they want a canvas for a chair, they send a paper pattern), then Aux Gobelins advises them on which model would suit them best.

There is a price list, in French, for rug squares, which vary in price from $20 to $80 and can be bought one at a time.

Dane, P.O. Box 900, DK-2100 Copenhagen, Denmark
Color catalogue, $2. Prices in $.

Dane is a new firm and it seems to be intended for the American market, so the catalogue is very easy to buy from. The designs are rather conventional but varied. They go from stylized traditional Scandinavian patterns of birds and plants through romantic cottage, country and sea scenes through flower bouquets both modern and traditional to painted canvasses for needlepoint of medieval or religious scenes. There is a page of table runners, bell pulls and small hangings with Christmas designs. Most of the kits are for cross-stitch on linen, counted thread or needlepoint, and prices are slightly lower than they would be for the equivalents sold in America.

Deighton Brothers Ltd., Riverside Road, Pottington Industrial Estate, Barnstaple, Devonshire, England
71-page catalogue, $2; $5 air mail (no checks).

Deighton Brothers say that they are one of the very few, and certainly one of the oldest, manufacturers who make hot-iron transfers for embroidery. The catalogue illustrates clearly their traditional flowery designs for cross-stitch, cutwork, beading, *broderie anglaise,* Jacobean panels and lettering, and there are a few designs for animals and antique cars too. Besides the embroidery transfers, there are transfers for Italian quilting and smocking. Although the catalogue is expensive, the transfers are inexpensive. Even the largest cost less than $1.

Luxury Needlepoint Ltd., 36 Beauchamp Place, Brompton Road, London S.W.3, England
Catalogue and wool samples, 50 cents; air mail $1.50.
Prices in $.

According to Luxury Needlepoint, doctors the world over recommend needlepoint, so if you feel you need this "finest form of occupational therapy," this shop will provide explanations (very helpful for beginners) of the ways that canvases come prepared, as well as painted or trammed kits in traditional designs suitable for chairs, cushions, stools, fire screens and carpets with their own special wools, from $5.50. But I like best their Tudor designs of some Chippendale flowers in antique coloring, $20, and four copies of old French pictures, each one showing a rustic boy or girl in a landscape surrounded by a frame of flowers, $20–$38.

The Needlewoman Shop, 146–148 Regent Street, London W1R 6BA, England
Price of catalogue not settled, write and ask.

The Needlewoman Shop in Regent Street must be the biggest shop of its kind in the world, and the outstanding catalogue for "those who embroider, crochet, knit or sew" should absolutely not be missed. Its virtue lies in its great variety, unlike the other needlework shops, which specialize in one or two styles. The Needlewoman Shop has works of every sort and every style imported from Austria, Denmark, Germany, Norway and Sweden. Tablecloths to embroider, rugs to make, felt appliqué and wool pictures, toys to sew, handkerchiefs to crochet, clothes to crochet and knit, and, of course, a bushel of cushions and pictures to embroider or needlepoint, guaranteed to entrap novices and entice devotees on to new heights. Designs change every year, the catalogue I looked at showed, among other things: Victorian samplers, regional Norwegian designs, London views imitating etchings, silhouettes of famous composers, animals, flowers, hunting scenes, abstracts, and some beautiful German cushions in gold thread on a white background. There is also a needlework-mounting service. Customers' work can be mounted on handbags, velvet cushions, writing cases, stools and various larger pieces of furniture.

In fact, a sewer's every need is covered: accessories, embroidery fabrics, "tools of the trade" are on sale, and what looks like a first-rate collection of inspirational and inexpensive "how to" craft books on tie and dye, patchwork, fashion crochet, flower making, costume dolls, metal-thread embroidery.

Eva Rosenstand A/S, Virumgårdsvej 18, Virum, Denmark
64-page color catalogue, $2. Prices in $.

Edwardian ladies drink tea on a tea cozy, a boy plays a pipe on a telephone-number book, huntsmen ride across a magazine rack, and little girls dance around a mirror. Eva Rosenstand specializes in whimsically designed embroidery

Hobbies

kits, mainly to be made into useful objects: glass cases, calendars, coffee cozies, bellows covers and pipe racks. Also bags of all kinds, from needlepoint and cross-stitch to silver thread on a Thai-silk background, and beads and gold thread on satin.

The catalogue also shows an appealing collection of cheerful Christmas kits for tablecloths, babies' bibs, cards, mobiles and tree decorations over which cavort bouncy elves, angels, children, snowflakes and stars.

Mounting kits, hangers and sewing accessories are on sale too.

Seldon Tapestries, Ltd., 10 Kings Mansions, Lawrence Street, London S.W.3, England
Brochure, $1.

How about a needlepoint picture of your dog, house, hobbies, or favorite landscape? Seldon Tapestries specializes in carrying out customers' own ideas. Write to them with your suggestion and they will quote you a price for a picture on a wall hanging, bedhead, handbag, belt, tray cover, card-table top, rug, etc. They also have an interesting collection of ready-made kits.

Clara Weaver, Østergade 42, 1100 Copenhagen K, Denmark
Color brochure, free. Prices in $.

This firm sells pretty fresh Danish designs for embroideries, tablecloths, place mats and tapestries. The designs are light and colorful with only a few traditional designs and with lots of wild-flower bouquets. Unlike most of the other needlework firms in this section, Clara Weaver sells charts instead of trammed or painted canvases, which means you have to count out the design yourself when you are embroidering. If you would like a trammed canvas, it can be done, but will take about three months and cost twice as much. As with all foreign needlework kits, prices are lower than American prices: there are a lot of kits for under $10, and almost nothing for over $20. The pieces can also be bought made up, but at about eight times the price.

Woolcraft, No. 4 Trading Building, Regina, Saskatchewan, Canada
26-page color catalogue, $1.25. Prices in $.

Delicate little sprays of needlepoint flowers to make into brooches, earrings or cuff links (everything provided) are available here, as are larger bouquets and flowers. Choose between petit-point or wool kits.

This is by far the best place for sentimental pictures— plenty of pekes, poodles, thatched cottages, geese at dawn and moonlit ruins.

POTTERY

Estrin Manufacturing Ltd., 1767 West Third Avenue, Vancouver 9, B.C., Canada
8-page leaflet, free. Prices in $.

A complete range of equipment for potters, including an assortment of wheels with or without motors. Wheels cost between $200 and $425, excluding shipping—which Estrin says is $30 to $100 less than competitors' wheels.

PUZZLES

Pentangle, Blacksmith's Farm, Over Wallop, Hampshire, England
Brochure, free; 50 cents air mail.

Perplexing puzzles for adults and persistent children are made by this firm, which will provide solutions on doctor's prescription. Puzzles include a glass marble to be removed from a cage, a silken cord to be removed from metal loops, and many wooden shapes to be constructed. Several of the puzzles have been chosen by the English Design Centre, and they are all coffee-table-worthy. On a lower level of humor, there is a tankard which only the owner will know how to drink out of, and a jug which can be made to suddenly start pouring from the center of the base "thus causing much jollification," claims the brochure.

RADIO

H.A.C. Short-Wave Products, P.O. Box 16, East Grinstead, Sussex RH19 3SN, England
Leaflet, free; 4 International Reply Coupons air mail.

H.A.C., suppliers of shortwave kits since the thirties, has updated its Model K. This battery-operated shortwave receiver kit is now called the K Mark 2, and is available in two versions. It can be built by anyone without specialized knowledge and is therefore good for the beginner who is interested in starting in ham radio. It can be used for the reception of all amateur transmissions, both phone and Morse code.

The H.A.C. one-valve receiver kit Model K Mark 2 costs $17.50. There is also an improved version, Model K Plus, costing $20, which has an enlarged panel with dial for easy calibration. Both versions can be converted to a two-valve receiver at a later date, and the conversion kit costs $6, including the extra valve or tube.

SCULPTURE

Alex Tiranti Ltd., 70 High Street, Theale, Berkshire, England
Sculptors catalogue, $1.

The London business of Alex Tiranti was started in 1895 by John Tiranti, a master carver from Turin. The firm is now run by the founder's grandson and sells tools for stone and wood sculpting and supplies for clay modeling, all made to the firm's own design either in its own workshops in Berkshire or imported from craftsmen in Italy.

SHELLS

Eaton's Shell and Rock Shop, 16 Manette Street, London W1V 5LB, England

Shells, coral, starfish and marine curios from all over the world. There is no catalogue, but if American customers list the shells they want, Eaton's will quote prices.

Hettie's Rock Shop, 110 Birdwood Avenue, Christchurch 2, New Zealand
Price list, free.

An assortment of New Zealand mineral specimens, fossils, sea shells, land snail shells, and old bottles from early gold-mining days are listed among the gemstones and minerals imported from other countries.

SPINNING

Ashford Handicrafts Ltd., P.O. Box 12, Rakaia, Canterbury, New Zealand
Leaflet, free. Prices in $.

A very good ready-to-assemble spinning wheel in silver birch costs only about $76, including postage, or even less—$57— if you buy five at one time. Wool is also sold here.

WEAVING

I have talked to a professional and an amateur weaver, both of whom said that weavers should always get their supplies from abroad, as prices are lower and colors better. They claimed that after mailing costs and duty are paid, you save about a $1 per pound of yarn.

DYES

Mr. C. D. Fitz Hardinge-Bailey, St. Aubyn, 15 Dutton Street, Bankstown NSW 2200, Australia
Price list, 25 cents (U.S. stamps accepted).
Fleece wools price list and samples, $6.50.

The dyes sold by this firm are produced mainly for use in the firm's own weaving, but they also sell their dyes to customers as a sideline.

World Wide Herbs Ltd., 11 St. Catherine Street East, Montreal 129, Canada
Brochure, free.

A very complete supply of dried-plant material, dyes and mordants, including cochineal at $7 a pound, and indigo root at $2.20.

LOOMS

Vävstolsfabriken Glimåkra AB, 280 G4 Glimåkra, Sweden
Brochure $1. Prices in $.

Lovely traditional Swedish handlooms and accessories at below American prices. Minimum order $100, and everything is sent sea freight.

YARNS

Cambridge Wools Ltd., P.O. Box 2572, Auckland, New Zealand
Price list and samples, free.

Yarns for weaving and knitting, and a spinning wheel that is half the price of the cheapest spinning wheels I have seen in America.

Wm. Condon and Sons Ltd., 65 Queen Street, Charlottetown, Prince Edward Island, Canada
Brochure and wool samples, free. Prices in $.

Beautifully colored wool yarns for knitting and weaving. Weavers should stick to the two-ply and up, as the single-ply yarns do not weave well.

Craftsman's Mark Yarns, Bronberllen, Trefnant, Denbigh, North Wales
Samples card, $2.

Exclusive yarn and fleece in lovely natural colors. "Best in the world," says one of my advisers.

J. Hyslop Bathgate and Co., Galashiels TD1 1NY, Scotland
Price list and yarn samples, $1. Prices in $.

Brightly colored homespun, botany and mohair loop wools are produced and sold by this carpet manufacturer. White slubby flax, white cotton, gray tapestry wool and remnants are also for sale. The price list gives postage rates and helpful advice on which quantities are most economical to ship.

The Multiple Fabric Co. Ltd., Dudley Hill, Bradford BD4 9PD, England
Samples card and price list, free. Prices in $.

Camel's hair, horsehair, mohair and wool yarn in natural colors.

Northwest Handcraft House, 110 West Esplanade, North Vancouver, B.C. V7M 1A2, Canada
Catalogue, 60 cents.
Sample cards of yarn listed, 25 cents per card.

This school for textiles sells imported and Canadian yarns for weaving, knitting and crocheting besides Ciba dyes for wool, Chlorentine (hot-water) dyes for cotton and other vegetable fibers, and Procion (cold-water) dyes for cotton, linen, jute and silk.

Texere Yarns, 9 Peckover Street, Bradford BD1 5BD, England
Samples, $1.

Texere Yarns is geographically in the middle of the English textile industry and sells a wide variety of yarns, some at extremely low prices. Samples change according to what is available. The batch I saw included woolen spun berber yarn in natural colors; brushed mohair, mercerized cotton and woolen spun silk; noil in natural colors only.

The Weavers Shop, Wilton Royal Carpet Factory, Wilton, Nr. Salisbury, Wiltshire SP2 PAY, England.
Price list and samples, $1.

The Wilton Royal Carpet Factory sells to weavers the same yarns that are used in their famous carpets (80 percent wool, 20 percent nylon, 2-ply, mothproofed). They also sell very inexpensive long ends of unsorted yarn in mixed colors.

Weinberger Bros. Ltd., Macroom, Co. Cork, Ireland
Price list and samples, $1. Prices in $.

Two very heavy types of hand-spun rug yarn are made by this firm in almost a hundred good, vivid colors. Price just under $8 per pound.

WINE MAKING

Loftus, 16 The Terrace, Torquay, South Devonshire, England
Brochure, 50 cents; $1 air mail.

W. R. Loftus has been supplying home wine and beer makers since 1855. In fact, they claim to be the original suppliers, and they say that they supply most of their smaller goods to American mail-order customers. Their complete homemade-wine beginner's kit costs about $9, and their ale or stout beermaking kits cost between $4 and $10.

WOODCARVING

Ashley Iles Ltd., East Kirkby, Spilsby, Lincolnshire, England
Leaflet $1. Prices in $.

Hand-forged wood-carving tools sold individually and in sets at fairly low prices. For example, a set of six boxwood-handled tools for the beginner costs about $25, while a set of eighteen boxwood-handled tools, including some for "high class" work and fine detail, costs about $75.

Carl Heidtmass, Box 140309, 563 Remscheid 14, Germany
Brochure, 2 International Reply Coupons.

Excellent wood-carving tools at prices below equivalent American prices.

13 House

BATHTUBS

Vogue Bathrooms, Bilston, Staffordshire WV14 8UA, England
Color catalogue, $1.25.

American bath takers are horribly discriminated against by manufacturers (who claim that most people take showers). Bathtubs are too short (5'), too shallow (14"), and their bases are covered by nonslip texture which is impossible to clean. If you look very hard, you might find a tub that is 5'6" long and 20" deep, but you won't get one at that size without the nonslip base. When I complained to a man at American Standard, he said there is such a demand for bathtubs because of the building down South that the manufacturers don't have to bother about bathtub fanatics. Anyone who enjoys a good bath should look at the catalogue of this leading English manufacturer, whose tubs come not only in better colors and better shapes (they don't have those thirties ripples on the outside that all American bathtubs have), but also in much better sizes. They are from 4'10" to 6'2" long and up to 21⅝" deep.

A few years ago I brought back a tub from England because there was none in America small enough to replace a fifty-year-old bathtub (when sizes were less standardized). I got the name Vogue from the catalogue, ordered the bathtub from a Southampton supplier and asked them to deliver it to the shipping office—exactly as you do with any large parcel you bring back by boat with you. On board I arranged to have an American carrier firm take the tub from the docks to my apartment, which they did after I had seen it through customs (yes, it did cause a bit of a stir on the docks). There were no boat shipping charges because it came under the baggage allowance for my family and only a few dollars of customs to pay. Anyone who wants to take a bath without getting cold knees can have one shipped.

BLANKETS

Wool blankets are heavier and more expensive than synthetic ones, but they have a much nicer texture, and don't mat or pile as much.

W. Bill Ltd., Mail Order Dept., 93 New Bond Street, London W1Y 9LA, England
Ask for the "Blankets" brochure, free. Prices in $.

Lan-Air-Cel, England's most famous cellular wool blankets, are woven with holes to trap air and give warmth by insulation while being comfortably light. They are made in all sorts of sizes, including crib size. Single bed, about $32; double, $44.

Hawick Honeycombe Blankets, Hawick, Scotland
Brochure, free.

Hawick's makes its own cellular wool blankets in cream, yellow, blue or red, and they also sell tweeds by the yard, knitting wool on the cone (which makes it cheaper) and made-to-measure clothes. Unfortunately, no prices are given in the brochure, but I imagine they are slightly lower than most.

Arthur Ellis and Co. Ltd., Export Division, Private Buag, Dunedin, New Zealand
24-page color brochure, free. Prices in $.

Arthur Ellis, who in the first edition of *The Catalogue of Catalogues* was listed only for sleeping bags and down-filled clothing, has now started making a down-filled blanket which may have some of the advantages of both blankets and comforters. This blanket, Ellis claims, has been proved by independent tests to give more warmth than four ordinary blankets, yet it is obviously lighter and easier to manage than four ordinary blankets. On the other hand, you do use this down-filled blanket with sheets and you tuck it in, too, so if you really prefer a conventional tucked-in bed to the Continental comforters (below), this might be the answer. The blanket comes in three sizes: single, double and queen. Single-bed size, about $47.

R. N. Peace and Co., 103 High Street, Witney, Oxfordshire OX8 6LZ, England
Price list, free. Prices in $.

The superb wool blankets sold by R. N. Peace are made by the famous three-hundred-year-old firm Charles Witney of Earley (By Appointment to the Queen). Witney blankets were originally brought over by English settlers who traded them for furs with Indians. (The Indians promptly dyed them blue or red.) Four qualities of blanket are available, each one substantially cheaper than when bought in America. Prices start at $14 for a single blanket in the lightest fabric, and go up to $64 for a king-sized blanket in the very best quality. Each blanket comes in white and about eight other colors, including orange and turquoise.

EIDERDOWNS

These eiderdowns have long been used in Germany and Scandinavia, and have more recently become popular in England, rightly so because they are a great advance—they put an end to bedmaking. The down-filled comforter is zipped into a sheet (rather like a pillowcase) and is used *instead* of blankets and sheets. It doesn't need tucking in, but settles around you as you move in bed. If you put a fitted sheet underneath, there is nothing to do in the morning but give the eiderdown a shake and lay it flat. Anyone who isn't convinced might experiment with their children. Eiderdowns are, of course, perfect for avoiding the agony of trying to tuck blankets into bunk beds.

Aenonics Ltd., The Duvet Center, 92 Church Road, Mitcham, Surrey CR4 3TD, England
Color leaflet, free.

A friend of mine who wanted to buy twelve eiderdowns for a new country house called me for some private advice on the best place to buy the cheapest comforter of all. In the course of my investigations and price comparisons, I discovered Aenonics, which sells do-it-yourself kits. (Meanwhile, my friend got tired of waiting and extravagantly ordered the comforters by phone from an address in *The American Catalogue of Catalogues*.)

Aenonics sells all the components to make your own eiderdowns with several kinds of fillings. They sell ready-made cases for anyone with an heirloom comforter of his own (perhaps with rare, genuine down from Eider geese) that needs a new case, and they sell ready-made eiderdowns. Prices are generally reasonable, and the do-it-yourself kits are about $5 cheaper than the same thing made up. There is one with a filling of Terylene which costs only $25 for a kit to make a bunk-size one. Slipcovers for the eiderdowns, fitted sheets, pillows, and valances to match are also available.

The German Bedding Center, 26 Connaught Street, London W.2, England
Color "Karo-Step" brochure, free. Prices in $.

The Karo-Step brochure quotes what must be the most banal folksaying ever: "Nobody can fall asleep with cold feet, and he whose feet are getting cold will soon awaken." Prices are higher here (see shops below), starting at $60, plus postage,

House

for a single-bed-sized eiderdown, but there are compensations. Judging by the pictures, the German-style eiderdowns are warmer, thicker and less flexible than the English or Norwegian ones. (However, as American houses are kept so much warmer than European homes, this may not be an advantage.) Many sizes are available, such as crib or king size, and any size can be made to order. The eiderdowns and their covers both come in many colors, and there are pillows and pillowcases to match. Finally, the brochure gives helpful information for anyone choosing an eiderdown for the first time.

Helios Home Supplies, Marlborough Mill, MacClesfield, Cheshire, England
Catalogue, free.

Helios stocks three brands of eiderdowns, including the most famous English quilt, Slumberdown. In fact, this is a very good place to get eiderdowns for children's bunks, as they have the right size for a 2′ 6″ mattress. There are many different types of covers to choose from, and everything is well explained. Bunk sizes start at $25; covers at $9.

Also for sale here are noniron sheets, twin size, $16 per pair; feather pillows start at $8 each. Moderna wool blankets start at $50 for double-bed size.

Sundt and Co., Export Department, P.O. Box 1063, 5001 Bergen, Norway

Sundt, a Norwegian department store, has a list of the "Continental quilts" that they sell by mail to America. Prices, including postage, start at $50 for a lightweight duck-down-filled eiderdown for a single bed. Covers in no-iron crepe cotton, in white or pastel shades, start at $20.

FLATWARE

BAHAMAS

Treasure Traders Ltd., P.O. Box N 635, Nassau, Bahamas
Leaflets on Alvin, Gorham, International, Georg Jensen, Lunt, Reed and Barton, Towle, Tuttle, Wallace flatware, free. Prices in $.
Leaflets on china by Ernestine, Richard Ginori, glass by St. Louis, and china and glass by leading British manufacturers, free. Prices in $.

Here is a fantastically useful address. Treasure Traders can order for you sterling-silver flatware by leading American manufacturers and Georg Jensen (Denmark) with good discounts. There is no U.S. duty to be paid on the American silver, so with all included you get about a clear 35 percent off the list price on most brands (25 percent off on International and Lunt), and after paying everything, including duty on the Danish silver by Georg Jensen, you save about 20 percent off the list price. China and glass are also available, but there are plenty of places to buy British glass and china at discounts and the minimum order here is $50, so perhaps the Ernestine and Richard Ginori American china and the St. Louis French crystal are of most interest. To get leaflets and information on prices and delivery dates, tell Treasure Traders exactly which brands you are interested in.

ENGLAND

Helios Home Supplies, Marlborough Mill, MacClesfield, Cheshire, England
Catalogue, free.

Helios stocks good English flatware, Spear and Jackson

1
Mothercare (see Clothes section) Reversible wool blanket.

2
David Mellor "Provençal" stainless-steel flatware with rosewood handles designed and made by David Mellor. Six-piece place setting, about $17.

3
David Mellor "Embassy" sterling-silver flatware designed by David Mellor for British embassies. Six-piece place setting, about $300.
photos Dennis Hooker

4
Rama Jewelry (see Jewelry and Silver section) Bronze flatware with bronze, teak, rosewood or buffalo-horn handles. 144-piece sets for twelve in teakwood chest cost between $35 and $150 each.

stainless steel, Old Hall stainless steel, and Cooper Bros. and Son Ltd. sterling silver and silver plate. Old Hall is very well known in England and has cutlery on display at the Design Centre. Their designs tend to be simple and clean lines. Prices go from $16 for a seven-piece place setting. Goblets, casseroles, tankards, butter dishes, salt and pepper shakers, etc., are also sold.

David Mellor, 4 Sloane Square, London SW1W 8EE, England, or 1 Park Lane, Sheffield S10 2DU, England
Leaflet, 1 International Reply Coupon.

David Mellor, Sheffield silversmith, cutler and designer, has recently opened a complete kitchen shop in London. By mail he sells the good-looking modern flatware he has designed and made. Patterns include chunky "Provençal" in rosewood and stainless steel; classically simple silver-plated "Pride," which has won a Design Centre award and is used on the *Queen Elizabeth II*; and hand-forged "Embassy" in sterling silver which was originally commissioned for use in British embassies and which is now made to special order. Prices start at about $5 for a five-piece place setting in stainless steel. David Mellor says that the Sheffield Cook's knives, penknives, scissors and hunting knives, "all of superb quality," have proved to be of special interest to American mail-order customers, but the firm also stocks top-quality knives and shears imported from Germany and Switzerland.

GERMANY

Rosenthal Studio-Haus, Dr. Zoellner Kg, Leopoldstrasse 44, 8 Munich 23, Germany

The big Rosenthal glass-and-china catalogue shows about ten handsome, modern flatware settings. I compared prices here with New York prices on one place setting, "Composition," German price was almost half. They start at about $12 for a four-piece stainless-steel place setting, and go as high as $75 for a four-piece sterling-silver place setting. Pieces all available individually or in sets.

Visitors Pavillon, A. Kazantzis K. G., Ditmarstrasse G, 6 Frankfurt am Main, Germany
Promotion for silver flatware made in the United States, free. Sterling and silver-plate trays, coffee and tea sets, candelabra, gift items made in the United States, free. German sterling and silver-plate trays, coffee and tea sets, candelabra, gift items, etc., free.
Silverware by Christofle, Paris, free.
Any of the above brochures, $1 air mail.

From this address, which was kindly given to me by a reader, you can get American flatware with 30 to 40 percent discounts, and German silver and excellent French silver plate by Christofle. Do look up the main listing for this shop under Glass and China in this section.

Franz Widmann und Sohn, am Karlstor Unter den Arkaden, 8 Munich 2, Germany
Manufacturers' brochures in German, free: Solinger stainless-steel ware; silverware; horn-handled steak knives and forks; carving sets; flatware in stainless steel, silver plate and sterling silver; scissors, manicure sets and electric razors.

Germany is well known for its first-rate stainless steel, and the old family firm of Franz Widmann sells the best-known of all such flatware. However, they do not have manufacturers' brochures and price lists for all their stock, so if you are interested in something in particular, write and ask for the price, otherwise specify whether you want stainless steel, silver plate or silver and Franz Widmann will send you what brochures they have.

If you are energetic, write to Widmann's for their brochures on other German specialties: real horn-handled knives, carving sets, scissors, manicure sets and Hummel figurines. But remember, everything is in German, so even though there are plenty of pictures, it is hard work translating.

HONG KONG

Langard Company, P.O. Box 13867, Hong Kong
Leaflet with some color, 1 International Reply Coupon; air mail, 3 International Reply Coupons. Prices in $.

An Englishwoman living in Hong Kong has started a small business selling stainless-steel and silver-plate flatware to personal shoppers, and imported Thai bronze flatware by mail. Her leaflet has clear photographs of four patterns of bronze flatware, and lists several gifts such as cake servers, letter openers, ice-cream spoons and baby sets. Mrs. Garland says that as there is a certain amount of substandard bronze flatware on sale in Bangkok, she buys very carefully, "only the best." Her prices are sometimes a little lower than Bangkok prices. It's worth comparing.

SWEDEN

PUB (Paul U. Bergströms AB), Box 40 140, Export Department, S-103/43 Stockholm 40, Sweden
Leaflets for glass, flatware and souvenirs, $1.50.

Swedish stainless-steel flatware was one of the first to break away from traditional shapes and has kept a reputation for streamlined design. The PUB department store says that their flatware is one of their most popular mail-order items to America. Leaflets show about four stainless-steel flatware settings. Ask about any KF, Gense or Nils-Johan flatware you are interested in because it's considerably cheaper when bought direct from Sweden.

THAILAND

S. Samran Thailand Co. Ltd., G.P.O. Box 740, Bangkok, Thailand
10-page brochure, free; $1 air mail. Prices in $.

Bronze tableware is a Thai craft that is very popular with tourists; it is a beautiful light gold color, but like silver, it must be polished. Samran is a leading maker. They sell large bowls decorated with Thai "angels" for about $20, sugar bowls, creamers, salt and pepper shakers for $3–$5. Complete sets of tableware, including postage, cost $60 for six place settings, $75 for eight, and $104 for twelve. There are ten patterns, and handles may be plain bronze, decorative bronze with Thai "angels" on the ends, rosewood or buffalo horn (buffalo horn should not be machine-washed). Tea sets and barbeque sets also for sale.

For more stainless-steel flatware, see Helios Home Supplies (Household Objects). For silver and silver plate, see Asprey, Carlo Mario Camusso, Garrard, Mappin and Webb, all in the Jewelry and Silver section.

FURNITURE

Furniture is usually so much less expensive abroad that it is well worth sending for. However, if your prime object is to save money, it is not usually worth sending for small single pieces, because shipping charges are disproportionately high. A single coffee table costs about $75 to ship to New York harbor, a three-seater couch between $150 and $250. For instance, Ashley tells me that their three-seater Chesterfield sofa costs $200 to pack and ship to New York harbor, and their matching Chesterfield armchair $100—yet the sofa and *two* chairs together cost $300 to pack and ship. The exception to the rule against buying single pieces is when the price difference between what you are buying abroad and in New York is very large. For example, leather couches cost $300 to $1,000 more in New York, and so are almost always worth sending for.

Shipping costs depend so much on where you live and what you are buying that it is hard to give a reliable rule of thumb as to what they will be. Marlau's, which is very experienced in shipping furniture to America, thinks that when you are looking at catalogues you should allow an extra 40 percent of the price if you live in the East, 45 percent if you live in the Midwest, and 50 percent if you live in the Far West. If you decide you are interested in a specific piece of furniture, you can get a better idea by asking the store for the cost of sea freight, and also asking them what the weight will be, as American trucking companies will give you an accurate estimate if you tell them the weight and destination of your load-to-be.

MODERN FURNITURE
DENMARK

These days "Danish Modern" furniture looks almost stately compared to the furniture being designed in Italy and England. It is streamlined, but carefully built to last. Dark rosewood, orangy teak or creamy oak are polished or oiled, and woolen fabrics are still used. The shapes are somewhat austere compared to the knockdown, switch-around, sink-in modules that other countries are experimenting with.

3 Falke Møbler, Falkonercentret, DK 2000 Copenhagen F, Denmark
30-page color catalogue, $1. Prices in $.
100-page color catalogue with leather and fabric samples, $10. Prices in $.

This large firm (which has furnished the General Time Corporation building in Stamford besides several hotels around the world) has its own workshops and makes a very wide range of furniture, lights and rugs, all in "Danish Modern" styles. The small catalogue will give you a perfectly adequate idea of styles and colors—it shows several living and dining rooms furnished mainly with rosewood furniture (there is some teak, oak and pine too, and most pieces can be made in any of the woods) covered in richly colored Scandinavian textiles or in leather. If you really mean business, send for the big catalogue, which gives the exact dimensions of each piece and includes samples of the fabrics. It is cumbersome, however, with lots of heavy plastic protecting the pictures, and heavy vinyl covers.

Although they aren't shown in the catalogue, this firm also stocks furniture by all the famous Danish architects such as Hans Wegner, Arne Jacobson and Fin Juhl which is now hard to find in the United States and is much more expensive if you do find it. 3 Falke Møbler says that they are always happy to send brochures illustrating special pieces you are interested in, such as bars or wall units.

Rud. Rasmussens Snedkerier, Nørrebrogade 45, 2200 Copenhagen N, Denmark
Composite-bookcases brochure, free.
Safari-chair leaflet, free.

Professor Kaare Klint has designed a safari chair which is beautifully made by this firm (I have two myself) and it has the advantage of being knockdown-able, so it will fit in a

5
3 Falke Møbler Bar table, width and length 39½", height 19½", bar top in black Formica. The bar portion is moved by gas cartridges and automatically lifts when press lightly. $227 in teak; $243 in walnut; $283 in rosewood.

6
Rud. Rasmussens Snedkerier Safari chair in natural ash with natural canvas, about $100. Chair in smoked ash with tan oxhide, about $300. Stool in smoked ash and oxhide, about $80.
photo Louis Schnakenburg

small box that can go by mail. The chair consists of canvas or leather stretched across a light wood frame with a thin, flat or buttoned cushion on the seat and leather straps for armrests. The chair is light and looks really lovely in natural linen with a pale ash frame; it has a footstool to match. Several years ago this chair was on sale in New York for over twice the price that it sold for in Denmark, but I haven't seen it at all lately, so it may not even be for sale here now. (The chair now costs $100 and up even from Denmark.)

This same firm also produces "composite bookcases" wall systems in a sort of intermediate style which is said to go well with modern or traditional furniture. The system is available in teak, mahogany, oak, Oregon pine or pine, and it can incorporate bookshelves, record dividers, drawers, hanging files, magazine (or catalogue) storage space, a wardrobe, and even a sofa.

Den Permanente (see Household Objects and Gifts) has an excellent collection of modern Danish furniture.

ENGLAND

Over the last ten years, young English designers have begun to organize their own firms to manufacture and sell their own designs. In a heroic effort to keep prices down, practically all the furniture that follows comes straight from the manufacturer in knockdown form (packed flat, but completely ready and easy to assemble). Shapes are simple, woods are pale and lacquered or painted in good colors, cushions are bright and removable, and prices are—low.

Habitat, Hithercroft Road, Wallingford, Berkshire, England
Color catalogue, $1. September.

There is nothing like this in America, though there should be. The first Habitat shop was opened several years ago by Terence Conran, who, like the owners of most successful shops, knew exactly what he wanted—a shop full of good design at low prices (American shops have either gone in for design and high prices or low prices and no design). Habitat style in furniture, linen, cookware and everything you need for the house is so distinctive that Habitat has become a byword, and it is hard to imagine any young English person with, to quote *Vogue*, "more taste than money" who hasn't bought *something* at Habitat.

The style is a combination of simple, almost classic shapes with bright solid colors, light woods and white paint. It has a sort of healthy simplicity about it all. To start with, Habitat carried furniture made to their own design. Now they stock things from other manufacturers (and even have some more expensive classics such as the Eames and Bauhaus chairs), so some of their things are also available in America. The main advantage of Habitat is that you can get a decent version of just about anything you need for the house from kitchen cabinets to a toothbrush holder. There are about sixteen different sofas and seating units, starting with their Harem seating, which consists of big floor cushions held together on a metal frame. A chair costs about $25, and a two-seat sofa about $100. There are a few shelving systems, in metal, painted white, or light-wood or metal dining tables and chairs (many of these are available in America), bedroom furniture in white or teak. But perhaps the most tempting things are not the furniture but the smaller items: richly colored matching sheets and wool blankets—bright-red, yellow, green or blue; classic, creamy-colored mixing bowls and chocolate-brown casseroles; sun blinds made from William Morris fabrics; filing cabinets and metal shelves in primary colors; shiny metal lampshades; classic English scenic china, or the toys (incidentally, in the catalogue I looked at there was a children's tent for $16 in cotton canvas, which I presume is less flammable than the synthetics almost always used in American tents). The catalogue also shows fiber-filled comforters to use instead of blankets at about $45 for single-bed size, and glasses, china, flatware, fabrics, wallpaper, paints, a few kitchen gadgets, medicine cabinets, shower curtains, etc.

However, although Habitat has always sold largely by mail order, and has a catalogue that makes my American friends green with envy, *they will only accept export orders of over £100* (about $240 at the moment). I consider it well worth while ordering with friends to make up the minimum, or, if you have friends in England, giving them Habitat presents (or better still, getting your own package sent to them and having them forward it). Within Great Britain the minimum Habitat mail order is about $12.

Christian Sell and Associates, 45 Camden Passage, London N.1, England
18-page color catalogue, free. Fabric swatches on request.

Christian Sell's "switch-around furniture" is all built in one basic design, thereby solving the problems of people who want a whole room (or house) to match neatly. Everything comes in solid laminated-birch hardwood, either simply lacquered or else painted and lacquered in white to what Christian Sell fondly hopes is a "diamond-hard" finish, and upholstery is in red, orange, navy-blue, dark-brown duck.

Peter Hoyte, Millbridge, Frenchsham, Surrey, England
Leaflet, free.

Peter Hoyte designs and manufactures mainly office chairs, but has only one chair which he sells by mail. It is a comfortable-looking sling chair with back and seat made of a buttoned cushion hanging on a frame of chromium-plated steel tubing. There is a stool to match, and Peter Hoyte says the two pieces look good upholstered in anything—real or imitation leather, tweed or even toweling for sea and pool use. The chair costs about $125 and the stool about $60, but unfortunately, even though both can be sent in a reasonably small box, they are too big for parcel post and have to go by freight.

George Sneed Furniture, Bacon's Barn, Saint Michael, South Elmham, Bungay, Suffolk, England
Catalogue, $1; $2 air mail.

George Sneed and two other craftsmen make simple country furniture in Scandinavian pine to standards they feel are much higher than those reached by mass-produced furniture. George Sneed has designed everything, and he doesn't attempt to imitate any styles of the past, so as it's made of pine, the furniture has a cozy, farmhouse feel without being in the least pseudo. The catalogue shows a pine battery-run clock, two tables available in various sizes, benches and chairs with canvas cushions, a small rocking chair and a good-looking modern version of the Welsh dresser. Chess tables and furniture can also be made in any wood and designed to customers' own requirements.

Sylvester Furniture, 23 Little Clarendon Street, Oxford, England
Brochures, free.

Sylvester Furniture was listed in the first edition of *The Catalogue of Catalogues* as manufacturers of wooden furniture. They now only make upholstered plastic foam furniture of various kinds. They have two big, comfy-looking sofas which can be covered in cotton or Elephant corduroy, one of which turns into a bed, and also scoop chairs in the same quilted cushions on a curved base that I mentioned

House

previously. However, Sylvester says that the above furniture *may* be on sale in America by the time this edition is published. The only thing they will be definitely selling themselves is their ingenious jigsaw puzzle chair-bed, which was the most popular with American customers anyway. It is three pieces of foam that can either be used as an armchair with a foot rest or can be rearranged and used as a single bed. In your own material it costs about $100. In cotton or Elephant corduroy it costs up to about $150.

FRANCE

Chapo, 14 Boulevard de l'Hôpital, Paris V, France
Leaflet in French, free; $1 air mail.

Just the place for anyone furnishing a Frank Lloyd Wright house. Pierre Chapo, owner of the firm, designs his furniture with a high regard for the natural properties of his materials, and there is lots of talk about function and sincerity in the brochure. Each piece is heavy and solidly made, no nails are used, and the best woods are oiled and polished by hand to show the natural grain. Tables, chairs, chests, beds, bunks, cribs, shelves and sofas—everything's here, and prices are low for this kind of very unusual work, although, of course, you can buy factory made furniture for much less. A thick round table that would look marvelous in a country kitchen costs just over $350, a sofa with big, squashy cushions, about $1,250.

Chapo represented France at the Montreal World Fair and is enthusiastically recommended by friends of mine living in France.

GERMANY

Wohnbedarf OHG, Mittelweg 166, D-2000 Hamburg 13, Germany
Catalogue in German, free.

Unfortunately, this catalogue is in black-and-white and printed in German, so it is hard to tell exactly how the furniture looks and works. Wohnbedarf sells mainly by mail and the furniture is all knockdown for easy shipping. Furniture designs are modern, ingenious and look just right for children's rooms or, say, remote summer homes where the transportation of furniture is a problem.

ITALY

Giovanetti, 51032 Bottegone, Casella Postale 1, Pistoia, Italy
Color brochure, free. Prices in $.

Italian designers are turning out the newest furniture designs in the world, and when you find them in America they are horribly expensive. Giovanetti has three models that you can buy direct from them at excellent prices. "Bauhaus" is a knockdown armchair and sofa made of plump but firm cushions which are assembled with the help of chrome fittings in the back which do not show in the front. In the brochure three small children are doing the assembling, presumably to show how easy it is. "Papillon" comes as a chair, three-seat or four-seat sofa; it is an inner structure of steel padded with polyurethene, and is covered with a loose cover of your choice. It has no legs, but looks just like a great big pillow, mysteriously half upright. In the brochure it is shown in a vivid yellow. And "La Papessa" is a long, comfortable-looking chair made of two slabs of polyurethene shaped to the body. As with the other pieces, it's all upholstery with no metal or wood showing, and it can be covered in fabric or leather.

7
Peter Hoyte Sling chair, about $125. Stool to match, about $60.

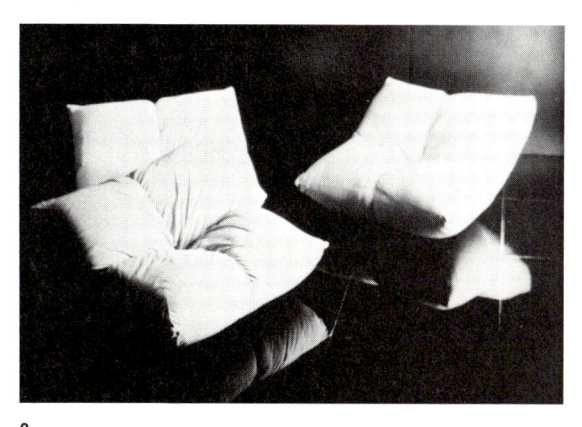

8
Giovanetti "Papillon" chair, also available as a three- or four-seat sofa.

9
Giovanetti "La Papessa."

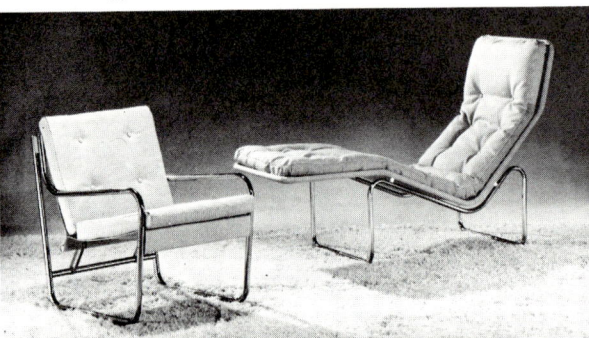

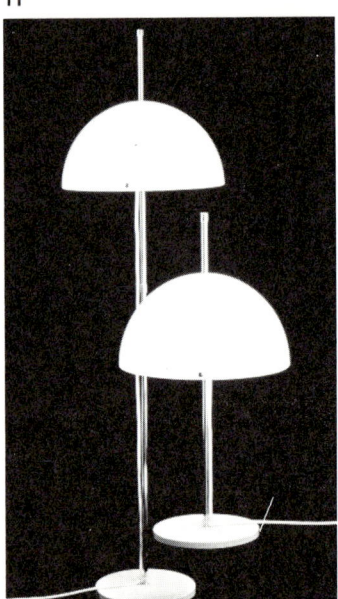

House

10
Ikea "Nikka" desk in oak or teak with a plastic lacquer finish. The pedestal on the left has a suspended filing system. About $70.

11
Ikea "Ögla" beechwood armchair in natural or white lacquered finish. About $15.

12
Ikea Chrome-plated tubular chairs upholstered in natural-colored canvas. The one on the left, "Lots," designed by Eric Wørsts, is about $45. The one on the right, "Kroken," designed by Christopher Blomquist, is about $65.

13
Ikea An adjustable light, "Amarant," can be raised to function as a standard lamp or lowered to be a table lamp. About $25.

14
Ashley Furniture Workshops 7'-long Chesterfield with button seat, available in 120 different shades of leather. $575.
photo S. S. Walia

House

SWEDEN

Ikea, 343 00 Älmhult, Sweden
200-page color catalogue in Swedish, free.

Ikea comes *fervently* recommended by Swedes and non-Swedes alike. Apparently this now-enormous business enterprise was started by a man who wanted to make very inexpensive, very good furniture. He managed it with spectacular success, and the big plant and shop outside Stockholm have become a favorite weekend-excursion goal—people drive out, dump their children in the Ikea nurseries, eat in the Ikea restaurant, wander around looking at the chair-and-carpet-torturing machines (everything is tested to see how it will stand up), buy something and drive home with it strapped on top of the car.

There is plenty of everything for the house in the (alas, Swedish-language) mail-order catalogue, including light fixtures and carpets. In general, Swedish prices are higher than Danish, but Ikea's furniture is less expensive than what you find in the grander Danish houses. The range is more catholic, too, because although the prevailing tone is bright and modern (lots of light and painted wood), Ikea happily copies anything popular: "Kolonial" bedroom suites, Louis XVI chests, chandeliers, puffy chrome-and-buttoned "*Italien-inspirerad*" sofas, Spanish and Oriental carpets. Prices: sofas $135 and up, dining-room tables from $55, and a bentwood side chair ("Lena") for $10—which costs $25 in Washington.

This is the place to furnish a child's room. A wooden highchair costs $7.50; a crib that turns into a sofa before and after babies, $27 (I had one of these and it was very useful; it saved storage space and was handy for visiting babies); for older children there are bunks that can also be used as two single beds, about $55 complete; five-drawer desks for $33, or for $55 you can put a top over ten drawers to make a desk; and for the astounding sum of $8.50 there is a desk chair that you can lower as the child grows taller. There are also lots of combinations of shelves, cupboards and toy chests that fit into each other and handy places. *All* the children's furniture is in pale wood or primary colors; not an elf or a flower to be seen anywhere.

REPRODUCTION FURNITURE

Some of these reproductions cost much less than they would in America, notably the furniture from England; others would be very hard to find here. The Spanish and Chinese shops will make pieces in any size you want, and will incorporate your own designs into their models.

ENGLAND

Ashley Furniture Workshops, 3a Dawson Place, London W.2, England
Brochure, free; $2 air mail. Prices in $.

This offshoot of a large modern-furniture manufacturer sells reproduction leather furniture to America by mail, and has what looks like excellent values. All the current and eternal favorites are here: Victorian-style Chesterfield sofas, $645–$745 (these cost around $2,295 in New York); Chesterfield chairs, $420 and up; the Victorian steel-and-leather rocking chair displayed at the Great Exhibition of 1851, for $215 (it is for sale in New York at a higher price and in vinyl instead of leather); a Sheraton tub chair from $230; a Hepplewhite wing chair from $345; a Georgian Winchester chair from $325; an open-sided eighteenth-century Gainsborough chair from $245. You can have most pieces either deep-buttoned or plain with feather-down cushions, and there is an astonishing range of leather.

Note: They are so pleased with the result of their listing in the first edition (they booked over $35,000 worth of orders because of it and sent me a batch of letters from happy American customers) that Ashley's is now going to add bookcases, desks and chests of drawers in Sheraton and Hepplewhite styles as requested by their customers.

C. P. Burge and Son, 162 Sloane Street, London S.W.1, England
Brochure, free. Prices in $.

This firm specializes in exporting reproduction furniture at very reasonable prices (the catalogue is in German, French and Italian, as well as English). Unlike any of the other shops, they make tables from old tops with new legs to match, so the tables look antique but are less fragile and less expensive than the real thing would be. In the brochure there is a nice one in "the Regency manner" which costs $185 and up (depending on size). There are usually plenty of tops in stock, so tables can be made according to customers' wishes at prices from $320 to $500.

Besides straightforward reproductions (leather chairs, folding library steps, butler's-tray tables, campaign chests), Burge has now started making extraordinary and charming nautical furniture—chests, tables, even wine racks are painted with ships, flags and nautical motifs, and decorated with fine yellow and red lettering, presumably in a style that was used on old ships. Prices go from about $125 for a nautical wine rack to $500 for a nautical trestle table.

Burge also stocks antiques in the same styles, and carved and gilded pieces, French marble mantelpieces and nautical items, but none of these are in catalogues, so you must write with a specific request.

Martin J. Dodge, Southgate House, Wincanton, Somerset, England
Photographs on request.

Martin J. Dodge, cabinetmakers, makes very fine pedestal tables in classic English styles, though he also has a few chairs. A small, oval coffee table, 40" by 27", costs $210; pedestal dining tables, from $430, according to size, with crossbanding around the edges in exotic woods $6.50 a foot extra; Chippendale (Queen Anne) side chairs with leather seats, $240; a child's Victorian chair in walnut, $150. Waiting time for furniture, ten weeks.

R. Tysack Ltd., Kitchener Road, High Wycombe, Buckinghamshire, England
Catalogue, $2.50.

This small manufacturer of high-quality furniture in eighteenth- and nineteenth-century styles produces an excellent catalogue of their sofas, chairs, dining and small tables, sideboards and desks. And besides the standard range shown in the catalogue, they are willing to adapt their designs to your specifications. There are masses of chairs, from dining chairs in Regency and Hepplewhite, and a couple of copies from the original designs of Thomas Chippendale, to unusual Victorian easy chairs and Georgian library and desk chairs. All of these can be upholstered in various fabrics (including your own) or in leather. In sofas there is the ubiquitous Chesterfield, or if you'd like something smaller and lighter, there is a charming buttoned Victorian settee (about $500 in leather) and a graceful Georgian-style settee. Three classic dining tables are shown; they are available plain or with cross-banding. A circular dining table in mahogany with a single pedestal of reeded legs and brass toe casters costs about $350. The smaller side tables cost from about $75 to $150.

House

15
C. P. Burge and Son Nautical wine rack, decoratively painted, about $150.
photo Jon Whitbourne

16
C. P. Burge and Son Porter's chair in tufted antiqued hide. About $1,080.

17
C. P. Burge and Son Nautical campaign desk, decoratively painted, $375.

18
Martin J. Dodge Oval pedestal coffee table (40″ × 27″, 20″ high). About $210.

19
Ziggurat A reproduction of the first steel rocking chair exhibited by R. W. Winfield at the Great Exhibition of 1851.

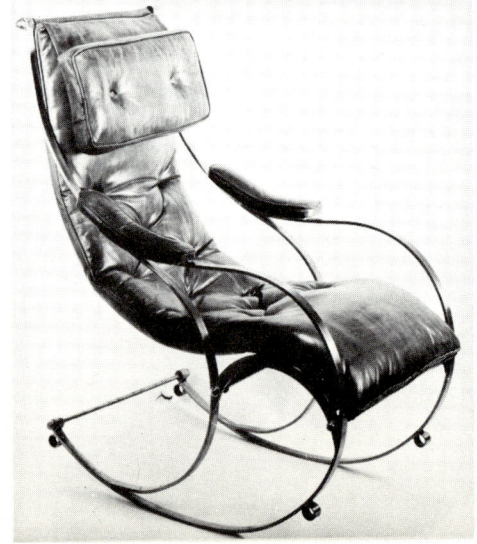

House

Upholstery Workshop, 13/14/15 North End Parade, North End Road, London W14 0S5J, England
Brochure, $5.

The Upholstery Workshop makes and sells its own handmade traditional sofas and armchairs. They say that their prices are high, so they are only able to sell to the "top end" of the market, but I wonder whether their prices will seem so bad in America where anything handmade is terribly expensive. Prices do not include fabrics; swatches will be sent on request. The comfortable-looking "London" for instance, costs $500, and a good-quality Dralon would be about $13.50 a yard. (There are less and more expensive fabrics.)

Ziggurat, 15 New Cavendish Street, London W.1, England
Brochure, free.

A marvelous collection of English leather chairs and sofas, many of them handmade throughout. The frames are hardwood and based on originals. Each piece is hand-sprung with horsehair and hessian filling. The supplest leathers are used, and given antique patina and coloring entirely by hand; wooden parts are hand-polished. There is a very authentic version of the Chesterfield for about $1,000. It can be made in any size and with several variations. A Georgian-style square-back settee costs from $900; a Chippendale camel-back settee from $800. Prices for chairs go from $325 for a Hepplewhite-style tub chair to $820 for a buttoned Chippendale-style library chair, and there is a charming Regency-style rocking chair for $275.

HONG KONG

Cathay Arts Co. Ltd., P.O. Box 5801, Kowloon, Hong Kong
48-page catalogue with some color, free; $3 air mail. Color leaflet, free (air mail).

This firm sells both wholesale and retail, and publishes a magnificent catalogue with photographs, many in color, of a wide range of teak and rosewood Oriental furniture "for those who appreciate the finest." There is furniture for every room, and some of it is very splendid. Besides sets for living and dining rooms as well as bedrooms, there are bars, hi-fi cabinets, silver chests, ottomans, serving trays, screens and planters. Sizes range from little jewelry boxes (in nineteen different designs) to enormous display cabinets with lighting and scenic inlay decorations.

Prices must be inquired about individually, and are higher than at the firms below.

Charlotte Horstmann Ltd., 104 Ocean Terminal, Kowloon, Hong Kong
50-page brochure, $1; $2 air mail. Prices in $.

A precise catalogue meticulously describes Charlotte Horstmann's handmade reproduction furniture. Each piece is constructed by only one man from start to finish, and no nails or screws are used on the Chinese pieces. Only tables, desks and chairs are shown, except for a Ming fourposter, a Korean divan and some library steps. Mostly there are restrained Chinese styles: Ming, Chinese Chippendale and Mandarin. But there are about twenty French and English pieces, notably five in the now fashionable "campaign" style:

The woods are Burma rosewood and teak, and the weight and moisture of the woods are most professionally described. Shipping information and prices are models of simplicity and clarity.

Ngai Fat Company, 132 Canton Road, Kowloon, Hong Kong
Brochure with color, free. Prices in $.

Ngai Fat Company has been manufacturing and exporting carved furniture since 1918. Well-seasoned camphor, teak and rosewood are made into ornate furniture in a large factory, and the most popular designs are illustrated in a brochure. Carved and inlaid chests, bars, screens and coffee tables seem to have flowers or Chinese garden scenes intricately carved or inlaid with ivory, soapstone or mother-of-pearl in a colored background. Prices of the illustrated pieces are all under $300, and shipping prices are not high. Like most Hong Kong firms, this one will also quote a price in response to any pictures, sketches or descriptions you send of anything special you want.

S. Y. Ma, 35 Hankow Road, Kowloon, Hong Kong
Furniture brochure, 50 cents air mail.

The large assortment of Ming and Western furniture (though only forty-three of the most popular pieces are shown in the brochure—photographs can be sent of others) is made from kiln-dried teak or rosewood, and pieces can be made to your own design.

Pewter and brass pots, plates, lanterns, and candlesticks (suitable for lamp bases, the brochure says) also available.

IRELAND

Abbey Crafts, Abbeyshrule, Co. Longford, Ireland
Leaflet, 25 cents.

Local craftsmen make Irish furniture in old country styles. There are trestle tables and stools, a hunting table, and the Crannog three-legged chair. There is also a wooden Curragh cradle which has been designed to fit a carry cot—when you don't need it for a baby any more, Abbey Crafts suggests that you use it for a wine rack, plant holder or blanket chest. The furniture is handmade and hand-finished in iroko, white pine or mahogany, and prices go from $35 for a Trinity stool to $375 for a Cloister dresser. Some of the furniture can be knocked down for shipping. Abbey Crafts also makes some chopping blocks, a meat-carving board and a fish-carving board in hand-finished iroko.

PORTUGAL

Fundação Ricardo do Espírito Santo Silva, Largo das Portas do Sol 2, Lisbon 2, Portugal
Photographs on request, free.

This unique museum and school of decorative arts was founded by a Portuguese banker who was anxious to keep alive the arts rapidly being taken over by machinery. There is a museum consisting of Mr. Santo Silva's private collection of furniture and beautifully bound old books, especially collected with this museum in mind. And in twenty-three workshops, experienced craftsmen and trainees copy, rigorously using the original techniques, furniture in the purest styles and periods of the past, mainly French. Wood-carvers, locksmiths, metal engravers, carpet weavers, tapestry restorers and bookbinders reproduce a wide range of decorative objects and luxurious pieces of furniture. A bookbinding department reproduces the "simplest to the most sumptuous" bindings from the sixteenth century to the Romantic period, including mosaic leather work in the style of Padeloup and Le Monier—the Fundação was completely

House

responsible for restoring Madame du Barry's library at Versailles.

As for prices—the Rockefellers, the Rothschilds and the palaces of Fontainebleau and Versailles shop here. If that doesn't put you off, write and tell them what kind of things you are interested in and the Fundação will give you information that "falls upon those."

Sociedade Inglesa Decorações e Antiguedades LDA, Rua da Emenda 26, Lisbon 2, Portugal
No catalogue; everything made to order.

The Sociedade Inglesa reproduces French and English eighteenth-century furniture and decorative objects. They are also decorators and have done the Sandy Lane Hotel in Barbados, and Reid's Hotel in Madeira, in modern styles. Prices are low: an extraordinary, very low country "saddle" chair with velvet cushions, $72 (apparently based on a sixteenth-century seat for riding a donkey); a low, 3′-long carved table with a marble top on gilt or painted base, $70; a black-and-gold-painted Regency chair copied from one left in Portugal by a Marshall Beresford after the Peninsula War, $56. There are also hand-embroidered carpets copied from seventeenth-century carpets in Lisbon museums, or designed especially for the Sociedade Inglesa, costing about $60 per square meter (1 sq. m. = 1.2 sq. yds.).

SCOTLAND

D. M. Kirkness, 14 Palace Road, Kirkwall, Orkney, Scotland
No catalogue.

The oak and woven-straw chairs produced by this small workshop are revivals of the traditional Orkney chairs that were very popular in the last century. Their square, rather graceless shape will delight anyone who is seriously interested in traditional crafts or who is looking for unusual countrified furniture. There is one basic form which can be bought in a hooded version in "gent's," "lady's" or "child's" size, and with rockers or a drawer and paneled base fitted. Sea-grass stools are also made.

SPAIN

Abelardo Linares S.A., Carrera San Jerónimo 48, Madrid 14, Spain
Brochure, free. Prices in $.

This famous Spanish antique shop in the middle of Madrid makes such authentic-looking reproductions out of old dry walnut, oak and mahogany that one can't help wondering whether they are being passed off as genuine somewhere. (Linares says they have been supplying American dealers for many years.) Most of the pieces are large carved Spanish chests and tables, costing around $700. There are some rush-seated chairs with carved pine backs at about $100 each, and an imposing studded and carved chair upholstered in tooled leather for $250; also a few plain English and French styles. State your interests, and photographs will be sent. Styles not shown can be made.

Perhaps of more general interest are the reproduction lanterns, a few of which are small enough to go by mail and which cost mainly between $40 and $60. There are also mirrors with ornate carved frames gilded in real gold leaf to be made in any size and costing from $65 to $95.

Marlau, Rey Francisco 8, Madrid 8, Spain
Color catalogue planned, $3. Prices in $.

An American couple, the Corcorans, turned a hobby into a business, got raves in all the shopping guides to Spain, and for several years were manufacturing superbly made Spanish reproduction furniture. Now Spain has become industrialized, wages are rising, and the Corcorans have mechanized and reduced their furniture to a few lines. Although the handmade pieces illustrated here will still be available, the Marlau catalogue will show mainly their mass-produced wall units (with a few chairs, tables and beds) at prices from $250 to $3,000. This is what the Corcorans say about their wall units: "We designed ours so that it is made up of a number of modules which, when coupled together, can fill a whole wall or can be just a single bookcase. Or it can be a number of free-standing serviceable units scattered throughout the household. Our largest single piece can be easily carried by two not too strong people. The catalogue includes six different types of doors (all very Spanish), three different cabinet heights, two different cabinet depths, plus a wide range of accessories like ball-bearing shelves for turn tables, tape and record storage drawers, gunrack assemblies, indirect lighting, felt-lined silver drawers, and on and on."

TAIWAN

Hsiang-Fu Teakwood Furniture Mfg. Co., 125-2 Wufu Second Road, Kaohsiung, Taiwan
Color brochure, free. Prices in $.

This address was given to me by a reader, Lillian Luke, who says that the prices are about half what you would pay for similar pieces in America. Screens, low tables with matching stools, chests and china cabinets are elaborately carved or inlaid with soapstone. There is a $2,000 minimum order, and as most prices are under $300, you'll have to either buy several pieces or get together with friends.

GARDEN ORNAMENTS AND FURNITURE

ENGLAND

Chilstone Garden Ornaments, Great Linford Manor, Newport Pagnell, Buckinghamshire, England
20-page catalogue, free. Prices in $.

Chilstone already sells garden ornaments to private customers and garden shops in America. Their specialty is handmade reproductions in reconstituted stone of sixteenth-, seventeenth-, eighteenth- and early-nineteenth-century original models. The texture of the stone is specially made to be almost indistinguishable from that of the original, and to be soft enough to pick up mosses and lichens so that it quickly looks old. Prices are reasonable, starting at $35 for an oval Regency basket, and only a few large objects—statues and sundials—cost more than $200. A baluster birdbath costs $80, a mid-Georgian urn with swags of drapery, bunches of flowers and fruit festooning the bowl, $150. (There are fountains, statues, lions, benches, pedestals, urns and even balustrades.)

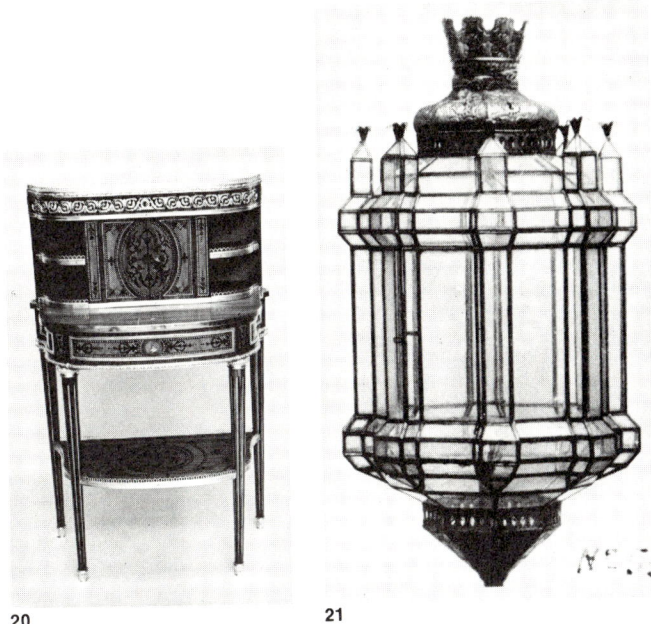

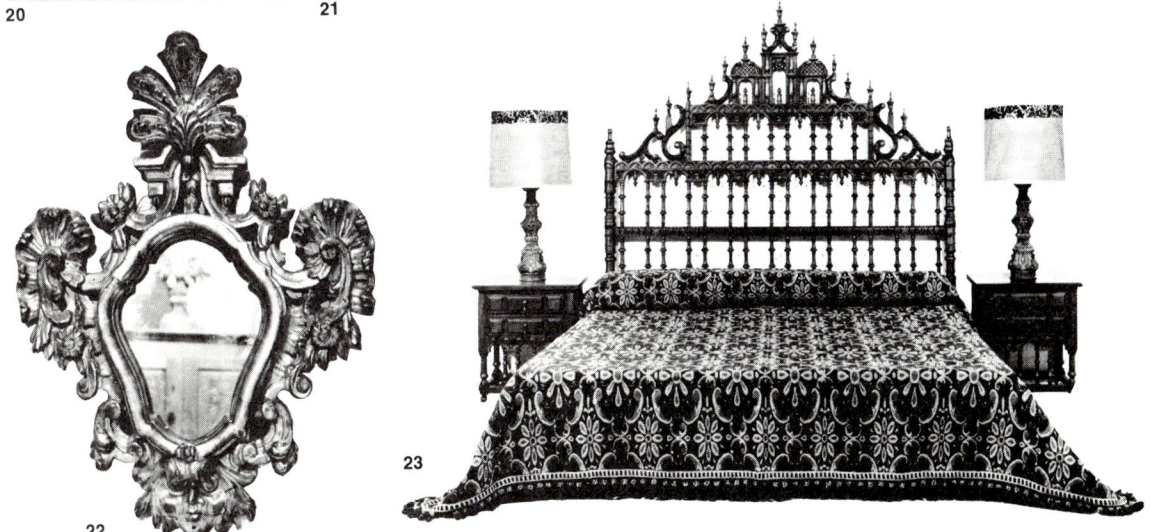

House

20
Fundação Ricardo do Espírito Santo Silva "Bonheur du Jour," a reproduction in precious woods of a Louis XVI piece made by the famous ebonist Roger Vandercruse, *dit* Lacroix, named master in 1755. $1,691.

21
Abelardo Linares Handmade wrought-iron lantern. About $70.

22
Abelardo Linares Carved mirror, gilded with real gold leaf (24" high, 20" wide). About $78. Can be made any size to order.

23
Marlau Gothic turned headboard: twin, about $737 up; double about $788 up. Bedspread in two colors: twin, about $87 up; double, about $113. End tables, about $180. Hand-carved wooden lamp bases, about $136. Lampshades, about $44.

24
Marlau Carved chest (28" high, 58" long), made from very old pine taken from demolished buildings. About $737.

25
Marlau Carved-leg dining table in various sizes. 6' long, about $490. Side chair, about $141; armchair, about $166.

House

HONG KONG

Kowloon Rattan Ware Company, 4 Hankow Road, Kowloon, Hong Kong
4-page illustrated brochure, free. Prices in $.

This firm seems to sell absolutely all the rattan screens, chairs and stools available in America, and at a third of the price. Curly, fantastic, Victorian styles, classic porch styles, and the smooth modern styles that go for high prices in New York shops. If you are planning to people a porch, garden or house with a forest of rattan, it is worth buying from here, otherwise the savings involved probably won't be worth the trouble. Most prices are from $5 to $15. They have other things not on the brochures—animal laundry hampers and tables, some small enough to go by mail. Ask for photographs of these.

GLASS AND CHINA

No one but a reckless spendthrift should buy imported expensive glass and china in America. Most of it sells for half the American prices in the country where it is made, so with little effort (but some patience), quite a lot of money can be saved, especially by people who are buying large quantities.

Like Scottish knitwear, the glass and china business seems to be one of the best organized foreign-mail-order activities; several of the shops say they have been at it for over twenty years. Goods are expertly packed, and on the rare occasion when something arrives broken, most of these shops will immediately replace the article simply on your say-so.

For some reason, English bone china, which has calcinated bone among its ingredients and is stronger than any other china, carries less duty than earthenware (the softest china) or regular porcelain. Duty on bone china comes to about 15 percent of the retail price, and shipping one five-piece place setting can cost about $5. So, for instance, at this writing on Wedgwood's "Colonnade Black," which costs $24.72 in England and $55 in New York, you save about $13 a place setting. And on Wedgwood's "Ascot"—$60.94 in England, $100 in New York—you save about $23 a place setting.

Duty on glasses for the table comes to between 11 and 13 percent of the price you pay, while surface-mail and insurance charges for eight glasses come to about $10.50, so you should add *roughly* $1.75 extra for each glass. High as that sounds, you will still save a great deal on certain glasses—for instance, about $36 on eight "Prelude" water glasses by Orrefors ($4 each in Sweden and $12.25 each in New York).

BELGIUM

Cristaux du Val St-Lambert, Etablissements Dubois, 57 Rue des Chatreux, Brussels, Belgium

This firm has many customers in America who buy Val St-Lambert glass directly from them to save money. At the moment there is no catalogue, but if you want to replenish your stock, or have seen the glass already, write and ask for the price of the style you are interested in (preferably giving style number as well).

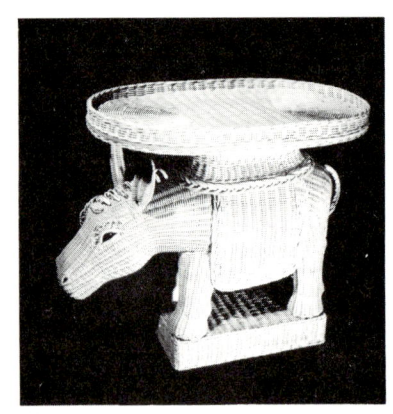

26
Kowloon Rattan Ware Company Donkey table, $10.

27
Chinacraft Ltd Royal Worcester "Hyde Park," an Italian Renaissance design raised in 24-carat gold. Five-piece place setting, about $26.

DENMARK

Frøsig, Nørrebrogade 9, DK-2200 Copenhagen, Denmark
Manufacturers' brochures: Bing and Grøndahl, Royal Copenhagen, Bjørn Wiinblad, free.

Frøsig has the very attentive Mrs. Buddig looking after American customers, who, she says, have been writing her long and interesting letters for the past fifteen years. The numbers of American customers have increased enormously, not through advertising but through the "mouth to mouth" method—not surprisingly, as you will see. Royal Copenhagen porcelain is sold here in both first and second quality, but the high standards of Bing and Grøndahl makes it possible for them to stock and sell only its second-quality porcelain, for the defects are very hard to see. Prices are consequently splendidly low for their porcelain figurines, misty-colored flowered vases, and pale-blue scenic ashtrays. When I compared prices, "Mary," a small girl in white cap and white flowered dress holding a baby in her arms, cost $63 in New York and $33, including postage, from Frøsig. "Reading Children" cost $57.50 in New York and $39.90, including postage, from Frøsig.

Also here are Bjørn Wiinblad's whimsical lovers frisking coyly through the seasons, she growing plumper and finally producing a baby—a series of twelve platters costing $3 each, including postage, available in any number from three up.

House

Old World Plates, P.O. Box 272, DK-1501 Copenhagen V, Denmark
Price list, free.

Old commemorative plates, Bing and Grøndahl for every year since 1895, Royal Copenhagen since 1908; from more recent years there is commemorative china or crystal from Denmark, England, Germany, Italy, Spain and Sweden.

ENGLAND

Chinacraft Ltd., 499 Oxford Street, Marble Arch, London W1R 2BH, England
24-page color catalogue, free. Prices in $.
Dinner China: John Aynsley, Royal Crown Derby, Royal Doulton, Minton, Royal Worcester, Wedgwood, Coalport, Crown Staffordshire, Royal Chelsea
Crystal: Stuart, Waterford, Tudor, St. Louis, Edinburgh, Thomas Webb, Royal Brierley
China Ornaments and Giftware: Crown Staffordshire, Wedgwood, Coalport, Royal Crown Derby, Aynsley, Royal Chelsea, Royal Doulton, Hammersley, Royal Worcester

Chinacraft shows the widest range of the London shops in their very good and complete catalogue, which includes sample shipping costs and customs duty. They show a little more china than the other shops, and a lot more traditional cut glass. They also have a whole section of giftware with quite a few pieces of Wedgwood's Jasperware illustrated — the famous pale-blue, green or black china, with Greek figures in white relief: earrings and brooches for $14 to $18, two ashtrays or heart-shaped boxes for about $17, three little cigarette cups for $18. Also, Crown Staffordshire flower clusters: eight place-card holders, $15.40; six pairs of tiny salt and pepper pots thoroughly disguised as pink flowers in white vases, $30; Coalport porcelain roses or posies in bowls, and Coalport houses. Finally, much more expensive pieces like the Wedgwood "prestige" pieces, vases and bowls at around $250 each; and Royal Worcester limited-editions.

Dent Glass, Risehill Mill, Dent, Sedbergh, West Riding of Yorkshire, England
Leaflet, free.

Dent Glass has chosen two goblets and a tumbler by Val St. Lambert which they will engrave in one of two type styles. Most requests are for anniversary goblets at a special price — at this time, a goblet with two initials with two dates costs about $18. At higher prices you can have additional letters and signs of the zodiac engraved.

Gered, 174 Piccadilly, London W.1, England
Wedgwood and Spode 20-page color brochures, free. Prices in $.

If you definitely want Wedgwood or Spode, write to Gered; they show more table settings from these companies than anyone else.

The Leach Pottery, Saint Ives, Cornwall, England
2-page leaflet, $2.

Bernard Leach, probably the most famous modern potter in the world, sells at agreeably low prices pottery designed by himself and made in his studios by apprentices. The first Western potter to study in Japan, Leach came back to Cornwall with Shoji Hamada and developed a classically simple style both in his own original pots and also in an appetizing collection of pottery to be used around the house: stewpots, jugs, coffeepots and baking dishes, soup bowls, sauce pots, casseroles and coffee cups. Some of them have an unglazed sandy outside and a smooth glossy glaze inside, others are glazed on the outside in tenmoko that varies between black and rust, oatmeal, gray, or pale celadon green. Prices vary between 95 cents for an egg cup and $9 for a large lidded coffeepot.

Leather and Snook, 167 Piccadilly, London W1V 9DE, England
12-page color brochure, free. Prices in $.
Royal Crown Derby, John Aynsley, Royal Worcester, Royal Doulton, Wedgwood, Minton, Coalport and Thomas Webb Crystal

Leather and Snook puts out a small and neat brochure showing just a few of all the patterns they can supply from the above companies. Prices are only given for five-piece place settings, but all details and prices can be supplied when you write.

John Sinclair Ltd., 266 Glossop Road, Sheffield S10 2HS, England
Leaflet, free. Prices in $.

This firm sells collector's plates and mugs, figurines and special issues produced by the leading English china and glass manufacturers. Every three months or so they send leaflets to their customers. The ones they sent me were for the Coalport china cottages, and various pieces that I hadn't seen before, such as a Wedgwood calendar plate, a Wedgwood children's story plate, and a Winston Spencer Churchill Centenary crystal bell.

Tabor Designs, 78 Northgate, Canterbury, England
Leaflet, 50 cents. Prices in $.

Here you can get craftsman-made pottery tableware in either a speckled oatmeal or a dark-brown glaze. No plates, just teapots, coffeepots, goblets and tankards, storage jars and spice jars. Prices are low, but as pottery is heavy and needs careful packing, postage will be expensive.

FRANCE

Limoges-Unic, Ventes par Correspondence, 12 Rue de Paradis, Paris X, France
120-page catalogue in French, $3 (refundable).

Limoges-Unic puts out a large and luscious color catalogue for their busy mail-order service. Elegant French Limoges porcelain by leading manufacturers with impressively literary names — "Balzac," "Colette," "Corneille," "Gide," "George Sand," etc.

Glass by Baccarat, Lorraine, Val St-Lambert, and modern glass by Daum, including their household objects.

Also French silver, which is a grayer color than most silver, and silver plate. But I compared one or two prices on the famous French "Cristofle" silver plate, and prices seem to be about the same in New York.

Obéron, 73 Champs-Elysées, Paris VIII, France
22-page catalogue, $1.50 (refundable with first purchase). Prices in $.

A large tax-free store for foreigners, Obéron is an excellent place to buy crystal gifts. The catalogue is in English and shows plenty of Baccarat and Lalique objects, some at half the American prices. A Baccarat squirrel paperweight costs $25 at Obéron and $150 in New York. A Baccarat caviar bowl is $94 at Obéron and around $100 in New York. Lots of table items, vases and smokers' sets, and also some Baccarat crystal stemware, each glass up to $9 less than in New York

House

28
The Leach Pottery Oven-proof stoneware with glazed interiors. Ashtrays, small bowls and lidded soup bowls, around $3; coffeepot and tall jug, around $7 and $9.

29
The Leach Pottery Glazed stoneware in black to rust, gray-brown, pale green or oatmeal. Small pieces at various prices from $2.50, large pieces around $12. *photo Studio St. Ives*

30
Leather and Snook Royal Crown Derby "Olde Avesbury." Five-piece place setting, $32.69.

31
Royal Tara Bone china "Georgian" shape, "Bird of Paradise" pattern. Five-piece place setting, about $20, including postage.

32
Dent Glass Presentation glass engraved with one initial, $17; extra initials and numerals, about $1 each.

House

(the Baccarat "Harcourt" water jug costs $83 at Obéron and $110 in New York).

Obéron also stocks porcelain gifts: Chantilly boxes; swan-shaped salt and pepper dishes at $10.40 the pair; blue-and-gold Limoges ashtrays, $3.10; informal Porcelaine de Paris baking dishes; and Fourmaintraux flowery earthenware.

GERMANY

Franz Widmann und Sohn, am Karlstor Unter den Arkaden, 8 Munich 2, Germany
This is the place for the renowned Hummel figures, the chubby children named things like "Little Wanderer," "Playmates" and "She Loves Me—She Loves Me Not." Prices are considerably lower than American prices.

German toy shops also sell Hummel.

Rosenthal Studio-Haus, Dr. Zoellner KG, Leopoldstrasse 44, 8 Munich 23, Germany
Leaflets.

Rosenthal's rather grand modern china by leading European designers ranges in style from thick blue and brown pottery to graceful white pieces painted with bouquets, and in such varied patterns that almost everyone is bound to find something he likes. Basically there are about twelve different shapes, each of which can be decorated with any of several patterns, and each one has glasses and stainless-steel flatware to match, often by the same designer.

In addition to the tableware, Rosenthal produces vases; ashtrays; candle holders; pretty little table lamps with molded white or colored bases and brightly colored shades; plates decorated by Bjørn Wiinblad with wide-eyed figures in rich reds, blues and gold; and also "smoker's sets" with an ashtray, lighter and cigarette box in each set. I compared American and German prices on the crystal star candleholders, which turn out to be one-third or half price in Germany; and the Bjørn Wiinblad Sarastro dinner service in white, decorated with hand-applied 18-carat gold, is also about half price (you'd save several hundred dollars if you bought a set for eight from Germany instead of in America). And the Rosenthal "Grill cutlery" with hand-painted china handles are also half price in Germany. (I chose these patterns to compare *only* because I have the American prices to hand. I am sure the price differences are typical.)

At the moment it isn't certain what literature will be available on the Rosenthal goods; the big catalogue probably won't be published any more, though there may be leaflets on individual patterns. I think the best way of buying will be to look at the china in your local store and then write to Germany asking about pieces that you like.

Visitors Pavillon, A. Kazantzis K. G., Ditmarstrasse G, 6 Frankfurt am Main, Germany
Promotion for silver flatware made in the United States, free.
Sterling and silver-plate trays, coffee and tea sets, candelabra, gift items made in the United States, free.
Lenox china and crystal, free.
Gorham china and crystal, free.
Franciscan china, free.
German sterling and silver-plate trays, coffee and tea sets, candelabra, gift items, etc., free.
German china, free.
German crystal glasses, free.
German crystal and china gift items, free.
Silverware by Christofle, Paris, free.
Any of the above brochures, $1 air mail.

This extraordinarily useful address was generously given to me by a reader, Roberta J. Frus, who writes: "Highly geared to mail-order business, particularly military. Sends free multi-catalogues on German crystal, china (Rosenthal, Johan Haviland, and others), silver, both holloware and flatware. Also gives special Spring promotion sales and special offers on over stock or on crystal with slight imperfections . . . I ordered beautiful crystal glasses and decanter set. It took three months, and as the dollar kept devaluing I had to send additional money. But their best offers are on all brands of American silver—both flat and holloware, 30% to 40% off. Order and money sent to Germany but silver is sent from American silver company. Friends of mine had just purchased twelve-piece place setting of sterling. When they saw my catalogue, they took back their silver, told store they were getting a divorce, and ordered the same thing from Frankfurt at $200 saving."

ICELAND

Glit Lava Ceramics, Hofdabakka 9, Reykjavik, Iceland
Color brochure, free. Prices in $.

Iceland is one of the most active volcanic countries in the world and Icelandic pottery is made mostly of volcanic lava. The unusual ceramics sold by Glit have shiny gray-blue glazes which fade into paler cream or are darkened by brown, and on the outside of the pots are rough bands of clay "inspired by bubbling volcanic craters and glowing streams of lava." Lanterns, hanging pots, candleholders, plates, bowls and mugs cost between $10 and $30 each.

HOLLAND

Focke and Meltzer, Kalverstraat 152, Amsterdam, Holland
Christmas gift brochure, $1, September; Christmas and Commemorative Plates brochure, $1, March; other manufacturers' brochures, free. Prices in $.

Founded in 1823, this international glass-and-china shop is visited by over twenty thousand Americans a year. Besides stocking Royal Delft and the best-known Dutch crystal hand-blown Leerdam and hand-cut Kristalunion, they also carry china and crystal from most other European countries: Val St-Lambert, Waterford, Rosenthal, Herend, etc., so if you are looking for something that you can't find elsewhere, try them. If you are interested in Christmas plates, Focke and Meltzer has a brochure showing most of them together with other commemorative plates ("The Moon," "Mayflower" and "Mothers"), all at about two-thirds the cost in America. Prices start at $11, including postage.

Royal Delftware, International Mailing Dept., Markt 45, Delft, Holland
Royal Delft brochures, free.

In 1969 this special department was set up to sell genuine Royal Delft (founded in 1653) by mail. Royal Delft was one of the first European earthenwares to show Chinese influence, and the familiar blue flower and bird designs are more robust and less formal than the leading china from other countries. Although plates are shown, the catalogues are mostly full of jugs, mugs, vases, candlesticks, table lamps, and traditional tiles with Delft designs which, this firm says, cannot be found in America at all. Prices are mainly in the $20–$50 range, including postage, with wall plates inspired by Rembrandt paintings costing over $100.

House

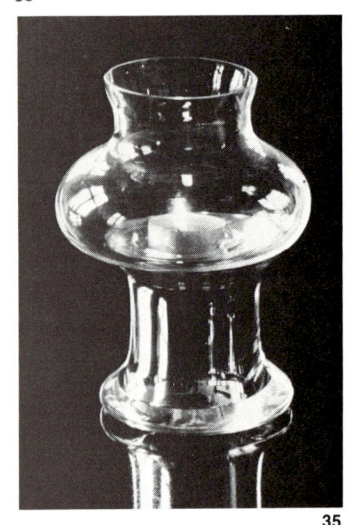

33
Cellini's Silver Factory Capodimonte figurine "Small Girl with Dog." $90.
photo Bazzechi

34
Nordiska Kristall Gift box with two glass plates, $10.35.

35
Nordiska Kristall Hurricane lamp, silver-colored base and clear glass, $14.10; gold-colored base, $15.55.
photo Stig T. Karlsson

36
H. L. Barnett A boxed pair of large Dartington crystal goblets. About $15 a pair. Surface postage $1.80.

37
Design Centre Candleholders, pepper mill, nut cracker, cigarette box and plate in wrought iron. Prices from $3.

House

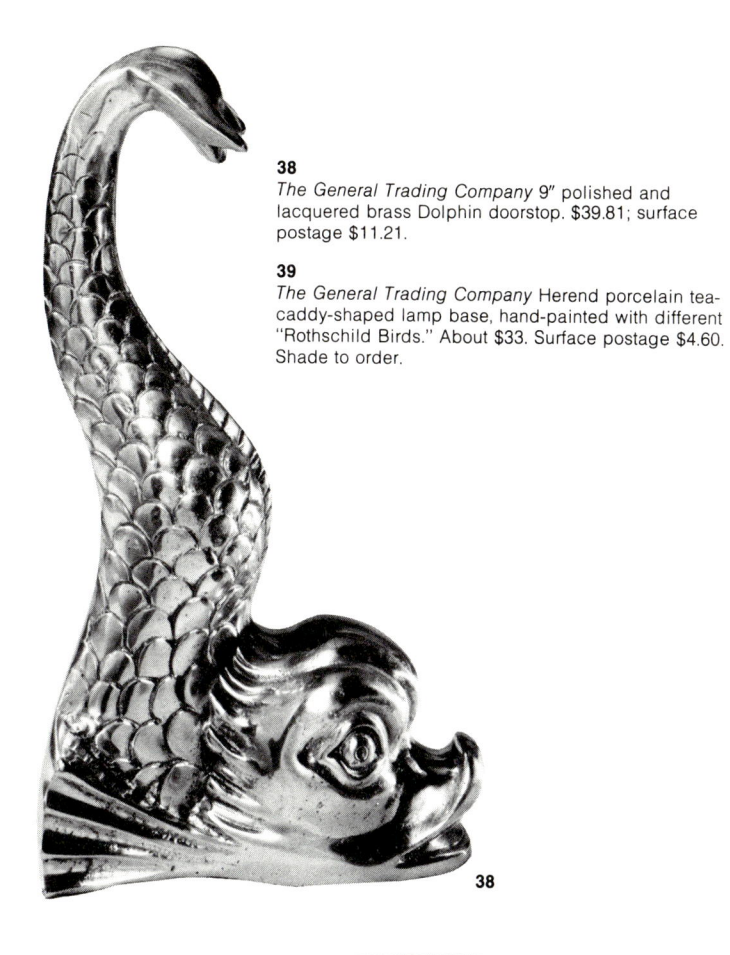

38
The General Trading Company 9" polished and lacquered brass Dolphin doorstop. $39.81; surface postage $11.21.

39
The General Trading Company Herend porcelain tea-caddy-shaped lamp base, hand-painted with different "Rothschild Birds." About $33. Surface postage $4.60. Shade to order.

40
The General Trading Company Black-and-white print wastepaper basket, about $10.14; surface postage $4.60. Black-and-white umbrella stand, $16.13.

41
Halcyon Days 1½" boxes enameled on copper inspired by eighteenth-century Bilston and Battersea enameled boxes. About $26 each.

IRELAND

Dublin Crystal Glass Co., Avondale, Carysfort Avenue, Blackrock, Co. Dublin, Ireland
Brochure, 25 cents.

This is what the managing director of Dublin Crystal wrote to me: "At the moment, we only have a stopgap brochure as we are bringing out a new range of items in Crystal such as ship's decanters, baskets, large plates, also a range of cased Crystal in various colors. We are the only firm in Eire producing this type of high-quality Crystal. We are also extending our sand-engraving business. We do such work as presentation pieces, Company award, Christmas gifts by large organizations (logos, company crests), and high-quality souvenir pieces. All of these pieces would be specially cut with a panel left clear for engraving with the customer's motif." I have seen the stopgap brochure and it shows two suites of hand-cut crystal at prices that are considerably lower than those of internationally promoted glass such as Waterford.

Stephen Faller, Industrial Estate, Mervue, Galway, Ireland
Manufacturers' brochures. Lladro figurines; Doulton, Minton, Waterford glass and Galway crystal, any or all of these for $1.

Apparently in the 1840s the Duchess of Sutherland had the novel idea of decorating her house with plates on the moldings around her rooms—within a few years the fad had caught on all over the country and has continued off and on ever since. Doulton makes a series of rack plates for people still doing it, mainly representing historic English buildings and famous authors such as Shakespeare and Dickens.

Waterford is available here too, and so are the very popular Lladro figurines.

Robert Hoggs and Co. Ltd., 10 Donegall Square West, Belfast BT1 6J, Northern Ireland
Information on Royal Doulton figures, Waterford glass, Belleek china, Old Country Roses, free. Prices in $.

In addition to the ubiquitous Royal Doulton and Waterford, Hoggs sells harder-to-find Belleek china—distinctive ivory-colored tea services with molded surfaces in imitation canework and shamrocks, vases with raised flowers and decorations. However, factory deliveries are so slow (six to twenty-four months on Coalport and Royal Doulton, and unknown on Belleek) that Robert Hogg asks customers *not* to pay in advance.

Royal Tara Ltd., Tara Hall, Galway, Ireland
10-page color leaflet, $1 (refundable).

Royal Tara has a leaflet illustrating their own bone china, and if you are longing for delicate old posies and rosebuds, write to them, as a few of their patterns are more romantic and country-cottage-ish than anything made by the better-known English companies. There are also mugs and tea sets decorated with hunting scenes.

ITALY

Cellini's Silver Factory, Piazza Santa Croce 12, Florence, Italy
Catalogue, free. Prices in $.

In the middle of this silver catalogue there are two full color pages of Italian Capodimonte figurines—humorous and "world renowned" as the catalogue says. Prices from $56 for "The Dog and the Butterfly" to $280 for "The Musicians"—a couple of down-and-out old men looking very pleased with themselves as they play on the guitar and violin, their pockets bulging with bottles of booze.

KENYA

Rowland Ward (East Africa) Ltd., P.O. Box 40991, Nairobi, Kenya
Leaflet, free.

The managing director of this firm says that they have a world-wide reputation as taxidermists and also sell high-quality East African goods. By mail they sell glasses, decanters, jugs and punch bowls engraved with big-game animals (lion, elephant, buffalo, giraffe and sable antelope). The glasses are available singly or in sets, and each glass costs between $7 and $12. The glasses are manufactured in, and mailed directly from, Bavaria. But they take three months to reach you from the time that Rowland Ward gets your order.

NORWAY

Porsgrunn Porselen, Karl Johansgate 14, Oslo 1, Norway
Leaflet, free.

I got a rather misspelled letter from this shop, whose card announces that it is a "store specializing in Norwegian porcelain." They tell me that "as a ruel our broshures will always be available," and they sent me a leaflet illustrating "very intresting Norwegian Mounten Flora porcelain." This is a coffee set with each of six place settings prettily decorated with a different wild mountain flower and described on the back in Norwegian and English. A plate and a cup and saucer together cost just under $9.

SWEDEN

Nordiska Kristall, Kungsgatan 9, S-111 43 Stockholm, Sweden
Catalogue, $1; $2 air mail. Prices in $.

This fifty-year-old firm in the center of Stockholm sells the best Swedish crystal by Orrefors, Kosta-Boda, Skruf and Strömbergshyttan. Their excellent catalogue shows a splendid assortment of possible gifts: perfume bottles, ice buckets, bells, smoker's sets, candleholders, hurricane lamps, chandeliers, decanters, bowls, vases, ashtrays and purely decorative pieces. This firm also has over sixty different stemware patterns in stock. Swedish glass is considerably cheaper when bought direct from Sweden, and is a really good buy.

PUB (Paul U. Bergströms AB), Box 40 140, Export Department, S-103 43, Stockholm 40, Sweden
Kosta, Orrefors, Skruf glass, leaflets $1.50. Rörstrand china, $1. Prices in $.

This large Stockholm department store sells Swedish glass by mail and also Rörstrand's famous modern china tableware. The most familiar pattern, "Mon Ami"—a regular design of stylized four-petal blue flowers on a white background—costs $3 per dinner plate, $8.50 for a coffeepot, and $22 for a casserole with lid.

TAIWAN

China Pottery Arts Co., 14 Central South Road, Section 2, Peitou, Taipei 112, Taiwan
Color catalogue $1; $3.50 air mail. Prices in $.

The big, magnificently presented catalogue introduces China pottery with a trumpet blast: "Mr. K. C. Jen, for the purpose of reviving and developing Chinese culture, making human life more pleasant and colorful, and promoting the mutual comprehension of those particularly in favor of Chinese culture, founded this company on February 10, 1958." The introduction goes on to say that the company manufactures Chinese classical pottery reproductions of different dynasties and that the designs, glazes and colors are patterned after pottery, porcelain and bronze articles in local museums. Much of the catalogue shows dignified vases decorated with flowers or Chinese scenes at prices mostly between $10 and $50, but there are also some functional pieces—punch bowls, tea sets and lamp bases. Non-pottery goods include imitation-bronze garden ornaments, wooden figurines, marble vases and goblets, and extraordinarily ornate furniture with carved dragons and other mythical beasts. Shipping prices are given for each piece and Mr. Jen says that the tourist industries in Taiwan and Japan have listed the China Pottery Arts workshops as a must for tourists, so they are obviously thoroughly used to shipping and mail order.

HARDWARE

Antique Handles, P. O. Box No. 1, Bolton, Lancashire, England
Period door-fittings brochure, 50 cents.
Reproduction cabinet-handles and fittings brochure, 25 cents.

A small collection of brass reproductions of period door fittings and furniture include Regency, Georgian and Victorian designs. For cabinets and antique furniture, there is a separate brochure illustrating reproduction handles and casters.

J. D. Beardmore, 3-5 Percy Street, London W1P OEJ, England
Illustrated leaves, free.

You will find twenty thousand different items stocked in this wonderland of reproduction furniture fittings and architectural metalwork in brass, bronze, copper and iron. Prices are not available now and whatever they are, they are clearly not low, though Beardmore's says that they are lower than they would be in America. For top-quality period reproductions of the "great eras in brass," write and tell them what you are looking for and in what style. People who crave just one fabulous door knocker and people who are trying to outfit an entire building in one style should be equally well served, because the range is very complete. There are decorative fittings for electric lights, curtains, bookshelves, cabinets, cloakrooms, clocks. If it is metal—or can be made more elegantly in metal—it is here. You can even have your keys fitted with a variety of grand cast-brass ends to match other period fittings.

Erme Wood Forge, Woodlands, Ivybridge, South Devon, England
Brochure, free.

Hand-forged door knockers, hearth furniture, weather vanes and gates, mainly to customers' orders. Weather vanes start at about $33 and go up to $350; there is a huge choice of models. A 3' gate starts at about $110, and other gates go up to $1,500.

Kingsworthy Foundry Co. Ltd., Kingsworthy, Winchester, Hampshire, England
Catalogue, $1.

Kingsworthy Foundry produces magnificent cast-iron reproduction antique firebacks, wall plaques and decorative castings. The firebacks (to go at the back of the fireplace) are adorned with winged lions, royal gatherings, angelic scenes, warriors and lions and unicorns, and they cost from about $30 to over $100 but will be very expensive to ship. Less expensive to ship because they can go by parcel post are the charming reproductions of Victorian doorstops of Wellington, a sphinx, a lion, a man with a twisted hat, or best of all, Punch or Judy. The doorstops are made of iron and painted black, but you can paint them yourself in bright colors as some of the originals were painted. The stops cost around $12 to $17 each.

Knobs and Knockers, 61–65 Judd Street, London W.C.1, England
Catalogue, free; $1 air mail.

A small but very varied collection of door knockers, door and cabinet handles, hinges, locks, bell pushes, mailboxes, coat hooks and house numbers are shown in this catalogue. The export manager says that "our fine range of English period door furniture seems to appeal tremendously to our overseas customers," but I would have thought that the most useful designs for Americans would be the very handsome, simple modern ones which are so hard to find in America and which are well represented at Knobs and Knockers.

S. C. Pierce & Son Ltd., Bredfield Ironworks, Woodbridge, Suffolk, England
General brochure for gates, window grilles, railing, free.

Pierce makes hand-forged gates at prices starting at $75 for a 3'-wide by 4'6"-tall gate.

HOUSEHOLD OBJECTS AND GIFTS

CANADA

Habitat Toronto, 277 Victoria Street, Toronto 200, Ontario, Canada
Brochure, free. October.

Habitat Toronto imports much, but not all, of its good-taste household items from England. If you haven't got a shop near you that sells modern and colorful things for the kitchen and house, then ask to be put on the Habitat mailing list. Glass candleholders, wooden pestle and mortars, bright enamel canisters, pottery oil-and-vinegar bottles, big cushions and educational toys—you know the kind of thing—and very pleasant it all is. Habitat says that it is now selling Canadian feather quilts at $70 for a single-bed size. Their American customers say they are cheaper than in the United States, but they are still more expensive than the European ones (and, of course, you do pay duty for imports from Canada).

DENMARK

Den Permanente, Vesterport, DK-1620 Copenhagen, Denmark
Catalogue, $3. Prices in $.

Everything shown and sold at "The Permanent Exhibition of Danish Arts and Crafts" has been chosen by an independent selection committee to represent the best in Danish applied arts, made both industrially and by craftsmen. The result is a stunning array of top-quality modern pots and pans, glass, cutlery, ice buckets, salad bowls, etc. Some of them are widely exported and familiar to people who like modern design: Dansk, Kastrup-Holmegaard glass, Kaj Bojesen wooden bowls and toys. Others, such as the "Cylinda" line (a superb new range in stainless steel; see the ice buckets, designed with some sort of collaboration from Professor Arne Jacobson) I have only seen in one New York shop. Prices seem to be roughly one-third lower than in America, so whether you save any money depends on postage and duty. A better reason for writing to Den Permanente is to get beautiful things not available locally. A lot of furniture is shown in the catalogue, too.

ENGLAND

Anything Lefthanded Ltd., 65 Beak Street, London W.1, England
Catalogue, 50 cents.

The owner of this store is left-handed himself and feels keenly the minor, daily miseries of this neglected minority, so the shop and catalogue are packed with gadgets to make life slightly less burdensome. Some seem to a (no doubt prejudiced) right-hander to be rather an exaggeration, like special pastry slicers and knives—surely lefties don't have much trouble with ordinary carving knives (but the shop owner writes: "Our pastry slicers/carving knives/bread knives ARE specific to the Left Hand. Ask any Left Hander if they like using a right hand carver!"). But left-handed scissors and fountain pens are very popular, and so are tailor's shears. And there are playing cards that show the pips whatever hand they are fanned in, left-handed pruning shears (secateurs), can openers and many more gadgets of all sorts, including a left-handed sink.

H. L. Barnett, Brunswick House, Torridge Hill, Bideford, North Devon, England
66-page catalogue, free; $1 air mail.

A good year-round mail-order service. The catalogue includes the usual gifts from first-rate firms: Smythson leather, Jacquard silk scarves, Fortnum and Mason food hampers, but also quite a few newer ideas. Pretty handmade Austrian kettle holders and oven gloves, about $2.25; framed reproductions of Piranese's Rome, $10; Celtic silver jewelry from $5; scarlet Portuguese embroidered aprons, $5. An assortment of calendars, including a special doodler's calendar with space and suggestions for doodling, $2.25; and a children's ark calendar with animals to be cut out on each page. There are children's toys from Galt, John Adams and Merrit, and for more expensive gifts, clothes from Peter Saunders, mohair tunics from Highland Home Industries, and Langmore sheepskin jackets and coats, $118 and up.

Beau Windows, Beauty Blinds Ltd., Priority Works, Gundry Lane, Bridport, Dorset, England
Color brochure, 25 cents.

It is hard to find inexpensive window shades in good colors. This firm makes shades to measure from well-known British woven fabrics or vinyl, all treated to be dirt-resistant and easily cleanable. The patented roller design enables you to change the fabric if you want to. The solid colors are above average (although not perfect), patterns tend to be stylized flowers or old-fashioned rose posies. Fabrics are sold by the yard so that you can make matching draperies, cushions and bedspreads (or in the case of vinyls, shower curtains).

The Design Centre, 28 Haymarket, London SW1Y 4SU, England
Color catalogue, $2.

Probably thousands of American tourists have, over the years, visited the Design Council's handsome exhibit center right off Piccadilly. The Council's aim has been to show to foreign tourists (and businessmen) the best in modern British design, and recently they have opened a small store selling exceptionally well designed souvenirs as well as their own publications. Now the Council has gone a step further and prepared an extremely useful if unfortunately expensive catalogue showing some of their best exhibits. If you want to buy any of the items shown, write to the Centre and you will be informed of who will sell it to you by mail. If you're interested in selling the goods in the United States, you can write directly to the manufacturer.

As you'd expect, the Centre catalogue is filled with lovely objects, a number of which are described separately in these pages, as the Centre has always been one of my first stops in London ever since I started doing research for *The Catalogue of Catalogues*. Probably the most useful items for Americans are the toys, which include some particularly charming gifts for small children; dolls; shoe and pajama bags with English motifs; delightful small cars; planes; and a brass-and-steam roller that I suspect most fathers would borrow permanently from their children. For adults, home accessories are probably the best choices, perfect presents—mostly in the category of terribly well designed versions of everyday items such as clocks, glassware, silver, etc. If you've decided that you're not going to be able to go to England for a while but would still like to give your friends (and yourself) some of the things that England makes so well, then the Design Centre catalogue will probably take care of your Christmas and wedding-gift lists for several years to come.

Egertons, Lyme Street, Axminster, Devonshire EX13 5DB, England
Catalogue, 25 cents; $1 air mail. Prices in $.

This "postal gift and shopping service" was expressly started to give people overseas an easy way of gift shopping for friends and relatives in Great Britain, though, of course, they do mail to America as well. Although it isn't very glamorously presented, this catalogue does look like the answer for a desperate would-be gift giver, as it has a large selection of standard gifts, from foods such as honey and cream (or even decorated birthday, aniversary and Christmas cakes) to cigars, whiskey, luggage and leather handbags, sheepskin goods, knitwear, jewelry, pottery, china, glassware, pewter, brass, blankets, clocks and a large section of children's toys.

The General Trading Company, 144 Sloane Street, Sloane Square, London S.W.1, England ♥
Export brochure, free. Prices in $.
34-page general catalogue, $2 (refundable).

The General Trading Company is housed in three discreetly converted Victorian residences and looks more like an elegant private home than a shop. They rather extravagantly call themselves "London's most fascinating store"—but you might well agree. Certainly their smashing catalogue is full of beautiful, unusual and decorative things for the home—antiques or in antique styles: pottery pomanders; animal-shaped brass doorstops; creamy Queen Victoria jugs made from an original mold; gold-tooled leather string boxes with gilt-handled Sheffield scissors; and nineteenth-century brass magazine racks. Lots of glass and porcelain, and a small, impeccable collection of reproduction and antique furniture: a buttoned Victorian sewing chair; cherry-wood end tables with brass-handled drawers; a leather-covered brass-studded library ladder that folds into a pole.

The smaller export brochure lists quite a bit of porcelain and other things specially suitable for mailing abroad.

Halcyon Days, 14 Brook Street, London W1Y 1AA, England
2-page color leaflet, free. October.

Halcyon Days has revived the eighteenth-century art of enameling on copper. In 1753 at Battersea, London, trinkets and curiosities—snuffboxes, scent bottles, bonbonnières—began to be produced and decorated with scenes and sentimental messages. Similar workshops were set up in Bilston, Staffordshire, and although the craft only lasted for a hundred years, "Battersea" enamels, as they are now called, are prized collectors' pieces. These fetching new Bilston and Battersea boxes are similar to the originals in design and coloring. For $20 each there are little 1½" boxes with flower or rose bouquets; eighteenth-century landscapes or messages, such as "Token of Friendship" or "Forget Me Not." For up to $40 there are round 2¼" and egg-shaped boxes with the same sort of designs, plus birds and animals, and one with a portrait of Napoleon.

Helios Home Supplies, Tytherington Center, MacClesfield, Cheshire, England
40-page catalogue, free.

A useful firm that sells an assortment of things, usually for the house, and always of reputable brands. The catalogue shows a fully illustrated collection of Old Hall cutlery and tableware, England's most famous streamlined stainless steel: vegetable dishes, casseroles, sauce boats, butter dishes, hors-d'oeuvre trays; a three-section hors-d'oeuvre tray in rosewood, $8; a four-piece tea set, $23. Fifty-piece flatware sets start at $80, three-piece carving sets at $18.

"Dorma"—Terylene-and-cotton sheets which have flower designs and deep colors like orange, with blankets and bedspreads to match—are much more expensive than American sheets. Twin size starts at $6.50. Twin-size Irish-linen sheets are $22 a pair.

There is also Bridge cut glass, $28 for six water goblets; Taunton Vale flowery kitchen accessories (pastry boards, spice racks, clocks, shopping lists); table mats from $6.50 for twelve: Dutch interiors, English birds, Turpin fruits, London scenes, Oxford and Cambridge colleges. Old prints of Oxford and Cambridge colleges are also reproduced on linen dishtowels, four for $4.50.

Mosesson Games Ltd., Creeting Road, Stowmarket, Suffolk, England
Color catalogue, $1.50.

Adult coffee-table games have become very modish lately, and here is a group of games redesigned to be left around as stylish decorations. The games are big and expensive and can be bought separately or as a set that fit into a support base to be a "Games Nest." There are two shiny modern chess sets (one with transparent acrylic chessmen, the other with black and white men); a silver blue-and-orange table hockey, a green-and-red maze; a red, white and mauve set of Bronx Bull (a ball game played on a 63" by 30" table); and red and blue table skittles. To match the games there is a modern games table on casters; four suede-covered hassocks fit into it for storage.

RD Design, 43 Derwent Road, Honley, Huddersfield, England
Leaflet, 1 International Reply Coupon; air mail, 2 International Reply Coupons.

Four young people started this firm hoping that there would be a market for well-designed, modern home accessories. I don't know how much of a market they found for the rest of their stuff, but their chess sets have been included in the Design Index and have been displayed by the London Design Centre, and, the designers say, have brought them international recognition. The leaflets show jazzy redesigned chess sets with half the pieces in clear acrylic and the other half in purple, green, or smoke-brown. Prices are from about $25 to over $50 per set.

Smythson's, 54 New Bond Street, London W1Y ODE, England ☙
Gift brochure, free. Proprietary list, free. Writing-paper samples, free.

The English *Harper's Bazaar* called Smythson's "an international status symbol" (along with Hardy's, sports, and John Lobb, clothes). They are famous for their blue writing paper, which, they say, is by far their greatest export to America, and will send samples of their poshly plain blue-and-cream stationery and their address dies. Paper can be bought plain, printed or initialed.

Smythson's also makes diaries, which are not sold by mail, since they are distributed in America. But other distinguished-looking things for the desk are sold by mail: loose-leaf morocco address books, from about $30; polished pigskin visitors' books embossed with your house name in gold, from about $55; wallets; onyx desk sets; a series of record books in which to make notes in an orderly way about hobbies and special interests: garden, golf, hunting, motoring, music, theater, wine, etc.; and the most expensive of the lot—$7 for one indexed "Blondes, Brunettes, and Redheads." And, in various sizes, indexed notebooks labeled "Christmas," "Gifts," "Menus" and "Guests," or a tycoonish three-city address book—"London-Paris-New York."

The gift catalogue contains lots of leather, and gadgets for fanatical golfers: gold-plated tees, golf-ball table lighters, and a home practice putter with a removable glass ashtray.

KITCHEN

E. Dehillerin, 18-20 Rue Coquillière, Paris I, France
12-page catalogue in French, free.

The world's most famous kitchen shop is in Paris, naturally enough, and sells by mail to America, *but* although they understand written English, they can only reply in French. They also advise customers to get together with friends and family for orders because only orders for merchandise weighing over 44 pounds are accepted (and go sea freight).

The catalogue, which is strictly for serious cooks, shows a workmanlike assortment of copper cooking pots and pans in all shapes and sizes: basic, nongimmicky utensils; good French chopping knives; and a range of classic molds (but no animal shapes or anything like that); Doufeu enameled cast-iron cooking pots; and what they call "*fantasie*" copper, including a jardiniere; lovely rustic stewpots; champagne buckets; and *hâtelets*, skewers decorated with fish, birds and animals. Prices are not in the catalogue, and are only given upon application.

House

42
Mothercare (see Clothes section) Blender grinds up meat and purées cooked fruit and vegetables for baby food. The transparent bowl at the bottom can be used as a feeding dish. About $4.

43
J. Jolles Studios Gros-point bag with black, beige, red or blue background. About $125.

44
J. Jolles Studios Gros-point purse. About $88.

45
Het Kantenhuis White, cream or pastel linen bun cozy with Battenberg lace. About $6.50.
photo Studio Hartland

46
Madeira Superbia Eight cut-work place mats and eight 18" square napkins in colored, white or ecru linen. About $55 the set.

47
Madeira Superbia Petit-point picture, canvas size 21" × 24", embroidery 11½" × 15". About $55.

J. Fröschl and Co., Schwanthalerstrasse 29, 8 Munich, Germany
160-page catalogue in German, $2.25.

Fröschl is the largest chain of electrical-appliance shops in Germany, and says they sell all German electrical appliances on the market. They are mostly 220 volts AC and can be used in America with a transformer. So if you are very design-conscious, you can get some sleek German appliances at lower prices than here (when available). Fröschl also carries excellent saucepans, including beautiful Silit, enameled in red, blue or green, with circles inside squares in a lighter shade of the same color. Prices are not given in the catalogue; you must write and ask.

Any electric appliance that runs on 220 volts instead of 110 volts will need a transformer, which can be bought through an American electrical supplies store.

LACE, LINEN, EMBROIDERY AND CROCHET

The lace shops in this section say that the art of making lace by hand is dying out, since fewer and fewer young people are learning it. And it is clearly such a specialized and delicate work that while people may continue to embroider as a hobby, few people will have the patience to make lace. So perhaps it would be sensible for people who like the idea of heirloom lace to get it while they still can.

AUSTRIA

J. Jolles Studios, Andreasgasse 6, Vienna VII, Austria
20-page catalogue of gros-point handbags, 30 cents; $1 air mail.
20-page catalogue of small petit-point articles, 30 cents; $1 air mail.
Two 40-page catalogues of petit-point evening bags, 30 cents each; air mail $1 each.

The world's most productive needlepoint producers, the Jolles Studios, won a Grand Prix at the Brussels World Fair. They design, make up and sell an enormous number of petit-point and gros-point purses and some tapestries at their Vienna shop, and for mail order they have four good catalogues.

Madeira Superbia (below) also has needlepoint.
Obéron (see Handicrafts and Special Local Products) has less expensive needlepoint.

BELGIUM

Maria Loix, 54 Rue d'Arenberg, Brussels 1, Belgium

Maison F. Rubbrecht, 23 Grand' Place, Brussels
Price lists, free.

Belgium is not only thought to produce the finest linen in the world, but is also renowned for comparatively inexpensive lace.

Both these top shops are very well known to American tourists for their "serious" prices and "perfect" service, and they supply unillustrated price lists for mail order. If you see something you like on one of their lists, write to them, and they will send a photograph of it. They stock a vast assortment of handmade lace—Duchess, Flanders, Princess, Venetian, etc.—but by far the most popular and least expensive is Battenberg, which is machine-made lacy tapes sewn by hand into the final lace shape. Prices seem to be roughly equal at both shops. Here are some prices for goods with lace: place mats, either linen-and-lace or all lace, $4–$9 each; 36" bridge-tablecloths with four napkins, $14 and up; tablecloth 71" by 55" with eight napkins, $60.

FRANCE

Pache—Aux Mille et Une Nuits, 21 Rue Godot de Mauroy, Paris IX, France

France has always taken "heirloom" trousseaus and layettes very seriously, and Pache is one of the few shops left where you can get entirely handmade lace on lingerie, blouses, layettes and tablecloths. There is no brochure or price list, so write only if you know just what you want and are prepared to pay through the nose. A handmade pure-silk crepe de Chine nightgown with handmade Valenciennes lace costs $135. A handmade, hand-embroidered muslin baby dress with machine-made lace costs $70.

HOLLAND

Het Kantenhuis, Kalverstraat 124, Amsterdam, Holland

Het Kantenhuis imports the very best handmade lace and embroidery from all over the world, so they have a marvelous selection. Antique Venetian, Swiss Embroidery, Brussels (Princess) lace and all sorts of other laces and embroideries are attached to anything you might hope to find belaced and embroidered: collars, cuffs, bun cozies, guest towels, bridge sets, tablecloths, table runners, mantillas and bridal veils. No price list, but they answer specific questions very efficiently.

HONG KONG

China Art Embroidery Co., T.S.T. P.O. Box 5811, Kowloon, Hong Kong

A *very* efficient catalogue is put out by this thirty-eight-year-old firm, which sells clothes and linen by mail. They list in detail a wide selection of embroidery and lace, and prices are lower than anywhere else (although apparently purists do not consider some Chinese laces "genuine" even when made in the same way as European laces). A 36" bridge set with five napkins in Irish linen, embroidery and cutwork costs $8. Venetian-lace oval place mats start at $54 for eight mats and eight napkins. The firm can monogram anything you buy.

IRELAND

Brown Thomas and Co., Ltd., Mail Order Dept., Grafton Street, Dublin 2, Ireland
38-page catalogue, 50 cents. Prices in $.

This well-known Irish store, winner of the "Coup d'Or du Bon Goût" (along with Marshall Field, Saks and others), has a thriving mail-order service to America and an excellent catalogue mainly of Irish products.

Their Irish Linen Shop has a good choice of the best Irish linen at prices one-third to half off American prices. Double-damask cloths start at $12; dozens of double-damask dinner napkins are $2.50 each; embroidered tea sets with four napkins, $12; ladies' handkerchiefs with crocheted edges, $2.10. Plain hemmed sheets cost $37 for a pair of single-bed size, and $46 for double (hand-drawn hem stitch is a dollar more). Besides plenty of linen to choose from, there is a selection of some other things that Ireland is famous for:

House

48
E. Bakalowits Söhne Hand-cut crystal lamp available in several sizes, the smallest 22″ wide × 13½″ high. About $225.

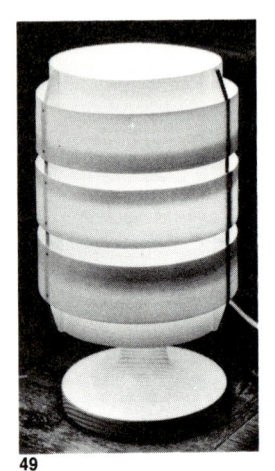

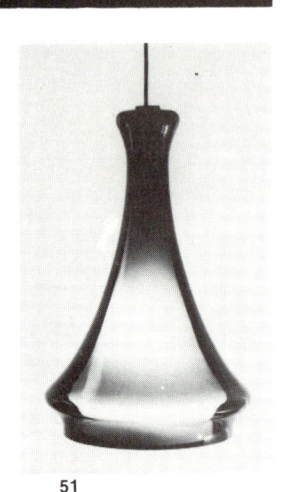

49
A.B. Ellysett 10″-high table lamp. Base in polished pine, and shade in pine splintwood; takes a maximum wattage of 60w. About $15.

50
A.B. Ellysett 11″-high table lamp. Base in polished pine and shade of frosted glass; takes a maximum wattage of 60w. About $20. 14″-high size takes a maximum wattage of 75w and costs around $22.
photo Hans Agne Jakobsson Ab

51
Fog and Morup Hand-blown glass lamp "Heliotrop"; inside glass white, outside blue or brown. About $65.

52
Fog and Morup "White line," lamps designed by Jo Hammerborg. About $21–$53.

53
The General Trading Company (see Household Objects section) Antique pewter: George IV quart tankard by Yates and Birch (circa 1820); baluster-shape tankard (circa 1830); plate by Samuel Duncombe (circa 1745); sandwich box (circa 1860). Similar pieces are usually available.

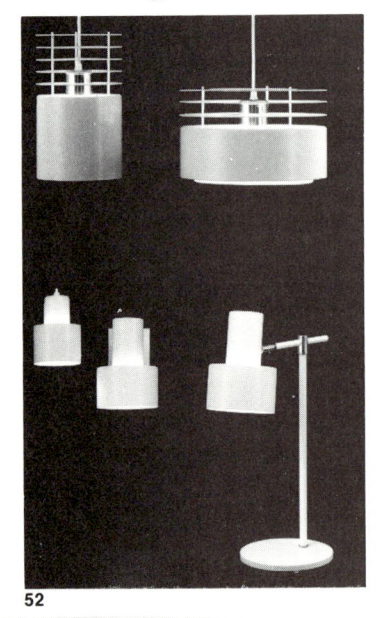

House

napkins, luncheon sets, mats, mantillas and bridal veils in handmade Carrickmacross lace; china and Waterford glass; and tweeds by the yard or made up into jackets for men, and coats for women; Donald Davies dresses; sheepskin coats; and the dramatic hooded Kinsdale cloak copied from a traditional County Cork cloak in black wool with a colored lining.

Donegal Linens Ltd., Bruckless, Co. Donegal, Ireland
Color brochure, 75 cents. Prices in $.

An easy catalogue to buy from, as each design is illustrated with a clear photograph. Donegal Linens makes machine lace, handmade lace and linen tablecloths, of which Michael McGinty, the chairman, says: "The linen is of a very high quality and in all cases the finish on our white linen surpasses anything in the trade. The hand-embroidered craftsmanship on all the goods far outweighs Madeira, Italian, Canarian in the finish and durability." Then he enthusiastically goes on to say: "Apart from the fact that it is traditional in the fullest sense and is the work of ladies, all nearing the century mark which brings it almost to the 'antique' bracket"—I can't quite understand whether it is the ladies or the lace which is nearing the century mark, but surely he can't mean that something produced by an antique person thereby becomes an antique itself. Anyway, for sale are handkerchiefs, tray cloths, beautiful scarfs, chair backs, pillowcases (with machine embroidery only), place mats and tablecloths. A set of six hand-embroidered place mats with six hand-embroidered napkins costs about $55.

ITALY

Jesurum, Ponte Canonica 4310, Venice, Italy
Venetian lace, probably the most expensive lace of all, is sold by this famous old shop, and made in its own lace-making school. Prices are high. Jesurum says that their tablecloths and place mats made with precious antique lace are extremely expensive, and with modern handmade lace are rather expensive. With machine-made lace, a napkin and place mat together cost about $9.50, so you can guess that when they say "expensive," they mean it. Tablecloths in batiste, organdy or linen start at $148; queen-size mixed-linen sheets with embroidery, $140 and up; six-piece machine-embroidered bath sets, $159 and up. Write to Jesurum and tell them what you are interested in, the size and price range you would like, and they will send you their "best offer" with a photograph of the item.

MADEIRA

Madeira Superbia, Rua do Carmo 27-1, P.O. Box 303, Funchal, Madeira, Portugal
52-page catalogue with some color, free. Prices in $.

Madeira Superbia, a large firm with many branches, has a very good catalogue illustrating their famous Madeira embroidery and needlepoint. The embroidery is mostly cut work or appliqué in flower or leaf designs, with an occasional animal thrown in. There are delicately monogramed handkerchiefs, moderately restrained for men, and going off into elaborate profusions of tiny flowers for women. Hand towels in various pastel shades with monograms or designs embroidered in the same or contrasting shade, $2 and up. There are place mats, tablecloths, napkins of course, and pretty embroidered cotton pillowcases, $11 the pair, for people who don't want to lash out vast sums for embroidered sheets. Sedate embroidered blouses cost $15, and there is a graceful collection of children's and babies' old-fashioned clothes, including a poplin party dress with cutout eyelets and tucks, for only $7.

To switch styles, Portuguese work is also sold here—simple stitches on brightly colored cotton—much more of a folk art. There are extraordinarily cheap hand-embroidered aprons for children, 75 cents; adults, $2.

Madeira Superbia is also known for its needlepoint reproductions in carpets, wall hangings, and pieces for chairs and cushions. A wall panel, "Summer" by Boucher—a voluptuous scene of luscious-looking ladies reclining by a waterfall—costs $220, and flower designs in the style of Dutch masters are worked onto rugs of all sizes. For cushions and chairs there are Chippendale, Regency, Baroque, Louis XV, and "conventional" designs in petit point and gros point.

MAJORCA

Casa Bonet, Tous y Maroto 46, Palma de Mallorca, Spain ♥

A famous linen shop with a museumlike display of fine old lace and embroidery. One of Casa Bonet's most popular items has been customer signatures hand-embroidered on the corner of handkerchiefs instead of a monogram or an initial. However, if you prefer to stick to monograms, women's handkerchiefs cost from $1.10 up, and men's from $1.65. Both fine white and multicolored Majorcan embroidery is sold here,

MALTA

Gozo 20, Gozo, Maltese Islands
Catalogue, $1.
Shade cards and samples, $1.25 (refundable).

This firm knits, weaves, crochets and makes lace to order, and makes wool or cotton bedspreads in traditional island designs that have never been written down. These cost about $125–$200, according to size. All crocheted bathroom sets—flannels, fringed bath mats and fringed towels—can be made to match any color scheme. A Victorian crochet pattern can be made into tablecloths or bedspreads. Knitted and crocheted clothes are sold—floppy hats, jackets and long skirts (there are long skirts in crocheted lace, too); embroidered hangings in island designs; and handwoven rugs and carpets made from tapestry wool and island sheep's wool.

SWITZERLAND

Ed. Sturzenegger AG, Postrasse 17, St. Gallen, Switzerland
Brochure, free.

This ninety-year-old firm publishes a small brochure illustrating their Swiss style hand-guided machine-embroidered white cotton, muslin or Terylene curtains and their Terylene tablecoths. At the moment a 36″ by 36″ tablecloth costs about $10.

LIGHT FIXTURES

Any lamp bought from abroad will need an adapter, an inexpensive little gadget on sale at electrical supply stores which enables the plug to fit into American outlets (or, of course, the plug can be replaced with an American one). British lamps don't take screw-in bulbs, so their bulb sockets have to be changed; with lamps from other countries, just make sure the metal tongue at the back of the socket is in contact with the bulb.

House

E. Bakalowits Söhne, Halirschgasse 17, 1171 Vienna, Austria
Photographs and prices, free.

Austria is a leading producer of fine hand-cut crystal, and this firm makes splendiferous modern chandeliers in what they say is A-1 quality, produced only in Austria. They have made lights for all sorts of theaters, government buildings, and posh hotels in Europe, and in America have supplied, among others, the John F. Kennedy Center in Washington, the House of Congress in Springfield, Ill.—and Alexander's department store in New York.

But all sizes of lights are made: little metal and crystal candlesticks, small wall or table lights, and small to huge ceiling lights. The designs range from fairly classic and unobtrusive compact shapes to dramatic sunbursts of glittering crystal. Prices are high; the candlesticks are about $38 each, and the lamps between $135 and $1,000.

AB Ellysett, Box 82, S-285 01 Markaryd, Sweden
23-page catalogue with some color, $1.

A designer, Hans-Agne Jakobsson, thought up these handsome pine lamps made in "darkest Småland," a forresty part of Sweden. Table, wall, floor and ceiling lights have shades made from slivers of natural pine. The lamps give a specially soft, warm light so appealing that the lamps have become very popular, and not only widely exported but also widely copied. Prices start at about $15.

Fog and Morup, STC 105 Bella Centret, DK-2400 Copenhagen NV, Denmark
30-page color catalogue, $1. Prices in $.

A good selection of modern lights for indoors and outside by leading Danish designers. Mouth blown-glass pendant lights in gracefully simple shapes, brass and copper wall and ceiling lights in more complicated shapes (and these are usually especially expensive in America); enameled lights in red, white, blue or yellow from $10; and a whole lot of lights for wall, ceiling or table in one design: a smooth round ball, half light-giving white plastic and half lacquered enamel, $14–$33. Also Royal Copenhagen table lamps in earthenware and porcelain, including one produced to commemorate Copenhagen's 800th jubilee with a delicate blue picture of the old city taken from a copperplate engraving.

For more modern lamps, see Ikea (Modern Furniture section); for pottery lamps, see Rosenthal Studio-Haus (Glass and China section); for hand-painted Indian lamps, see Central Cottage Industries Emporium (Handicrafts and Special Local Products section).

PEWTER

HOLLAND

Focke and Meltzer, St. Lucien Shop, St. Luciensteeg 18, Amsterdam, Holland
Pewter catalogue, free. Prices in $.

A very good choice of classic and typically Dutch pewter, including a page full of spoons. But ask specifically for the pewter catalogue, because glass and china are also sold here and at Focke and Meltzer's other branch.

Schiphol Airport, Tax-Free Shopping Center, Amsterdam, Holland
The shop at the Amsterdam airport will send you a brochure of Royal Holland Pewter by Daalderop with a price list for the pieces they keep in stock.

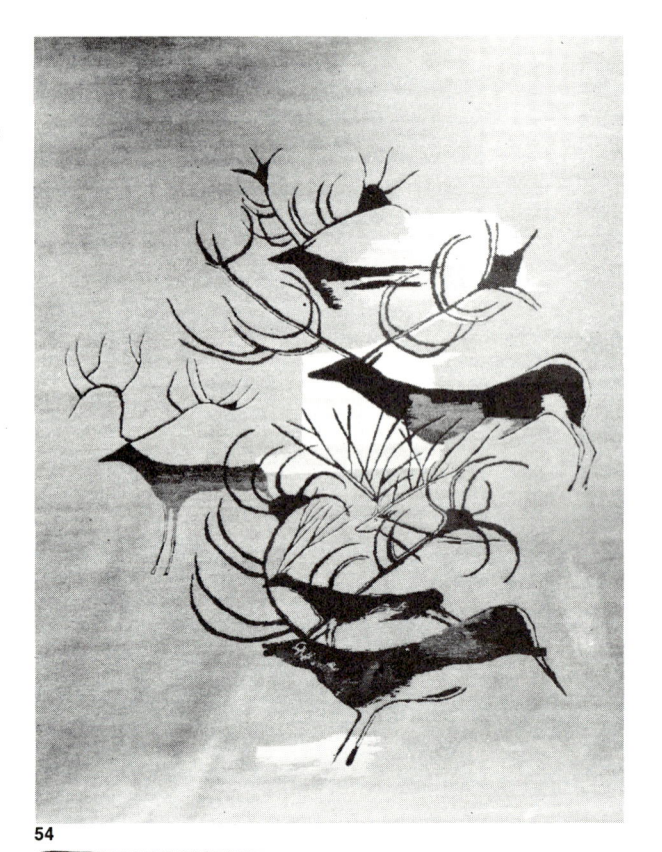

54

56

58

House

54
Folklore "Cuernos" hand-knotted rug in cream and brown (or any color to order); several sizes. $15 per square foot.

55
Folklore "Curiquinge" hand-knotted rug in red, brown, pale blue and pale yellow on beige background (or any color to order). 4' × 6' to any size. $15 per square foot.

56
National Welfare Organization Needlepoint rugs, about $84 per square meter (1.2 sq. yds.). Available in several sizes.
"Strawberries," red and green on cream background.
"Birds and Cypress," orange, blue, green, red on cream background.
"Cyclamen," pink, blue and green on cream background.

57
Fernandez Angulo SA "Selecta 152" twin bedspread in black, white and green-gray, about $75. Bedspreads in two colors start at $49.48; floor rugs in the same designs start at $13.95.

58
Märta Mååås-Fjetterström "Gula Trädet" rug in flossa technique, yellow, red, blue or white-gray, designed by Marianne Richter. $554 per square yard.

59
Märta Mååås-Fjetterström "Tuppamattan" tapestry 5'1" × 5'11", designed by Marianne Richter, main color green, blue and red or orange-red. $4,820.
photo Pål-Nils Nilsson

House

A. Tobben, Haven 5–9, Volendam, Holland
10-page brochure, free. Prices in $.

Lead-free Royal Holland pewter in simple classic and modern designs at lower prices than anyone else's.

MALAYSIA

Selangor Pewter Co., Mail Order Dept., 231 Jalan Tuanku Abdul Rahman, P.O. Box 15, Kuala Lumpur, Malaysia
14-page brochure, free. Prices in $.

Apparently Malaysia, too, is known for its pewter. Selangor is a large old family firm employing over three hundred pewtersmiths in two factories. But unlike some firms, they use new machinery and methods to make lead-free pewter in modernish styles. You can choose to have your pewter plain, hammered, part hammered, or with a local picture (of, say, a bullock cart) engraved on it. Tankards start at about $8, candlesticks about $5. No plates illustrated, but there are napkin rings, cigarette boxes and photograph frames, among other things.

For antique pewter, write to the General Trading Company, (Household Objects); and Harrods (General).

RUGS
ECUADOR

Folklore—Olga Fisch, P.O. Box 64, Quitó, Ecuador
Rug brochure in color, $3. Prices in $.
Handicrafts brochure, $1. Prices in $.

Folklore has a staggeringly top-notch list of clients: embassies, famous people and museums. In New York, Folklore hand-knotted rugs are owned by the Museum of Modern Art, the Museum of Primitive Art, the United Nations, and the Metropolitan Opera House (fourteen of them). The rugs are designed for Folklore by Mrs. Olga Fisch and cost about $15 per square foot (with roughly $30–$40 extra per rug for handling and air-freight charges). They come in several sizes from 4' by 6' to 12' by 14'. Most designs can be made to order in special sizes and colors, and color samples can be matched ("to perfection," they say).

The most distinctive and original carpets are inspired by old textiles and cave paintings and are in subtle dark browns, reds and cream. But there are also more conventional rugs: "Georgia," a very beautiful colonial carpet with pale-blue, gray and brown flowers on white; or "Caceria" with a pattern of people, plants and animals based on Colonial embroideries. There are several modern designs in gorgeously rich reds, blues and greens—in fact, this is a terrific place for unusual rugs.

FINLAND

Sotainvalidien Veljesliiton Naisjarjesto r.y.n, Ryijypalvelu, Kasarmikatu 34, 00130 Helsinki 13, Finland
Color catalogue in Finnish, $3; $5 air mail.

Rya-rug kits and the same rugs made up are sold by this firm in rather wild and beautiful designs that are more like abstract paintings than the traditional rug patterns; more colors and busier patterns here than in most Ryas.

Suomen Käsityön Ystävät, Yrjönkatu 13, Helsinki 12, Finland
Color brochure, $1. Prices in $.

Rya rugs, the shaggy Finnish carpets, in large, blurry, abstract designs and magnificent colors: suns in fiery yellow and orange; squares within squares of magenta and brown; icicles of gray on white. The rugs here are particularly finely and subtly colored, but humbler versions can be bought at the Scandinavian furniture stores at much lower prices. A do-it-yourself kit here costs about $121 for a 4' by 5' rug (the same thing made up costs $392, and there is a waiting time of three months).

For more Rya rugs, see Ikea (Modern Furniture).

GREECE

A. Karamichos, 3 Mitropoleos Street, Athens 118, Greece
6-page color brochure, free. Prices in $.

Greek Flokati rugs are rather like the Finnish Rya but longer-haired, silkier and traditionally made in white. Karamichos make the heaviest and most sumptuous by hand in qualities not often exported because foreign stores prefer cheaper versions, though if you buy them directly from Greece the prices are low, under half the New York prices I have seen. Made with a 4" pile from sheep's wool and fluffed under waterfalls, the rugs are available in plain, natural colors or simple designs—squares, triangles, etc. For a few extra dollars they can be custom-dyed, *really* custom: you are not allowed to say airily "red" or "blue," you have to send a color swatch you want matched. Nine sizes and two qualities. Prices start at $41 for a 3' by 5' rug; and one, 6' by 9', costs $146.

Note: These new prices are slightly higher than New York prices, but cheaper, machine-made rugs are also available.

National Welfare Organization, Handicrafts Dept., 6 Ipatias Street, Athens 117, Greece
22-page crafts catalogue with some color, free.

The National Welfare Organization (previously Their Majesties Fund) has encouraged and promoted carpet making by peasants as a means of increasing family income. Instead of trying to compete with Oriental carpets, they have developed unusual and beautiful Greek designs, knotted, woven and embroidered. Based on folk art and Hellenic motifs, styles are simple and graceful, leaning toward small, repeated pictures of stylized flowers, birds and geometric patterns. Prices start at $84 per square meter (1 sq. m.= 1.2 sq. yds.), but rugs are not illustrated in the catalogue.

HONG KONG

Carpet House, 313 Hong Kong Hotel Arcade, Kowloon, Hong Kong
Color leaflet, free; 20 cents air mail. Prices in $.

Carpet House makes pure-wool carpets, chrome-dyed and chemically washed. Sixteen designs in color are shown on their leaflet in Floral, French Aubusson, Peking or solid-color embossed design, or to special order. Background color can be beige, maroon, blue, gold or green. Sizes are 3' by 5', 4' by 9', 8' by 10', 9' by 12', 10' by 14', 12' by 15', and as I write, prices start at $10 per square foot for the solid-color embossed carpets.

House

Tai Ping Carpet Salon, 3 Middle Road, Kowloon, Hong Kong
Color catalogue, $4.

Excellent, informative catalogue showing the kinds of custom-tailored carpets that Tai Ping has made for firms all over the world, including the Columbia Broadcasting System, First National Bank, Ford and General Motors, the Time-Life Building in New York and Grauman's Chinese in Hollywood. The carpets, manufactured in a large modern factory in Taipo, are made by hand from a blend of New Zealand and Scottish wools in any shape—any design—any size, so this is a marvelous place for anyone having trouble in finding what they want. The catalogues show lots of "contemporary," "periodic," "Chinese" and "Moroccan" designs, but as each carpet is made up to order, there is always a waiting time. Prices for standard designs vary from about $4 to $8 a square foot, with 15 percent extra for custom colors.

MEXICO

Zarapes de San Miguel, Carrada de la Calzada Aurora No. 1, San Miguel de Allende, Guanajuato, Mexico
Catalogue, $1. Prices in $.

I haven't seen this catalogue because Tomas L. Alvarez says that it is usually sent out at the end of the year. However, if listed in this edition, he will make sure his catalogue is available all year. His firm makes handwoven rugs and wall hangings which have won a gold medal—the first prize for design of goods for export given by the Mexican Institute of Foreign Trade. Mr. Alvarez also says that his customers tell him that the U.S. Customs says theirs is one of the best merchandise crossing the border, which makes him very proud. He sent me a thick woven rug which is certainly of excellent quality. It has a stylized design based on the folk tale about the animals climbing on each other's backs and all making their respective noises to frighten thieves away. The background is natural and the colors of the animals—olive, mustard, bright-red—are good. Rugs have names like Violetas, Pescados (fish), Navajos, Turista, Moderno and Figuritas Mexicanas ("Rugs with old Mexican figures"). All the rugs are small enough to go by mail, which saves trouble with air freight or whatever, and prices go from $20 for a 2' by 4' (including fringe) to $287 for a round rug with a 10' diameter.

NEW ZEALAND

The Sheepskin Rug Shop, Mail Order Dept., P.O. Box 12-175, Penrose, Aukland, New Zealand
6-page brochure, free.

New Zealand is, of course, known for its sheep, and the manager of this shop chauvinistically says that the sheepskins he has seen on sale in America are poorer quality and two and a half to three times the price. Rugs made out of one or two lamb or sheep skins can be bought dyed in any of fifteen colors. Prices are from $9 to $33, and postage is only about $1.75 per rug. Clipped, rectangular rugs in sizes up to 3' by 6' cost from $22 to $36 in various colors. All are washable.

There is also an imaginative collection of other things in sheepskin: toys, poodle and cat pajama cases, purses, handbags, cushions in all colors (12" by 12", only about $8, other sizes made to order), muffs, hats, all manner of slippers, and even sheepskin-lined, lace-up leather shoes for $13. Sheepskin stools, and car-seat covers—warm in the winter, cool in the summer (they stop you from sweating).

SPAIN

Fernandez Angulo S.A., Calle de Toledo 4, Madrid 12, Spain
30-page color catalogue and wool samples, free; $2 air mail. Prices in $.
Wall hangings brochure, free. Prices in $.

These brilliant baroque bedspreads and carpets from Spain have been copied all over the world, usually in strong blues and greens or reds and orange. Fernandez Angulo makes them in several patterns and any combination of a hundred colors (although service, which is slow anyway, becomes even slower if you don't choose the standard color combinations).

Outside Spain the very fetching bedspread versions seem to be most popular, although in a New York department store prices started at $90 for a twin-bed size. At Fernandez Angulo, twin sizes start at $50 and double at $62. This firm was recommended to me by a friend and both of us have satisfactorily bought rugs. The only hitch is that although the catalogue is in English, English is not spoken (or written), so if you need to ask about anything special, you'll need a translator.

SWEDEN

Märta Måås-Fjetterström, Myntgatan 5, Stockholm C, Sweden
Brochure in Swedish, free.

A weaving studio that makes very beautiful but very expensive original designs in tapestries and carpets. Orders take at least four months to complete, and small tapestries cost $107 and up. Carpets start at $180 per square meter (1 sq. m. = 1.2 sq. yds.).

TUNISIA

Office National de l'Artisanat, Ministère des Affaires Economiques, Den Den, Tunisia
68-page color catalogue, Vol. 1, "Tapis" (Rugs), $4.50.
100-page catalogue, Vol. II, "Divers (Miscellaneous), $1.50.

The Tunisian government has a splendid full-color catalogue published in Paris illustrating sixty-four carpets made by hand in the workshops of the Office de l'Artisanat. Styles vary from very traditional intricate geometric designs to simpler modern versions based on the old patterns. Most carpets come in about eight sizes up to 10' by 13'. Prices on request, but service is puzzling—I wrote two letters in English which were answered in French, and then one in French which was answered in English.

WEST INDIES

Tropicrafts, P.O. Box 43, Roseau, Dominica, West Indies
Leaflet, free.

Tropicrafts makes the kind of grass hats and bags that tourists are always drawn wearing in cartoons, but they also make traditional grass mats in many designs and sizes which are not expensive and can be sent by mail.

House

DO-IT-YOURSELF RUGS
The Rugcraft Centre, Croft Mill, Hebden Bridge, Yorkshire HX7 8AP, England
Rug-kits color catalogue with samples, free.
Church Kneelers brochure, free.

Kits to make Rya, Oriental, traditional or solid-color pure-wool rugs are illustrated in color in the rug catalogue, and so are very inexpensive kits to make rugs from "thrums." Thrums are end pieces of yarn in mixed colors left over from weaving manufactured carpets. All the rug kits are at least a third off similar kits bought in America, even after postage and duty have been paid.

The Rugcraft Centre also publishes a brochure showing the kits for needlepoint church kneelers that they sell to church groups and individuals all over the world. Besides stocking standard designs, the Centre can provide canvasses painted with customers' own designs and yarns in customers' own colors, and the brochure has a page of symbols to inspire church groups that would like to design their own motifs. The Centre can also provide "Donate a Kneeler" cards to church groups that would like to finance such a scheme by sending out the cards or putting them in the church.

For do-it-yourself rugs, see the shops in the Needlework section and PUB (General).

TILES

Tiles are expensive, but they can be very decorative and their glazed surface is exceptionally dirt-resistant.

The Portuguese tiles cost from as little as 20 cents, yet in New York I have seen the same tiles for $1 each, and very similar ones for $2. They are fairly compact to ship, and you can save quite a bit of money if you want to tile a large area. But even if you have just a few mailed, you can get a bargain. Fabrica Ceramica Viuva Lamego says that fifty blue-and-white tiles (1 square meter, enough for a coffee table or small counter) would cost $33 to mail to America: $10 for the tiles and $22 for postage and insurance of two parcels. Duty is 24 percent of the cost of the tiles, so you should save about a third of the New York price.

PORTUGAL

Fabrica Sant'Anna, Calcada da Boa Hora 96, Lisbon, Portugal
52-page catalogue in Portuguese, $2.

This large firm has done *"grandes"* works for clients in Portugal and abroad, and finished the catalogue with a list of them—mostly municipal offices, hotels, embassies and palaces. But don't be daunted, their catalogue shows plenty of unusual antique style ceramic objects for private homes in prices around $15 each: plates, mugs, jugs, jars, name plates, candlesticks and table lamps hand painted in flowery fold art styles. For more ambitious decorators there are fountains, benches and decorative panels, from a 12-tile eighteenth-century gentleman on a horse to a whole wall-sized view of old Lisbon which is now pleasing guests in a Brussels hotel.

Royal Delft (Glass and China) has Dutch tiles. Marlau (Reproduction Furniture) has Spanish tiles.

60
Fabrica Sant'Anna 20" platter, handmade and hand-painted. About $9.

61
Fabrica Sant'Anna "Artistic Panel." About $22 to $30.

14 Jewelry and Silver

Jewelry and Silver

The jewelry is divided into two sections: *International*, for famous jewelers who make fairly classic, conventional and extremely expensive jewelry in worldwide styles, and *National*, for jewelry either made in local styles, or with local stones. Some of the prices in the National section are high, too, but quite a few are not at all. For less expensive and very interesting jewelry, see the Handicrafts and Special Local Products section. For antique jewelry and silver, see the Antiques section.

INTERNATIONAL JEWELERS
AUSTRIA

Heldwein, Graben 13, 1010 Vienna, Austria
18-page color brochure, in German, $3. October.

Heldwein makes diamond jewelry and animal brooches, but their specialty is unusual modern jewelry, often to customers' own design. Gold is squashed and ribbed into naturalistic shapes, vaguely petal- or shell-like, usually without stones but sometimes studded with irregularly shaped aquamarines or crystals. Lapis lazuli and coral are worked into golden chains and twisted, tasseled cords for necklaces and bracelets; smooth circles and balls of gold make hanging earrings. This is the only catalogue to show a couple of pages of modern silver jewelry: lighters, boxes, etc.

BELGIUM

Kornreich Diamond Manufacturing Co., Hoveniersstraat 53, 2000 Antwerp, Belgium
Price list, free. Prices in $.

Belgium and Holland are old rivals as world's diamond cutting centers. This Belgian firm gets rough diamonds from De Beers Co. in South Africa and polishes them in their own factories. They sell only loose diamonds so that the diamonds can be appraised correctly, and say that their classifications are very strict. They also say: "Our diamonds are so in demand not only for jewelry and gifts, but also very much for investment . . . Our prices are insurance, postal charges, etc., included. We usually tell our clients to give us their requirements concerning size, color, purity and price range, and we are then in a position to give them the best advice and a judicious offer, which generally proves to be right." Minimum order, $1,000.

ENGLAND

Asprey and Co. Ltd., 165–169 New Bond Street, London WIY OAR, England ♕
24-page color catalogue, free. September. Prices in $.

Asprey's won gold medals at all the famous nineteenth-century exhibitions, and have been "by appointment" to every reigning sovereign since Queen Victoria—but their grand reputation goes back to the eighteenth century when William Asprey started a silver and leather working firm. His descendants have been making dressing cases, fine writing paper, jewelry and silverware for top people ever since.

The gift catalogue is called "The Art of Giving"—an art which must be easy to master with the help of Asprey's and a lot of money. Gifts suggested are classic, and highly expensive, but consummately well made, often in Asprey's own workshops. Diamond jewelry, golden cigar cutters, wine goblets, onyx-marble cigarette boxes, silver nutcrackers, golden-edged crocodile wallets, silver-edged cut glass, and the *Memoirs of Casanova* bound in red calf. There are antique bibelots, and prices go happily over $3,000 (for a mosaic box given by Pope Pius VII to a British warship captain, in 1816).

Garrard and Co. Ltd., 112 Regent Street, London W1A 2JJ, England ♕
33-page color catalogue, free. September.
Regent plate catalogue, free.
Sterling-silver catalogue, free.
William Tolliday at Garrard brochure, free. Prices in $.

Garrard (by appointment to the Queen, goldsmiths and crown jewelers—need I say more?) sends its catalogues to a selected list of important business people in America, but say that they have no mail-order service as at the moment their American customers buy when they come to London. They would, however, be happy to mail catalogues and goods to anyone else.

The gift catalogue shows very expensive modern and antique silver and jewelry. The lowest price I could find was $65 for a pair of cuff links.

The sterling-silver catalogue has interesting handmade and reproduction silver tea sets, candelabra, tankards, wine goblets (one Charles II reproduction wine goblet, $175), and punch bowls. Six-piece sterling-silver place settings start at about $170.

The silver plate is in traditional designs and is not priced in place settings but by the dozen, as is the English habit. Twelve table forks start at $65. Tea sets to match start at $200 for four pieces.

A color brochure shows pictures made out of gold and jewelry collages by William Tolliday, who exhibits his work only at Garrard's. Prices for signed and limited editions range from $520 to $1,700.

Mappin and Webb Ltd., 170 Regent Street, London W1R 6JH, England
32-page gift catalogue, free.
Sterling-silver brochure, free.
Mappin plate brochure, free.

On the other hand, Mappin and Webb, silversmiths to the Queen, says that they have many customers in America; perhaps it is because their gift catalogue isn't as glossy and expensive as Garrard's. No antique jewelry or silver; instead glass, leather, dressing-table sets and stainless-steel flatware. There are gold tie tacks and green onyx table lighters for as little as $27.

The sterling-silver brochure shows "the twelve great designs" in flatware. Prices for twelve forks, $490–$807, depending on the great design.

The silver-plate brochure has, besides the regular flatware, seven canteens (chests) in veneered oak. Six five-piece place settings in a chest at $275.

NATIONAL JEWELERS
DENMARK

Buch and Deichmann, Kulhus, 3500 Vaerlose, Denmark
Leaflet, free. Prices in $.

Ten Scandinavian designers make jewelry at the Buch and Deichmann center, an old manor house north of Copenhagen. As the firm puts more emphasis on design than materials, the jewelry is made in anything from solid gold or silver to pewter, brass, copper and leather. Works of enormously varying prices are sold in Denmark and also exported to the United States. By mail the firm sells a small and attractive collection of modern silver-plated jewelry at prices mainly between $5 and $30 (prices include air-mail postage). Spiky rings, swirling bracelets and chunky pendants are occasionally set with tiger's-eye or amethyst, but are more often simply in silver, relying on their design for effect.

Jewelry and Silver

1
Heldwein Sterling-silver rose pin, $70.

2
Heldwein Gold ring with lapiz lazuli, $300.

3
Asprey and Co. Ltd One-pint sterling-silver tankard with acanthus-leaf decoration, reproduction Charles II. Around $600.

4
Garrard and Co. Ltd Set of four gilt salt or sweetmeat dishes, complete with salt spades. Height 5-3/4". Recently sold.

5
Buch and Deichmann Handmade silver-plated jewelry designed by Jacob Hull. Top: brooch, $19; bracelets, $33 each. Left: ring, $10. Right: ring (sterling silver), $19.

6
Buch and Deichmann Handmade silver-plated jewelry designed by Erik Dennung.

7
Buch and Deichmann Handmade silver-plated jewelry designed by Jacob Hull. Necklace with tiger's-eye or amethyst. Bracelet, $19; adjustable ring, $9.

8
Frank and Company Jade section bracelet with Chinese good-luck symbols, gold-plated, $12.50. Sterling silver, $15.50.

Jewelry and Silver

HOLLAND

A. Van Moppes and Zoon, Albert Cuypstraat 2–6, Amsterdam, Holland
20-page brochure, free. Prices in $.

Holland and Belgium are the world's diamond-cutting centers. This large and reputable diamond factory in Amsterdam is open to visitors, and thousands of tourists go through the plant every year. Van Moppes and Zoon imports diamonds directly from South Africa, then two hundred employees are involved in the sawing, shaping and polishing. Some diamonds are sold loose, others are made into jewelry, and for that, Van Moppes uses only top-quality diamonds: "blue/white and flawless" is the official grading. They say that their jewelry prices are 30 percent lower than American prices, but I haven't been able to check, as each piece is individual and settings vary, so I leave checking to anyone who considers buying. The brochure comes with a useful leaflet giving general information on cut and quality of diamonds. Prices for rings illustrated, $50–$780; pins, $60–$340; earrings, $225–$666. If you want anything not shown, professional drawings will be sent and you can have pieces made to order. The part I like is that each diamond comes with a written guarantee of the exact quality and weight. The guarantee allows you to trade your purchase for another piece, with no time limit, and full credit of the original price. Van Moppes refunds half of any duty you pay on their goods.

HONG KONG

Hong Kong Jade Center, 20-B Carnarvon Road, Kowloon, Hong Kong
Brochure, free; $1 air mail. Prices in $.

A big shop selling 14-carat gold jewelry set with jade, diamonds, star sapphires, emeralds, pearls and semiprecious stones. Designs are uninspired and tend to be souveniry (lots of charms), but it should certainly be possible for most people to winkle out something they like, as styles vary and some are respectably plain. Prices are low, specially for jade—jade cuff links cost $55—and opal, moonstone or garnet rings are $45, aquamarine or onyx rings $30, all set in gold.

ITALY

Giovanni Apa, Torre del Greco, Naples, Italy
46-page catalogue, some color, free. Prices in $.

Since Romans took over the Egyptian craft, Italy has been the place to find cameos, and anyone looking for inexpensive shell cameos will be very pleased with this famous store. A large catalogue illustrates a plentiful selection made in the Apa factories. Mythological scenes, Roman warriors, religious figures, cherubs, women's heads, flowers—they come mounted or unmounted in sterling silver or 14-carat gold and there are all kinds of ornaments for men and women. Prices start at $7 for lockets and rings, and go up to over $220 for plaques of scenes like "The Dance of the Muses" and "Cupids on the Lake" signed by the artist.

9
Giovanni Apa "The Muses" extra-quality cameos mounted on a sterling-silver bracelet. About $60.

10
Cellini's Silver Factory Silver rose bracelet, $38. Ornate bracelet with semiprecious stones, $70.

11
Cellini's Silver Factory Sterling-silver tray, $680; four-piece sterling-silver coffee and tea service, $1,500.
photo Bazzechi

Apa also make another Italian specialty: coral jewelry, not rough but polished into beads or carved into roses and fruit. Brooches and earrings mounted on gilded silver cost under $10, heavy necklaces with multiple strands start at $45. "Extra" quality coral mounted on gold costs considerably more; prices start at $58 for earrings.

Cellini's Silver Factory, Piazza Santa Croce 12, Florence, Italy
28-page catalogue, free. Prices in $.

Cellini's makes sterling silver by hand with the same methods and in some of the same styles that were used in the Renaissance by the famous Florentine silversmiths, and have a world-wide mail-order service. It is an excellent place for small, inexpensive objects. There is a page full of tea and coffee spoons; the cheapest, $5, is a coffee spoon with an effigy of Michelangelo's "David" on the handle; an hors-d'oeuvre fork with a Venice lion on the handle costs $5.50. Engraved cuff links, tie tacks, rings and earrings cost under $10. Pillboxes, powder compacts, cigarette lighters—plain or engraved in the curly feathery Florentine style and filigree jewelry—cost not much more. You can also get anything you want in silver for the house in impressively regal shapes—Baroque, Empire, or several Italian styles: coasters ($2.70 up); napkin rings, goblets; dishes, photograph frames; salt and pepper mills; tea and coffee sets; trays; five-piece dresser sets (three brushes, comb and mirror) in Louis XVI or Chippendale style cost only $115 (postage free). Presumably the set is light, as it costs *much* less than anywhere else, but if you are willing to sacrifice some weight in the interests of economy—a terrific buy.

Peruzzi Bros. Silversmiths, 60 Ponte Vecchio, 50125 Florence, Italy
Catalogue with some color, $4.

The Peruzzi brothers say this about themselves: "Our firm is the oldest silversmith's factory in Florence. It was established in 1880 by Giuseppe Peruzzi and is still led by the family. Present owner Mr. Gustavo Peruzzi, with the cooperation of his sons Gilberto and Gino. Our firm has overcome the bumping down of German mines in 1944 which destroyed Borgo S. Jacobo and the terrible flow of 1966, and will celebrate its hundredth anniversary in the best of spirit."

Besides some very grand and ornate pieces such as hand-chiseled ice buckets and hand-chiseled four-piece coffee and tea sets with matching samovars, there are plenty of smaller pieces: charms, cuff links, lighter cases, salt and pepper sets, photograph frames, solid-silver animals, and what they call "small gift items": sugar spoons, cigar holders, money clips, cake servers, grape scissors, etc. Some jewelry is illustrated in color; besides the typical Florentine silver, there is gold-plated filigree and a little gold jewelry. Because of rapidly changing prices of gold and silver, prices are not sent out with the catalogue, but prices of specific pieces are given on request.

JAPAN

Amita Jewelry Corp., Mail Order Service, Kyoto Handicrafts Center, Kumano Jinja Higashi, Sakyoku, Kyoto, 606 Japan
29-page brochure, free. Prices in $.

Amita Jewelry Corp. in the Kyoto Handicrafts Center is visited by thousands of tourists each year and sells little things most of which cost less than $20: silver and gold charms, ivory flowers, heart-shaped crystal pendants, initialed cuff links, silver pen knives, and Damascene jewelry with Japanese scenes or birth flowers worked in silver and gold into a black background. Also for sale are other modern Japanese offerings such as lacquerware, brocade purses and ornamental dolls.

Imperial Pearls Co., 3–4, 7-Chome, Roppongi, Minato-Ku, Tokyo, 106 Japan
Color brochure, free.

Imperial Pearls has been recommended by a reader of the first edition of The Catalogue of Catalogues. A clear brochure illustrates gold and silver jewelry for men and women set with cultured (fresh-water) seed and South Sea pearls. The color photographs make this a very convenient place to buy from. The only trouble is that the prices are given in yen.

Matoba and Co., Inc., Central P.O. Box 451, Tokyo, Japan
Say what you are interested in, and designs with prices will be sent.

A shop with a large stock and excellent reputation, Matoba specializes in cultured pearls. As price depends not only on size but also on quality, i.e., thickness of nacre, roundness, smoothness, color, cleanliness and brilliance of luster, mail-order customers write and tell Matoba what price, size and quality of necklaces and bracelets they want, and Matoba does the choosing. Where designs are variable (pins, rings, earrings, cuff links, etc.), there are drawings, but customers can still indicate what size and color of pearl they prefer and what setting. Everything is available in either silver or 14-carat gold. A pendant with a pearl inside a heart costs $9 in silver and $29 in gold; earrings, $8 in silver, $29 in gold.

K. Mikimoto, Inc., Mail Order Section, 5–5, 4-Chome, Ginza, Tokyo, Japan
48-page brochure with some color, free. Prices in $.

Natural pearls are made when pieces of shell, bone or sand accidentally get into an oyster and the oyster covers the particle with layers of nacre. Cultured pearls are made when a nucleus of shell is put inside the oyster on purpose. The value of a cultured pearl depends, among other things, on the thickness of the nacre formed.

Kokichi Mikimoto invented cultured pearls, and the firm has kept a very high reputation. With a superefficient brochure, they have a worldwide export service of their necklaces and other jewels.

Queen Pearl Co., CPO Box 1446, Tokyo, Japan
Price list, free. Prices in $.

For their more expensive cultured pearls, Queen Pearl Co. makes individual offers according to what customers want. But for customers who want more than anything to spend as little as possible, there is a list of bargains neatly divided according to price. It starts at $14 for 14" necklaces with round and baroque (off shape) pearls; price includes sea mail.

Besides pearls in standard colors, Queen has black cultured pearls which are not superficially dyed but have gone through some sort of secret chemical transformation. Also South Sea cultured pearls, larger and rarer than Japanese pearls and more expensive.

MAJORCA

Nacar S.A., 115–119 Avenida Jaime 111, Palma de Mallorca, Spain
Price list, free. Prices in $.

This large gift shop is an excellent place to buy Majorca artificial pearls by mail and, indeed, already has over a

Jewelry and Silver

thousand foreign mail-order customers. Their list gives prices for single-and double-strand necklaces, bracelets and earrings, and there is a millimeter scale so you can see the exact size of the beads. Prices are the same as at Majorica's own factory shop; a 24" necklace in 8-mm. beads costs $6 less that at Perlas Manacor (below).

Perlas Manacor S.A., Rector Rubi 8, Manacor, Mallorca, Spain
16-page brochure with some color, free. Prices in $.

Majorica is the trademark of the world-famous artificial pearls made by Heutch from "natural essences extracted from marine species in the Mediterranean warm waters." Majorica are generally considered the tops and are often imitated by other manufacturers who give their artificial pearls deceptively similar names. In Majorica, where they are made, Majorica cost two-thirds of what they cost in America. When I compared prices, a 24" necklace in 8-mm. beads (8 mm. is apparently the most popular size) cost $50 in New York and only $33 at Perlas Manacor. Postage is only $1.50 and hopefully you will not be asked, on these small packets, to pay duty, but even if you are, you still save a lot—especially on the long double strands.

There is a price list of necklaces and bracelets by Majorica, and a good glossy and clear little catalogue of rings, earrings and pins in sterling silver with artificial pearls of various makes, including Majorica.

PERU

Carlo Mario Camusso S.A., Avenida Mariscal Oscar Benavides 679, Casilla Postal 650, Lima, Peru
Flatware leaflet, free. Prices in $.
Gift leaflet, free. Prices in $.

Peru is, like America, a leading silver producer. Carlo Mario Camusso is one of Peru's top silversmiths. Eighteen fairly classic sterling-silver flatware patterns are shown, and prices for six-piece place settings vary between $60 and $80. (This includes a 15 percent discount from the listed prices—part of Peruvian trading customs, I suppose.) Pieces can be bought individually or in sets. There are also serving pieces in the same patterns.

The gift leaflet shows trays, ice buckets, pitchers, etc., in various patterns, and Empire pattern plates and platters starting at $10 for 4" ones.

Purchases are delivered ten to sixteen days after the order and money have been received. They are sent air freight, which, Camusso says, costs about 5 to 7 percent of the price of your purchase. You pay for the shipping on arrival.

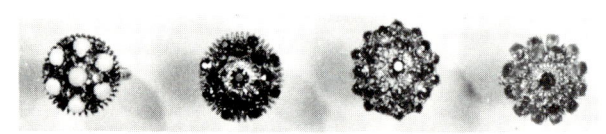

12
Rama Jewelry Variations on the Thai "Princess" ring in 14-carat gold which traditionally has nine different stones, but can be made in any combination to order. About $34–$54.

SCOTLAND

Cairncross, 18 St. John Street, Perth, Scotland
Brochure, free.

Cairncross makes pins and rings with Scottish fresh-water pearls that have formed naturally inside mussels. Apparently Scottish pearls are smaller than oyster pearls, have a softer bloom and vary in color from pale gray to pink. The small and delicate pins are mostly in the shape of flowers and plants. Prices start at $38 for two pearls set in 9-carat gold wild-"blaeberry" sprig and go up to $330 for fifteen pearls in a branch of heather. Ask about exact sizes—they're not given in the brochure.

Shetland Silvercraft, Sounside, Weisdale, Shetland, Scotland
Leaflet, 25 cents; 50 cents air mail.

Shetland Silvercraft started as a one-man business in 1953 and has expanded to a workshop staffed by local men and women. Very attractive silver jewelry is made based on traditional local designs, many of which have been influenced by Shetland's long association with Norway. There are about thirty pieces, mostly brooches, earrings and cuff links, but there are also a few bracelets, small spoons and napkin rings. Most of the prices are between $10 and $25. Shetland Silvercraft can also make anything you want in gold, silver or other metals, and set it with precious stones. Sketches and estimates are free.

TAIWAN

Frank and Company, P.O. Box 58428, Taipei, Taiwan
28-page color catalogue, $2. Prices in $.

A good selection of jade and coral jewelry set in 14-carat gold at low prices. There are simple jade bangles ($3 to $15) and cuff links, decorative wedding rings set with semiprecious stones, plenty of pendants, rings and earrings for under $30, and also some Chinese figurines.

THAILAND

Rama Jewelry Ltd., 987 Silom Road, Bangkok, Thailand
Color leaflet illustrating only Princess Rings, free. Prices in $.

Rama Jewelry has been manufacturing and exporting jewelry for the last ten years, and in 1970 expanded into a new seven-story building of their own. They make all sorts of jewelry, including reproductions of traditional Thai jewels, but by far the most popular with tourists is the Princess Ring. A big domed ring studded with multicolored stones, the design is hundreds of years old and is supposed to bring the wearer good luck. Mr. Prapanth, the store manager, says that now when "the world of fancy fashion has taken place," the ring's design is often changed and customers can choose their own stones, sticking to one color if they like. The rings are set in 14-carat gold, and traditionally have nine stones in hierarchical order—diamond, ruby, emerald, topaz, garnet, sapphire, moonstone, zircon, cat's-eye. They cost only $34–$54 each, and air-mail postage for up to three rings is $4.

15 Music

INSTRUMENTS

Tony Bingham, At the Sign of the Serpent, No. 47 Poland Street, London W1V 3DF, England
Price list, free.

A gentleman with a sense of style, Tony Bingham sends out his mimeographed price lists with a beautifully lettered cover and his envelopes adorned with sealing wax. This is what his lettering says: "All Sorts of Old Rare and Unusual Musical Instruments Bought and Sold by Tony Bingham . . . Where may also be had a Variety of Old and New Books, Music and Tutors Oil Paintings, Watercolors and Engravings of Musical Interest. All Instruments Sold to the Publick by the Above Establishment have been carefully restored to the Greatest Perfection to enable them to be played with care." He sent me a price list of double-reed instruments at prices starting at about $250, a price list of flutes and flageolets starting at about $150, and one of old books, tutors and prints.

M. G. Contreras, Mayor 80, Madrid 13, Spain
Price list in Spanish, free.

This workshop makes guitars and mandolins of various kinds and at various prices. As I write, the most expensive folk guitars cost about $375, and the most expensive classical guitars cost about $425, made in special Brazilian palisander wood. Although prices start well below, M. G. Contreras feels that it isn't worth sending instruments costing less than about $50, because the air freight (which they always use with foreign customers) is more expensive than the actual instrument. Although there is a brief price list, this firm prefers that you write to them (in English if you like) telling them exactly what you are after, and they will answer (in Spanish) giving you the appropriate information.

Lindberg, Sonnenstrasse 15, 8 Munich 15, Germany
51-page color brochure in German, free.

"Das Paradies der Musikfreunde" puts out a jolly catalogue full of laughing groups playing away on pianos and accordions (thirty Hohner models at prices from $26 to $2,800), "Organettas," "pianets," over thirty kinds of guitars—Western Spanish, electric ("Wanderlust," the least expensive, costs $16)—two electric Hawaiian guitars, six banjos, a ukelele, zithers, saxophones, clarinets, trumpets and horns, drums, violins, and even a lyre. Lindberg says that a lot of folk-music instruments are bought by mail from America, especially concert zithers, Hackbretter recorders, harmonicas, violins, also German sheet music. Unfortunately the catalogue is in German, and it is essential to have someone to translate the technical information.

The London Music Shop Ltd., 218 Great Portland Street, London W.1, England
Catalogues and price lists, free.

Providers of a complete music service, including instruments, records, music and books, this large London store is obviously worth looking at if you know what you want in musical items and need more than a new recorder for the children. Music is, as would be expected, a basically international field and much of what is for sale here is imported, so comparison shopping makes sense. For instance, the shop sells twelve different kinds of flutes, including a Yamaha, ranging in price from a little over $100 to close to $300. They also sell oboes, bassoons, school violins and just about every other instrument or accessory that you can think of. Much of their equipment is geared, as would be expected, to the school market, and before buying or renting a very expensive instrument for your child, it may be worth your while looking at their catalogue.

Morley Harpsichord, Pianoforte and Harp Galleries, 4 Belmont Hill, Lewisham, London SE13 5BD, England
Complete catalogue, $1.25, including air-mail postage.

Morley's specializes in both new and second-hand pianos, harps and early keyboard instruments and antiques. Americans, apparently, are most interested in classical early keyboard instruments, as well as some of the antique and restored pieces. Morley lists early-nineteenth-century pianos starting around $1,000, though obviously going up to much more. Old lutes, spinets and a double-manual harpsichord made by John Broadwood in 1799 at close to $20,000 is the most expensive item in the catalogue I looked at. A similar price range exists for harps, from about $1,200 for an early-nineteenth-century Grecian to over $7,000 for a new Obermeyer. Their well-illustrated and extremely helpful catalogue has photos of spinets, virginals, clavichords and the simpler, modern pianos. These include a large number of British makes as well as the increasingly widespread Japanese and other models.

John Nicholson, Bream House, Hungershall Park, Royal Tunbridge Wells, Kent ETN4 8NE, England
Catalogue, 35 cents or 3 International Reply Coupons.

John Nicholson builds organs and other instruments, most of which are sold directly to American customers, many of them university music departments and other specialized music groups. All his instruments, including the organs, can be shipped to the United States. The portative organs cost over $5,000 and can cost up to twice as much. On the other hand, Nicholson also offers a range of much less expensive instruments, mostly replicas of early music instruments, such as psalteries of various sorts, rebecs, pibgorns and panpipes. These cost from under $100 to two and three times that for the more complex models.

Paxman Musical Instruments Ltd., Pattenden Lane, Marsden, Kent TN12 3QJ, England
Price list, $2.50 for air mail.

Paxman is a maker of musical horns and accessories which they export all over the world. They are the only British manufacturer of these instruments and one of the few left in the world who still build horns to order. Their horns are made in different alloys, at different prices, and cover the classic range of single, double, dual-bore and triple horns.

Henri Selmer and Co. Ltd., Woolsack Lane, Braintree, Essex CM7 6BB, England
Brochure, free.

Selmer sells a range of electronic home organs which are available for export. The instruments, called Kentucky for some reason, are small, compact home models, which however have a full 49-note keyboard. The manufacturers boast of their voicing authenticity and the provision of sustain on all models. Prices range from slightly over $1,000 to roughly twice that for the most expensive models with all accessories.

Waltons Musical Instrument Galleries Ltd., 2–5 North Frederick Street, Dublin 1, Ireland
Price list, free. Prices in $.

Waltons makes and sells Irish harps, and also sells other musical instruments, sheet music and records related to Ireland. They sell knee harps, ballad harps and several different models of classic bardic harps, as well as a number of harp accessories. They also have a large selection of words and music for Irish ballads, records of Irish songs, dances and marches, and bagpipes and accordions.

Music

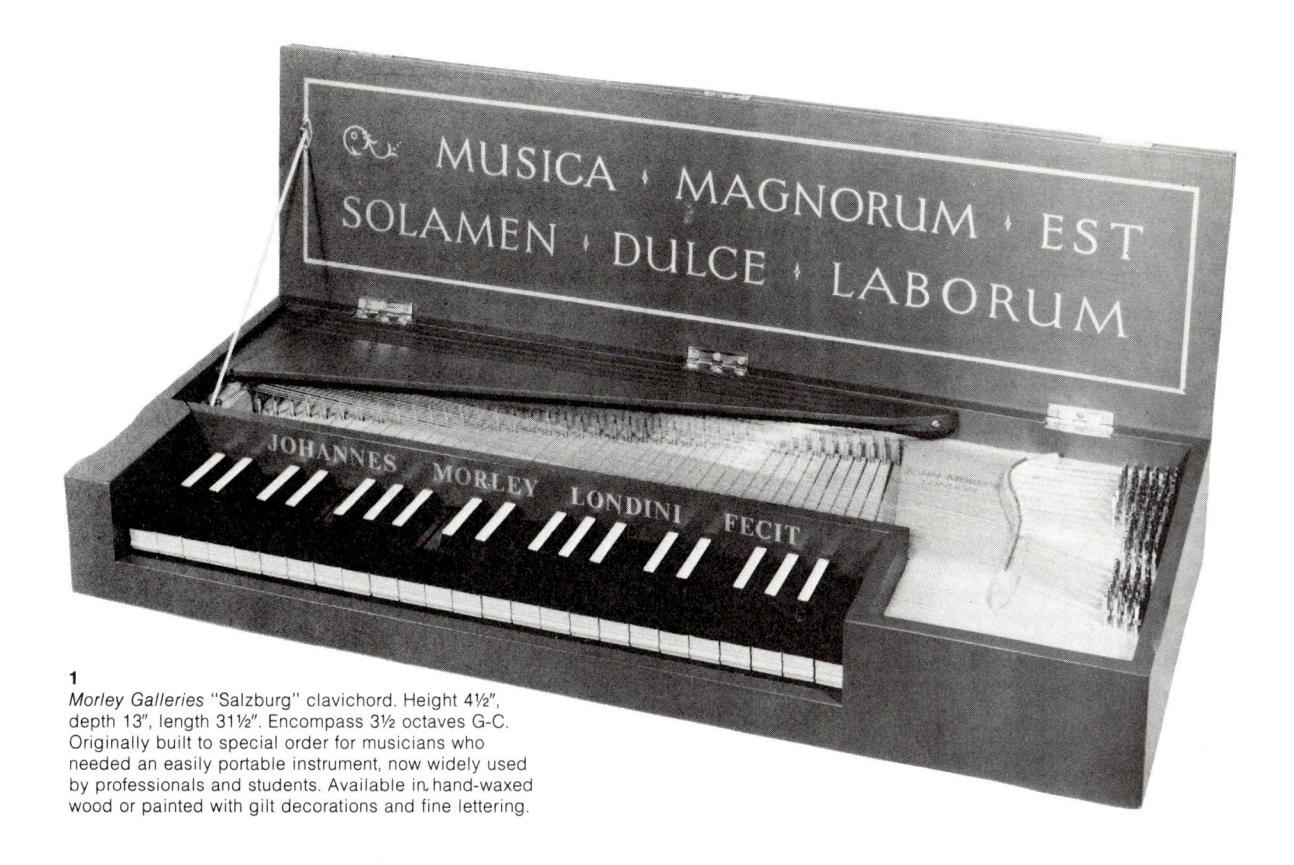

1
Morley Galleries "Salzburg" clavichord. Height 4½", depth 13", length 31½". Encompass 3½ octaves G-C. Originally built to special order for musicians who needed an easily portable instrument, now widely used by professionals and students. Available in hand-waxed wood or painted with gilt decorations and fine lettering.

Firma Kurt Wittmayer, Cembalobau, D-8190 Wolfratshausen, Postfach 1120, Germany
Brochure in German, free.

In their Upper Bavarian workshops, Kurt Wittmayer and his assistants make clavichords, harpsichords and spinets for customers all over the world, including American colleges, universities and professional harpsichordists. Kurt Wittmayer (whose work has been recommended to me by two customers) lectures, writes, exhibits his instruments, and has developed a patented precision shaft action that works in an "irreproachable way" in any climatic conditions.

Apparently the greatest demand nowadays is for small, reasonably priced instruments with modern "backpost construction," but Kurt Wittmayer also copies historical prototypes either to customers' exact specifications or after consultation and advice. Prices for clavichords and spinets are about $390–$780. One-manual harpsichords sell for $1,000 and up, and two-manual harpsichords from $2,250 and up. These are ready for delivery within one to four months after they are ordered. Copies of Baroque and Renaissance instruments take six to eight months and cost $1,650 and up.

PRINTED MUSIC

Blackwell's Music Shop, 38 Holywell Street, Oxford OX1 3SW, England
Catalogues:
General Music Books, free.
Piano and Organ Music, free.
Instrumental Music, free.
Orchestral Music, free.
Operas and Oratorios, free.
Solo, Madrigal and Folk Music, free.

A division of Blackwell Bookshop, Blackwell's Music Shop has just expanded into a specially designed new building, and now thinks and hopes that this is the largest shop in the world devoted to books on music and printed music. They stock English, European and American music, and are going to enlarge their antiquarian and second-hand departments.

I am told that although American records are less expensive than any others, foreign records cost less if bought directly from abroad. Blackwell's sells records by all the major English companies, and the complete Erato range from France.

William Elkin Music Services, Deacon House, Brundall, Norwich NOR 86Z, England

William Elkin Music Services supplies (promptly, they say) sheet music and books on music from all publishers in the United Kingdom and Europe. No catalogue; write and tell them what you want.

The English Folk Dance and Song Society, 2 Regent's Park Road, London NW1 7AY, England
Price lists, free; air mail, 3 International Reply Coupons.

I have often passed by the Society's handsome town house in London without realizing that within blossomed an extensive mail-order operation. The Society now runs a program called Folk Mail, an outgrowth of their folk shop, which mails out hundreds of books, records and other material every day. There are excellent catalogues on folk dance (including the required music), folk-song books, and records of songs and dances. These are, of course, primarily English, Irish and Scottish, though some American and other material is available. A marvelous list, not just for folk-song specialists, but for music teachers, community organizers or just plain parents—there are, for instance, several books of children's songs and games. The Society also sells a number of instruments—melodeons, dulcimers, kalimbas, guitars, whistles, pipes, etc., but you must write for information about these. And what English group catalogue would be complete without a selection of club ties, dishtowels, badges, car stickers, etc. A delightful list with no exact American counterpart that I know of.

Heugel et Cie., 2 bis Rue Vivienne, Paris II, France
Various price lists, free.

Heugel is one of France's leading and, I suspect, oldest publishers of choral and instrumental music. I say oldest because the firm's catalogues reprint their old price lists (with prices updated, of course), and the typography suggests that some of these were first printed at the turn of the century. It must be marvelous to work in a field where the products can so clearly last forever. Newer pieces have been added, so the choice is very wide, though naturally more complete when it comes to French composers. Among the lists available are orchestral, ancient, choral, instrumental and dramatic scores as well as a special catalogue of recorder music.

Musica Rara, 2 Great Marlborough Street, London W.1, England
Miscellaneous price lists, 25 cents; $1.25 air mail.

This unusual firm specializes in the publication of first editions of the classics and contemporaries in brass and woodwind music. In addition to the classic European repertory, the firm supplies music for pre-Columbian musical instruments, and for the increasingly popular medieval and Renaissance ensembles. A small selection of music for piano and stringed instruments is also available. Besides selling music, Musica Rara deals is pre-Columbian musical instruments as well as medieval and Renaissance musical instruments and recorders.

RECORDS

James Asman Ltd., Mail Order Department, 63 Cannon Street, London E.C.4, England
Price lists, 25 cents.

Asman sells both new, used and out-of print records by mail and is accustomed to supplying new discs that overseas readers have seen reviewed or advertised. In addition to this, their catalogue lists a selection of new records in all categories. On the whole, English record prices are still higher than ours, but firms like Asman can be of particular interest to overseas buyers, since their stock may include many records, including American popular and jazz music, that is much harder to find here except at high premiums.

Leslie Brown, The Showman's Record Shop, 95 High Street, Stockton on Tees, Teeside TS18 1BD, England
Price list, $1.

For showmen and for people who love fairs, fairgrounds and mechanical music, Leslie Brown publishes an irresistible list of books, cassettes and records. There are fair and carousel-organ records from all over the world, and such things as original recordings from Paul Eakins Gay Nineties Organ Museum and White's Mammoth Gavioli Organ. The books are about fairgrounds (one is called *Ups and Downs and Roundabouts*), gypsies, traction engines, musical boxes and even steam rollers—"everybody loves a steam roller" says the book list.

James H. Crawley, 246 Church Street, London N9 9HQ, England
List Vocal Art, one issue, 85 cents; annual subscription, $5.

James Crawley buys and sells rare vocal 78-rpm records, mostly ones that look and sound absolutely new. They also have some rare recordings transcribed onto 12" long-players for about $11 each, and will transcribe others at customers' requests. A selection range of vocalists goes from "French Opera Stars," "Famous Tenors," and great French, German, Italian, Russian singers to music-hall songs and stars like Gertrude Lawrence in the original version of *The King and I* (four records for about $4) or Noel Coward singing "Don't Let's Be Beastly to the Germans." Also a few talkies like Ellen Terry delivering the "Quality of Mercy" speech from *The Merchant of Venice*, and Herbert Beerbohm Tree doing "Antony's Lament" from *Antony and Cleopatra*.

Dobells Jazz Record Shop, 77 Charing Cross Road, London W.C.2, England
Monthly bulletin, $1.20 yearly subscription.
Price list of own records, free.

This shop specializes in hard-to-find jazz, folk and blues records and also issues a small number of records on its own label, "77." These cost $5 each, while the other items stocked by the store may cost considerably more. These include a great many rare discs which, the store warns, are in very limited supply and should be ordered quickly.

HMV Shops, Mail Order Department, 363 Oxford Street, London W1R 2BJ, England
No catalogue.

The largest tape and record store in Europe says that they stock most British records besides many issued on the Continent. They have many customers who send the mail-order department lists of records and tapes they want that can't be found locally; HMV replies with a *pro forma* invoice giving the prices of the records and tapes, along with the charge for packing and mailing.

Saydisc Specialised Recordings Ltd., The Barton, Inglestone Common, Badminton, Gloucestershire GL9 1BX, England
Price list, free; air mail, 2 International Reply Coupons.

Saydisc is a small record company specializing in esoteric fields neglected by the larger firms. They have no distributor in America and therefore sell a great deal by mail. Americans are most interested in the "American blues, old time country and ragtime reissues as well as the recordings of musical automata, English bell change ringing and English dialect issues." Saydisc's records include selections from old Wurlitzers, mechanical organs and honky-tonk nickelodeons. Others range from "Furry Lewis in Memphis" to "Cotswold Characters," the latter a record about the traditional English countryside.

The Swing Shop, 1B Mitcham Lane, Streatham, London S.W.16, England

Being specialists in new and second-hand jazz and blues records in all speeds, The Swing Shop was recommended to me by a New York jazz enthusiast who says that jazz has become so neglected in America that he finds more records in England. Dave Carey, who runs The Swing Shop, says that customers' "want lists" are given careful attention, but as the shop is always frantically busy operating at "full steam" and "battling against the clock," he *wholeheartedly* recommends that jazz fans subscribe to (either or both)

Jazz Journal, Borough Green, Sevenoaks, Kent, England
Storyville, 66 Fairview Drive, Chigwell, Essex 197 6HS, England

which always have a full-page, detailed advertisement of Swing Shop offers and also well-written reviews of jazz issues available in England.

16 Perfume and Cosmetics

Perfume and Cosmetics

Cathay of Bournemouth Ltd., Cleveland Road, Bournemouth BH1 4QG, England
Catalogue, $1.

Cathay's ("Herbalists of the highest repute and integrity") is the largest dealer in herbs in England and offers a fascinating contrast with its counterparts in the United States. While in America herbal remedies are part of rural folklore or buried within the subcultures of hippie experimentation of Puerto Rican botanicas, Cathay's catalogue exudes scientific respectability. A spotless factory, packaging equal to posh Bond Street shops, a wide range of natural cosmetics side by side with Tiger Headache pills, Emerald Jade (diuretic) tablets and a little old-fashioned booklet on *Male and Female Sexual Difficulties and how to SAFELY Overcome Them*. Here we find that Black Pearls or Yellow Emperor drops were useful for some of the classic masculine complaints, with ginseng appearing discreetly, as it does in our local drugstore.

Still, with the Chinese showing that traditional medicine is an important part of any pharmacopoeia, it may well be that Cathay Liver Stimulant is what you need, but Cathay's is circumspect about ingredients and it may be wiser to stick to remedying that "run-down" feeling where the chances are excellent that Cathay's is as useful as the stuff advertised so stridently on television.

Whatever your feelings about medicine, you may want to try the attractively packaged and not all that expensive herbal creams, balms and soaps which occupy a large part of this intriguing booklet.

J. Floris Ltd., 89 Jermyn Street, London SW1Y 6JH, England
Brochure, free; 50 cents air mail.

Floris, which claims to have been perfumers to the Court of St. James's since 1730, was started by Juan Famenias Floris, who sailed to England from Majorca, and has remained in the family ever since. The shop, which until a few years ago was the only place that sold the perfumes, is the original shop, although it has been extended and adorned with mahogany fittings brought from the Great Exhibition of 1851. The perfumes are especially nice because they are flower perfumes which catch the smells of the original English flowers beautifully without spoiling and cheapening them, as so often happens with flower scents. Perfumes include English violet, gardenia, honeysuckle, jasmin, lily of the valley, rose and stephanotis, and they come in colognes, powders, bath oils and soap, and red rose even comes in a mouthwash. In other scents there are potpourris, pomanders, vaporizers and candles. For men there are shaving creams and lotions, shampoos, brilliantine in lime, verbena, new-mown hay and other rustic smells.

French perfume and cosmetics are among the best buys in this book. The shops listed below are beautifully organized to make buying easy, and when you buy by mail the goods are exempt from high French taxes, so they end up costing two thirds of the American price, even after you've paid the postage and duty.

See Addresses of Import Information ("Trademark Information") at the end of this book, with hints on what to do about import restrictions on certain brands of perfume.

Freddy, 10 Rue Auber, Paris IX, France
Price list for perfume, free. Prices in $.

Grillot, 10 Rue Cambon, Paris IX, France
Price list for perfume and Antoine, Lancôme, Orlane and Stendhal cosmetics; also, at great savings, the famous scented "Rigaud" candles, free. Prices in $.

Michel Swiss, 16 Rue de la Paix, Paris II, France
Price list for perfume and Orlane cosmetics, free. Prices in $.

Obéron, 73 Champs-Elysées, Paris VIII, France
Price list for perfume and Orlane and Lancôme cosmetics, free. Prices in $.
General catalogue, $1.50. Prices in $.

1
Obéron "Step" purse atomizers. Limoges porcelain. About $5 each.

17 Pets

Pets

Harrods Ltd., Knightsbridge, London S.W.1, England
Harrod's pet shop sends lion cubs, pumas, bush babies, otters, Siamese and Burmese cats, decorative waterfowl, aviary birds, etc., all over the world. In 1967 they sent an elephant called Gertie by air to Los Angeles. They will gladly give a quotation for any animal which doesn't have to undergo American quarantine, and say that British-bred dogs are in great demand in America.

A permit is needed to import an animal, for details write to the Commissioner of Customs, Washington, D.C. 20226, and ask for the leaflet "So You Want to Import a Pet."

18 Photographic Equipment

Photographic Equipment

The best place, by far, to get photographic equipment is Hong Kong, a free port which does not pay local taxes and has lower overhead charges. In fact, I first heard about Cinex (below) from a professional Washington photographer who gets his equipment from them because Hong Kong discounts make their prices even lower than professional discount prices available in America. He says that the firm is highly professional and packs superbly. Write and ask the firms below for their prices and mailing charges for still and movie cameras, interchangeable lenses, movie projectors, slide projectors, sound projectors, electronic flash, light meters, fish-eye conversion lenses, tele converters, binoculars and tripods.

T. M. Chan and Co., P.O. Box 3881, Hong Kong
Catalogue, free. Prices in $.

Two of my friends recommend this firm, one of them bought here a Miranda Sensorex Single Lens Reflex Camera f/1.8 for $148 including surface postage and duty. He claims that the lowest American price at the time for this camera was $216, and that it sold for up to $322.45.

Cinex Ltd., General Post Office Box 724, Hong Kong
Price list, free (International Reply Coupons appreciated). Prices in $.

Cinex no longer mails out the Hong Kong camera buying guide. Instead, they send out a brief price list for the leading brands of cameras, hi-fi equipment and Seiko watches.

Photo Hobby, Rotelstrasse 29, 8042 Zurich, Switzerland
Catalogue in German, free; air mail, 3 International Reply Coupons.

This chain of four photographic-equipment shops in Zurich says that they have a 20 to 40 percent discount on regular prices. However, as Swiss prices are not low and the catalogue is in German, this address should only be used by people who are looking for something specific.

Universal Suppliers, P.O. Box 14803, Hong Kong
Catalogue, free; air mail $1.80. Prices in $.

Universal Suppliers publishes its own catalogue for cameras and accessories, binoculars, telescopes, rifle scopes and spotting scopes, all at the usual low Hong Kong prices. For $1.80 they will air-mail several of their catalogues, but be specific as to what you are interested in, because they have catalogues for many things including stereo equipment, watches, china and embroidered linen.

19 Services

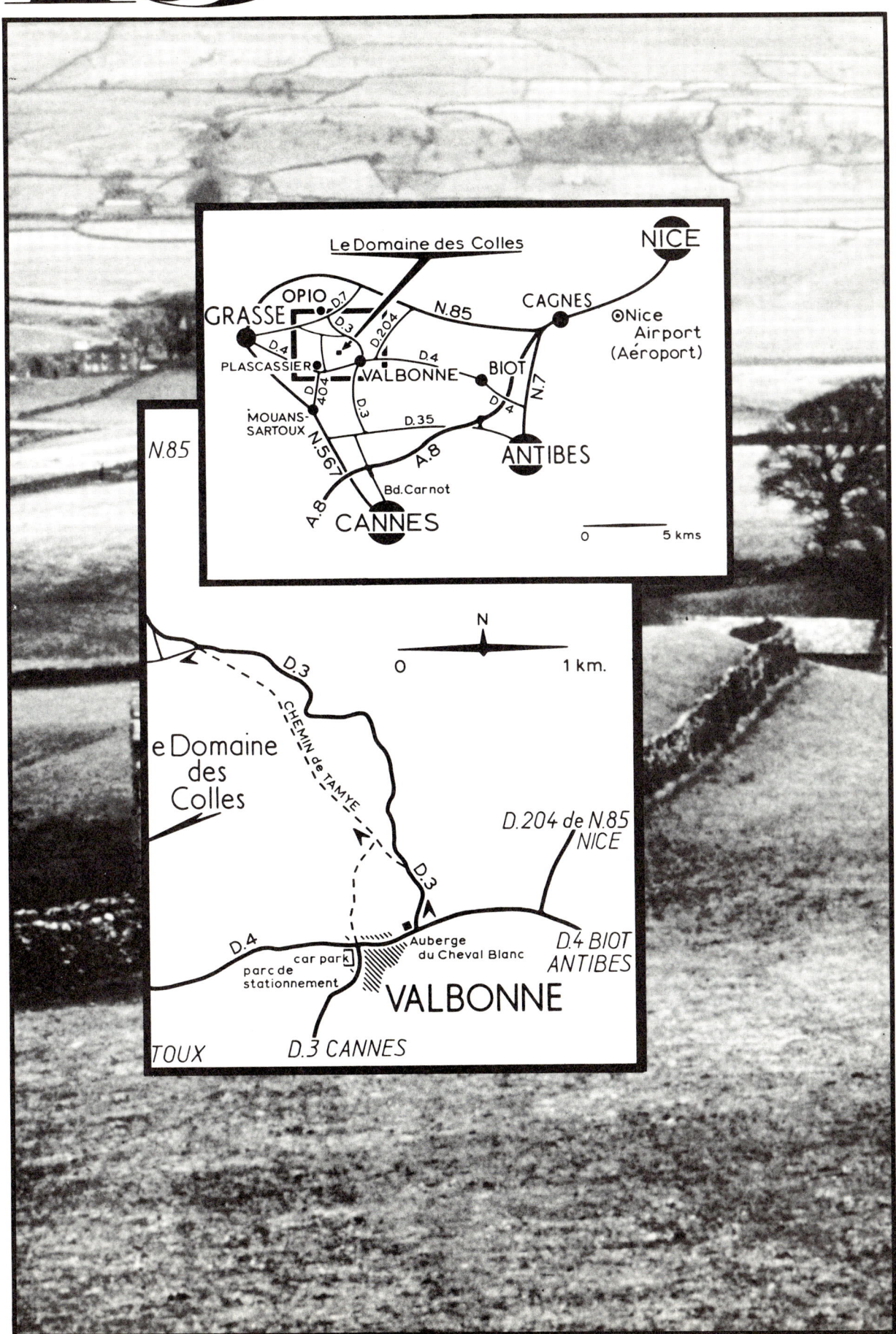

Services

BOOKBINDING

George Bayntun, Manvers Street, Bath BA1 IJW, England ♕
List of modern reprints bound in leather, $1.

A family firm, bookseller and bookbinder, owning a large—possibly the largest in the world—collection of books in new leather bindings: first or fine editions of English literature, standard sets, illustrated and sporting books, poetry, biography and travel.

They also bookbind, mainly for collectors, in leather only, calf or morocco, with gold tooling, and have over ten thousand brass-engraved tools for finishing, many following the designs of important binders of past centuries so that old bindings can usually be copied faithfully. Prices are from $50 upward to any amount.

López Valencia, Bárbara de Braganza 9, Madrid 4, Spain
Price list in Spanish, free.

As both leather and labor are cheap in Spain, bookbinding is astonishingly inexpensive. López Valencia has several American customers and they correspond in English. They will send a brief price list in Spanish, but it is much more useful to write giving them some idea of what you would like done. López Valencia will send a small sketch at the customer's request which serves as a pattern. Prices for a 10" book start at $3 for a fabric binding and go to $7 for a plain leather binding.

FORTUNETELLING

Roger Elliot, The Manor, Cossington near Bridgwater, Somerset, England

Roger Elliot, who calls himself "up and coming" (he should know) and has appeared on the English *David Frost Show*, tells fortunes. He is a graduate of a correspondence course run by the Faculty of Astrological Studies, Burnham-on-Sea, England, comprising two years of study followed by fifteen hours of exams. To tell a fortune he needs $25 and the date, place and, as closely as possible, the time of his client's birth. He also likes a few details about present circumstances, especially if there are problems, e.g. "mother semi-invalid, husband wants to get out of insurance job into something more creative, hoping to move to the West Coast." He then makes a map of the sky as it appeared when the person was born. The map, he says, is really a diagram of the psyche and shows the disposition, character and potential skills of the person, and it also shows when particular facets of the personality will be emphasized or subdued. From this, he says, he can assess the probability of a person behaving a certain way at any time. He tries to cover the following points: basic outlook on life, superficial temperament, inner emotional disposition, chief motivations, potential conflicts within the psyche, major aptitudes and talents, interpersonal relationships, the kind of work that is suitable, the major emotional and spiritual experiences of the lifetime (including partnerships and love liaisons). He also plans each analysis to suit the needs of the client: a brisk, no-nonsense (no-nonsense?) businessman gets a crisp, tabulated report, while a teen-ager gets a more psychologically oriented work-up. Charge: $100 per fortune. No mention of money-back guarantee.

Note: A reader wrote and told me that she sent Roger Elliot money but never got her fortune. Roger Elliot claims that he is especially punctilious about answering letters with money enclosed because he knows that many people regard fortunetellers as charlatans. Although I haven't checked

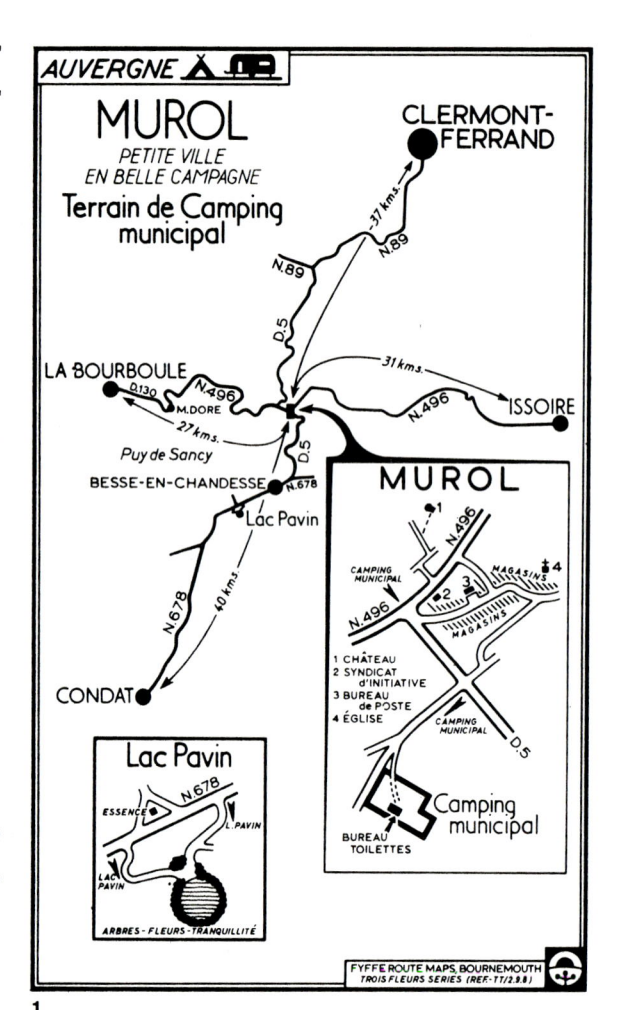

1
Anthony Fyffe "How to Find Us" maps can be made to order in quantities of 200 and up.

further with the disappointed reader to find out if she eventually got her fortune told, I have, after thinking about it, decided to leave this entry in, with this note as a warning.

MAP MAKING

Anthony Fyffe, 30 Chantry, Madeira Road, Bournemouth, Dorset, England

Anthony Fyffe makes "How to Find Us" maps both for businesses and for private homes. Two hundred copies of a 7" by 10" functional but not beautiful "social" map cost $95 plus postage. The customer sends the name and address of the place to be pinpointed, and a map of the area, which can be a local map or a rough sketch. The rough sketch is sufficient because Mr. Fyffe has official maps of the United States on a 1:24,000 scale.

ROCKING-HORSE RESTORATIONS

Andrew Booth, The Antique Shop, Bishop's Waltham, Southampton SO3 1BE, England
No catalogue.

Mr. Booth, a rocking-horse expert, restores old horses for their owners and also sells tails, manes, harnesses, etc., for people who have horses that just need sprucing up a bit. Unfortunately, old rocking horses are now so prized that they rarely come up for sale, so Mr. Booth can't sell restored antique horses. He can, though, when asked, make a magnificent new horse in the old-style Gilpin stance with Georgian rockers, hand-carved in mahogany. The horse costs around $750. Delivery takes about a year, but judging by the photograph, is well worth the wait.

SIGN CARVING

Rusticraft Signs, Woodland Forge, Covert Lane, Scraptoft, Thurnby, Leicestershire, England
Leaflet, 50 cents.

House signs made to order by a small group of English craftsmen. Signs are made out of African hardwood, hand-lettered and hand-carved, or wrought iron, and prices are very much lower than American prices.

20 Special Needs

Special Needs

I have made an exception of this section and included some American institutions because these nonprofit organizations don't advertise and there are many people who never hear about the services they could be using.

Duk Kwong Optical Co., 17 A Cameron Road, Kowloon, Hong Kong
Leaflet, free.

If you have your own prescription, you can buy glasses by mail from this firm. They send a picture page illustrating forty-two shapes that you can have made up with clear or tinted glass or plastic lenses. The shapes are a good, up-to-date assortment, and John Pong, the manager, says that folding glasses, metal frames and lorgnettes are the most popular with his American customers. As I write, glass lenses cost $7, plastic $14, and frames from $6 to $15 for metal.

Universal Suppliers, P.O. Box 14803, Hong Kong
Assorted catalogues, $1.80.

Universal Suppliers makes prescription glasses from American optical lenses made by A. O. Company of America with simple modern frames made in France, Spain and West Germany. Prices, which include frames and air-mail postage, are mainly between $20 and $30 except for certain 14-carat gold-plated frames by Rodenstock of West Germany, which are around $40. Hard contact lenses are also made for $30 per pair. Once you have been properly fitted in your own country for contact lenses and are used to wearing them, if you need replacement lenses, send a full prescription, which should include the fit as well as the graduation, to Universal Suppliers.

American Foundation for the Blind Inc., 15 W. 16th Street, New York 10011, U.S.A.
Aids and Appliances brochure, free. Catalogue of publications, free. Prices in $.

The American Foundation for the Blind runs a nonprofit mail-order service selling commercial, adapted or special devices to help reduce the problems arising from blindness. Their catalogue is available in Braille or inkprint and has aids to help the blind or partially sighted: writing equipment, sewing aids, travel aids, music aids, games, watches and all sorts of things for the kitchen: a specially chosen frying pan, a dispenser to measure teaspoonfuls, a "flame tamer" for people who have trouble keeping the heat or gas or electric fires low enough to prevent burning.

The catalogue of publications contains a list of both free and priced publications available, most of them for families, teachers and professionals who deal with blind people, but sources for Braille and talking books are also given.

Royal National Institute for the Blind, 224 Great Portland Street, London W1N 6AA, England.
Catalogue of apparatus and games for the blind, free.

The Royal National Institute for the Blind has a big export mail-order service with a special export price list. Prices tend to be lower than in America, and although many goods are the same in both countries, many are not. Perhaps predictably, England does not have as many kitchen gadgets but has many more games: card games, a solitaire board with instructions in Braille, a bridge scorer, jigsaw puzzles which can also be used by partially sighted children. Also more mathematical aids, writing equipment and devices for speaking to the deaf-blind, and a phonograph pickup control which enables the user to pick out particular passages from long-playing records.

Science for the Blind, 221 Hill Rock Road, Bala-Cynwyd, Pennsylvania 1900, U.S.A.

A nonprofit organization with a $10 annual membership fee that develops and sells sophisticated aids to its members. Besides instruments to help with technical work, there are low-cost ham radios, tape recorders, disc players and cassettes, as well as free monthly taped periodicals such as *Radio Digest* (a collection of articles about ham radio chosen from electronic and ham-radio magazines), *Timely Topics* (nontechnical scientific material taken from publications like *Time* and the *New York Times*) and selections from *Consumer Reports*.

Royal National Institute for the Deaf, 105 Gower Street, London WCIE 6AH, England
Booklet, "Special Aids to Hearing," 70 cents.

This booklet describes various aids for the deaf or hard-of-hearing which the technical department of the R.N.I.D. has tested or developed. For just over $1 there is a harness to keep hearing aids in place for young children; for 40 cents a little celluloid note pad for communicating; there are also several light-flashing door bells, and a vibrating pillow (instead of an alarm clock), which would need adapters for American voltage. For people who would like to make their own, or have a local electrician make one, a flashing door bell or television adapter (so that those hard-of-hearing can listen at the volume they need without disturbing others), there are do-it-yourself instructions. If you are interested, the R.N.I.D. can explain necessary electrical adjustments.

Evergreen Travel Service Inc., 19429-44th Avenue West, Lynnwood, Washington 98036, U.S.A.
Catalogue, free.

Group trips abroad for mentally handicapped, physically handicapped and blind people.

Handy-Cap Horizons, 3250 Loretta Drive, Indianapolis, Indiana 46227, U.S.A.
Leaflet, free.

The most useful of these travel organizations, Handy-Cap Horizons is an international club that provides meetings, tours within America as well as abroad, and a magazine. It is a nonprofit organization, so it has the lowest prices.

Kasheta Travel Inc., 139 Main Street, E. Rockaway, N.Y. 11518, U.S.A.
Catalogue, free.
Rambling Tours Inc., P.O. Box 1304, Hallandale, Florida 33009, U.S.A.
Leaflet, free.

Group trips, mainly abroad, for the physically handicapped.

The Helping Hand Company, Church Road, Sandhurst, Kent TN18 5NT, England
Leaflet, free.

This company makes five different reaching aids for people who are disabled, bedridden or simply have trouble bending or stretching for things out of their immediate reach. The lightest model, for instance, has a magnet attached to the claw for small metal objects such as pins and nails. Another model has a special handle for people with hand disabilities. Now The Helping Hand is producing and exporting a second gadget of general interest called the Litter Picker. It is a long metal stick with a nylon claw at the end with which you can pick up anything from tin cans and rags to broken glass,

Special Needs

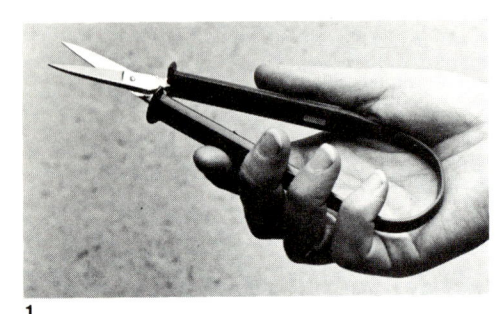

1
ICTA The "Styrex" scissors used for precision cutting in industry and also useful for people with a poor grip. About $3.50.

2
ICTA Playing-card holder consisting of two plastic disks that can be easily screwed onto any table. About $1.50.

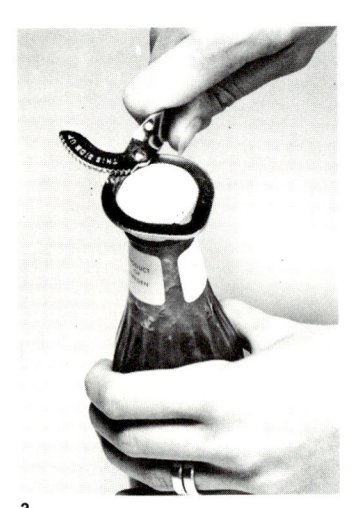

3
ICTA Crestella screw bottle opener, designed for people with weak hands. About 75 cents.

cigarette butts and matches. Without touching anything dirty, you can reach litter in thick grass, hedges, under benches and even under water; the stick sounds terrifically useful for private groups who are trying to keep public places clean, and costs under $10, including postage. (Discounts for larger orders.)

ICTA Information Center, Fack S-161 03, Bromma 3, Sweden
Information sheets on technical aids, $8 for a year's subscription.
List of literature, free.
Prices in $.

ICTA distributes information to private patients, institutions and organizations on new technical aids from all over the world for handicapped people. The multilingual information sheets, which cost $8 for a year's subscription, or $15 for a year of back numbers, are illustrated, and give clear descriptions of the aids and their uses, and the address of the manufacturer or designer. The sheets ICTA sent me included English tableware for use by people with hand disabilities, a Swiss semiautomatic feeding device, a Danish typewriter for the severely disabled, a Swedish chair for people who find it hard to rise from a sitting position, an Italian walking aid for children, a German aid for dressing and undressing. While distributing information, the center is anxious to be advised about new aids.

There are also various practical publications, such as a motel guide (55 cents) that gives information about motels along two European highways conveniently set up for handicapped people: on E1, London–Palermo, and on E4, Lisbon–Helsinki.

Central Council for the Disabled, 34 Eccleston Square, London S.W.1, England
List of publications, free.

This council is campaigning to make public buildings and facilities accessible to the disabled. As part of their work they have produced several pamphlets for planners and architects with ideas on how to design buildings and facilities so as to make them manageable by the disabled. For the disabled themselves there is a series of twenty-two guides to England's most interesting towns; they are $1 each surface, $2 air mail. The London guide (55 cents surface, 90 cents air mail) is in its third edition, and like the others, lists places where chairbound and other disabled people can most easily shop, eat, stay and visit—places of interest such as churches, important buildings, parks and gardens. There is also a pamphlet, "Holidays for the Physically Handicapped" (85 cents, including surface mail), which lists suitable hotels in Scotland and Wales, and includes a few on the Continent; and two pamphlets on easy-access "sights," in the county of Dorset and another for Sussex, $1 each, including surface postage.

Information Officer, National Society for Mentally Handicapped Children, 86 Newman Street, London W1P 4AR, England
Book list, $2. (No checks).

The list of books on sale is, unfortunately, just a list and does not describe the books, though quite often the title is informative enough. Most of the books give advice and information to parents and teachers of mentally handicapped children; the books range from generally helpful books, such as Spock and *Simple Puppetry*, through others, such as *Story Telling for the Slow Learner*, to studies mainly of interest to professionals in the field.

Special Needs

Supplies Officer, the Spastics Society, 12 Park Crescent, London W1N 4EQ, England
"Best Buys" brochure, 25 cents.

A list of aids sold especially cheaply by the society, including such things as a double-handled mug, dresses for children with changeable front panels, and a new multivariable chair for children two to eight years old with adjustable height and various adjustable supports.

21 Sports Equipment and Clothes

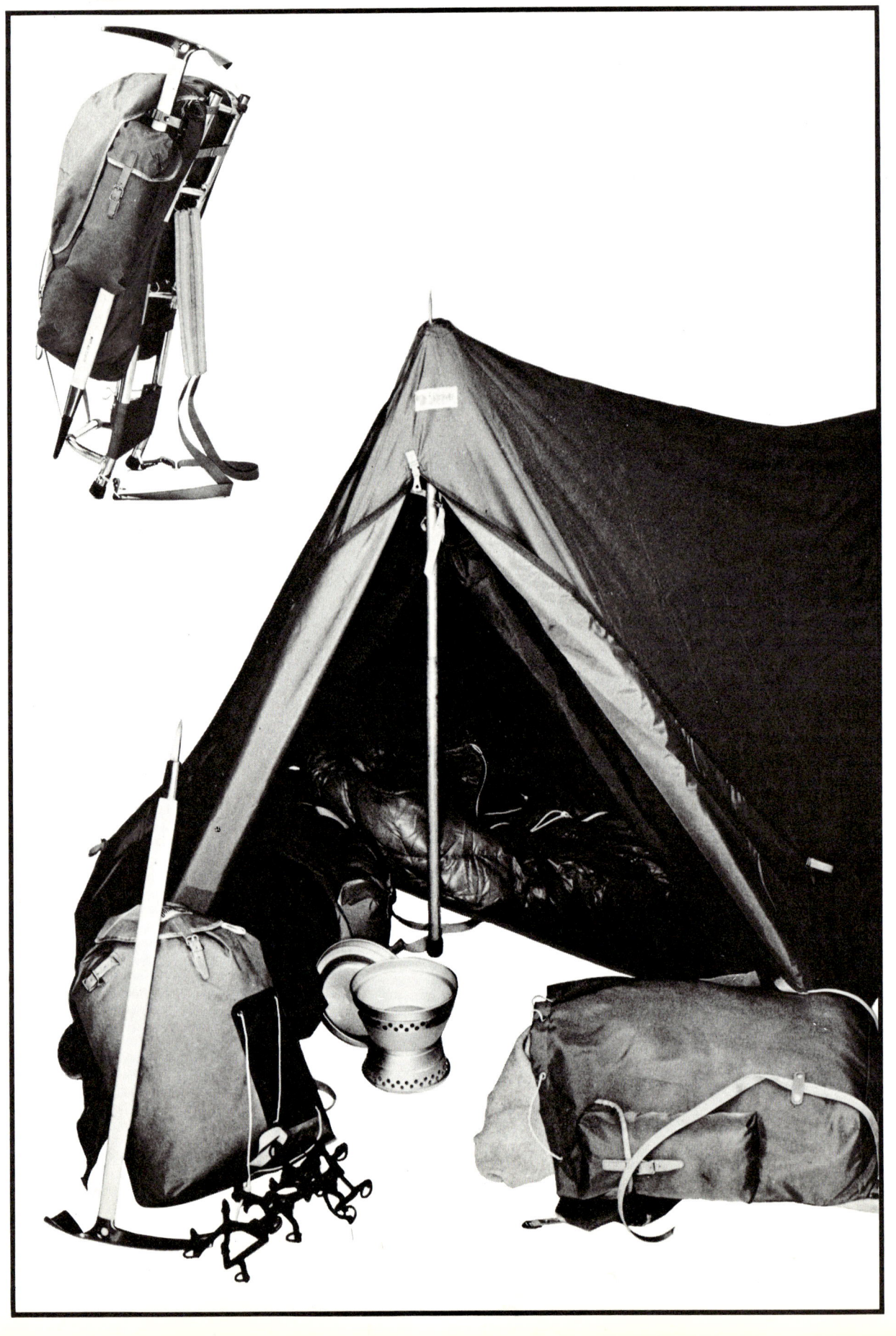

Sports Equipment and Clothes

BICYCLES

Condor Bicycles, 90/94 Gray's Inn Road, London WC1X 8AA, England
Leaflet, free.

This firm says that top amateurs and the MacKeson professional racing team have been instrumental in obtaining the Condor frame design which has been used in the Tour de France, world championships, Olympic games, Commonwealth games; however, if, in spite of this, you wish to alter their specifications, they would be pleased to discuss your needs. By far their most popular frame is the Condor Italia, which is roughly $140. It is built with Reynolds 531 DB tubing and has long Prugnat lugs, and many variations can be made on the frame, some of which are listed on the leaflet. There are five frames described on the price list, which comes with a forty-seven-part questionnaire you must answer to have the bicycle custom-built for you.

Cyclists' Touring Club, 69 Touring Club, 69 Meadrow, Goldaming, Surrey, England
Annual subscription, one adult, $7; whole family, an additional $1.45.

"The national association devoted to the encouragement of recreational cycling and the protection of cyclists interests" warmly welcomes new members (Her Majesty the Queen is a patron of the society; this conjurs up a nice picture of biking royalty). The benefits of joining include a bimonthly magazine with articles on travel, touring lesser-known areas, small ads and "Companions Wanted" features; a touring service to help with plans, routes, etc.; an annual handbook (for an extra 65 cents) with 3,000 addresses of accommodation, repair shops and local information officers; touring and general biking information; technical advice and information; leaflets dealing with biking and details of bike hiring facilities, and organized tours of the British Isles and Europe. All in all it sounds like excellent value for anyone thinking of taking a bike holiday or doing a little biking as part of a lazy holiday in Europe.

BOATS

Aquaquipment, 4 Ashwell Street, St. Albans, Hertfordshire, England
Wetsuit kits brochure, free.
Inflatable-boat kits brochure, free.

Here are yet more things you can save money on by making them yourself from a kit. Aquaquipment claims to be the BIG name in wetsuit kits, and besides making ready-made wetsuits in standard sizes, they make kits in standard small and large sizes. Prices for standard-size jacket and pants kits start at about $57. Aquaquipment also says that as far as they know, they are the only suppliers of do-it-yourself inflatable-boat kits in the world. They contain everything you need to build a boat except for the few woodworking tools for the floorboards. They also contain test seams so that you can make a few seams and undo them to check whether you are making them correctly before starting the boat, and Aquaquipment will even sell you a set of seams for $2.50 so that you can check before buying the kit. There are four boat models, and prices start at about $225 for a 8'3" boat that can carry three people and takes a 3-hp engine.

Downer International Sails Ltd., Charlemont Avenue, Dun Laoghire, Ireland
Price list, free.

Downer manufactures Terylene (same as Dacron) sails for small boats at prices which sailing friends tell me are slightly over half American prices; they also make dinghy-boat covers in vinyl and hatch tarpaulins in finest quality canvas and PVC; riggings and rope work. They can supply aluminum mast and booms, and mast and boom kits.

The London Yacht Center Ltd., 13 Artillery Lane, London E17LP, England
Specific inquiries for major equipment (electronic equipment, inflatable boats, outboard motors, windlasses and winches) are answered individually.

The center says that the best buys for Americans are British sea motors, Avon inflatable boats, Seagull motors, and Brookes and Gatehouse electronic equipment. Here, you can save a little if you send for them by mail, but more if you buy in person and bring purchases back with you.

Moyle Marine Products, 73 Walton Road, Woking, Surrey, England
Catalogue, $2.50.

Moyle Marine Products, a special division within a foundry, manufactures and sells boat fittings principally made from castings: winches, ventilators, port lights, etc. Most of their products are small enough to go by mail.

Ship Shop, Andries de Jong BV, Muntplein 8, Amsterdam, Holland
Catalogue, 3 International Reply Coupons.

The Ship Shop has been selling ship's lanterns, ship's clocks, bells, pennants, flags, flagpoles and a huge range of nautical articles since 1787. The catalogue contains a very handsome collection of lamps and lanterns, barometers, compasses, brass name plates (in English) and smaller things such as corkscrews, ashtrays and cuff links. A terrific place for nautical presents. The Ship Shop says that they have quite a few American clients who all realize that "our articles are comparatively cheap and of excellent quality."

Captain O. M. Watts Ltd., 48 Albemarle Street, Piccadilly, London WIX 4BJ, England
20-page sailingwear catalogue, free.
20-page Christmas catalogue, free.
Simpson-Lawrence hardware catalogue, $2.50.

"Everything for the yachtsman and his yacht," says the letterhead. Watts makes a big thing of foreign mail order and is the only yachting shop in London to provide catalogues in dollars. The clothes catalogue has lots of inexpensive waterproof garments for adults and children: reefer jackets, heavy sweaters for around $20; shirts; marvelous sailcloth fishermen's smocks for about $12; footwear, headwear and bags. Also "regalia": nautical badges, buttons and ties.

The Christmas catalogue has gifts for sailing fiends: books, trophies, tankards, ashtrays, badges engraved with yachts or flags, nautical nutcrackers, sea-horse cuff links. Galley cloths with fishy scenes, and a gimball oil lamp for $19, exactly the same as one I saw for $35 in an American catalogue.

The Simpson-Lawrence catalogue has hardware for above and below decks. If you are looking for anything special, Captain Watts will send information.

Tyne Canoes Ltd., 206 Amyrand Road, St. Margaret's Twickenham TW1 3HZ, Middlesex, England
Tyne touring canoe brochure, free.
Streamline competition kayaks brochure, free.

This firm sells its very reputable canoes and kayaks by mail and says that although they have exported almost every model, the most popular abroad are the folding models which

Sports Equipment and Clothes

can be sent by mail, and the do-it-yourself kits from which you can make a complete wood and cotton duck one- or two-seater for about $100. Other popular export canoes are the child- or adult-sized "Beaver," a traditional birch-bark shaped canoe made of fiberglass most suitable for inland waterways. Canoe prices start at about $150. Lots of accessories (various bags, knee pads, roof racks, trolleys and repair outfits) are on sale, and so is an inexpensive collection of booklets published by the British Canoing Association: *Choosing a Canoe and Its Equipment, Canoe Camping, Canoe Building, Canadian Canoing and Long Distance Racing Handbook.* All cost about $1 each.

Yachtmail Co. Ltd., 7 Cornwall Crescent, London W11 1PH, England
Illustrated price list for kites, free. Prices in $.
Price list for sailing goods, free.

Yachtmail, which was listed in the first edition of this book for their kites, now wants to be listed in the Sports section as well. They sell a basic range of sailing goods by top British manufacturers at discount prices and say that echo sounders, compasses and inflatable dinghies seem to be most popular with American customers.

CAMPING

Brown Best & Co. Ltd., 47 Old Woolwich Road, Greenwich, London SE10 9PU, England
20-page catalogue, 35 cents; $1.40 air mail.

Brown Best is one of England's leading makers of rucksacks, having equipped the British Everest Expedition and others. They sell nylon as well as canvas packs, pack frames and various accessories at prices that are still very reasonable for America. For instance, canvas packs start at $5 to $35, and a portable air bed for around $15. Certainly a list worth consulting before buying here.

Export Division, Arthur Ellis and Co. Ltd., Private Bag, Dunedin, New Zealand
24-page color brochure, free. Prices in $.

Arthur Ellis and Co. makes duck- and goose-down sleeping bags that have been used on all sorts of international expeditions. "The best that can be obtained anywhere," say Hillary and Tenzing, who took them up Mount Everest. Prices are very low, starting at about $40 for a duck-down bag intended for motorists, trailer owners and home use, and the most expensive bag is still under $90—the goose-down "Everest Sierra," good for mountaineering under extreme conditions. Down-filled clothes are also sold: gloves, slippers, trousers, racy slim-cut ski jackets, and monsterish polar jackets that have been tested in "the major cold areas of the world."

Fjällräven SE-AB, Fack 209, S-891 01 Örnsköldsvik, Sweden
20-page color brochure, free. Prices in $. Summer, winter.

A first-rate little brochure from this manufacturer of sophisticated camping equipment. Most things are photographed in color, and there are good descriptions of each article, materials used, and the advantages of that particular model. There are five tents sleeping two or four people, including "Thermo G66," which was developed with experts involved in the 1966 Greenland expedition. It is a double-walled thermo tent, cooler in summer and hotter in winter. Total weight of tent, 3½ pounds; cost, about $120. Also five carrying frames; ten bags; and extra pockets to be sewn on the bags; four down sleeping bags; a professional-looking

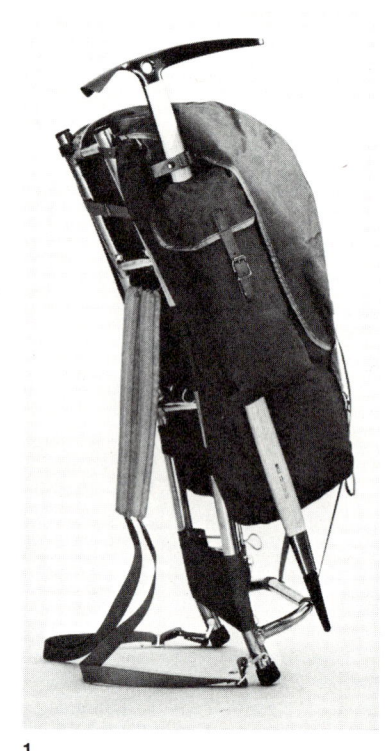

1
Fjällräven SE-AB "Expedition no. 505" rucksack with extra-large flap and inside waterproof pocket fitted with optilon lock. Snow locks inside the bag as well as in the pockets. Bulge seams reinforced with leather. Welded frame adjustable to fit different shoulder widths. Weight 3.8 lbs. $46.

fishing jacket "ideal for advanced pleasure fishing"; a down jacket; Greenland pants; a poncho that can be used as a tent floor; a metal match; and a storm stove developed by Swedish commando units which needs no assembling.

Trend, 336 Rayners Lane, Pinner, Middlesex, England
Brochure, 25 cents.

This large firm deals primarily in army surplus, including rucksacks and camping equipment, and supplies retail stores throughout England. Their brochure is, unfortunately, a very small selection of their stock—backpacks, a nylon tent for about $40, and twelve bush hats and sports caps, each under $2. For most army-surplus items, they say, "It's common for people to write and ask for what they require."

FISHING

Cambrian Fly Fishers, The Old Vicarage, Trevor, Llangollen, Wales
Color catalogue, 75 cents; $1.25 air mail.

Fishing-tackle makers who, according to the owner of the firm, Mr. Diggory, use only traditional methods. Each rod is hand-built by a craftsman to meticulous specifications prepared by Mr. Diggory, who personally designs the tapers, selects the cane, works out the number and type of rings, how and where to position them, and matches each section of the cane to provide exactly the kind of action required. Instead of using prefabricated handles, each one is shaped by hand and follow-through ferules with strengthening bands are used. Cambrian Fly Fishers makes only one fiberglass rod because although Mr. Diggory thinks that the light weight of fiberglass is useful in reservoir fishing where you have to cast long distances all day, he feels that for close-quarter work and general all-round fly fishing, "The precise and delicate presentation of a first-class cane rod is unequalled." Mr. Diggory also says in a letter to me: "We have recently extended our business into the manufacture of specialist clothing for the Fishing and Shooting man. We make trousers and breeches in Moleskin and Corduroy. We make shooting jackets in pure Welsh tweed. We have a large range of hats and woolen sweaters. We are at present doing a very considerable business in the United States of America with our Moleskin trousers. These seem to have found considerable favour among the Field sportsmen." Moleskin (twilled cotton fabric) is apparently a material which hasn't been easily available for many years, although it is very tough, yet soft and flexible. Before the war it was used for making road mender's trousers, and after much searching Cambrian Fly Fishers found an English firm that was making moleskin pants for export to Australia and New Zealand for the sheep farmers.

Hardy Bros. (Alnwick) Ltd., 61 Pall Mall, London S.W.1, England
22-page color catalogue, $1 surface; $2 air mail. January.

The most famous rod makers in the world, Hardy Bros. is even more—an international status symbol according to the English *Harper's Bazaar*. They make tackle and are fanatically interested in improvement and innovation, and say that all their management people are "ardent anglers." An excellent catalogue gives full explanations of all their products, most of which are cheaper when bought directly from England. The exceptions are single rods that are too long to be mailed; shipping these costs so much that it is better to buy them from Hardy agents in your own country.

Hardy also organizes Angling Courses in Scotland, Ireland, Wales and Norway (ladies and young anglers welcome). Ask for "Angling Course" brochure.

MOTOR-RACING EQUIPMENT

Les Leston Products, 141 George Street, London W.1, England
Catalogue, $3 (refundable).

Specialists in motor-racing equipment. They have gadgets for the car and clothes for the driver: helmets and flameproof gloves, suits and shoes; also ties, cuff links and lighters with car badges on them, and umbrellas decorated with international racing flag signals. The Les Leston people say that although their products are sold in America, you save about 50 percent by buying direct from them.

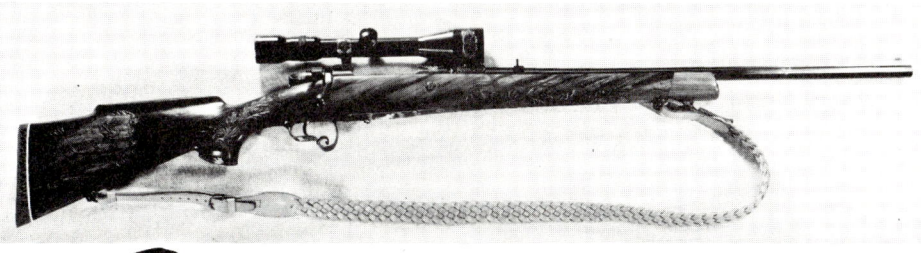

2
Sport & Waffen Dschulnigg Dschulnigg Super De Luxe rifle with mounted scope in cal. 7 mm. Rem. Mag.
photo Thuma Seekirchen

3
Functional Clothing Ltd. 33"-long waterproof jacket, five pockets, fitted for hood. One or two detachable foam linings can be added over the regular lining to provide three or five layers of air for warmth. Available in navy, olive, slate, black, blue or orange. Sizes small to extra large; price about $35.

MOTORBIKES

Paul Dunstall, Crabtree, Manorway, Belvedere, Kent, England
Brochure, free. Prices in $.

Top-quality touring motorbikes. There are three basic models, and each one has features that can be varied to suit individual customers. Prices start at about $1,500. Brochure quotes ecstatic press reviews and lists races Dunstall Norton motorbikes have won.

RIDING

W. and H. Gidden Ltd., 74 New Oxford Street, Bloomsbury, London W.C.1, England
Catalogue, $3.

The top name in saddles and riding equipment in England (as they, themselves, correctly say), W. and H. Gidden makes saddles by hand and sells only to private customers. Seventy percent of their production goes abroad, and is approximately 50 percent less expensive than American equivalents. A horse-loving acquaintance of mine adds that it is also 100 percent better.

Moss Bros. Ltd., Bedford Street, Covent Garden, London WC2E 8JB, England
Catalogue, 5 International Reply Coupons.

Although Moss Bros. is a household name and often a household joke in England because they rent out clothes for grand occasions, they are better known in other parts of the world for what they call their "superb riding and saddlery equipment and clothing." A large catalogue shows riding and polo clothes, saddles, reins, halters, snaffles, gags, weymouths, hunting and stable equipment and a few horse-related gifts, such as a stirrup barometer and shooting sticks.

George Parker and Sons (Saddlers) Ltd., 12 Upper St. Martin's Lane, London W.C.2, England
Catalogue planned, $1. Fall.

Another very reputable English saddler says that the reason English saddlery is so popular in America is not only the fine quality and competitive prices but also that some of the things sold in England are not available in America.

SHOOTING

Churchill, Atkin, Grant and Lang Ltd., 7 Bury Street, St. James, London SW1 6AF, England
Catalogue, $5.

This smart firm of gun ad rifle makers has sold guns to people as disparate as Annie Oakley and King Constantine of Greece, and they are so proud of themselves that they have almost more about their history than their guns in the catalogue. There is even a family tree that shows exactly who Churchill, Atkin, Grant and Lang were and how their descendants fit into the firm. Although their shop is very traditional, they claim to have the most up-to-date gun factories in the country. There is an elaborate questionnaire for people ordering guns, but Churchill, Atkin, Grant and Lang Ltd. encourages new gun owners to go to the West London Shooting Grounds as "the importance of visiting a shooting school for fitting a new gun cannot be underestimated." Practice may be had at Driven Partridges, Grouse Shooting, High Pheasants or through trees, walking up, etc., for both beginners and the experienced.

Firma Edward Kettner, Krebsgasse 5, Postfach 18 02 05, 5 Cologne 1, Germany
Color catalogue in German, $4.

A reader recommended this firm, praising it for very good service. A splendid 300-page catalogue shows an enormous selection of guns and hunting accessories, dog-grooming supplies, bags to carry catch home, plaques to mount antlers, bird whistles, hideouts for hunters and a great deal more than I've ever seen in any American catalogue. There is also an excellent clothes section showing all green loden coats, capes, jackets, sweaters, pants, hats, shoes, boots, socks, gloves, and even slippers for men. For women the same, with some additional dirndls and blouses, and there are even a few corduroy pants and loden coats for children. And finally, this is obviously a good place to find presents for hunters, as hunting motifs decorate just about anything for the house: beer mugs, ashtrays, glasses, cigarette boxes, coasters, dinner services, clocks, wall plaques, lampshades and even wallpaper.

Sport & Waffen Dschulnigg, P.O. Box 89, 5021 Salzburg, Austria
Rifle catalogue, free.
Hunting and sportswear color catalogue in German, free.

Guns made to order, but these must be imported through an American dealer. This firm says they send quite a few rifles to the U.S.A. and seems to make their own as well as selling those made by Steyr.

The sportswear catalogue shows boots, sleeping bags, stoves, knives, but also clothes and "gifts" of interest to hunters—bottle corks with gilt animals on them, plates with animals on them and, appropriately enough, carving knives with animals on them.

GENERAL

J. Barbour and Son, Simonside, South Shields, County Durham, NE34 9PD, England
Catalogue of waterproof and protective clothing for fishing, shooting and country wear, free. September.
Catalogue of waterproof and protective motorcycle clothing, free. September.

Barbour thornproof, waterproof clothing is well known and highly thought of. If you don't know it, you'll find out about it from reading the press quotes in the catalogue. Meanwhile, this is what the American magazine *Fly Fisherman* writes about one of the Barbour jackets: "The Durham Thornproof four-weather British fishing jacket is a classic. This is for Spring, Fall, Winter, and north country wear, although it is only 27 ounces in weight . . . the workmanship and design is superb, that thorough, well-thought-out British craftmanship we just can't seem to duplicate here . . . the tailoring is excellent, and you can spend hours finding little design features which place this rain jacket on a pedestal all its own." (It costs about $40.) The catalogue illustrates a large selection of jackets, pants, coats, hats, boots, mitts and socks. Prices for jackets and coats are between $40 and $50. There is a separate catalogue for waterproof motorcycle clothing.

Beaver of Bolton Ltd., Middlebrook Works, Gilnow Lane, Bolton BL3 5EW, Lancashire, England
Brochure, free.

Beaver of Bolton says they have quite a few American customers who have either seen their polyester insulated clothing when on vacation in England or else have been told about them by satisfied customers. Their flame-colored waterproof shooting jacket (price about $41 to $45, including surface postage) is especially popular in the United States. But there are also riding and shooting vests, jackets and coats, riding capes and an underwear suit useful for trailer dwellers and people with rheumatism or arthritis. Prices are mostly $16 to $25. By far the most expensive thing in the catalogue is a two-piece yachting suit for $61.

Functional Clothing Ltd., 20 Chepstow Street, Manchester M1 5JF, England
Catalogue 75 cents; $1 air mail.

The foam-lined clothing for sports and people doing outdoor work is on display at the London Design Centre and has also been warmly (so to speak) praised by organizations using it and by the press. The clothes in this small collection are less expensive than Barbour's and are available only by mail from Manchester. They are made in children's sizes as well adults'. Prices are the same for individual and bulk buyers—a light jacket costs about $25 and a heavier one up to about $35 according to size.

Greaves Sports Ltd., 23 Gordon Street, Glasgow G1 3PW, Scotland
Manufacturers' brochures for clothes and equipment for bowls, camping, climbing, cricket, ice skating, squash, soccer, table tennis and tennis, $1.

Greaves describes itself as "a retail sports outfitting shop with a very broad coverage of the trade in general. There is virtually no sporting requisite which we cannot obtain, and we pride ourselves in the fact that we provide a good back-up service." If you tell Greaves which sports you are interested in and send them $1, they will send you (surface mail) brochures from the best English manufacturers of clothes and equipment in that field, many of which have international reputations and sell their products for much higher prices abroad.

Husky of Tostock Ltd., 115 Bury Street, Stowmarket, Suffolk, England
26-page color brochure, 30 cents. Prices in $.

A United States colonel moved to England for a peaceful retirement, but soon found himself making the insulated clothing he had learned about in the Air Force, for his sporty friends battling with the windy and damp English climate. In 1961, as more and more people asked for the clothes, Colonel Gulyas decided to turn the hobby into a business, and now, after more than ten years' work, he has a factory with a staff of fifty, showrooms for personal customers, a color brochure for mail order, and a classy clientele that includes peers, baronets and royalty.

A good and informative brochure describes the waterproof, insulated clothes made of polyester fiberfill and nylon in standard sizes *or sizes to order*. There are specially designed golf coats, $30; fishing jackets, $56; shooting and riding vests, as well as car coats, trousers, underwear and hats for men and women. Also thermoinsulated tweeds which, the brochure says, will make a woman look like a French countess stepping out of a Paris couturier house—well, they won't quite, none of the clothes are highly fashionable but the tweeds do look perfectly serviceable and the insulation is cleverly disguised.

Lillywhite Ltd., Piccadilly Circus, London S.W.1, England
Golf catalogue, free.
Subaqua catalogue, free.
Ski catalogue, free.
Christmas gifts, free.
Cruisewear catalogue, free.
Riding catalogue, free.
Each catalogue only available during the appropriate season.

Lillywhite is London's largest sports shop, and stocks equipment and clothes for *all* sports. Their catalogues are excellent—the ski catalogue has some swish outfits, a few from Switzerland and Scandinavia—after-ski wear, hats, goggles, bags, boots and skis—the lot. Prices start at $51 for a one-piece nylon ski suit from Switzerland; a Finnish nylon jacket costs $18. Even though the ski catalogue is only available during the winter, you can buy the contents all year round.

The golf catalogue shows clubs, clothes, shoes and golf gifts—putting improvers, portable golf nets, ball washers, pocket warmers, etc. (No prices at the moment.)

Lillywhite says their subaqua department is the largest in Europe. The catalogue has what looks like everything to me— all the essential equipment and underwater communications sets, cameras, gauges, torches, watches and compasses. Also equipment for water-skiing.

Sports-Schuster, Rosenstrasse 5–6, 8 Munich 2, Germany
100-page color catalogues in German, surface, free; $1 air mail. April, October.

This large sports shop puts out two luscious catalogues a year crammed with famous brands of gear and clothes. An excellent place for anyone who wants to buy ski clothes by mail, because although prices are higher than in Austria, there is a terrific selection: smart sweaters, $23–$34; over fifty glossy jackets, around $45 each; goggles at up to $6; pages of shaggy-fur boots that cost between $25 and $57; and every sort of ski boot; and ski outfits for children.

The summer catalogue shows tennis clothes and parkas, and for camping and the great German pastime—hiking— pages and pages of boots, ropes, rucksacks, picks, sleeping bags, tents and other necessary things. Also skin-diving gear and sailboats with motors.

Alas, the catalogue is in German. However, prices are right next to pictures and Sports-Schuster will answer letters in English *when asked* (otherwise they assume you know German).

22 Stereo Equipment

Stereo Equipment

Most stereo belongs to that awkward group of things, just too large or heavy to go by mail and not worth paying sea-freight costs on. However, buying from abroad *is* worthwhile for hi-fi fanatics who are trying to assemble a complete stereo system from the best components made by different specialized firms. You can either send for parts that are small enough to be sent by mail or buy several things at once, so that freight charges are small compared to savings. Hong Kong shops stock an enormous variety of equipment, and are very experienced in mail order. As I write, minimum sea-freight charges from Hong Kong to an American port are $68 to the West Coast and $78 to the East Coast. For that price one amplifier, one turntable and two loudspeakers can be shipped. As Hong Kong prices are only one third or one half of American list prices, quite a bit of money can be saved. But, as always, take into consideration at what prices the same things are actually available to you locally, and whether you can go down and collect the stuff from the port yourself or whether you have to pay someone else a lot extra to see your equipment through customs and deliver it.

ENGLAND

Audio T, 190 West End Lane, West Hampstead, London NW6 1SQ, England

Japanese units are obviously not worth buying from England as they are no cheaper than in America. The following European brands are likely to be less expensive in England than in the United States (but do check the Hong Kong prices): Revox, Cambridge, Lecson, Spendor, Linn-Sondek, IMF, Celestion, Monitor, Audio, Era, J. E. Sugden, Sonab, Lustraphone, Naim, Leak, Scan Dyna, Thorens, Transcriptors and KEF.

I have recently heard about some new components from English friends which they say might be of interest. One is the pickup arm produced by Keith Monks Audio, it is damped, has magnetic bias compensation, tracks even freer than the SME pickup arm, and is less expensive. Another component is a new amplifier by Lecson which performs superbly, but its main appeal is that it looks like something from outer space—it is a thin upright cylinder with a control box that has colored sliders. There are also Spendor speakers, which are considered by some people in England to be far better than anything in their price range. But speakers are too big and heavy to go by mail, so aren't worth sending for, though the drivers (called "chassis" in England) are. My own speakers are made with a KEF midrange and KEF woofers imported from England (KEF are the tops—they are used in some of the best and most expensive American speakers; however, the KEF tweeters are not as good, so I bought a Phillips tweeter at a discount place in New York, where it was cheaper than in England).

***Hi-fi Answers*, Haymarket Publishing Co. Ltd., Gillow House, 5 Winsley Street, London W1A 2HG, England**

"The Transition Line Monitor Speaker," by C. J. Rogers. Reprint, 50 cents.

Hi-fi Answers published an article in its August 1973 issue on how to make speakers for about $250 the pair. The components are KEF B139 base unit, KEF midrange, KEF T27 tweeters and ITT-STC 101 super tweeter. The speakers have been highly praised, and are considered, by disinterested parties, to be better than most speakers and as good as the best—which, of course, cost almost three times the price. Reprints of the article are available (mark the back of your envelope "Reprint" to hurry things up); the article gives full instructions on how to make the speakers as well as

1
Klinger hi-fi stereo, beautiful teak cabinet, outlet for the connection of a radio tuner or tape recorder. Available from Fortnum and Mason (see Food section).

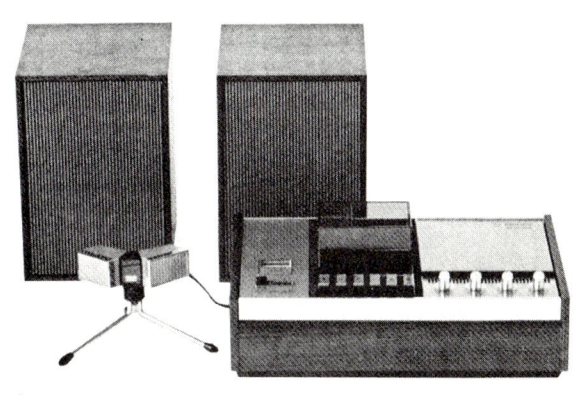

2
Stereo cassette recorder in rosewood-veneered cabinet. Maximum playing time twelve hours; with automatic changer and automatic stop at the end of the last tape. Available from Fortnum and Mason (see Food section).

generally useful information on where to get the parts.

A friend of mine who lives in New York subscribed to English hi-fi magazines because they give more objective reviews of equipment than American magazines. He thinks that American magazines don't mention faults because they are afraid of the advertisers. He recommends *Hi-fi Answers* (U.S. subscription $15 per year) and *Hi-fi News*, Link House, Dingwell Avenue, Croydon CR9 2TA, England (U.S. subscription $18 per year).

Laskys, Audiotronic House, The Hyde, London NW9 6JJ, England
Monthly price lists, free.

The largest hi-fi retail group in Europe exports goods all over the world and produces monthly up-to-date price lists. According to a reader of the first edition of *The Catalogue of Catalogues*, English hi-fi firms have identical export prices, even the places that claim to have cut-rate prices. So although it is worth getting English-made equipment that is small enough to come by parcel post from abroad, check with Hong Kong to see which has the lower prices.

Incidentally, a friend of mine had dreadful trouble with Laskys. They shipped some things that were small enough to go parcel post air freight C.O.D. to America, so they had to be returned because you can't send things C.O.D. internationally. The air freight is a minimum charge from England of $29, so if after hearing this you still feel like buying from Laskys, remember to insist on parcel post.

Michael O'Brien, 95 High Street, Wimbledon Village, London S.W.19, England
Manufacturers' brochures, $2.

Michael O'Brien specializes in top-class hi-fi equipment, and also has a personal export service. He says that these components seem to be of special interest to American customers, prices are very roughly:

Quad amplifiers $301
SME pickup arms $85
Tannoy speakers $180
Ferrograph tape recorders $278

HONG KONG

The Radio People Ltd., 25 Chatham Road, Kowloon, Hong Kong
Audio-equipment price list, free.

The Radio People's price list is in Hong Kong dollars, so if you already know what you want you can avoid the list and write direct asking for the price, including shipping, of what you want. Otherwise write for shipping costs, etc., after studying the list. The Radio People sells all parts and all accessories to do with stereo equipment, and tape recorders, public-address amplifiers, etc., of most leading makes. They also make cabinets to customers' own designs.

Universal Suppliers, P.O. Box 14803, Hong Kong
Hi-fi price list, free; $1.80 air mail. Prices in $.

Universal Suppliers has an excellent price list for stereo, but it is essential to specify that this is what you want, as they sell glass, china, linen, watches, and goodness knows what else. In electronics, Universal Suppliers lists amplifiers, tuners, receivers, changers and turntables, hi-fi systems, tape recorders, speakers, headphones, color TV (though I checked Sony and their sets cost the same as in America), radios, video equipment, electronic calculators. Manufacturers stocked: Akai, Dual, Garrad, Kenwood, Miracord, Pioneer, Sharp, Sensui, Sony, Tandberg, Teac, Thorens.

23 Toys

Toys

I have bought more toys from abroad than anything else—often in large batches, ahead of time, for birthdays and Christmas, and often chosen by my daughters to give to their friends. Toys are an ideal mail-order buy, easy to choose from a catalogue, easy to ship, and the best toys are less expensive abroad. Many of the most attractive and unusual toys sold in New York stores have been imported, and by going direct to the source, you get a wider choice at lower prices. Take the German Steiff furry animals, for instance—five hundred of them are shown in the German catalogue, far more than you can see in any American shop. On even the smallest you save about $1 each, after shipping, and much more on the larger toys.

Note: Any electric toy that runs on 220 volts instead of American 110 will need a transformer. An American electrical supplies store can order this for you when they know the voltage of the toy.

DENMARK

Priors Dukke Teatre, Købmagergade 52, 1150 Copenhagen K, Denmark
Leaflet, free.

Toy theaters became popular in England in about 1800 and then spread to the rest of Europe. Priors says that this wonderful hobby for grownups and imaginative toy for children has been praised by great writers like Robert Louis Stevenson, Goethe and Hans Christian Andersen—all keen toy-theater owners. If you'd like to follow in their illustrious footsteps or if you have a child who might benefit from "opening the mind for the world of fantasy" (to quote the Priors leaflet), Priors has two replicas of old Copenhagen theaters, which can be bought assembled in wood and cardboard with footlights and accessories, or in inexpensive (about $5 each), build-it-yourself sheets (much easier to mail). Besides many plays in Danish there are several in English—Andersen fairy tales, several Harlequin and Columbine plays, and a detective play.

ENGLAND

Beaver Toys, Marlborough, Wiltshire, England
Brochure, 25 cents; 50 cents air mail.

Beaver Toys makes mainly strong wooden components for children to make toys or buildings of their own. These have been praised in the English press for being, like all Beaver toys, "enormously carefully thought out to give maximum amount of pleasure for the minimum cost." But mailing costs will, unfortunately, put up the prices of these larger, heavier toys, so perhaps mail-order customers should concentrate on the lighter toys, which are equally carefully thought out. There is a complete "Paint and Make" set with brilliant foils and tissues, adhesive tape, safe scissors, card and cellophane, washable but intensely colored paints, crayons, brush, etc., with a book of suggestions for things to make. "Splendid, keeps them happy and absorbed," says the *Daily Telegraph*. Another interesting-looking toy is a roundabout (merry-go-round) in nine brilliant colors which can be taken apart, and then there is a painted wooden transport set in thirty-eight pieces which Beaver liberatedly says is popular with boys *and* girls who use it to make trucks, fire engines and buses. Prices: $5 to $15.

Birdmobile Card Sculptures, The White Gate, Ballards Crowhurst, Battle, Sussex TN33 9DA, England
Leaflet, free.

Malcom Topp has designed a series of birds on cards to be cut out and glued into sort of small paper sculptures and hung up. The colors of the birds are realistic, and the kits come with a bit of information about the bird to be made (I saw a kingfisher and an owl). Several birds together would make a beautiful mobile. But they do require skill, so any child under twelve would probably need the help of an adult.

Mrs. E. M. Brickdale, Mousehole, Widford, Ware, Hertfordshire SG12 8SE, England
Price list, free; air mail, 2 International Reply Coupons.

Mary Brickdale makes dressed mice for children and adults. Unfortunately, there are no illustrations on the price list, but I have seen the mice in person. They are tiny, delicate and beautifully dressed, especially the ladies. Possibly the best for children are the family mice dressed as grandmothers or a mother with baby; souvenir mice are dressed as Irish, Scottish or Welsh men; and mice for special occasions are dressed as Santa Claus, or brides (in a presentation box) or fairies (fairy godmothers?). There are also mice couples for wedding anniversaries. "Special orders receive special attention." You can have a bride dressed in silver or gold, or in a costume of your own choosing if the quantity you order is large enough. The mice are about 1¾" high and cost from about 75 cents to $3. Mary Brickdale says the mice are so light that postage doesn't cost much, but she says firmly that she will only accept payment in pound sterling, as banks charge for converting foreign checks—disastrous on small orders.

Margaret J. Brown, Old Bell Cottage, Bisley, Stroud, Gloucestershire, England
Leaflet 50 cents.

Margaret Brown makes somewhat larger dressed animals (about 4" high) and I find them irresistible. My daughters had some of Miss Brown's mice when they were younger, and I think I liked them more than they did, which makes me think perhaps the animals are more suited to older children of, say, eight and up, who appreciate little toys that are not played with so much as looked at. Creatures include a goose in bonnet and cloak; a squirrel; a rabbit; a gardener mole with an apron and a piece of straw in one hand and a flower in the other; a husband-and-wife mouse pair (he wears a print vest that matches her dress); a bride and bridegroom, he in morning coat with top hat and pink vest, she in pink with lots of lace; and a rabbit-egg cozy. There are magnetic mice (I'm not quite sure what you'd do with them) and finger puppets with a hanging cloth bag designed as a house to keep them in. Most things cost about $1.50 each.

Channel Island and Guernsey Toys, 48 and 50 the Bordage, St. Peter Port, Guernsey, Channel Islands, England
Color leaflet, 25 cents; 50 cents air mail.

A collection of soft and fluffy toys, some of which are quite ordinary, while others have outstandingly charming personalities. Badgers, pandas, penguins, koala bears and woolen-haired rag dolls look as though they could become well-loved and long-lasting possessions. (Some of them have received Design Centre awards.) There is a lilliput range of little cats, birds and mice dressed in aprons which will be appreciated by older children. Prices are low. Everything except a furry camel, which is also a stool, costs around $5 or under.

Toys

1
Cuckoobird Productions Little 6" Alice lavender-sachet doll, $1.90.

2
Cuckoobird Productions U. S. Mail laundry bag. About $6.
photo Council of Industrial Design

3
Cuckoobird Productions Washpacks designed by Dick Bruna containing one mitt and one hand towel. Each pack $2.60, postage 50 cents. "Teddy" is in yellow, red and white; "Miffy" (rabbit) is in red, white and blue.

4
Cuckoobird Productions Pocket tidy in red, white and blue. Holds eight pairs of children's shoes. $5.43.
photo Council of Industrial Design

Cuckoobird Productions, St. Michael's House, Peckham Bush, Tonbridge, England
Color leaflet, $1 (refundable). Prices in $.

A small family firm that manufactures handsome "useful presents" in cotton, at very low prices: some beautiful, big bags for laundry or toys: the bags unzip at the bottom and the one I like shows Punch and Judy in orange, yellow, turquoise and green; also pillowcases with grinning lions or tigers, $3.80; wash packs (washing mitten and hand towel) showing an English guardsman or Dick Bruna animals, $3.85. And a wonderful London-bus shoe bag. I gave one to my six-year-old for Christmas, and somewhat to my surprise, she was delighted with the possibly overpractical gift—and has used it ever since.

Dobbin Designs, Gwithian, Hayle, Cornwall, England
Brochure, 36 cents. Prices in $.

One of the few places left making rocking horses. Dobbin Design's carved hardwood model has been blessed by London's independent and fussy Design Centre, which exhibits in its showrooms the best of British design. The horse comes in two sizes, in dapple gray or palomino with shiny white mane and tail, red rockers, and real leather saddle and bridle. The smaller horse's back is 26" high, the larger 30". They cost $172 and $218, respectively. Dobbin Designs has found that freight to America comes to about $200.

The Dolls House, 4 Broadley Street, London NW8 8AE, England
Leaflet, 1 International Reply Coupon; air mail, 2 International Reply Coupons.

This is a good source of dollhouse furniture for both children and adults. My daughter who is a dollhouse owner and miniature collector comments: "The Dolls House seems to have combined the 20-cent accessory with the $500 Georgian dollhouse with everything in between. They were opened in October 1971 and have accumulated a lot of variety since then. They have for 8 cents a plastic baby or for $1.50 twin beds, or three radiators for 50 cents. For the more collector type of miniature-lover they have a $5 hand-carved dining-room chair, or how about a pine dresser for $25?" There are dollhouses for children and dollhouses for collectors. Most of them, however, are too expensive to ship, as they are too big to go by mail, but there is one small house (by the firm John Adams) which has no roof and is knockdown-able, so it can easily be mailed packed flat. It has a nice red-and-blue front and costs only about $22. Antique dollhouses at prices between $75 to over $250 are usually in stock, and so is antique miniature furniture.

Fabra, 1 New North Place, London EC2 4JA, England
Brochure, 5 International Reply Coupons; air mail, 7 International Reply Coupons.

Most children love making things with a adult, and Fabra has produced some toy kits which can be made up in harmonious cooperation. In felt there is a giraffe, a buffalo, and a kangaroo with a baby in its pouch—all of them rather nicely designed for about $2 each (not including stuffing). There is a rag doll with a long dress, a petticoat and pantaloons, and a bathtub boat for a beginning woodworker aged between six and eleven for about $5. There are also made-up dolls and felt animals, and new toys are added as they are designed.

Toys

5
Dobbin Designs Carved wooden rocking horse in dapple gray or palomino, red rockers and leather bridle and saddle (back 26″ high).
photo Green Lane Studio

6
Fabra Toys Complete kit to make a rag doll, about $7.

7
James Galt and Co. Ltd Brightly colored "See Inside" jigsaw puzzles for children one and a half to three years old. Around $6 each.

8
Tridias Felt-jack-in-the-box in a wooden box painted red, blue, green, orange or yellow. About $5.50.

9
Tridias Wooden farm building with a gray removable roof, blue doors and green base, about $15. One of a set of three farm buildings, made in scale with Britain's farm animals, about $27 the set.
photos Photography West

Toys

7

8

9

Toys

Ron Fuller Toys, Laxfield, Woodbridge, Suffolk 1P13 8DX, England
Leaflet, 25 cents; 60 cents air mail.

Several years ago I was given a magnificent toy—an acrobat in a brightly colored shiny cardboard box turns somersaults. It is more of a decorative piece to be looked at by adults and children than a toy to be played with. Now I find that it is one of the few exceptional toys handmade by Ron Fuller. The other toys, which are painted in beautiful glossy color combinations, might offend anti-violence parents, but are unusually ingenious. One is a submarine with a torpedo which you shoot at a ship; if the torpedo hits the right place, the ship flies apart. Another is a biplane based on a World War I model which can be bought alone or with a factory that collapses when bombed. Prices under $10.

Halfpenny Houses, Orleigh Court, Buckland Brewer, Bideford, Devon EX39 5EH, England
Brochure, 2 International Reply Coupons; air mail, 3 International Reply Coupons.

Mark Heal, woodworker, and Gillian Heal, painter, call their firm "a small but successful business run from an efficient workshop in the outbuildings of a dreaming manor house in a quiet corner of North Devon." For years they have made dollhouses (there is still one small doll cottage), and now they have added some lovely little painted shops (butcher, baker and post office), and some money, sewing and odds-and-ends boxes to their collection. Also a few other toys, wooden dollhouse furniture and people, magnetic fish, etc. The designs are the Heals's own, and are charming. I've seen the toys and I know that the black-and-white brochure doesn't do them justice.

James Galt and Co. Ltd., Brookfield Road, Cheadle, Cheshire, England ♥
38-page catalogue with some color, free.

England's leading "educational" toy manufacturer, with a store at the end of Carnaby Street, makes handsome, strong toys, in wood rather than plastic, which are moderately experimental and are generally pleasing to design-conscious parents as well as to many English schools. Prices here are considerably lower than the U.S. equivalents, and the catalogue is excellent. It gives the ages that each toy is suitable for.

Hamleys, 200–202 Regent Street, London W.1, England ♥♥
Hamleys is the F. A. O. Schwarz of England—a huge toy store selling every kind of traditional toy and most leading brands. It also has many catalogues:

General catalogue, 27 pages, free.

Selections from each floor including art, books, games, puzzles, kits, planes, dolls, crafts, music, science, mechanical toys, sports, and very helpful for parents, a back page full of aids to party giving: novelties, favors, magic tricks, disguise outfits, surprise ball and snappers.

Britain's Toy Models, 31 pages illustrated with colored drawings, 10 cents.

A huge range of these tiny plastic animals and people at war and peace. Confederate and federal gun teams, which I have seen in New York for $7.50 each, costs $4.35 at Hamley's, and a farm set imported and sold by a New York department store for $10 costs $3.75 at Hamley s.

Triang, Hornby and Minic Motor Racing and Model Railways, 44 pages in color, 25 cents.

British trains: electric, clockwork and battery. Bridges, stations, scenic materials and people. Also electric car-racing sets and scale-model plastic construction kits. Transformers for electric toys should be bought locally.

Scalestric Home Motor Racing, 32 pages in color, 15 cents.

Cars, tracks, track accessories, buildings, figures to be painted, and kits to build stands, etc. Also some electric steeplechasing sets.

Philips Young Engineer Kits, 8-page leaflet, free.

Seven kits. Electronic engineer, mechanical engineer, interphone engineer, and radio construction kits, ranging in price from $11 to $18.

Homebound Craftsmen, 25A Holland Street, Kensington, London W.8, England
Leaflet, 30 cents.

A good cause that one can support very agreeably. This small shop in Kensington sells fetching soft toys made by disabled workers—rosy-cheeked rag dolls cost about $5.15; mohair teddy bears start at $5; soulful panda families; cheery Humpty Dumptys; and some adorable little mice in long skirts or aprons and jackets which cost only $1.25 each—these seem to appeal to older children as well as to little ones. Puppets are very inexpensive: a penguin, a donkey and a bear, $2.50 each, and unusually sweet-faced Punch and Judy, $2.30 each. But do be sure to add enough postage. Homebound Craftsmen only gives local internal English costs, and they say that their American customers often forget to allow $1 for small parcels and $2 for larger ones.

Noah's Ark Toys Ltd., 325 Birmingham Road, Wylde Green, Sutton Coldfield, Warwickshire, England
Brochure, 1 International Reply Coupon.

Noah's Ark Toys says that they are best known for their children's vinyl aprons with London bus and London guardsmen designs that have been used by the British Tourist Authority and other official agencies. However, the firm also makes soft toys and nursery accessories, and this is a good place to get small children practical presents such as coat hangers in the shapes of animals, or pajama bags in the shape of a floppy clown or a mobcapped doll. Other toys include a growing chart, jumping jacks, dominoes, lotto, and jigsaw puzzles of animals with their babies curled up inside them. Prices mostly under $5.

John Paige, The Manor House, Kings Cliffe, Peterborough PE8 6XB, England
Brochure, $1. Prices in $.

John Paige, a free-lance graphic designer, publishes and sells his own animal and train friezes. The paper friezes are sophisticated, in restrained realistic colors, and can be joined together to stretch right across a wall. The British trains are just the thing for a train buff. Bought by the carriage, entire walls can be covered with them. John Paige suggests that until he publishes some (which he is planning to do), customers can add their own lineside features by making drawings or pasting up photographs of signal boxes, bridges, stations, smoke or anything else. The train friezes are 3" high, and engines cost 38 cents each, carriages 25 cents. Also two complete trains: the Silver Jubilee, which is 8'6"long, is hauled by a Silver Fox engine and costs $1.30, and the Coronation, 10' 9" long, is hauled by a Dominion of Canada engine and costs $2.30.

There are three animal friezes: mustard-and-dark-brown

Toys

10
Charlotte Weibull Handmade dolls 8″ high: bride from Skåne, about $9; bridegroom, about $7.50; fiddler, about $6.50.

11
Charlotte Weibull Handmade dolls, peasant children Åsa Gåsa Piga and Nils Holgerson on a bench. About $13.50.
photo Alice Strid

giraffes galloping across a toast-colored background; black-and-white zebras galloping across a blue background; brown-and-green lions standing and lying on a white background.

Pollock's Toy Museum, La Scala Street, London W.1, England
Leaflet, free.
An old toy-theater maker, now well known for reproductions of its original wares. Six different theaters are now produced in book form for about $2.50, including postage: each book includes a theater printed on card with scenery, characters and text for one play. It measures about 11″ by 11″ by 9″ when set up. Additional plays adapted from fairy tales to fit the theaters cost about $1.50. A larger and very handsome theater, the Redington, comes ready cut out and complete with two plays, characters and scenery. It measures approximately 21″ by 18″ by 15″ and costs about $7.50. If you want to ensure a longer life for your theater, Pollock's will sell you materials to build a wooden stage.

The Stratford Games Ltd., Merelles House, Henley Street, Stratford-upon-Avon, Warwickshire, England
Leaflet, $1 (60 cents refundable).
For adults and children this firm makes "high class period games" including a few mentioned in Shakespeare's plays. There is Nine Men's Morris, which, like many old games, was originally played outside, cut into the ground. The design has been found carved in Egyptian roofing slabs, on benches in cathedral cloisters, on church walls. Stratford Games has followed a later version, a popular indoor board game, where the object is to form a straight line of three men and prevent your opponent from doing the same thing. Another game is Shove-groat, mentioned in *The Merry Wives of Windsor*, in which you roll a coin on a wooden board. It has survived almost unchanged; in England it is called Shove-Half-penny. There are about ten games in all, made out of light wood, and although they are old in origin, they are modern versions which do not look ancient. Prices from $1 to $15.

Three Four Five, 33 West Hill, London SW18 1RD, England
Color leaflet, free.
Three Four Five produces a sort of educational course for three-year-olds that has been very well reviewed by the English press. Parents who want to help their children prepare for school can subscribe to this series of twelve packets of activities for preschool children which will arrive by mail, one parcel every month, for a year. The packages look more like play than work, and taking this course certainly isn't going to produce a young Einstein, but as all the activities need the cooperation of a parent, they should be stimulating as well as very enjoyable for the child. Activities include things like cards to build stories around, action rhymes to learn, and number activities. As I write, the course costs $30, including surface postage to America.

Tridias, 8 Savile Row, Bath BA1 2QP, England
14-page catalogue, free.
Another good-taste toy shop, well worth looking at. Tridias sells mostly carefully chosen English and Continental toys by other manufacturers, but when driven to it, because they can't find something they like, they make their own. They have made a nice musical carrying box with a handle. It can be used for things like pencils and comes plain with a set of transfers so that the owner can decorate it himself, $6. They also have their own beautiful Georgian dollhouse for $45, good for anyone returning from England by boat, but otherwise disproportionately expensive to ship, as it is too

large to be sent by mail. Also their own wooden trucks, trains, forts, farms, etc.

Compared to Galt's (above), Tridias tends to go for more old-fashioned toys and are less "educational." I bought a big box of party favors from them—animal and bird transfers, furry mouse pins, magnetic ladybugs, whistling birds in cages, cutout farms—it was *much* easier to find novel things at Tridias than in my neighborhood.

GERMANY

Germany produces vast quantities of superb toys, and the leading toy shops below are all quite used to sending them abroad (Spielzeug-Rasch says they have over a thousand foreign customers, and answer letters in French and Spanish as well as in English). Many of the toys are 50 percent less expensive in Germany than in foreign stores—electric trains in O, HO or N gauge, Schuco mechanical toys and Steiff plush animals, for instance, all of which are very popular German mail-order buys. The shops below, in addition to a general catalogue, will send, if you ask, brochures produced by the famous German manufacturers. The full lists of manufacturers' brochures available are in the general catalogues and include model trains by Trix, Fleischmann, Marklin and Arnold Rapido; lineside buildings by Faller and Kibri; mechanical toys by Schuco, soft toys by Steiff (about five hundred in the catalogue), card toys by Ravensburger (see below), figurines by Hummel.

All the catalogues are in German, but they are illustrated by full-color photographs with the prices in Deutche Mark (often written DM) right next to the toys.

Spielwaren Behle, Kaiserstrasse 28, Frankfurt/M, Germany

Spielzeug-Rasch, Gerhart-Hauptmann-Platz 1, Hamburg 1, Germany
Special models catalogue, $4.
Color catalogue in German, $1. October.

Spielwarenhaus Virnich, Luitpoldstrasse 6, 85 Nuremberg, Germany
Color catalogue in German, $2. October.

These three shops all send out the same very good general catalogue, showing colorful German versions of most toys. (Spielzeug-Rasch also puts out a very serious and professional catalogue of specialized models.) Germany is particularly strong on all sorts of models: little wooden villages and the model buildings that are so expensive in America—castles cost about $13, old-fashioned gabled farmyards about $15, a ranch about $10, and "Fort Texas," $12. German construction sets are shown: Baufix, Fischertechnik, and Plasticant; cars and garages; Schuco; Gama; Faller; and a few of the model trains. Plenty of cozy doll cradles, pretty tea sets and some very distinguished dolls (though no cheaper than American dolls)—a delectable ash-blond one costs $16, and the famous Käthe Kruse dolls are stocked.

Kinderparadies, Neuer Wall 7, Hamburg, Germany
Summer brochure in German, 50 cents. April.
Main catalogue in German, 50 cents. September.
Electric Trains and Building Hobbies Catalogue, 50 cents. September.

The summer catalogue that I have looked at has a bit of what the main catalogue has—Leggo (with a hand pointing at a Leggo plane, Leggo dollhouse furniture, and a Leggo family with the words "DAS IST NEU"), Fischertechnik construction sets, box games, and also some summery things like kites, sailboats, roller skates, ball games and a whole lot of jolly plastic dump trucks and cement mixers for the sandbox. The main catalogue shows a little from several of each of the best-known German toy manufacturers: Steiff stuffed animals, Schuco cars, Marklin and Kibri railroads, Ravensburger box games, dolls, model buildings and dollhouse furniture. Kinderparadies also sent me manufacturers' brochures for Steiff animals, Käthe Kruse dolls, Bodo Henning dollhouse furniture, and Fischertechnik wooden construction sets but— warning!—this was the only German toy shop to actually write to me in German, so you'll probably need a translator to deal with them.

Ask any of the above shops for the Ravensburger catalogue.
24-page color catalogue in German, free.

This catalogue is in German and unnumbered, but the boxes are partially printed in English and it is well worth the trouble, as Ravensburger makes widely exported and beautifully printed board games and hobby kits. The designs and colors are excellent and most of the games have instructions in English (you can tell by the pictures in the catalogue whether they do or not).

HOLLAND

Dovina, Hollandsestraat 18–22, Rotterdam 25, Holland
Color postcard, free.

Beautifully made plastic dolls 11" high, dressed in eighteen different regional Dutch costumes; doll and surface postage, about $12 each.

SWEDEN

Charlotte Weibull, Box 4042, 203 11 Malmö 4, Sweden
List of costume dolls, free.
7-page brochure in Swedish, $1.

Charlotte Weibull has a seventeenth-century house at Lilla Torg, Sweden, which is a doll shop and puppet theater, and she hopes to add a doll museum. Tourists already make special trips to see her well-known collection of lovely souvenir dolls in good Swedish taste—handwoven fabrics and hand-painted faces. There are dolls in the costumes of every Swedish province, dolls from Swedish fairy tales, doll bookmarks, and dolls to hang up. Some are about $3.50 and others are about $6.50, and now there is a little folding theater for about $8 with hand puppets at $3.75.

WALES

J. & F. Butler Toymakers, Groes Afon, Cefn Coch, Welshpool, Powys, Wales
Leaflet, 50 cents.

A husband and wife make a nice collection of old fashioned toys: rag dolls, peg dolls, wooden dolls and puppets—all wide-eyed and tousle-haired. Also very simple painted wooden planes and boats, and a magnetic fish game. Prices exceptionally low.

24 Watches

Watches

Watches are easy to buy from abroad, being light and small to air-mail, but you have to be careful with duty, which depends on various things such as thickness of watch and number of jewels—watches with over seventeen jewels are charged $4 extra.

HONG KONG

T. M. Chan and Co., P.O. Box 3881, Hong Kong
116-page catalogue, free. Prices in $.

Seiko watches and Omega and Rolex for roughly what they sell for in Switzerland, about a third less than in America.

Universal Suppliers, GPO Box 14803, Hong Kong
Rolex and Seiko watch leaflets, free; air mail $1.80 for both. Prices in $.

Seiko Japanese watches are being heavily advertised in America, where they sell for $55–$100. Universal Suppliers has them for $20–$70, mostly $30–50; prices include air-mail postage and insurance.

SWITZERLAND

Itraco Watch Co. Ltd., P.O. Box 289, 8027 Zurich, Switzerland
Catalogue 43, $1.

Itraco was, naturally enough, pretty peeved about my description of their watches in the first edition (they said it was "catastrophical, besides of it being untrue") because I said: "These watches are Roskopf escapement and pin-lever watches, 'drugstore' quality, and the kind of thing my watch mender refuses to fix on the grounds that it will break again immediately . . ." Itraco says that they have watches of all kinds and except for a very few of the cheapest, they are guaranteed for the duration of one year "and we have instituted a REPAIR SERVICE WORLD-WIDE." I still think that anyone buying Itraco watches should do it for their glamorous exteriors rather than their inner worth. The new catalogue has picture watches for children, watches in zodiac pendants, knobbily rings and in glittery bracelets, cigarette lighters, key rings and on the cover the "latest world novelty" Hudson-instalite, the flashlight digital. "No reason to be angry anymore, HUDSON-INSTALIGHT gives you correct time even in the darkest corner . . . (Press a button for light at night) . . . finding the keyhole, the door bell, to open the doors of your car, in the theater or cinema, in the woods, in the plane or even at a date at night!" Price about $16. There are plenty of watches for under $10, and I think that they are all under $30.

A. Turler, Paradeplatz, 8001 Zurich, Switzerland
Vacheron and Constantin, Eterna-Matic, International Watch Co. Longines brochures, free.

Switzerland's largest retail watch stores say they have been sending watches to America since the first GIs came by. Eterna prices start at about $110, International Watch Co. at about $110—and Vacheron and Constantin, which are *very* de luxe, at about $600.

1
Heldwein (see Jewelry and Silver section) Jeweled pendant watch by Piaget.

2
Heldwein (see Jewelry and Silver section) Piaget wrist watch with turquoise dial and diamonds.

TRINIDAD

Stechers Ltd., 62 Independence Square, Port of Spain, Trinidad
No general catalogue.
Prices quoted for specific Delaneau, Audemars Piguet, Girrard Perregaux.
Patek Philippe and Seiko watches on request.

Stechers Jewelers is very well known, indeed, to American tourists in the Caribbean. They stock famous brand-name watches, glass, china, perfume, etc., at prices which they say are an average of 40 percent below American prices. If they do not have what you want in stock, they will order it.

Appendices

CLOTHING SIZE CHARTS

As clothing sizes vary according to the manufacturer, always add measurements.

LADIES

Dresses, Coats, Suits, Skirts

Junior

American	7	9	11	13	15	17
English	9	11	13	15	17	
Continental	34	36	38	40	42	44

Misses

American	10	12	14	16	18	20
English	32	34	36	38	40	42
Continental	38	40	42	44	46	48

Women

American	38	40	42	44	46	48
English	20	22	24	26	28	30
Continental	46	48	50	52		

Blouses and sweaters

American	34	36	38	40	42	44
English	36	38	40	42	44	46
	42	44	46	48	50	52

Stockings and gloves are standard.

MEN

Suits, Overcoats and Pajamas

American and English	34	36	38	40	42	44	46	48
Continental	44	46	48	50	52	54	56	58

Shirts

American and English	12½	13	13½	14	14½	15	15½	16	16½	17
Continental	32	33	34	35-36	37	38	39	40-41	42	43

Sweaters

American	Small	Medium	Large	Extra Large
English	34	36–38	40	42–44
Continental	44	46–48	50	52–54

Hats

American	6⅞	7	7⅛	7¼	7⅜	7½	7⅝	7¾
English	6¾	6⅞	7	7⅛	7¼	7⅜	7½	7⅝
Continental	55	56	57	58	59	60	61	62

Shoes

American	6½	7	7½	8	8½	9	9½	10	10½	11	11½
English	5	5½	6	6½	7	7½	8	8½	9	9½	10
Continental	38	38½	39	39½	40	41	41½	42	42½	43	43½

Appendices

ADDITIONAL IMPORT INFORMATION

Office of Information and Publications, Bureau of Customs, Treasury Department, Washington, DC 20226 give out several free leaflets:

"Know Before You Go" gives general information about what is and is not allowed into the country. It is intended for tourists but most of the information also applies to shopping by mail. It also lists current duty rates for about eighty items, and is revised whenever necessary. Telephone or write your nearest Customs Office or District Director of Customs for anything not covered.

"Trademark Information." This leaflet lists those foreign articles bearing "prohibited" trademarks recorded in the Treasury Department, such as certain perfumes, cameras, watches, stereo equipment, which must not be brought into the country with the trademark on. However, it is perfectly legal to bring in the articles with their trademarks removed, and if you want to bring something in that has a registered trademark, you can do one of two things: you can ask the shop you buy the article from to remove the trademark, or you can wait until it arrives and is inspected by American customs officers. If they feel it is necessary, a form will be sent for you to sign declaring that you agree to remove the trademark yourself. After signing the form, you mail it back and the goods will be forwarded to you in the normal way.

Appendices

CONVERSION TABLES

	.10	.15	.25	.50	.75	1.00	5.00	10.00	12.50	15.00	20.00	50.00	75.00	100.00
United States Dollars (U.S.$)														
Great Britain Pound Sterling = 100 New Pence	.04	.06	.10	.21	.31	.42	2.08	4.17	5.21	6.25	8.33	20.83	31.25	41.67
France Franc = 100 Centimes	.44	.65	1.09	2.18	3.26	4.35	21.75	43.50	54.38	65.25	87.00	217.50	326.25	435.00
Austria Schilling = 100 Groschen	1.67	2.50	4.17	8.34	12.50	16.67	83.35	166.70	208.40	250.00	333.40	833.50	1250.00	1667.00
Germany German Mark (D.M.) = 100 Pfennig	.23	.35	.58	1.17	1.75	2.33	11.65	23.30	29.13	34.95	46.60	116.50	174.75	233.00
Spain Peseta = 100 Centimos	5.60	8.40	14.00	28.00	2.00	56.00	280.00	560.00	700.00	840.00	1120.00	2800.00	4200.00	5600.00
Switzerland Swiss Franc (S.F.) = 100 Rappen	.26	.40	.66	1.32	1.97	2.63	13.20	26.30	32.88	39.45	52.60	131.50	197.25	263.00
Hong Kong Hong Kong Dollar (H.K.$) = 100 Cents	.48	.71	1.19	2.38	3.57	4.76	23.80	47.60	59.50	71.40	95.20	238.00	357.00	476.00
Sweden Swedish Krona (S.KR.) = 100 Öre	.40	.60	1.00	2.00	3.00	4.00	20.00	40.00	50.00	60.00	80.00	200.00	300.00	400.00
New Zealand N.Z. Dollar (N.Z.$) = 100 Cents	.08	.12	.20	.41	.62	.82	4.11	8.22	10.28	12.34	16.45	41.12	61.68	82.24
Portugal Escudo (ESC.) = 100 Centavos	2.44	3.66	6.10	12.20	18.30	24.40	122.00	244.00	305.00	366.00	488.00	1220.00	1830.00	2440.00
Denmark Danish Krone (D.KR.) = 100 Øre	.56	.83	1.39	2.78	4.17	5.55	27.78	55.50	69.44	83.33	111.10	277.75	416.63	555.50
Norway Norw. Krone (N.KR.) = 100 Øre	.52	.78	1.30	2.60	3.90	5.20	26.00	52.00	65.00	78.00	104.00	260.00	390.00	520.00
India Indian Rupee (I.RP.) = 100 Paise	.73	1.09	1.82	3.64	5.46	7.28	36.40	72.80	91.00	109.20	145.60	364.00	546.00	728.00
Netherlands Guilder (HFL) = 100 Cents	.25	.38	.63	1.25	1.88	2.50	12.50	25.00	31.25	37.50	50.00	125.00	187.50	250.00
Tunisia Dinar (T.D.) = 1000 Millimes	.05	.07	.12	.24	.36	.48	2.42	4.84	6.04	7.25	9.67	24.18	36.27	48.35
Turkey Turkish Lira (T.L.) = 100 Kurus	.71	1.07	1.78	3.57	5.35	7.14	35.70	71.40	89.25	107.10	142.80	357.00	535.50	714.00
Italy Italian Lira (LIT) = 100 Centesimi	63.00	94.00	156.00	312.00	469.00	625.00	3125.00	6250.00	7812.00	9375.00	12500.00	31250.00	46875.00	62500.00
Japan Yen = 100 Sen	29.00	43.00	72.00	145.00	217.00	290.00	1450.00	2900.00	3625.00	4350.00	5800.00	14500.00	21750.00	29000.00

Based on rates prevailing as of March 1975. Most currencies are on a floating rate basis and subject to daily fluctuations.

Compiled by
Deak—Perera International, Inc.
41 East 42nd Street
New York, N.Y. 10017 and
J. F. Kennedy International Airport
Jamaica, N.Y. 11430

LIST OF CUSTOMS CHARGES

ANTIQUES made at least 100 years before date of entry   free
AUTOMOBILES, passenger   3%

BAGS, hand, leather   10%
BINOCULARS
   prism   20%
   opera and field glasses   8½%
BOOKS
   foreign author   free
   foreign language   free

CAMERAS
   motion picture, over $50 each   6%
   still, over $10 each   7½%
   cases, leather   10%
   lenses   12½%
CANDY
   sweetened chocolate bars   5%
   other   7%
CHESS SETS   10%
CHINA
   bone   17½%
   nonbone, other than tableware   22½%
CHINA TABLEWARE, nonbone, available in 77-piece sets
   value over $10 but not over $24 per set   10¢ doz. + 55%
   value over $24 but not over $56 per set   10¢ doz. + 36%
   value over $56 per set   5¢ doz. + 18%
CIGARETTE LIGHTERS
   pocket, value over 42¢ each   22½%
   table   12%
CLOCKS
   value over $5 but not over $10 each   75¢ + 16%
   value over $10 each $1.12 + 16%

DRAWINGS (works of art)
   original   free
   copies, done entirely by hand   free

EARTHENWARE TABLEWARE, available in 77-piece sets
   value over $7 but not over $12 per set   10¢ doz. + 21%
   value over $12 per set   5¢ doz. + 10½%

FIGURINES, china   22½%
FUR
   wearing apparel   8½% – 18½%
   other items made of   8½%
FURNITURE
   wood, chairs   8½%
   wood, other than chairs   5%

GLASS TABLEWARE, value not over $1 each   22½% – 50%
GLOVES
   wool   37½¢ + 18½%
   fur   10%
   horsehide or cowhide   15%
GOLF BALLS   6%

HANDKERCHIEFS
   cotton, plain   25%
   other vegetable fiber, plain   9%

IVORY, items made of   6%

JEWELRY, precious metal or stone
   silver chief value, value not over $18 per dozen   27½%
   other   12%

LEATHER
   pocketbooks, bags   10%
   other items made of   4% – 14%

MOTORCYCLES   5%
MUSICAL INSTRUMENTS
   music boxes, wood   8%
   woodwind, except bagpipes   7½%
   bagpipes   free

PAINTINGS (works of art)
   original   free
   copies, done entirely by hand   free
PAPER, items made of   8½%
PEARLS
   loose or temporarily strung (without clasp)
     genuine   free
     cultured   2½%
     imitation   20%
   permanently strung (with clasp attached or separate)
     12% – 27%
PERFUME   8¢ lb. + 7½%

RADIOS
   transistor   10.4%
   other   6%
RATTAN
   furniture   16%
   other items made of   12½%
RECORDS, phonograph   5%

SHOES, leather   2½% – 20%
SKIS AND SKI EQUIPMENT   8% – 9%
   ski boots   free to 20%
SLIPPERS, leather   5%
STERLING FLATWARE AND TABLEWARE
   knives and forks   4¢ each + 8½%
   spoons and tableware   12½%
STONES, cut but not set
   diamonds not over ½ carat   4%
   diamonds over ½ carat   5%
   other   free to 5%
SWEATERS, of wool, over $5 per lb.   37½¢ lb. + 20%

TAPE RECORDERS   5½% – 7½%
TOILET PREPARATIONS
   not containing alcohol   7½%
   containing alcohol   8¢ lb. + 7½%
TOYS   17½%
TRUFFLES   free

WATCHES, on $100 watches duty varies from $6 to $13
WEARING APPAREL
   embroidered or ornamented   21% – 42½%
   not embroidered, not ornamented:
     cotton, knit   21%
     cotton, not knit   8% – 21%
     linen, not knit   7½%
     man-made fiber, knit   25¢ lb. + 32½%
     man-made fiber, not knit   25¢ + 27½%
     silk, knit   10%
     silk, not knit   16%
     wool, knit   37½¢ + 20% – 32%
     wool, not knit   25¢ – 37½¢ lb. + 21%
WOOD
   carvings   8%
   other items made of   8%

Index

Abbey Crafts, 117
Abelardo Linares S.A., 19, 118
accordions, 146
Adachi Institute of Woodcut Prints, 30
address books, Smythson's, 129
Aenonics Ltd., 108
Aero Nautical Models, 66
aids: for the blind, 159; for the deaf, 159; for the disabled, 159-60
Africa, books about, 34
Akios Industries, 43, 82
Alajarven Huvilaveistamo, 85
alchemy, books about, 39
Allwood Bros. Ltd., 100
Alpengrow Gardens, 99
American Foundation for the Blind, Inc., 159
Amita Jewelry Corp., 143
anarchy, books about, 34
Ancrum Craig, 54
Kinloch Anderson and Sons Ltd., 91
Anderson's Rose Nurseries, 99
Fernandez Angulo S.A., 137
Animal Health Division, address, 96
animalier bronzes, 19
animals, 152
animal skins, 91
Anticoli Gloves, 52
Antique Export Establishment, 18
Antique Handles, 127
The Antique Lovers Coterie, 18
antiques, 14-20; beds, 14; carpets, 14; classes in, 41; clocks, 14, 18; curios, 15, 18; cushions, 76; furniture, 18-19, 115; glass, 15-19; jewelry, 15, 19, 140; mirrors, 19; music boxes, 20; nautical, 115; silver, 15-20; 140-44; watches, 15
antiquities, 14
Anything Lefthanded Ltd., 128
Giovanni Apa, 142
aprons: with lace, 133; Mexican, 91; Portuguese, 128, 133
Aquaquipment, 163
archeology, classes in, 41
architectural metalwork, 127
architecture, classes in, 41
Argalius, 71
Argyle Models, 66
Arima, 68
armor, antique, 14
The Armourer's Shop, 14
Art Needlework Industries Ltd., 104
Art Nouveau, decorative objects, 18
Arts Council Shop, 28, 35
Artwork, 83
Ashford Handicrafts Ltd., 105
Ashley Furniture Workshops, 115
Ashley Iles Ltd., 106
ashtrays: crystal, 87, 121, 126; Indian, 89; Limoges, 123; onyx, 82; pewter, 88; Rosenthal, 123; Wedgwood, 121
James Asman, 148
Asprey and Co. Ltd., 140
Astley's Ltd., 46

astrology, books about, 39
Atkinson-Ward Shirts, 56
atlases, 37, 40
attaché cases, leather, 52
Audio T, 169
Au Printemps, 78
Australia, stores, 61, 74, 99, 100, 106
Australian Gem Trading Co., 101
Austria, stores, 47, 50, 68, 75, 131, 134, 140, 166
autographs, 65
Aux Gobelins, 104
The Aviation Bookshop, 35
aviation posters, 30
Avis Avouris, 87

Bahamas, stores, 109
Bakalowits Söhne, 134
Ballet School Supplies Ltd., 52
balustrads, 118
A. C. Bang, 60-61
Bangkok Dolls, 93
banjos, 146
barbeque sets: bronze, 110; wrought iron, 93
J. Barbour and Son, 166
H. L. Barnett, 74, 128
Barton Children's Holidays, 40
baskets: rushwork, 90; trugs, 85
bassoons, 146
J. T. Batchelor and Co., 102
Les Bâteaux Leclerc Inc., 67
bath oils, Taylor of London, 85
bath robes: Indian, 89; tweed, 90; Viyella, 79
bathtubs, 108
batik, supplies for, 96, 97
George Bayntun, 156
beaded trim, by the yard, 58
J. D. Beardmore, 127
beauty cases, 56
Beau Windows, 128
Beaver of Bolton Ltd., 166
Beaver Toys, 172
bed linen, 77-79, 129, 131, 133
beds, fourposter, 14
bedspreads: Aran knitted, 58; crochet, 133; Indian, 89; Spanish, 137; Welsh tapestry, 94
Belgium, stores, 29, 120, 131
belts: beaded African, 91; for evening, 97; made to measure, 97; for men, 50-55; for women, 97; zebra skin, 91
benches: reconstituted stone, 118; tile, 138
Kunstschmiede Manfred Bergmeister, 87
Paul U. Bergströms AB, see *PUB*
Berner and Co., 93
bicycles, 163
W. Bill Ltd., 49, 70, 108
Tony Bingham, 146
binoculars, 79, 154
birdbath, 118
bird cage, Tunisian, 93
bird house, 83
Birdmobile Card Sculptures, 172
bird pictures, 83
birds, 152

Blackmore and Langdon Ltd., 100
Blackwell's, 33
Blackwell's Music Shop, 147
blankets, 78, 108; embroidered, 82; Icelandic, 89
N. Bloom and Son Ltd., 19
Blower Bentley car, electric, 76
Boat Enquiries Ltd., 41
Bodant Garden Nursery, 99
N.V. Boekhandel & Antiquariaat B. M. Israel, 37
Robert Bolton and Sons, 100
bookbinding, to order, 34, 117, 156
Book-Care, 40
book ends, Italian, 30
book plates, 40
books, 33-41; on Africa, 34; architecture, 35; art, 35; aviation, 35; for the blind, 159; about brass rubbing, 96; building, 35; about cabala, 39; children's, 39; cinema, 35; about crafts, 96, 104; about deafness, 159; about diets, 39; Dutch, 40; about flower arranging, 97; French, 39; French for children, 40; gardening, 36; geneaology, 36; German, 40; about graphology, 39; guides for the handicapped, 160; holiday guides, 40-41; interior design, 40; leatherbound, 156; magic, 39, 103; about mentally handicapped children, 160; military, 36; model railroads, 67; modern first editions, 38, 39; music, 146; music boxes, 20; natural history, 36; needlework, 104; numerology, 39; occult and allied subjects, 39; old, 37-39; palmistry, 39; paper flowers, 97; playing cards, 68; rare, 38; Russian, 37; sailing, 163; science, 37; Scotland, 92; stamps, 68; tarot cards, 39; transport, 37
Andrew Booth, 157
boots: fur, 167; sheepskin, 89; ski, 167
botany equipment, 103
bowls: Indian, 89; wooden, 83, 128
boxes: Chantilly, 123; decorated with reproductions, 30; enameled, 129; Indian, 89; silver, 140; Tunisian, 93; Wedgwood, 121
Boyne House (Kington) Ltd., 15
Branners Bibliofile Antikvariat, 39
brass rubbings: equipment for making, 96; reproductions of, 30
bread-dough figures, 43, 82
Paul Breman Ltd., 35
Brentano's, 39
Mrs. E. M. Brickdale, 172
briefcases, leather, 52, 56
Broadleigh Gardens, 99
bronze tableware, 110
Brown Best and Co. Ltd., 164

Brown Thomas and Co. Ltd., 71, 131
Bede Brown (Metal Craft), 102
Leslie Brown, 148
Margaret J. Brown, 172
Brunings (Holborn) Ltd., 103
Buch and Deichmann, 140
buckles, 96
Buderim Ginger Factory, 74
The Building Bookshop, 35
bulbs, 98-99
Burberry's Ltd., 55
C. P. Burge and Son, 115
Bushland Flora, 100
J. F. Butler Toymakers, 178
butterflies, 96
buttons, 97

cabala, books about, 39
cactus plants, 99, 100
Leo Cady's Cacti Gardens, 99
Cairncross, 144
cakes, 74-76
Caldron Promotions, 28
calendars, 128; Japanese flower arrangements, 97
Cambrian Factory Ltd., 49
Cambrian Fly Fishers, 165
Cambridge Wools Ltd., 106
cameos, 142
cameras, 154
Camphill Products, 84
camping: clothes, 164-65, 166-67; equipment, 164-65, 166-67
Carlo Mario Camusso, 144
Canada, stores, 24, 35, 65, 70, 76, 82, 98, 99, 100, 105, 106, 127
candies, 74-76
candleholders, 15, 43, 138; antique, Russian brass, 19; brass, 88, 117; crystal, 134; Ethiopian, 85; pewter, 136; Rosenthal, 123; Swedish glass, 126
Candlelight Associates, 88
Candle Makers Supplies, 96
candles: beeswax, 84, 96; Rigaud, 150; supplies for making, 96
candlesticks, 15, 87
capes, 50-51; children's, 51
caps, Norwegian knitted, 54
Carpet House, 136
cars, racing clothes and equipment for, 165
car-seat covers, sheepskin, 137
carvings, ivory, 88
carving tools, 106
Casa Bonet, 133
cash registers, antique, 18
Catello D'Auria, 52
Cathay Arts Co. Ltd., 117
Cathay of Bournemouth Ltd., 150
caviar, 89
Cellini's Silver Factory, 126, 143
Central Cottage Industries Emporium, 71, 89
Central Council for the Disabled, 160
Ceylon, see Sri Lanka
champagne, 76
T. M. Chan and Co., 154, 180

185

Ascot Chang Ltd., 56
Channel Island and Guernsey Toys, 172
Chapo, 113
Charbonnel et Walker, 74
charms, 78, 142; Dutch, 88; English, 78
Chater & Scott Ltd., 37
cheese, 75-76, 89
cheese boards, 83, 93
Cherry's Ltd., 67
chess sets, 82, 97, 129
children: books, 39; books in French, 40; cushions, 83; engineering kits, 176; fancy dress, 43; records, 39; shoe tidy, 173; toy bag, 173; wall charts, 29; wall friezes, 176; wash packs, 173
Children's Book Centre Ltd., 39
children's clothes, 62-63, 78, 167; capes, 51; Juul Christensen knitwear, 54; coats, 50; dirndls, 50, 62; fancy dress, 43; gloves, 52; Happi coats, 54; Indian, 89; Iroquois, 82; with lace, 133; Norwegian sweaters, 54; party dresses, 62; rainwear, 63; sailing, 163; ski, 167; snowsuits, 63; Wellington boots, 62
Chilstone Garden Ornaments, 118
Antranig S. Chiluirian, 89
china, 79, 120-27, 128; antique, 18; Danish, 120-21; Dutch, 123; English, 121, 126; German, 123; Herend, 123; Irish, 126; Limoges, 87, 121; Porcelaine de Chantilly, 87; Swedish, 126; Wedgwood, 121
China Art Embroidery, 131
Chinacraft Ltd., 121
China Pottery Arts Co., 127
Constance and Anthony Chiswell, 19
Chocolaterie Dauphine, 74
Chocolaterie International, 75
chocolates, 74-76; liqueur, 74
chokers, 97
V. Juul Christensen and Son, 54
W. D. Christianson, 65
Christie, Manson and Woods, 15, 27, 75
Christmas: cards, 43-44; cookie molds, 88; decorations, 43; embroidery kits, 105; musical balls, 93; plates, 123; puddings, 74-76
church furnishings, 83, 87
Churchill, Atkin, Grant and Lang Ltd., 166
cigar cutters, 140
cigarette boxes: Indian, 89; onyx, 140; pewter, 136
Cigarette Card News, 65
cigarette cups, Wedgwood, 121
cigarette holders, meerschaum, 46
cigarette lighters: crystal, 121; onyx, 140; pewter, 129; silver, 140, 143; with watches, 180
cigars, 46, 76
Cine Books, 35
Cinex Ltd., 154

clarinets, 146
clavichords, 146-47
Cleo, 60
clockmaking supplies, 27
clocks: antique, 14-15, 18; antique reproductions, 93
clogs, 55
clothes, 49-63, 78-79, 82, 87-94, 133; African, 90; ballet, 52; Berketex, 51; boots, 50; Ceylonese, 93; Donald Davies, 49, 133; down-filled, 164, 167; Ecuadorian, 82; for female impersonation, 49; French, 87; Greek, 87; Guatemalan, 88; Highland Home Industries, 58, 128; Hong Kong, 88-89; Icelandic, 89; Indian, 89; Iroquois, 82; Jaeger, 51; Lacoste, 87; Langmore sheepskin, 128; leather, 50; Mexican, 91; mohair, 84; moleskin, 165; patchwork, 84; Philippine, 91; rubber, 60; Peter Saunders, 128; Scottish, 91-92; sports, 49-51, 163-67; Thai silk, 71; Viyella, 51, 78-79; Welsh tapestry, 60, 94; Windsmoor, 51
clothes, made to measure, 49-51, 54, 56-57; belts, for women, 97; crochet, 133; insulated, 167; knitwear, 54; pajamas, 56; Scottish, 91-92; shirts, 56-57; shoes, 57
Clothkits, 62
coffeepots, copper, 88
coffee sets, 120-27
coins, old, 15, 65
The Collector, 19
Collectors Treasures Ltd., 25
Collett's, 37
comforters, 108-9
compasses, 163, 164
Wm. Condon and Sons Ltd., 106
Condor Bicycles, 163
Confiserie-Schatz, 75
construction kits: airplanes, 66; railroads, 67; ships, 67; shortwave radios, 105; villages, 67
M. G. Contreras, 146
cookies, 74-76
Bruce Coombes, 65
copper pots, 89, 90, 93
Coptic crosses, 85
coral, 105
J. C. Cording and Co. Ltd., 49
Cornelius Furs, 61
cosmetics, French, 150
Cottage Crafts Ltd., 70
Cottage Industries, 90
cottages, 85
Council of Industrial Design, 40
Country Cousins, 83
Covent Garden Bookshop, 38
cowbells, Swiss, 93
Craftsman's Mark Yarns, 106
craft supplies, 97
G. Cramer, 27
James H. Crawley, 148
Creation Boutique, 49
crèches, 43
D. J. Cremin and Son, 90
Cristaux du Val St-Lambert, 120
crochet: bathroom sets, 133;

blouses, 90; clothes, 58, 133; shawls, 90; supplies for, 104
Crowther of Syon Lodge Ltd., 18
C. A. Cruickshank Ltd., 98
Cuckoobird Productions, 173
cuff links, 140-44; decorated with animals, 56
curios, 15, 18
cushion covers, 133; kits to make, 104-5; Thai silk, 71
cushions: antique, 76; Ecuadorian, 82; Greek needlepoint, 88; needlepoint, 133; patchwork, 83; sheepskin, 89, 137; Tunisian, 93
P. Cutler Ltd., 49
Cyclists' Touring Club, 163

Dalecarlian horses, 79
dancing, classes, 41
Dane, 104
Danfood Ltd., 75
L. Davenport and Co., 103
David and Joe Trading Co., 49
Davidoff et Cie, 46
Dawson's of Pall Mall, 37
Wm. Dawson & Sons Ltd., 40
Margery Dean Antiques, 19
Deane and Adams, 96
Deepak's Rokjemperl Products, 102
E. Dehillerin, 129
Deighton Brothers Ltd., 104
Denmark, stores, 19, 39, 46, 47, 54, 60, 68, 104, 105, 111, 120, 121, 128, 134, 140, 172
Den Permanente, 128
Dent Glass, 121
The Design Centre, 128
desk sets: leather, 52; onyx, 129
diet, books about, 39
Dillon's University Bookshop, 34
dirndls: German, 50; Swiss, 62
dishcloths, 96, 129
dissection equipment, 103
Dobbin Designs, 173
Dobells Jazz Record Shop, 148
Yvonne Docktree, 98
Martin J. Dodge, 115
Dodo, 28
dogs, Tibetan Apso, 89
doll houses, 65-66, 173
dolls, 65; African, 91; antique, 18; Dutch, 178; Ecuadorian, 82; Ethiopian, 85; French, 87; from Hong Kong, 88; Irish, 90; Polish, 91; Swedish, 178; Swiss, 93; Thai, 93; Tunisian, 93; Welsh, 94
The Dolls House, 173
Dominican Republic, stores, 82
Donegal Linens Ltd., 133
door knockers, 127
doors, Spanish, 118
doorstops, 127
Dovina, 178
Downer International Sails Ltd., 163
drama, classes in, 41
drawings, 22
dresser sets, 140, 143
dressing cases, gentlemen's fitted, 56
drinking flasks, 56

drums, 146
Dublin Crystal Glass Co., 126
Duk Kwong Optical Co., 159
R. S. Duncan and Co., 102
Paul Dunstall, 166
dusting powder, Taylor of London, 85
Dutch crafts, 88
Dutch Gardens, Inc., 98
dyes, 96, 106; Sennelier, 96

Eaton's Shell and Rock Shop, 105
Ecuador, stores, 43, 82, 136
Educational Graphics Ltd., 29
Francis Edwards Ltd., 37
Egertons, 128
egg cups, for children, 43
Egypt, stores, 82
eiderdown comforters, 108
Eileen's Handknits, 54
electrical appliances, 131
electronic calculators, 170
electronic flash, 154
William Elkin Music Services, 147
Roger Elliot, 156
Arthur Ellis and Co. Ltd., 164
AB Ellysett, 134
embroidery, 131; antique English, 14, 15; kits, 78, 103-5; kits designed to order, 105; Portuguese, 133; supplies, 103-5; Tunisian, 93
Emerald Crafts, 90
England, stores, 14-43, 46-71, 74-78, 83-85, 96-110, 112-13, 115-18, 121, 127-29, 138, 140, 146-52, 156-78
The English Folk Dance and Song Society, 147
engravings: antique, 15; musical subjects, 146
entomology equipment, 96, 103
Erme Wood Forge, 127
Estelle, 60
Estrin Manufacturing Ltd., 105
Ethiopia, stores, 85
Euston Gallery, 27
Evergreen Travel Service, 159

Fabra, 173
Fabrica Sant'Anna, 138
fabrics by the yard, 70-72, 78; African, 91; antique, 15; Liberty, 70; Thai silks, 71, 93; tweed, 49, 50, 70, 90, 102, 133; Welsh flannel and tapestry, 94; woolens, 54
Stephen Faller, 126
fancy-dress costumes, for children, 43
Farm Holiday Guides Ltd., 41
Fauchon, 75
Joan Faulkner Miniatures, 65
feather pillows, 108
Felin Newydd, 72
figurines: Baccarat, 121; Bing and Grøndahl, 120; Capodimonte, 126; Chinese, 28; Hadeland, 79; Hummel, 110, 123, 178; Lalique, 121; Lladro, 126; Royal

Copenhagen, 43, 120; Royal Doulton, 126; Swedish glass, 65
Filmdocumentatie, 35
Finland, stores, 78, 85, 136
E. Fioravanti and Co. Ltd., 90
firebacks, 127
fishing: clothes, 49, 163, 165; courses, 165; equipment, 165
C. D. Fitz Hardinge-Baily, 106
Fjällräven SE-AB, 164
flatware, 109-10, 129, 140-44
J. Floris, 150
flower arranging: classes in, 41; classes by mail, 97-98; club, 97
flower pictures, 83
flowers: Coalport china, 121; Crown Staffordshire, 121; paper, kits for making, 98; pictures for framing, 30, 83
flutes, 146
Focke and Meltzer, 123, 134
Fog and Morup, 134
Folio Society Ltd., 39
Folklore—Olga Fisch, 82, 136
food, 74-76; hampers, 128; Icelandic, 89
R. W. Forsyth, 75
Fortnum and Mason, 43, 75
Fortune Hand Work Family Co. Ltd., 28
fortuneteller, 156
Fountain House Antiques, see Chiswell
fountains, 118; Portuguese tile, 138
frames, Mexican, 91
France, stores, 25, 39, 41, 52, 65, 71, 75, 78, 85, 87, 101, 104, 113, 121, 129, 131, 148, 150
Denise Francelle, 52
Frank and Company, 144
Fratelli Alinari, 30, 43
Freddy, 85, 150
Freedom Bookshop, 34
Freemans of London, 78
J. Fröschl and Co., 131
Frosig, 120
Ron Fuller Toys, 176
Functional Clothing Ltd., 167
Fundação Ricardo do Espirito Santo Silva, 117
furniture, 78; antique, 18-19, 129; for children, 78; Congolese, 91; garden, 18, 118, 120; Hong Kong, 127; Icelandic chairs, 89; modern, 111-15; Muurame, 78; rattan, 120; reproduction, 115-18, 129; sheepskin stools, 137; Spanish colonial, 91
furniture fittings in metal, 127
Anthony Fyffe, 157

James Galt and Co. Ltd., 176
games, 129; for the blind, 159
Ganymed Original Editions Ltd., 22
garden ornaments, 118, 127
gardening: books, 36; supplies, 98-101
Garrard and Co. Ltd., 140

A. Garstang and Co. Ltd., 56
gates, wrought-iron, 127
Ernst Geissendorfer, 25
gems, 101-2
geneaology, books about, 36
General Trading Company, 128
geology, equipment, 103
Gered, 121
The German Bedding Center, 108
Germany, stores, 24, 25, 40, 43, 50, 66, 78, 87, 97, 106, 110, 113, 123, 131, 146, 166, 167, 178
Stanley Gibbons Ltd., 68
W. and H. Gidden Ltd., 166
ginger, 74
Giovanetti, 113
Giovanni Apa, 142-43
glacéed fruits, 74-76
glass, antique, 18, 19
glass cases, leather, 52
glass figures, 65
glassware, 80, 120-29, 140; antique, 18; Belgian, 120; Carnival, 15; English, 84, 121; French, 87, 121; German, 123; Irish, 90, 126; Swedish, 79, 126
Glit Lava Ceramics, 123
globes, 40
gloves, 52, 78; crochet, 90; down-filled, 164; French, 87; Norwegian knitted, 53; oven, 83, 128; string, 49
gobelins, *see* Tapestries
Edward Golemberski, 15
golf: accessories, 129, 167; clothes, 49, 167
L. S. A. Goodwin and Sons, 100
A. Goto, 15
Gozo 20, 133
graphology, books about, 39
grates, antique, 18-19
Greater London Council, 30
Greaves Sports Ltd., 167
Greece, stores, 61, 71, 87, 136
greeting cards, 43-44
Martyn Gregory, 22
Grillot, 87, 150
Luis Grosse Ltd., 83
Guatemala, stores, 88
guide books, 40-41; for the disabled, 160
guitars, 146, 147
guns, 166; cabinets for, 118
Cadwyn y Cwch Gwenyn, 94

Habitat, 112
Habitat Toronto, 127
H.A.C. Short-Wave Products, 105
Haiti, stores, 88
Halcyon Days, 129
Halfpenny Houses, 176
Hall Green Wools, 102
Hamblings Ltd., 67
Hamleys of Regent Street, 43, 176
Hammersmith Books, 37
ham radio kits, 105
handbags, 52, 55, 56, 85; deerskin, 91; Ecuadorian, 82; fur, 59; Greek tagari, 87, 88; Mexican, 91; needlepoint, 87,

88, 131; sheepskin, 89, 137; Welsh tapestry, 94
Handi-Cap Horizons, 159
handicapped, *see* Aids
James Hanna Workshop, 90
Gilbert Hansen, 68
Happi coats, 54
Keith Harding Antiques, 20
Hardy Bros. (Alnwick) Ltd., 165
harpsichords, 146-47
Harrods Ltd., 78, 152
Douglas Hart, 83
Harvie and Hudson Ltd., 56
Hatchards, 34
hats: African beaded, 91; Aran knitted, 58, 90; Borsalino, 52; crochet, 133; fur, 59; sheep-skin, 89
Hawick Honeycombe Blankets, 108
Hayashi Kimono, 54
Health 4 All Products Ltd., 76
hearth furniture, 127
Heather Valley Ltd., 54
J. Heemskerk, 98
Heffer's Children's Bookshop, 39
W. Heffer and Sons Ltd., 33; children's bookshop, 39
Carl Heidtmass, 106
Heldwein, 140
Helios Home Supplies, 109, 129
The Helping Hand Company, 20
Henke Schachspiele, 97
Heraldry Today, 36
Het Kantenhuis, 131
Hettie's Rock Shop, 105
Heugel et Cie, 148
Hi-fi Answers (magazine), 169
Highland Home Industries, 60
Hillier and Sons, 99
HMV Shops, 148
Hobby Horse Ltd., 43, 97
A. T. Hogg (Fife) Ltd., 55
Robert Hoggs and Co. Ltd., 126
Holland, stores, 27, 31, 35, 37, 40, 74, 88, 98-99, 123, 131, 134, 136, 142, 178
Holland Handicrafts, 88
Holly Gate Nurseries Ltd., 100
Holy Trinity School Gift Shop, 88
Homebound Craftsmen, 173
Hong Kong, stores, 28, 44, 49, 55, 56, 60, 88-89, 110, 117, 120, 131, 136-37, 142, 154, 159, 170, 180
Hong Kong Jade Center, 142
hope chests, antique, 18
horns, musical, 146
Charlotte Horstmann Ltd., 117
Peter Hoyte, 112
Hsiang-Fu Teakwood Furniture Mfg. Co., 118
Thomas Humphrey Ltd., 15
Hungary, stores, 40
Hunt and Winterbotham Ltd., 54, 70
H. Huntsman and Sons, 57
hurdy-gurdies, 18
Husky of Tostock Ltd., 167
J. Hyslop Bathgate and Co., 106

IA Produkter AB, 68
ice buckets, 128

Iceland, stores, 89, 123
Icemart, 89
ICTA Information Center, 160
Ikea, 115
Ikebana International, 97
Imperial Pearls Co., 143
Inderwick and Co. Ltd., 46
India, stores, 71, 76, 89, 102
The Inland Waterways Association, 41
The International Model Mail Order House, 84
Ireland, stores, 49, 50, 54, 55, 60, 71, 76, 78, 90, 106, 117, 126, 131, 132, 133, 146
Irish Cottage Industries, 49
iron, brass, 88
Iroqrafts Ltd., 82
Iroquois crafts, 82
Israel, stores, 19
B. M. Israel, see *N. V. Boekhandel*
Italy, stores, 22, 30, 43, 44, 52, 90, 113, 126, 133, 142, 143
Itraco Watch Co. Ltd., 180
ivory, carved, 88

S. and M. Jacobs Ltd., 50
Jahn-Markl, 50
Jannabags, 52
Japan, stores, 15, 24, 25, 30, 54, 97, 98, 143
Jazz Journal (magazine), 148
Jesurum, 133
jewelry, 82, 128, 140-44; African beaded, 91; antique, 15, 18, 19, 140; Canadian Indian, 82; Celtic, 90, 128; Ecuadorian, 82; Ethiopian, 85; Greek, 88; Hong Kong, 88, 89; Icelandic, 89; made to order, 140, 142; making, 102; needlepoint, kits to make, 105; Scottish, 91; Tunisian, 93, Wedgwood, 121
jewelry boxes: Chinese, 117; leather, 52, 56
jewelry cases, leather, fitted, 56
jewelry-making supplies, 102
jigsaw puzzles, 176
Jillian Junior Fashions, 62
H. Johnson Ltd., 90
Herbert Johnson Ltd., 52

La Joie de Lire, 39
J. Jolles Studios, 131
Judaica, 19
jugs: copper, 88; Portuguese, 138

Kandelka Native Seeds, 100
A. Karamichos, 136
Kasheta Travel, Inc., 159
Kause Oy, 85
Lee Kee Ltd., 55
Kegan Paul, Trench, Trubner and Co., 22
Kendal Playing Card Sales, 68
Kennedy's of Ardara, 54
Kenya, stores, 90-91, 126
Kernowcraft Rocks and Gems Ltd., 102

Firma Edward Kettner, 166
Kevin and Howlin Ltd., 71
kimonos, 54
Kinderparadies, 178
Louise King, 25
Kingsworthy Foundry Co. Ltd., 127
D. M. Kirkness, 118
kitchen appliances, 131
kitchen gadgets, 129; for the blind, 159
kitchen utensils, 129; decorated, 129; enamel, 78
kites, 102
kits: children's engineering, 176; children's hobby, 178; inflatable boat, 163; model railroad, 67; to make petit-point jewelry, 105; to knit Norwegian sweaters, 102; to make shortwave radios, 105; toys, 173
Klods Hans, 43
Kløverhuset, 54
knitting supplies, 102, 106
knitwear, 54-55, 58, 78-79, 87, 89, 90, 92; Aran, 54, 55, 71, 90; Barrie, 54; beaded, 58; Braemar, 51, 54, 70; Juul Christensen, 54; Fair Isle, 55, 71; French, 87; Guernsey, 55; Harris, 71; Lyle and Scott, 55; Morley, 51; Pringle, 51, 54, 70, 78
knives: Ethiopian, 85; German, 110
Knobs and Knockers, 127
Joseph Kober, 68
Konn's Fine Arts, 44
Kornreich Diamond Mfg. Co., 140
Kow Hoo Shoe Co. Ltd., 55
Kowloon Rattan Ware Company, 120
Kristine Leather Goods Workshop, 52
Richard Kruml, 22
Kuja Crafts Ltd., 91
Kultura, 40
Kunstschmiede Manfred Bergmeister, 87

labels, old, 29
lace, 131, 133; Tunisian, 93
Carlo Lambardi, 52
G. Lambor, 14
lamps, 133-34; Delft, 123; hand-carved and gilded, 30; Indian, 89; Portuguese, 138; Rosenthal, 123; wood, 83, 134
G. G. Lang sel. Erben, 43
Langard Company, 110
lanterns, 163; wrought-iron, 118
W. Larsen, 46
Laskys, 170
laundry hampers, 120
Victor Laurence, 50
R. G. Lawrie Ltd., 92
Leach Pottery, 121
Leather and Snook, 121
leather for dressmaking, 70
leather goods, 50, 52, 55, 56, 57, 128, 140; Ethiopian, 85; Smythson's, 128, 129

Leather School, 52
leather supplies, 102
Lebanon, stores, 91
Lecuyer, 29
John Lees, 102
left-handed, implements for, 128
Les Leston Products, 165
letter openers, see Paper Knives
letters, old, 38
Liberty and Co. Ltd., 57, 70
Liechtenstein, stores, 18
Gertrude Liechti, 62
lighting fixtures, 133-34; antique, 19; in brass, 127
light meters, 154
Lillywhite Ltd., 167
Limoges-Unic, 121
Lindberg, 146
Daniel Lloyd, 36
Llyswen Welsh Craft Center, 94
John Lobb, 57
Priscilla Lobley Flower Kits, 98
Glen Lockhart Knitwear, 54
loden, 50, 166
Loden-Frey, 50
Loewe, 52
Loftus, 106
Maria Loix, 131
London Cigarette Card Co. Ltd., 65
The London Music Shop Ltd., 146
London Transport Poster Shop, 29
London Yacht Center, 163
López Valencia, 156
Lords Gallery Ltd., 30
P. G. de Lotz, 36
Julie Loughnan, 62
Lumley Cazalet Ltd., 22
Luxury Needlepoint Ltd., 104
lyres, 146

S. Y. Ma, 117
MacGillivray and Company, 71
macramé, 82
Märta Måås-Fjetterström, 137
Madeira Superbia, 133
magazine racks, 129
magazines: cigarette cards, 65; flower arranging, 97, 98; foreign subscriptions, 40; French fashion and decorating, 39; jazz, 148; model railway, 67; Science for the Blind, 159
magic, books about, 39, 103
magicians' supplies, 103
Mailmaster Film Productions, 103
Maison F. Rubbrecht, 131
Majorca, stores, 133, 143-44
Malaysia, stores, 136
Malta, stores, 133
mandolins, 146
manicure sets, 110
mantelpieces, antique, 18, 115
manuscripts, old and rare, 37-39
Mappin and Webb, 140
maps, 40; made to order, 40, 157; old, 25, 37, 38; reproductions of old, 30, 91; wall, for children, 82
marble bowls, 90

marine curios, 105
Marlau, 118
masks: false-face, 82; Inca reproductions, 82
maternity clothes, 61
Maternity Kits, 61
Alister Mathews, 22
Matoba and Co. Inc., 143
Matthes Ltd., 76
May Fashion House, 60
Alan McAfee, 57
medals, 15
Medieval English Brasses, 30
David Mellor, 110
Merion Mill, 60
Mexico, stores, 30, 91, 137
microscopes, 103; antique, 20
K. Mikimoto, Inc., 143
Millhaven Knitting Services, 54, 102
Millholme Models, 67
minerals, 65; Swiss, 93
miniatures, doll house, 65-66
Minutiques, 65
mirrors: antique, 18, 19; carved and gilded, 118
Misrachi, 30
mobiles, Christmas, 43
models: airplanes, 66; Britain's, 176; castles, 178; ranches, 178; ships, 67; soldiers, 68; villages, 178
Modern Coins and Banknotes (journal), 65
Moffat Weavers, 51
Mohilla, 47
Pascual Iniguez Montoya, 93
Morley Harpsichord, Pianoforte, and Harp Galleries, 146
Mosesson Games Ltd., 129
Moss Bros. Ltd., 166
Mothercare Ltd., 62
motorbikes, 166
Motor Books and Accessories, 37
motor-racing equipment, 165
movie projectors, 154
movies, home, 103
Moyle Marine Products, 163
muffs, sheepskin, 89, 137
Multiple Fabric Co. Ltd., 106
music: aids for the blind, 159; classes, 41; printed, 147-48
musical instruments, 146-47; African, 91
Musica Rara, 148
music boxes, 20; antique, 18; Swiss, 93

Nacar S.A., 143
name plates, Portuguese tile, 138
napkin rings, pewter, 136
napkins: butterfly-decorated, 96; damask, 131; embroidered, 131, 133; with lace, 131, 133; linen, 133; Thai silk, 71
National Gallery, 30
National Palace Museum, Tapei, 31
National Society for Mentally Handicapped Children, 160
National Welfare Organization, 87-88, 132

Nativity scenes, 43
natural history, books, 36-37
The Needlewoman Shop, 104
needlework, classes in, 41
Nepal, stores, 91
Nepal Craft Emporium, 91
netsukes, 15
New Central Jewelry Stores, 102
New Zealand, stores, 101, 105, 106, 137, 164
Ngai Fat Company, 117
Henry J. Nicholls and Son Ltd., 66
John Nicholson, 146
Noah's Ark Toys Ltd., 176
Nordiska Kristall, 126
Northwest Handicraft House, 106
Norway, stores, 54, 61, 109, 126
notebooks: decorated with Japanese flower arrangements, 98; Smythson leather, 129
numerology, books about, 39
Numismatic Circular (journal), 65
nutcrackers, silver, 140

Obéron, 87, 121, 150
oboes, 146
Michael O'Brien, 170
occultism: books about, 39; witchcraft symbols on jewelry, 89
Fergus O'Farrell Ltd., 90
Office National de l'Artisanat, 93, 137
Ohara School, 97
oil lamps, 43, 163
Old Hall Gallery Ltd., 28
Old World Plates, 121
Olive Wood and African Curio Shop, 85
Una O'Neill Designs, 55
oology equipment, 103
Orangerie Verlag, 24
organs, 146
A. W. G. Otten, 55
oven gloves, see Pot Holders

Pache—Aux Mille et Une Nuits, 131
John Paige, 176
paintings, 15, 18, 27-28; Canadian Indian tribes, 82; Dutch reproductions, 88; Ecuadorian, 82; Ethiopian, 85; miniature, 15, 28; of musical interest, 146; reproductions, 30-31; of ships and horses to order, 28; Spanish, 19
paints, 97
Paisley Ltd., 92
pajama cases, 128; sheepskin, 137
pajamas, 78
palmistry, books about, 39
paperweights, antique, 19
Paris House, 97
The Parker Gallery, 25
George Parker and Sons (Saddlers) Ltd., 166
party supplies, 43, 176; magic tricks, 103, 176

passport cases, 56
Patches, 84
patchwork, 82, 84
Pâpér Textiles Ltd., 70
pates, 74-76
Paxman Musical Instruments Ltd., 146
R. N. Peace and Co., 108
pearls: artificial, 143-44; cultured, 143; fresh-water, 144
Al Pellegrino Cattolico, 90
Pels Backer, 61
Pentangle, 105
Perez, 14
perfume, 79; French, 85, 87, 150; sachets, 85; Taylor of London, 85
Perlas Manacor S.A., 144
Peru, stores, 144
Peruzzi Bros., 143
pets, 152
Pettits, 60
pewter, 18, 78, 117, 134, 136; antique, 19
Philippines, stores, 91
Phillips and Page, 96
Phillips Auctioneers, 18, 68
photograph albums, leather, 52
photography, classes in, 41
Photo Hobby, 154
pianos, 146
picnic baskets, 56
picture frames: leather, 52; pewter, 136; silver, 143
S. C. Pierce and Son Ltd., 127
Manuel Antonio Pilón, 88
Hayim Pinhas, 46
Pipe Dan, 47
pipes and accessories, 46-47; antique, 15, 46; made to order, 47; make your own, 47; Peterson, 78; racks, 85; repair service, 46
place-card holders, Crown Staffordshire, 121
place mats, 129; butterfly-decorated, 96; Ecuadorian, 82; embroidered, 131, 133; English views, 78, 129; with lace, 131, 133; Mexican, 91; Scottish views, 91; Thai silk, 71; tweed, 90
Plaistow Pictorial, 30
plant importation permits, 98
plants, 99-100
plates: brass, 117; collectors', 68, 123; Indian, 89; pewter, 134, 136; Portuguese, 138; Tunisian, 93
playing cards, 68
Poland, stores, 91
Pollock's Toy Museum, 177
Pollyanna by Post, 62
pomanders, Taylor of London, 85, 129
Denise Poole, 20
Henry Poole and Co., 60
M. M. Poonjiaji and Co., 76
Porsgrunn Porselen, 126
Portugal, stores, 117-18, 138
postcards, 31, 79, 98
posters, 15, 28-30
pot holders: Austrian, 128; Mexican, 91
pot lids, antique, 18

Pottenbakkery, 88
Mary Potter Designs, 31
potters' supplies, 105
pottery, 121, 127; antique, 15, 19; classes in, 41; Fourmaintraux, 87; Icelandic, lava, 89; Irish, 90; Portuguese, 138; Tunisian, 93
powder compacts, silver, 143
princess rings, 144
prints, 25; British scenery, 38; Japanese wood-block, 25; reproductions of Japanese wood-block, 30; reproductions of old prints, 38
Priors Dukke Teatre, 172
Paul Prouté, S.A., 25
PUB, 79, 110, 126
public-address amplifiers, 170
purses, *see* Handbags
puzzles, 105

Bernard Quaritch, 38
Queen Pearl Co., 143
Quelle Inc., 78
quilts: Iroquois, 82; patchwork, 83
Quinta Fdo. Schmoll, 100

P. J. Radford, 25
Radio Digest (magazine), 159
Radio People Ltd., 170
radios, 170
rainwear, 51, 55, 63; Aquascutum, 51; Burberry's, 55; Dannimac, 51; Quelrayn, 51; Rodex, 51
Rama Jewelry Ltd., 144
Rambling Tours, 159
Rud. Rasmussens Snedkerier, 111
RD Design, 129
recorders, Hackbretter, 146
records, 148; for children, 39; Erato, 148; jazz, 148
The Red Lantern Shop, 24
Redpath Campbell and Partners Ltd., 70
Chris Reekie, 84
Rélais du Silence, 41
religions, books about, 39
religious articles, 90
Research Publications Services Ltd., 41
Otto Richter and Sons Ltd., 100
riding: clothes, 49, 166; equipment, 166
Mark Rimmell, 28
Ritchie Bros., 76
W. S. Robertson Ltd., 54
rocking horses, 76, 157, 173; parts and restoration, 157
rocks, Swiss, 93
Rodin, 71
Romanes and Patterson, 54
rosaries, 90
Eva Rosenstand A/S, 104-5
Rosenthal Studio-Haus, 110, 123
Bertram Rota, 38
Rowes of Bond Street, 62
Rowland Ward (East Africa) Ltd., 126
Royal Delftware, 123

Royal National Institute for the Blind, 159
Royal National Institute for the Deaf, 159
Royal Tara Ltd., 126
The Rugcraft Centre, 138
rug-making supplies, 103-5; kits, 136, 138
rugs, floor: 111, 115, 118, 136-38; antique, 14, 15; Aubussons, 14; Ecuadorian, 82, 136; Ethiopian, 85; Henequen, 91; needlepoint, 133; Portuguese, 118; Rya, 136; sheepskin, 137; Tibetan, 89
rugs, travel: Foxford, 90; mohair, 84
Rusticraft Signs, 157

R. Saggiori, 65
sailing: canoes, 82, 163-64; clothes, 55, 163, 166-67; equipment for, 163-64, 167; nautical furniture, 115; nautical gifts, 163
St. Andrews Woolen Mill, 71
samovars, 19
S. Samran Thailand Co. Ltd., 110
sandwich boxes, silver-plated, 56
Sango Inc., 98
Santa Rosa de Lima, Inc., 82
saucepans, antique copper, 15
saunas, 85
saxophones, 146
Chas. J. Sawyer, 34
Saydis Specialised Recordings Ltd., 148
scarfs, 52; designer, 87; Jacquard, 128; Thai silk, 71
Ron Scarpello, 94
Schiphol Airport, 76, 99, 134
Marga Schoeller Bücherstube, 40
The School Shop, 62
Schweizer-Heimatwerk, 93
Science for the Blind, 159
scientific instruments, antique, 19, 20
scissors, 110, 129
Scotch House, 51
Scotland, stores, 51, 54, 55, 60, 66, 71, 75, 76, 91-92, 99, 106, 108, 118, 167
Scottish Merchant, 55
sculpting tools, 105
sculptures, 19, 82, 90
seat sticks, 56
seat umbrellas, 56
seaweed, 76
Seaweed Ltd., 76
seeds, 100-1
Selangor Pewter Co., 136
Seldon Tapestries Ltd., 105
Christian Sell and Associates, 112
Henri Selmer and Co. Ltd., 146
Selva Technik, 97
T. Seng and Son, 93
shades, window, 128
Shannon Free Airport, 76, 78

sheepskin clothes and goods, 55, 133, 137
The Sheepskin Rug Shop, 55, 137
shells, 105
Sheppard's Place Antiques, 14
Shetland Silvercraft, 144
Ship Shop, 163
shirts for men, 56-57, 71
shoes, 51, 55, 57, 78-79; for men, 51, 55, 57; sheepskin, 137
shooting: accessories, 56, 166; clothes, 49, 166, 167; guns, 166
shopping bags, butterfly-decorated, 96
shrubs, 99-100
Shuttles and Seawinds Limited, 82
Sifton, Praed and Co. Ltd., 25
sign carving, 157
Signum Press Ltd., 24
silver, 76, 121, 140-44; antique, 15, 18, 19, 20, 140; flatware, 109-10; reproduction, 18, 78, 92; Royal Irish, 90
silver plate: antique, 19; Cristofle, 121, 140
George Sim Mfg. Co., 62
John Sinclair Ltd., 121
J. A. Sistovaris and Sons, 61
sleeping bags, 164, 167
slide projectors, 154
slippers, sheepskin, 137
Brian and Cherie Smazlen, 94
G. Smith and Sons, 47
smoked salmon, 74-76, 89
smokers' knives, 46
smokers' sets, 87; crystal, 121
Smythson's, 129
snappers, 43
George Sneed Furniture, 112
Snowflake Kit, 102
snuff, 47
snuffboxes, antique, 19
soap: French, 85, 87; Taylor of London, 85
Sociedade Inglesa Decorações e Antiguedades LDA, 118
socks: hand-knitted, 49; Welsh, 94
Sombol, 88
Somerset House Wedmore Ltd., 84
Sotainvalidien Veljesliiton Naisjarjesto, 136
Sotheby and Co., 15, 27, 75
Henry Sotheran Ltd., 38
sound projectors, 154
South Bucks Rainwear Co., 55
Spain, stores, 19, 52, 68, 93, 118, 137, 143-44, 146, 156
Spastics Society, 161
spears, Ethiopian, 85
spices, 74-76
Spielwarenhaus Virnich, 178
Spielzeug-Rasch, 66, 178
spinets, 146-47
Spink and Son, 18, 65
spinning wheels, 105
spoons, 109-10, 140-44; horn, 91; silver, 92; Welsh, 94
"sporting" gifts, 56, 129, 163-67
sports clothes, 49, 163-67

189

Sports-Schuster, 167
Sport & Waffen Dschulnigg, 166
Sri Lanka, stores, 93, 102
stainless steel, 79
stamps, 68; albums, 68
Edward Standford Ltd., 40
Mairtin Standun, 90
Stanza del Borgo, 22
starfish, 105
Starfish Books Ltd., 41
stationery: Italian, 44; Smythson's, 129
statues: African, 90; garden, 18, 118
Stechers Ltd., 79, 180
Stedelijk Museum, 31
stereo: cabinets, to customer's design, 170; equipment, 169-70
stevenographs, 18
Stockmann, 78
stone rubbings, 28
stools, 82
Storyville (magazine), 148
The Stratford Games Ltd., 177
Strength and Co. Ltd., 63
Strike One, 14-15
string boxes, 129
Ed. Sturzenegger AG, 133
sub-aqua equipment, 167
suede: for dress making, 70-71
sundials: antique, 18, 20; reproduction, 118
A. S. Sundt and Co., 79, 109
Suomen Käsityön Ystävät, 136
surprise snowballs, 43
Sutton and Sons Ltd., 100
Svenskt Glas, 65
Swaine Adeney Brigg and Sons Ltd., 56
Swan and Edgar Ltd., 51
Swatow Weng Lee Co., 88
Sweden, stores, 68, 79, 106, 110, 115, 126, 134, 137, 160, 164
The Swing Shop, 148
Michel Swiss, 150
Switzerland, stores, 46, 51, 93, 133, 154, 180
Switzers Department Store, 90
Christopher Sykes, 19
Sylvester Furniture, 112
Andrzey Szczepka, 91

tablecloths: Ecuadorian, 82; embroidered, 90, 131, 133; Greek, 88; Indian, 89; Irish, 90; lace, 131, 133; linen, 88, 89, 90, 131, 133
Tabor Designs, 121
tailors, 57-58
Tai Ping Carpet Salon, 137
Taiwan, stores, 31, 118, 127
tape recorders, 169-70
tapestries, 104, 105, 117, 137; antique, 14, 15, 19

tarot cards, books about, 39; packs, 68
Tartan Gift Shops, 92
Tate Gallery, 31
Audrey Taunton, 84
taxidermy equipment, 103
Taylor of London, 85
teaching aids, 34
tea cozies, 90, 94
teas, 76
tea sets, 120-27, 129; bronze, 110; pewter, 134, 136
tele converters, 154
telephones, antique, 18
telescopes: accessories and books, 103
television sets, 170
tennis clothes, 167
tents, 164, 165, 167
Tesoro's International Inc., 91
Texere Yarns, 106
Thailand, stores, 71, 93, 110, 144
Thai Silk Company, 71
Theatreland Ltd., 71
Thompson and Morgan Ltd., 101
3 Falke Møbler, 111
Three Four Five, 177
Tibet, stores, 89
Tibetan Self Help Refugee Center, 89
tiles, 88; Delft, 123; Portuguese, 138
Timely Topics (magazine), 159
Alex Tiranti Ltd., 105
tobacco, 46-47
A. Tobben, 136
toys, 78, 128, 172-78; Arnold Rapido, 178; Baufix, 178; Faller, 178; Fischertechnik, 178; Fleischmann, 178; Gama, 178; Hornby, 176; Kibri, 178; Käthe Kruse, 178; Marklin, 178; Minic, 176; Plasticant, 178; Ravensburger, 178; Scalestric, 176; Schuco, 178; Steiff, 178; Triang, 176; Trix, 178
toy soldiers, 18, 68
toy theaters, 172, 177
Trade Exchange (Ceylon) Ltd., 93
trains: friezes, 176; model, 67, 176, 178
transport, books about, 37
Charles W. Traylen, 38
trays, 30, 129
Treasures of Italy, 44
Treasure Traders Ltd., 109
trees, 99-100
Trend, 165
Le Tricoteur, 55
Tridias, 177
Trinidad, stores, 79, 180
tripods, 154
Tropicrafts, 137
trumpets, 146

The Tryon Gallery, 31
Elsie Tu Ltd., 60
tubs, bath, 108
Tulipshow Frans Roozen, 99
Tunisia, stores, 93, 137
Turkey, stores, 46
A. Turler, 180
Turnbull and Asser, 57
Tyne Canoes Ltd., 163
R. Tysack Ltd., 115

Uchida Art Co. Ltd., 25
ukeleles, 146
umbrellas, 52, 56, 85
Union Handiwork, 89
Universal Suppliers, 154, 159, 170, 180
W. J. Unwin Ltd., 101
Upholstery Workshop, 117
U.S.A., services, 159

vacations, English guides to, 40-41; fishing, 165
A. Van Moppes and Zoon, 142
W. P. Van Stockum, 40
Van Tubergen, 99
vases: crystal, 121; Delft, 123; Japanese lacquerware, 98; Rosenthal, 123
Vävstolsfabriken Glimåkra AB, 106
Charles Veillon, 52
Erik Vejerslev, 19
Vicky, 91
video equipment, 170
Vilmorin-Andrieux, 101
violins, 146
virginals, 146
Visitor's Guide to Country Workshops, 41
Visitors Pavillon, 110, 123
Vogue Bathrooms, 108

Wales, stores, 49, 60, 72, 94, 99, 106, 165
walking sticks, 56, 90; African, 91
wall charts: butterfly, 96; Canadian Indian tribes, 82
wallets, leather, 52, 129, 140
wall hangings, 31; African, 89; for Christmas, 43; kits to embroider, 104-5; needlepoint, 133; woven, 137
Wallis Woollen Mill, 60
wallpaper, hand-painted, 28, 88
L. A. Wallrich, 39
Waltons Musical Instrument Galleries Ltd., 146
wastepaper baskets, 52
watches, 79, 88, 180; antique, 15; for the blind, 159
watercolors, 22
Watkins and Doncaster, 103

Watkins Bookshop, 39
Watkins Seeds Ltd., 101
Watts, Captain O. M., 163
weapons, 166; antique, 15, 68; guns, made to order, 166; reproduction, 68
weather vanes, 127; made to order, 127
Clara Weaver, 105
The Weavers Shop, 106
weaving supplies: looms, 106; yarns, 106
weekend cottages, 85
Charlotte Weibull, 178
Weinberger Bros. Ltd., 106
Welfare Handicrafts, 89
Welsh Cottage Craft Shops, 94
West Indies, stores, 137
William Weston Gallery Ltd., 24
Westport House, 55
wetsuits, 163
Wheldon and Wesley Ltd., 36
whips, 56
Franz Widmann und Sohn, 110, 123
J. B. Wijs & Zoon, 99
Wilkinson and Gaviller Ltd., 85
Wilson of Hawick, 54
Wilton Royal Carpet Factory, 101
wine, 75
wine bags, 93
wine labels: antique silver, 20; reproduction, 68
wine-making equipment, 106
Firma Kurt Wittmayer, 147
Wohnbedarf OHG, 113
Margaret E. Wolverson, 28
wood, bowls and household objects made of, 85, 90, 91
wood-carving tools, 106
wood paneling: African, 90; antique, 18
Woolcraft, 105
Workshop, 94
Worldwide Butterflies, 96
World Wide Herbs Ltd., 106
Walter Wright, 60
writing: cases, 56, 129; classes, 41; equipment for the blind, 159
Wyatt Druitt, 68
Harriet Wynter, 20

Yachtmail Co. Ltd., 102, 164
Yahya el Miligi and Co., 82
yarn: knitting, 102; weaving, 106
Yogini Gems, 102
Yoseido Gallery, 25
Den Young, 66
The Young Idea, 63
William Yu, 60

Zarapes de San Miguel, 137
Ziggurat, 117
zithers, 146
A. Zwemmer Ltd., 35

ABOUT THE AUTHOR

MARIA ELENA DE LA IGLESIA was born in Madrid in 1936, and attended Dartington Hall School and Newnham College, Cambridge, England, from which she was graduated with honors and where she also received her M.A. degree. She has written articles for *The Times* (of London) and is the author of two children's books, *The Cat and the Mouse* (1966), and *The Oak That Would Not Pay* (1968), both of which were published by Pantheon Books. She is also the author of *The Catalogue of American Catalogues*. She is married to publisher André Schiffrin and they live in New York City with their two daughters, Anya and Natalia.